LAFAYETTE

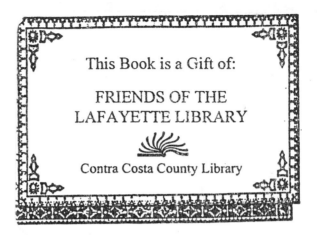

This Book is a Gift of:

FRIENDS OF THE
LAFAYETTE LIBRARY

Contra Costa County Library

MUGGLES AND MAGIC

D0469883

Books by George Beahm

The Vaughn Bode Index (Heresy Press, 1975)

Kirk's Works (Heresy Press, 1977)

How to Sell Woodstoves (George Beahm, Publisher, 1980)

How to Buy a Woodstove—and Not Get Burned (George Beahm, Publisher, 1980)

Notes from Elam (editor) (George Beahm, Publisher, 1983)

Write to the Top: How to Complain & Get Results—Fast! (The Donning Company, 1988)

The Stephen King Companion (Andrews McMeel Publishing, 1989)

The Stephen King Story (Andrews McMeel Publishing, 1990)

War of Words: The Censorship Debate (Andrews McMeel Publishing, 1993)

Michael Jordan: Shooting Star (Andrews McMeel Publishing, 1994)

The Stephen King Companion (Rev.) (Andrews McMeel Publishing, 1995)

The Unauthorized Anne Rice Companion (Andrews McMeel Publishing, 1995)

Stephen King: America's Best-Loved Boogeyman (Andrews McMeel Publishing, 1998)

Stephen King from A to Z (Andrews McMeel Publishing, 1998)

Stephen King Collectibles (Betts Bookstore, 2000)

Stephen King Country (Running Press, 1999)

Patricia Cornwell Companion (St. Martin's Press, 2002)

The Essential J.R.R. Tolkien Sourcebook (New Page Books, 2003)

How to Protect Yourself & Your Family Against Terrorism (Brasseys, 2003)

WITHDRAWN

MUGGLES AND MAGIC

J. K. Rowling and the Harry Potter Phenomenon

CONTRA COSTA COUNTY LIBRARY

George Beahm

Illustrations by Tim Kirk

HAMPTON ROADS
PUBLISHING COMPANY, INC.

3 1901 03748 9194

Copyright © 2004 by George Beahm
All rights reserved, including the right to reproduce this work in any form whatsoever,
without permission in writing from the publisher,
except for brief passages in connection with a review.

This book is not endorsed, approved, or authorized by Warner Bros.,
J. K. Rowling, or her publishers. Harry Potter is a trademark of Warner Bros.

Cover design by Steve Amarillo
Cover design elements: picture frame © 2004 PhotoDisc,
owl © 2004 Nova Development Corp., hand/wand © 2004 Steve Amarillo
Interior photo album cover © 2004 Anne L. Louque

"The Magic of Harry Potter" © 2004 by Colleen Doran. "The J. K. Rowling Story" by Stephen McGinty © The Scotsman Publ. Ltd., Edinburgh, is reprinted with permission."A Brit's View of Its Book Publication" © 2004 by Allan Harvey. Book reviews © *Publishers Weekly* are reprinted with permission of Reed Business Information. "Lives Changed by J. K. Rowling: The *Real* Magic of Harry Potter" was originally published as "Spellbound" in *The Scotsman* (June 14, 2003) and is reprinted with permission. © 2003 The Scotsman Publ. Ltd., Edinburgh. www.scotsman.com. Art © 2004 by Tim Kirk is reprinted with his kind permission. *Photos*: Unless otherwise credited, photos are © 2004 by George Beahm. Photos from *The Scotsman* are © by The Scotsman Publ. Ltd., Edinburgh. Photos by Britain on View are © by www.britainonview.com. Owl photos by photographer Nick Derene are published with the permission of Marge Gibson and Nick Derene of the Raptor Education Group, Inc. Photos from *The Guardian* are © The Guardian and reprinted with permission. Every effort has been made to locate and secure the permission of copyright-holders when making use of copyrighted materials beyond the scope of Fair Use under the law of copyright.

Hampton Roads Publishing Company, Inc.
1125 Stoney Ridge Road
Charlottesville, VA 22902

434-296-2772
fax: 434-296-5096
800-766-8009 (orders only)
e-mail: hrpc@hrpub.com
www.hrpub.com

Beahm, George W.
Muggles and magic : J.K. Rowling and the Harry Potter phenomenon / by George Beahm.
    p. cm.
  ISBN 1-57174-412-6 (6 x 9 tp : alk. paper)
  1. Rowling, J. K.--Criticism and interpretation. 2. Children's stories,
English--History and criticism. 3. Fantasy fiction, English--History and
criticism. 4. Rowling, J. K.--Characters--Harry Potter. 5. Potter, Harry
(Fictitious character) 6. Wizards in literature. 7. Magic in literature.
I. Title.
  PR6068.O93Z53 2004
  823'.914--dc22

2004001560

10 9 8 7 6 5 4 3

Printed on acid-free paper in Canada

To the memory of my mother-in-law,
Mildred "Lib" Bryant,
and her magical grandchildren:
Courtney, Melissa, Patrick, and Kevin.

"You'll never make any money out of children's books, Jo."
—Barry Cunningham, then co-partner of the Christopher Little Literary Agency, who pointed out to Joanne Rowling prior to the publication of her first book that, for the most part, most children's book authors make very little money.

Gringotts Bank

Contents

Part Two: A Writer's Life

Part Three: Harry Potter–Screen Magic

Part Four: A Look at the Books

Part Five: Harry Potter Merchandise (a selection)

Part Six: Harry Potter Websites

Appendices

A Note to the Reader

"Harry Potter," according to a 2003 year-end Google search summary, ranks second in popular queries for the year. That's not surprising, since 2003 was a big year for J. K. Rowling and Harry Potter. After a three-year interval between Harry Potter book four and book five, readers worldwide searched for any tidbit of news about *Harry Potter and the Order of the Phoenix* (book five) and for news about the third movie in the works.

Though there are dozens of books about J. K. Rowling (mostly quickie biographies) and Harry Potter (mostly academic texts), no book exists that looks at both Rowling and Potter in the context of the popular culture—a serious omission given the sheer breadth and scope of material available on both subjects, especially for new readers who saw the movies first and then decided to read the books.

This book is intended as a general interest companion guide to J. K. Rowling and her most famous fictional creation, Harry Potter.

I hope you enjoy dipping into this book, written to be read by topic rather than straight through, so there's some necessary repetition.

Tim Kirk

Foreword:
The Magic of
Harry Potter

by Colleen Doran

Plush Harry Potter doll

Reams of paper have been devoted to dissecting the Harry Potter phenomenon. Stone-faced intellectuals scoffed at the boy with the round glasses and the magical powers. "Fun literature rots kids' brains," they intoned. "Anything that makes that much money must be bad."

As if reading those books wasn't bad enough for kids, their parents had started glomming onto the volumes with childlike enthusiasm. "Glory be! How could an adult be caught dead reading that nonsense!" Grown-ups across the planet lined up to get the latest Potter tome with faces as eager and bright as those of their children. You could almost hear the faces of the literati squeal as they pinched themselves into a squeeze heretofore unknown outside acts such as the consumption of particularly sour lemons.

I, too, was a skeptic. For years I had managed to skirt the rim of the Potter event horizon without ever being sucked into the singularity. A life-long fantasy reader, I managed to turn my nose up as volume after volume of Harry Potter adventures flooded the market. I suppressed a sneaking admiration for the Hogwarts school sweaters I saw kids wearing to the bookstore and instead noted Potter's more than passing resemblance to Neil Gaiman's Tim Hunter in his *Books of Magic,* certain Rowling's young hero was a riff of Gaiman's work.

Why bother giving Harry Potter a read? Anything that popular just couldn't be that good—could it?

The author of this book, George Beahm, finally managed to coax me to the theater to catch a look at the first of the Harry Potter films. There was more than a month to go before the release of the first *Lord of the Rings* films and I expected to be able to spend some wicked typewriter time giving a couple of reviews comparing the two most popular fantasy epics of the century, certain Potter would be found wanting and I'd be able to rack some wickedly delightful poison pen time. And what the heck, George was buying the movie tickets.

I came out of the theater a convert, a satellite, caught in the grip of the Hogwarts gravity well, and I have been delightfully captivated ever since.

While the films may have introduced me to the Potter world, the real charm is found in the books. Their clever and musical language gilds a seemingly simplistic story line that is as intricately plotted as many far more "sophisticated" works. The Potter books are riveting page turners that are also beautifully crafted works of great charm, warmth, and humanity, encompassing classic fantasy story elements and then wrapping them up in a world that reflects the concerns of modern boys and girls and modern grown-ups, all awash in the glow of a golden-hued fantasy image of middle-class England.

The most obvious nod to classic fantasy is Harry himself—the orphaned boy with magical gifts and a Destiny with a capital *D.* Fantasy literature often features a child sans parents in Jungian fashion, as the child achieves the great Destiny only after being freed from the shadow of the adult.

Also, Harry is the cuckoo in the nest, a boy living with an adopted family in which he is the miraculous and strange odd-man-out, reflecting the alienation most children feel as they grow and develop their own identities. The need to be acknowledged as a special, unique being is universal, and almost every little boy or girl wonders if their parents really *are* their parents, or perhaps, like Harry, wonders if beyond their banal existence, there's a world of adventure and dreams waiting for them, perhaps to be delivered into their hands by a white owl carrying an extraordinary letter.

These are just two of the powerful, archetypal themes that resound throughout the Harry Potter books, masterfully executed by Rowling in such a way that they grab the mind and heart of readers as few books have in the history of literature.

Rowling herself is a dream girl for every aspiring artist or writer, the woman from impoverished circumstances who spends years carefully crafting her work with heart and skill, one day plucked from complete obscurity and a life on the dole to become one of the wealthiest and most celebrated women in the world.

Rowling's success is more rare than winning the lottery, only there was no luck involved. She is an immensely talented writer, extraordinarily clever and hard working, and no magic ticket will buy that for anyone. Her unique combination of ability and popular appeal, and the romanticization of her climb to success make her one of the most appealing figures in popular literature today as millions of the creatively inclined dream of creating their own Potter-level publishing empires.

The need to devalue the popular is strong: that which is popular must, somehow, appeal to the lowest common denominator, and people of extraordinary vision, talent, and wisdom can't be attracted to anything low or common.

Kurtis Wiley, a Harry Potter look-alike who works for Barnes & Noble

However, many of the elements that account for the astounding universal appeal of Harry Potter are in no way low, but are thankfully common to all people of good will: friendship, loyalty, love, and self-sacrifice.

Harry Potter books don't just tweak our sense of adventure and appeal to our sneaking need for a little escapism. They appeal to our finest human qualities, our loftiest and noblest aspects, qualities that may seem simple to jaded minds, but are the purest and best features of any human being. Any parents who see their child immersed in the act of reading one of Potter's adventures can count themselves lucky, as their child isn't only engaging in the glorious act of reading a book (something parents for generations have had to bludgeon their children into doing), that child has entered a world where friends behave like true friends, where moral character is a virtue instead of a variable, and where problems aren't just solved with raw power but with brain power.

Now that I think of it, more adults should be reading the Harry Potter books.

From far away, I hear some intellectuals making the sound of sucking sour lemons. If they went to Hogwarts, I bet they'd be in Slytherin House.

Colleen Doran created, writes, and draws the critically acclaimed graphic novel series *A Distant Soil* for Image Comics. A professional cartoonist with hundreds of book credits from D.C., Marvel, and other publishers, Doran recently illustrated *Orbiter, Reign of the Zodiac,* and *The Essential J. R. R. Tolkien Sourcebook.*

Acknowledgments

Writing a book is a solitary activity, but publishing it is a team effort. The following people deserve to take a bow:

Stephen McGinty, a Scottish journalist from the *Scotsman* who allowed me to reprint his biographical piece on J. K. Rowling.

Thomas N. Thornton, COO of Andrews McMeel Publishing, who encouraged me to write this book, championed it, and urged its publication. I am privileged to know him and to have books published by his house.

Allan Harvey, a Londoner with a dry wit who, time and again, dropped whatever he was doing to help out on matters large and small for this book.

Tim Kirk, who graciously allowed me to reprint his art to grace the pages of this book. His works add the right touch throughout.

Colleen Doran, a treasured friend and an artist who took a pen to create not art but words, her foreword that sets the stage for the main show. We shared many hours at Starbucks during which we talked about all aspects of this book, immeasurably improving it. *Elen sila lumenn' omentielvo.*

Ned Brooks, who served as my research assistant on matters both large and small. Drawing from his considerable knowledge of fantasy and, especially, children's literature, Ned was indispensable.

The staff at Barnes & Noble in Newport News, Virginia, especially **Barbara,** who has promoted my books with several signings, and **Kurtis Wiley,** who helped with the photography.

My friends at Hampton Roads Publishing, who believed in me and this book: **Robert S. Friedman,** an old friend from when we both worked at the Donning Company, a book publisher he founded in southeast Virginia; **Richard Leviton,** a senior editor at HRP, whose eagle eyes took my raw manuscript and improved it immeasurably; **Sarah Hilfer,** who cared for my manuscript in-house; and the artful **Jane Hagaman**.

For timely and much appreciated assistance on rights and permissions, I'd like to thank **Gary Ink** of *Publishers Weekly*; **Bill Bradley, Kerry Black,** and **Stephen McGinty** of *The Scotsman* in Edinburgh, Scotland; **Jonathan Crabbe** of the British Tourist Authority; **Judith Caul** of *The Guardian*; **Marge Gibson** of the Raptor Education Group, and photographer **Nick Derene**.

Mary, my wife, who gave encouragement and support, and was an indispensable source of editorial input. And our niece **Courtney Bryant,** who introduced me to the Harry Potter books, for which I am eternally grateful.

Thank you, one and all.

Introduction:

J. K. Rowling: A Sorceress with Words

Time magazine cover story

When *Harry Potter and the Philosopher's Stone* was published in 1997, with its tiny print run of 500 copies, which sold principally to libraries and a handful of independent booksellers in England, it had—according to experts in the book industry—a number of strikes against it.

First, its length: Considered a children's book, industry experts regarded its 80,000 words as a major liability. Children, the experts intoned, won't read a book of that length.

Second, the gender of its author: Boys, those same experts agreed, won't read a book penned by a woman. Therefore the name should be gender-free: Joanne Rowling became J. K. Rowling.

Third, it was a first novel by an unknown author. More to the point, she had never published anything professionally—not even a magazine article or short story. The odds, the experts said, were against her—odds so daunting that no Las Vegas bookie would have taken bets on the possibility of her success as a novelist.

But as the saying goes, three strikes and you're out. The experts not only missed the mark, they could not have been more wrong. Against all odds, J. K. Rowling would go on to become the most popular author in book publishing history.

Book length a deterrent? Hardly. The most recent novel, *Harry Potter and the Order of the Phoenix,* is the longest yet: 870 pages in the U.S. edition, with a quarter-million words, which fans read until some literally developed what was humorously termed "Hogwarts headaches" by a pediatrician.

Gender an issue? Forget it. Young boys snap up the Harry Potter books as eagerly as their female counterparts. A well-told story appeals not only to both sexes but to the young as well as the young at heart.

Harry Potter mania is a worldwide phenomenon the likes of which we haven't seen since another British invasion, back in the 1960s when the Beatles, four mop-topped lads from Liverpool, took the world of popular culture by storm.

Judging from the brouhaha surrounding the July 2003 publication of *Harry Potter and the Order of the Phoenix* and the forthcoming Harry Potter movies, the excitement shows no signs of abating. Indeed as momentum continues to gather for the publication of the sixth Potter, fever pitch will be reached with the seventh, and last, Potter novel.

Book magazine cover story

In the seventh novel, Harry Potter will come of age and leave Hogwarts permanently behind; so, too, will J. K. Rowling, who has adamantly refused to even entertain the notion of writing about Harry's post-high-school career. Will he become an Auror and fight dark wizards? Will he assume a position at the Ministry of Magic? Or will he remain at Hogwarts in a teaching capacity?

We shall likely never know, although Rowling knows because she's already written the final chapter, which is under lock and key in an undisclosed location. That chapter sums up the

series, ties up all the loose ends, and as an artifact is a manuscript of incalculable worth.

J. K. Rowling is, as Stephen King explained in an *Entertainment Weekly* book review of *Order of the Phoenix,* currently at the top of her game and writing a series that (in his estimation) will stand the test of time. Harry Potter, asserts King, will take his place among the other literary greats, like Alice and Huck and Tarzan.

I think the bogeyman from Bangor is right. Harry Potter is in good company indeed—a frightening thought to highbrow literary types who consider Harry Potter lowbrow fare. How it must rankle them to know that Rowling, in a few short years, not only became a best-selling author, but became *the* best-selling author in book publishing history.

Part One:
The Real World of
Joanne Rowling

Tim Kirk

I would have been crazy to have expected what has happened to Harry. The most exciting moment for me, against very stiff competition, was when I found out Harry was going to be published. It was my life's ambition to see a book I had written on a shelf in a bookshop. Everything that has happened since has been extraordinary and wonderful, but the mere fact of being able to say I was a published author was the fulfillment of a dream I had had since I was a very small child.

—*J. K. Rowling, quoted in Kidsreads.com*

Chronology

The *Only* Authorized Biography of J. K. Rowling

CONVERSATIONS WITH

J.K. ROWLING

Author of
HARRY POTTER

SCHOLASTIC

Cover of *Conversations with J. K. Rowling*

1965 March 14: Pete Rowling and Anne Volant marry at All Saints Parish Church.

July 31: Joanne Rowling is born at Chipping Sodbury general Hospital (Gloucestershire, England).

1967 June 28: Her only sibling, a sister named Dianne, is born.

1970 At age five, she attends St. Michael's Church of England Primary School.

Family friends include the Potter family. The Rowlings live in a town called Yate.

1971 The family moves to Winterbourne (near Bristol).

1974 When Joanne is seven, the family moves to Tutshill, near Chepstow in Wales.

She attends Tutshill Church of England Primary School.

1975 She becomes a Brownie and joins the Second Tidenham (St. Mary's) Brownie Pack.

1976 She attends Wyedean Comprehensive in Sedbury.

1980 Her mother, Anne, is diagnosed with multiple sclerosis.

1982   She is selected as Head Girl at Wyedean Comprehensive.

1983   Her mother, suffering from multiple sclerosis, makes her will.
Turned down for Oxford, she attends the University of Exeter.

1985   Joanne spends time in Paris.

1987   She graduates from the University of Exeter with a degree in French and the classics, moves to an apartment in Clapham (South London), and spends free time during lunch and after hours writing two adult novels (both unpublished).

1990   June: On a train ride between Manchester and London, she dreams up Harry Potter.
December 30: Her mother, Anne, dies at age 45.

1991   She takes a job teaching English at Encounter English Schools in Porto, Portugal.

1992   October 16: She marries TV journalist Jorge Arantes at the civil register office in Porto.

1993   April 2: Her father, Pete Rowling, remarries; his new wife is his former secretary, Janet Gallivan.
July 27: Joanne's daughter, Jessica, is born.
November 17: Joanne's husband throws her out of their house, but she goes back in to get Jessica; she makes plans to leave for England with her daughter in tow.
December 21: Settled in Scotland, she applies for public assistance from the Department of Social Security in Edinburgh.

1994   March 15: After discovering that Jorge Arantes is in Edinburgh and looking for her, she starts proceedings to get a temporary restraining order against her husband.
November 23: She renews the temporary restraining order against Arantes.

1995   June 26: The restraining order against Arantes becomes permanent; she is officially divorced from him.
She finishes writing the first Harry Potter novel and begins submitting it to agents for literary representation.

1996   February: She signs on with the Christopher Little Literary Agency.
July: She receives certification to teach, a Postgraduate Certificate of Education, and begins teaching French at Leigh Academy, in Edinburgh.

1997   February: Receives £8,000 from the Scottish Arts Council. She uses most of the money to buy a word processor, replacing her £40 typewriter.
June 26: The first Harry Potter novel, *Harry Potter and the Philosopher's Stone*, is published in the U.K., with a print run of 300 in hardback and 200 in paperback. She splurges, spending £100, on a jacket to wear when meeting the press.

September: Scholastic buys the book for the U.S. market for $100,000, with plans for a first printing of 50,000 copies.

She quits teaching to become a full-time writer.

She moves from a rented apartment in South Lorne Place to a new residence at Hazelbank Terrace, which she buys.

1998   July 2: *Harry Potter and the Chamber of Secrets* is published in the U.K.

October: *Harry Potter and the Sorcerer's Stone* is published in the U.S.

1999   June: *Harry Potter and the Chamber of Secrets* is published in the U.S.

July: *Harry Potter and the Prisoner of Azkaban* is published in the U.K.

September: *Harry Potter and the Prisoner of Azkaban* is published in the U.S.

She signs a major movie deal with Warner Bros.

2000   July 8: *Harry Potter and the Goblet of Fire* is published simultaneously in the U.K. and the U.S.

September: She accepts a post as an ambassador for a charity, the National Council for One Parent Families.

Hagrid holding Norbert the Dragon

2001   April: A patron of the Multiple Sclerosis Society in Scotland, she attended the opening of one of its resource centers in Aberdeen.

She publishes two books, *Quidditch Through the Ages* and *Fantastic Beasts and Where to Find Them,* the proceeds of which benefit Comic Relief.

November: *Harry Potter and the Sorcerer's Stone* is released as a movie.

December 26: She marries Dr. Neil Murray.

2002   September: A U.S. judge dismisses the lawsuit filed by Nancy Stouffer against Rowling.

November: *Harry Potter and the Chamber of Secrets* is released as a movie.

2003   March 23: Their son, David, is born.

June 21: *Harry Potter and the Order of the Phoenix* is published in the U.K. and the U.S.

June 26: She appears at the Royal Albert Hall in London for a reading.

November: The sales of Harry Potter novels reach 250 million, according to Christopher Little.

2004   June: *Harry Potter and the Prisoner of Azkaban* is released as a movie.

2005   The movie *Harry Potter and the Goblet of Fire,* directed by Mike Newell, is scheduled for a November 18 release.

The J. K. Rowling Story
by Stephen McGinty

Before Harry Potter, before the novels, before the films, before the millions and millions of pounds, there was a little girl who liked to play witches and wizards. During the sleepy summer months, in the English town of Winterbourne, a half-hour journey by car from Bristol, Joanne Rowling, then six years old, first encountered a wizard called Potter. The game of Let's Pretend was played out in the front garden of number 35 Nicholls Lane, one of a row of grey brick, three-bedroom houses, into which Pete and Anne Rowling and their two young daughters had recently moved.

The game was Joanne's idea and involved raiding her mother's cupboard for costumes, the neighbours' garages for brooms, and corralling the children next door to make up the numbers. Joanne, her younger sister, Dianne, and friend Vikki were all witches while the solitary wizard was five-year-old Ian Potter. As he recalled almost 30 years later: "I used to wear my Dad's long coat back to front to look like a wizard. I think there were a pair of joke specs in the box as well—a bit like Harry's."

The life of J. K. Rowling began with the meeting of two strangers on a train in 1964. Pete Rowling was an 18-year-old soldier when he met Anne Volant, a WREN (Women's Royal Navy Service), also 18, on the train from King's Cross bound for the headquarters of 45 Commando in Arbroath. Introductions across the seated compartment led to a long conversation and stolen kisses beneath duffel coats. By the time they alighted in Scotland, Pete and Anne were a confirmed couple.

A few months into their courtship Anne became pregnant with her first child (Joanne). The young lovers decided to discard their uniforms to marry on 14 March 1965 before setting up home in Yate, ten miles outside Bristol. Four months later, on 31 July 1965, their daughter was born at the Cottage Hospital, in the more affluent suburb of Chipping Sodbury, where Rowling would later claim her family lived. While her father secured employment as an apprentice engineer at a Bristol factory, her mother cared for Joanne and her sister, Dianne, born two years later on 28 June 1967. A year later the family moved to the larger house at Winterbourne, where Joanne first discovered the magical world of books, and created her own adventures in the front garden.

A childhood bout of measles, at the age of four, provided the author's earliest memory of books, when her father raised her spirits by reading aloud to his bed-bound daughter the adventures of Toad of Toad Hall, from *The Wind in the Willows*. Books were spread around the house, crammed in every room, and although young Joanne had little interest in the adventures of the Famous Five, she would later praise the work of Richard Scarry, whose anthropomorphic work inspired her earliest work of fiction: a story called "Rabbit" written at the age of six. By this time she was a happy pupil at St. Michael's Church of England Primary School, five minutes' walk from the family home. But another move was afoot. In 1974 her parents purchased an old stone cottage in Tutshill, on the Welsh border, close to the Forest of Dean, which would become a blueprint for Harry Potter's Forbidden Forest, just as it had inspired the work of another local author, the late Dennis Potter.

The idyllic Church Cottage, which had a flagstone floor and a covered well, was just a goblin's throw from the local graveyard, and was surrounded by countryside in which the Rowling sisters would enact their adventures. But for the young J. K. Rowling, the first day at Tutshill Church of England Primary School in September 1974 was not a success. She scored only half a mark out of ten in a test that led to her being positioned on the less intellectual side of the class. Her natural ability soon shone through and she was promoted, but as she explained: "The promotion was at a cost . . . Mrs Morgan made me swap seats with my best friend." The teacher, Mrs Sylvia Morgan, was a strict, intimidating woman, who frightened Joanne as a child and whose presence would work its way into the less sympathetic masters of Hogwarts. By the age of ten, Joanne was a keen Brownie, a voracious reader, and a serious student who raced to get her hand up first. "I was the epitome of a bookish child, short and squat, thick National Health glasses, living in a world of complete daydreams."

When she made the move to secondary school, Joanne found herself accompanied by her mother. After 12 years of bringing up her daughters, Anne Rowling secured the position of laboratory technician at Wyedean

Comprehensive under the supervision of John Nettleship, the school's head of science. Nettleship remembers Joanne, whom he taught, as a bright but quiet girl and considers himself an early inspiration for Professor Snape. "I think chemistry maybe made the most impact on her because I did teach her about the philosopher's stone, the alchemist's stone. Possibly she knew about it already, but I did include it in my lessons and explained how it turned things to gold." He then chuckles before adding: "It seems to have worked for her, hasn't it?" Although bright, she was not the most enthusiastic student, as Nettleship, who is now retired, recalls: "Her attitude in the science lessons was more like Harry's in the potions class rather than Hermione's."

Anne Rowling, meanwhile, was delighted to be around the beakers and chemicals and working once again after such a long absence. "She was absolutely brilliant, a sparkling character, totally reliable, very interested in words and stories and things like that. Although her job was on the technical side, she was also very imaginative," says Nettleship.

A brief encounter with bullying led Joanne to spend her break walking to the science block to collect her dinner money rather than face the intimidating atmosphere of the playground. A larger girl in her own year picked a fight with her. "I didn't have a choice. It was hit back or lie down and play dead," recalls the author. "For a few days I was quite famous because she hadn't managed to flatten me. The truth was, my locker was right behind me and it held me up."

Throughout her teens Rowling honed her taste in reading material. It is unsurprising that she was greatly influenced by J. R. R. Tolkien's *The Lord of the Rings,* but she also loved Jane Austen, whose work *Emma* she has read over 20 times. Another seminal influence was Jessica Mitford, whom she adopted as a personal heroine, and whose autobiography, *Hons and Rebels,* became a significant text for Rowling.

But as with all teenagers, Rowling became more and more interested in pop music. It was the early 1980s and so she was inspired by the Smiths and Siouxsie Sioux, whose look she adopted early on and maintained for many years; when she began university, she still sported startling back-combed hair and heavy black eyeliner.

At this point Rowling's home was a happy and stable environment. Her father, Pete, was now an executive engineer at the Rolls Royce plant and her mother was working in a job she adored. But things were about to change dramatically, casting a shadow over Rowling's life and tearing apart her close-knit family.

The spectre of her illness first appeared to Anne Rowling in 1978 when her hand began to tremble while she was pouring tea. At first the symptoms were fleeting and she dismissed them with a shrug but over the next two years her loss of physical control intensified. She began breaking beakers at work and often dissolved in tears of frustration. On a good day she could still play guitar, but the bad days began to mount up. When Joanne was 15, her mother was diagnosed with multiple sclerosis. The disease was triggered by the lack of a certain protein in her spinal column, which served to scramble the signals from her brain and resulted in a loss of control of her limbs. Anne was broken-hearted at having to give up her lab technician's job, but busied herself by volunteering to clean the local church.

Rowling could only watch helplessly as her mother succumbed to this destructive disease. In an article the author wrote, published in *Scotland on Sunday,* she described how at one point her mother was reduced to crawling upstairs. The "galloping" progression of the illness meant that within a few years Anne Rowling moved from walking with difficulty to using a walking frame and then a wheelchair.

A depression settled over Church Cottage, leaving Rowling feeling trapped and miserable. Escape came in the form of a new pupil at Wyedean Comprehensive, Séan Harris, who quickly became a firm friend. In 1982 he drew up outside the family home in his blue Ford Anglia and whisked her away from the grim stillness of Tutshill to the concerts and bars of Bristol. He would park under the Severn Bridge and together the pair dreamt up better futures for each other. Harris's blue Ford Anglia would become immortalised in Rowling's fiction as Ron Weasley's family car and he would be described in the dedication in her second book as "getaway driver and foul weather friend."

Joanne's academic achievements led to her being appointed Head Girl at Wyedean and her ambition was to study languages at Oxford. Her A-levels in English, French, and German (two A's and a B) were good enough on paper to secure an Oxbridge place, but she wasn't accepted. Her teachers were surprised, believing she was the victim of institutional prejudice against comprehensive pupils. The dreamed of spires of Oxford were instead replaced by the red-brick halls of residence at the University of Exeter.

Lecturers remember Rowling as nervous and insecure, but a fellow student, Yvette Cowles, told Sean Smith, her unofficial biographer, that she was popular and striking. "She wore long skirts and used to have this blue denim jacket she liked to wear. Jo was very shapely and she had this big hair, kind of back-combed and lacquered, and lots of heavy eyeliner. I think she was quite popular with the guys."

In her first year she signed up for French and classics, but an attitude to academia best described as minimum work, maximum fun led to her abandoning classics after she failed to register properly for an exam. Her third year was spent teaching in a school in Paris and sharing a flat with an Italian, a Russian, and a Spaniard. She found the Italian disagreeable and would

avoid him by spending whole days in her room reading. During this time she read Charles Dickens's *A Tale of Two Cities,* a literary discovery that may have influenced her alleged intention to kill off Harry Potter at the end of book seven. The death of Charles Darnay, sacrificing his life for a friend, and his moving last words—"It is a far, far better thing that I do than I have ever done; it is a far, far better rest that I go to than I have ever known."—had a major impact on Rowling.

Anne Rowling attended her daughter's graduation in 1987 in a wheel-chair and watched with pride as she was awarded a 2:2 in French. The next four years were to see her daughter work through a variety of temporary jobs including posts with Amnesty International and the Manchester Chamber of Commerce, a post so brief there is no record of her ever being there. During this time she began a parallel life as a writer, toiling over two adult novels, which were never published, and developing a passion for classical music.

It was while Rowling drifted aimlessly through these years that the most important moment of her life occurred. In the summer of 1990, Rowling's boyfriend had moved to Manchester and she found herself returning to London by train after a weekend spent flat-hunting with him. Quite sponta-neously during that trip an idea took shape: "All of a sudden the idea for Harry just appeared in my mind's eye. I can't tell you why or what triggered it. But I saw the idea of Harry and the wizard school very plainly. I suddenly had this basic idea of a boy who didn't know who he was, who didn't know he was a wizard until he got his invitation to wizard school. I have never been so excited by an idea."

The birth of Harry Potter was followed six months later by the death of her mother. Anne Rowling passed away on 30 December 1990 at 45. Joanne had visited home six days earlier but had not realised the seriousness of her mother's illness. "She was extremely thin and looked exhausted. I don't know how I didn't realise how ill she was, except that I had watched her dete-riorate for so long that the change, at the time, didn't seem so dramatic." The death of her mother sent Rowling into a tailspin. Within months her relationship ended, she moved into a hotel and would soon leave the coun-try altogether.

An advert in the *Guardian* for English teachers in Portugal held out the promise of warmth and a fresh start. Rowling was soon living in the bustling city of Porto in a shared flat with Aine Kiely, from Cork, and an English girl, Jill Prewett. Between 5 P.M. and 10 P.M. the trio taught classes at the Encounter English School before heading out to Swing, the town's largest nightclub. Rowling spent her days in local cafés, sipping strong coffee and writing in longhand the first draft of the first Harry Potter. Maria Ines Augiar was the school's assistant director and became a close friend, remem-bering Rowling as a "very nervous person, anxious" and one who was "desperate for love." Only after she had been resident in the country for 18 months did Rowling find love, albeit briefly, with Jorge Arantes, a dashing journalism student three years her junior.

Arantes was drinking with friends in Meia Cava, a downstairs bar when, as he recalled: "This girl with the most amazing blue eyes walked in." He approached her, they began to chat in English and found they were both fans of Jane Austen. The night ended with an exchange of kisses and phone numbers and within a couple of days they were sleeping together. But if Arantes, who had an abundance of Latin machismo, thought he could treat her in a casual manner, he was mistaken, as his new girlfriend made clear when he began chatting to other girls while they were on a date. Rowling approached him and whispered in his ear that it was her or them. She won that contest, but a volatile passion came to exist between the pair. Against the odds their relationship continued, with Rowling providing money through her work, which Arantes spent while looking for employment he never seemed to find.

The couple had been together for only a few months when Rowling became pregnant, just as Arantes embarked on eight months' national service. They agreed that Rowling would move in with Arantes's mother, who lived in a small two-bedroom apartment on the rua Duque de Saldanha, and await his return. Unfortunately, the pregnancy ended in miscarriage. The disappointment brought Rowling and Arantes closer together and on 28 August 1992 he proposed. Friends in Portugal were taken aback when Rowling accepted.

Maria Ines Augiar believed Jorge to be both possessive and jealous, while Steve Cassidy, who ran the school where Rowling worked, viewed him as rough and untrustworthy. His perception was not altered by an incident at the language school prior to their wedding. The couple had been drinking coffee in a café across the street when an argument broke out during which Jorge violently pushed his fiancée. Rowling burst into tears and ran back to the school, but the intensity of Jorge's outburst led one onlooker to inform the police, who arrived to find a large crowd surrounding Arantes as he cried, "Joanne, forgive me, I love you." According to Maria Ines Augiar, Rowling was soon shouting back, "I love you, Jorge."

The marriage lasted 13 months and one day. Later, when Rowling was writing *Harry Potter and the Prisoner of Azkaban*, she had one character, Professor Trelawney, inform a pupil that the thing he was most fearful of would take place on 16 October—the date of her wedding in 1992. The ceremony took place in Porto's registry office and was attended by Rowling's sister, Dianne, and her boyfriend. Photographs suggest a subdued affair with Rowling in black holding a bunch of deep red flowers. The girls' father did not attend. The speed of Pete Rowling's decision to move in with his secretary after his wife's death distressed both sisters and a fault line now separated them and their father.

The marital home remained that of Arantes's mother and was far from happy. Two months after the ceremony Rowling found herself pregnant once again. She continued her job and, worryingly, discovered she was losing weight due to the stress of arguments with Arantes. Prior to the birth of her daughter, Jessica, named after Jessica Mitford, on 27 July 1993, Rowling's friends were urging her to leave her husband, but she was determined to make her marriage work. Arantes's behaviour made this impossible. Rowling has never spoken publicly about her marriage, except to dismiss her former husband's claims to have helped shape the first Potter novel, with the withering line: "He had as much input into Harry Potter as I had in *A Tale of Two Cities.*"

But Arantes has described his shameful and violent behaviour. The extent of the domestic violence Rowling endured is not known, but Arantes admits slapping her "very hard" early in the morning on 17 November 1993 and throwing her out of the house without her daughter. When Rowling returned the following day with Maria Ines Augiar, a policeman accompanied them and it did not take long before Jessica was handed over.

For two weeks Joanne and Jessica stayed in hiding with friends whom Arantes did not know. Then she boarded a flight to Britain and flew from Arantes and his terrifying temper. Her precious cargo included a cherished daughter and three chapters about Harry Potter, her surrogate son.

Trains run through J. K. Rowling's life with timetabled frequency. Her parents met on a train, the idea for Harry Potter was first conceived on a train, and now in the winter of 1993, a train carried both mother and daughter north toward a new life in Scotland. After arriving back in Britain, Rowling had nowhere else to turn. Her father had married Janet Gallivan, his secretary, and relations were strained, but Dianne had recently married in Edinburgh and swung open her door. Despite her sister's hospitality, the next few years were to be Rowling's nadir. Although never quite as bad as the press has painted in terms of poverty—she always had food and clothes, heat and light—Rowling did endure a deep depression brought about by circumstance and frustration.

For the first few weeks Rowling and her daughter stayed with her sister Dianne and restaurateur brother-in-law, Roger Moore, in their home in Marchmont Road, but it was an arrangement that could not continue indefinitely. Social services organised a small flat at 28 Gardner's Crescent. So began Rowling's experience of government bureaucracy as she was forced to fill in endless forms and attend demeaning interviews in order to secure a weekly allowance of £69. A Christmas present she received, REM's new album *Automatic for the People,* only added to the gloom. The album was viewed by critics as REM's nihilistic best and Rowling seized on the spirit-sapping track "Everybody Hurts," which she began to play incessantly.

The new year brought with it a new flat, but her depression deepened. Shortly after her return to Britain her old friend Séan Harris had offered to lend her money, but she refused. By midwinter she was so unhappy in Gardner's Crescent that she changed her mind and borrowed £600 from him to use as a deposit on a rented flat. Finding one was more difficult than she thought and it was only after enduring rejection after rejection from owners unwilling to rent to an unemployed single mother that she secured the keys to a flat in South Lorne Place. It was a pebbled and brick-faced four-story flat, furnished thanks to contributions from friends.

It was here that Rowling was overcome by a feeling of hopelessness. Her despair was compounded by the arrival in March 1994 of her estranged husband in search of his wife and daughter. Since her departure from Porto, Arantes had succumbed to drug abuse and his wife was so concerned for the safety of her and her daughter that she was forced to obtain an Action of Interdict, an order of restraint that prevented Arantes from "molesting, abusing her verbally, threatening her or putting her in a state of fear and alarm by using violence toward her anywhere within the sheriffdom of Edinburgh." Arantes returned to Portugal and Rowling filed for divorce in August 1994.

The sense that she was failing her daughter was unbearable to Rowling. Whenever she visited the homes of other mothers, Rowling gazed covetously at their children's bright bundles of toys. Her own daughter's toys could fit comfortably in a shoe box. Yet when an insensitive, if well-meaning, health visitor brought around a raggedy teddy bear and a small plastic phone, she junked them in a fit of shame.

Only after a period of counselling was she able to tackle her depression and begin writing again. But once she did, it was the writing that elevated her self-worth. The first three chapters of *Harry Potter and the Philosopher's Stone* had made her sister laugh, a reaction that kindled hope in Rowling. In the long evenings at home, with little else to do, she set about working on further chapters. In the mythology of J. K. Rowling, Nicolson's restaurant is where the majority of Harry Potter was written. Yet the brightly coloured restaurant has now gone, long since replaced by a Chinese restaurant, King's Buffet. The new owner, Winnie Yau, still receives pilgrims from all over the world, asking about the building's most famous customer.

Rowling went to Nicolson's either as a respite from a freezing flat or through a passion for good coffee, depending on which version you believe. Nicolson's was scarcely convenient, half a mile from her flat and at the top of 20 steps, quite a hike for a mother with a young child in a push-chair, but it was owned by her brother-in-law which allowed her to draw out a single coffee over a few hours, and the primary colours in which it was painted couldn't help but lift the spirits of even the most despondent visitor. A second establishment she visited regularly was the Elephant House, on George

IV bridge, whose much patronised back room has windows overlooking Greyfriars cemetery. A sign at the entrance now reads: "Experience the same atmosphere that J. K. Rowling did as she mulled over a coffee, writing the first Harry Potter novel."

The writing of *Harry Potter and the Philosopher's Stone* was slow. Rowling wrote in longhand then typed up the finished work on a second-hand manual typewriter. In the meantime she needed a job. At first she took on secretarial work for a few hours each week, but a full-time job was a necessity. She wanted a career, not just a means to make money, and so applied to study for a Postgraduate Certificate of Education in modern languages at Moray House, now part of Edinburgh University. A generous friend supplemented a small grant and in August 1995 she became a student once again. Staff at St. David's High School on Dalkeith Road and Leith Academy, where she taught as part of her teaching training, remember her as keen and well-organised. She graduated in June 1996 around which time she heard the news that Harry Potter was to be published at last.

In early 1996, with the manuscript of *Harry Potter and the Philosopher's Stone* complete, Rowling visited Edinburgh Central Library to look up the *Writers' and Artists' Year Book* in search of a literary agent. Her first approach had been unsuccessful: a brief rejection letter. She then posted a sample of three chapters and a cover letter to the Christopher Little Literary Agency, based in Fulham. It was here that a young reader, Bryony Evens, read the first chapter and laughed. Evens passed the chapters to Fleur Howle, a freelance reader, who agreed with her assessment and together they persuaded Little to sign up Rowling. A few days later Rowling received a letter asking for the remainder of the manuscript. The agency sent Rowling's 200-page manuscript to 12 publishers, all of whom, to their eternal regret, turned down the book. Harper Collins showed interest but was too slow in formulating a bid and so the first book by the most lucrative writer in the world was picked up by Bloomsbury for an advance of £1,500.

When Barry Cunningham, head of children's fiction at Bloomsbury, invited Rowling to lunch in London, he praised her book but told her to be prepared as there was no financial reward in children's books. Rowling did not care. To hold a hardback copy in her hand was reward enough.

Anxious to finish the second novel, *Harry Potter and the Chamber of Secrets,* Rowling applied for a grant from the Scottish Arts Council and was awarded £8,000, which allowed her to purchase a word processor and steady her turbulent finances. The publication date for *Harry Potter and the Philosopher's Stone* was set at 26 June 1997 and Joanne Rowling was rechristened J. K. Rowling. Christopher Little had discovered that boys were unlikely to read a book written by a woman and so pushed for Bloomsbury to use the ambiguous initials in order to attract both sexes.

But before Harry Potter and Hagrid, Hermione and Ron Weasley, Professors Albus Dumbledore and Severus Snape could bewitch the children of Britain, they had cast a collective spell over an American publisher. Arthur Levine, the editorial director of Scholastic, a large American publishing house, first read the novel at 36,000 feet as he flew over the Atlantic to attend the Bologna Book Fair. He became so engrossed that he had no wish to land. Little had organised an auction for the American publishing rights to Harry Potter and Levine became determined to be the highest bidder. Three days after the British publication date, Rowling received a call from her agent to say that Scholastic had bid $100,000—an unprecedented sum—for a children's book that already had the makings of a phenomenon.

In the Eye of the Storm

In the autumn of 1999 J. K. Rowling arrived in America for yet another nationwide tour. *The Prisoner of Azkaban,* her third novel in as many years, had just been released three months after its British edition, a delay that had caused thousands of eager Americans to order Bloomsbury editions over the Internet. Her American publishers, Scholastic, were anxious to develop Rowling's profile with a series of book-signing sessions. Previous tours in 1997 and 1998 had seen the number of excited children and patient parents rise from dozens to a few hundred. No one expected to see thousands.

When Rowling's black Lincoln arrived at Politics and Prose, a popular bookstore in Washington, D.C., and Rowling saw a queue that snaked out the door and two blocks back, she assumed there was some kind of sale. On that visit she managed to sign 1,400 copies before her handlers dragged her on to the next event. The same delighted crowds of children and, for the first time, unaccompanied adults, met her at every city on the tour. Chat-show hosts such as Katie Couric of the *Today Show* and Rosie O'Donnell were delighted to share their sofas with the hottest author in America.

In the season of Halloween, Harry Potter reached critical mass and exploded. Across the country six giant printing presses were spinning 24 hours a day to maintain demand for his three adventures. The *New York Times* had J. K. Rowling at the first three slots on their best-seller lists and would eventually have to a create a new children's book list in order to evict her. *Time* magazine placed the boy wizard in the company of world leaders when it granted him a cover story. When embarking on the writer's life, the height of Rowling's ambition was for a sales assistant to recognise her name off her credit card and declare herself a fan. "In my wildest fantasy I could not have imagined anything like this," she told Katie Couric on the *Today Show* that autumn. "I could not even come close."

In Britain the books had been a slow steady burn. *Harry Potter and the*

Philosopher's Stone had a first print run of 500 copies, but Bloomsbury knew they had a hit when new orders began to arrive and the book ran into reprint after reprint. British sales had been assisted through the publicity generated by her $100,000 advance from the American publisher. Although in later years Rowling would have cause to regret her portrayal as "poverty-stricken single mum makes good," those stories gave her a profile most first-time authors could only dream about. Yet all the hype and publicity would have faded like the steam off a cauldron if children had not grasped the books as their own. Teachers and parents who presented the novel to their children could almost hear an audible "click." They got Harry Potter and they wouldn't let him go. The first Harry Potter sold 70,000 copies in the first year and won the Smarties Prize for Children's Literature.

The advance from Scholastic for the American rights had allowed Rowling to purchase a two-bedroom flat in Hazelbank Terrace. Jessica soon settled into Craiglockhart Primary School and a nanny was hired to allow Rowling extra time to write and attend signings and readings. While Rowling remained nervous and unsure around adults and particularly during interviews, she adored visiting schools and attending children's events. By the time her second novel, *Harry Potter and the Chamber of Secrets,* was released in July 1998, an anxious audience was already waiting. The book became a number one best-seller and the hype continued to build, this time infecting adults who overcame their embarrassment to lose themselves in a pacy, humorous read. In order to lasso a wider audience and spare the blushes of commuters, Bloomsbury released the books with moody adult covers.

Rowling's ambition was to release one book a year for seven years, taking young Harry up to graduation and no further. By the time the *Prisoner of Azkaban* was released in July 1999 Rowling was on the verge of her first million and had maintained her tight writing schedule. She had also taken the next step toward ensuring her creation's global dominance—a film deal with Warner Bros. had finally been agreed upon. An executive at Heyday Films, Tania Seqhatchian, had read the first Potter book, spotted its potential, and passed it onto her boss, David Heyman, an experienced producer who was representing the Hollywood studio in Britain.

Christopher Little, Rowling's agent, was aware of the tremendous potential in the film rights and urged a slow, cautious approach, while the author herself was highly protective. "I would do everything to prevent Harry Potter from turning up on fast-food boxes," explained Rowling. "That would be my worst nightmare." The deal Rowling finally consented to gave her unprecedented powers for an author, who is usually handed a cheque with one hand and shown to the door with the other. Under the deal she took a lower fee, said to be around $1 million, but had veto on the director, the script, and merchandising ideas.

Rowling showed she shared the pluck of Harry Potter when she disagreed with Steven Spielberg, who took an interest in directing the film. The director of *ET* and *Raiders of the Lost Ark* wished to merge the plots of the first two books and cast Haley Joel Osment, the American child actor who starred in *The Sixth Sense,* as Harry Potter. Rowling insisted each film tackle one book and that Harry had to be British. Spielberg walked away.

The Harry Potter phenomenon was to be driven by America, where 55 percent of all Rowling books are sold, and it was there, at the buckle of the Bible Belt, that the backlash began. In autumn 1999 the board of education in South Carolina agreed to review whether the novels should be available in schools after receiving complaints from parents. One outraged mother criticised them for possessing "a serious tone of death, hate, lack of respect, and sheer evil." A few Christian schools in Australia banned them on account of their tone, but the Catholic Church later rode to their defence and praised them for instructing children on good and evil.

For the feminist academic Dr. Elizabeth Heilman, the trouble was not broomsticks, but boys. The males were forever rescuing the females, who, she believed, were "giggly, emotional, gossipy and anti-intellectual." It was a charge Rowling dismissed out of hand. The more serious charge of plagiarism levelled by Nancy Stouffer required the judgment of the American courts.

Stouffer was the author of *The Legend of Rah and the Muggles,* a children's book published in 1984 that featured a hero called Larry Potter, who also had black hair with glasses. In her book Muggles were imps; in Rowling's work it is a term given to ordinary non-magic folk—but still Stouffer believed she was the inspiration for a now multimillion dollar success story. Rowling defended the case through the courts and was vindicated in September 2002.

By the time *Harry Potter and the Goblet of Fire* was published in July 2000, Rowling was struggling to cope with her new status. The pressure to complete her longest novel to date had been intense, compounded by a plotting error that forced her to rip up chapters and begin again. The manuscript was delivered in March and so concerned were her publishers about plot leaks that it was placed in a safe. Bloomsbury's marketing campaign meant no copy was available to anyone prior to the publication date, 8 July, and even the title was a closely guarded secret, to be revealed as part of a slow press campaign. The book sold one million copies in Britain and more than five million in America.

The success of her books had made Rowling inaccessible to fans. Book signings were increasingly difficult due to the volume of demand. When Bloomsbury converted King's Cross into Platform Nine and Three-Quarters from which the Hogwarts Express departs in her books, Rowling was unable to meet the children who had gathered because of the press scrum and could only shout an apology out the window as the antique train hired for the event steamed off. She had greater success at communicating her message at the University of Exeter, where she returned that summer to collect an honorary degree, urging the students never to fear failure.

Rowling's success in cash terms was staggering. The *Sunday Times* Rich List of 2001 estimated her wealth at £65 million, a sum Rowling used to insulate herself from the world. The small flat in Hazelbank Terrace was donated to a close friend, a fellow single mother, while Rowling and Jessica moved into a Georgian mansion in Merchiston whose nine-foot-high wall would deter even the most intrusive snooper. She also paid £4.5 million for a second home in London's Kensington, complete with indoor swimming pool. A country house on the banks of the River Tay called Killiechassie was added to her property portfolio in 2001. In previous years Rowling was regularly spotted around Edinburgh in cafés and restaurants, but her success restricted her movements to dinner parties with friends. When Giles Gordon, the literary agent, announced in his column in the *Edinburgh Evening News* that the author regularly frequented Margiotta, the popular city deli, Rowling never returned.

The next stage of the Potter phenomenon was triggered by the success of the first film, *Harry Potter and the Philosopher's Stone*. Rowling approved Chris Columbus as director and was delighted by the casting of Daniel Radcliffe as Harry and pleased that Robbie Coltrane had accepted the role of Hagrid. Writing on the next book was set aside as she discussed set designs and script notes, and watched rushes on what would become the second-highest-grossing film of all time (after *Titanic*), grossing $926 million and creating millions of new readers. Escorting Rowling to the premieres in London and Edinburgh was Dr. Neil Murray, an anesthesiologist whom she had met at a friend's dinner party. Murray, then separated from the wife whom he later divorced, brought love and a new balance into Rowling's life.

The couple married on Boxing Day 2001 in a private ceremony at Killiechassie attended by close friends and family including her father, with whom relations had thawed, and his second wife. The couple's first child, a boy, was born in March 2003 and the world breathed a sigh of relief when it was announced he would be christened David and not Harry.

There are now only four days to endure before the publication of *Harry Potter and the Order of the Phoenix* and Rowling can gaze with considerable pride on what her work has achieved. In just six years more than 160 million Harry Potter books have been sold in more than 100 countries, and both films have achieved box office records. Harry Potter licensing deals have been struck with the biggest companies in the world, with Coca-Cola bidding £65 million for the rights. Next week Rowling will become the first artist since Madonna to participate in a live webcast at the Albert Hall, at which 4,000 children will have the chance to ask her questions as Stephen Fry tries to contain them. Even Prince Charles has swooned in her presence, commenting, "I'm staggered that someone can write so beautifully."

The tragedy for fans is that they are one book closer to the end. The final chapter has already been written and is tucked in a yellow folder in an anonymous safety deposit box. We may think we're experiencing a literary phenomenon—but just wait until that box is unlocked. . . .

The Legacy of Harry

It was, she later said, "the best moment" in "one of the best weeks of my life." It was the summer of 1998, and J. K. Rowling was touring the country reading extracts from her second book, *Harry Potter and the Chamber of Secrets.* She had just finished a reading and the children had begun to drift away when a mother approached her for a quiet word. She explained that her nine-year-old son was dyslexic and Harry Potter was the first book he had ever managed to finish on his own. "She said she'd burst into tears when she found him reading it in bed the morning after she'd read the first two chapters aloud to him," Rowling recalled. "I'm not sure I managed to convey to her what a wonderful thing that was to hear, because I thought I was going to cry too."

That scene has since been repeated in bookshops, libraries, and school-rooms around the globe, as the adventures of Harry Potter have drawn an entire generation, previously bewitched by television and computer games, back to the traditional comfort of a book. Rowling's Harry Potter novels have been a godsend to teachers and parents who feared they could not open a book in front of a child without evoking a yawn. This love of reading in young children is part of a long legacy spawned by the Harry Potter books and by Rowling herself. It has been noted, too, that Harry Potter has become a trusted guide through the difficulties of childhood, tackling fears, death, and disappointment in a most admirable manner.

"We cannot sing the praises of Rowling high enough," says Charlie Griffiths, director of the National Literacy Association. "Anyone who can persuade children to read should be treasured and what she's given us in Harry Potter is little short of miraculous. To see children queuing outside a store, not for concert tickets or computer games, but for a book, is brilliant."

Griffiths says that the books themselves rise above the massive publicity campaigns that now surround the release of a new Harry Potter book.

"I know people will insist it's all down to clever marketing, but if there is not a story that a child wants to read then no amount of marketing will persuade them. Her novels have created positive peer pressure in favour of reading. A child might not have that great an interest in reading but he wants

to keep up with his friends and so he'll get sucked in. She's also helped shine a light on other wonderful children's writers."

The works of Jacqueline Wilson, Philip Pullman, Lemony Snicket, and Eoin Colfer have all been given a boost by young readers who, having torn through the four Potter novels, are anxious to kill time before the release of the fifth. In an unprecedented reversal, Harry Potter has also been responsible for the swelling hordes of adults reading children's literature. It is unlikely, for example, that Sir Tom Stoppard would be scripting an adaptation of Pullman's *Northern Lights* trilogy were it not for the interest in children's fiction triggered by Rowling. Children remain her principal audience, though, and there is no way to quantify the sheer delight and happiness she has brought to their lives. As one Scottish mother explained it: "She's made bedtime less of a struggle than it once was and for that alone I'm grateful."

But Rowling is determined that her legacy will encompass more than book sales and pencil cases. It will be to make a difference in the lives of those who struggle. She's determined to reduce the stigma attached to single mothers, ease the pain borne by multiple sclerosis sufferers and simultaneously raise their standard of care. She has said she will not be satisfied until Scotland has a chain of centres designed to comfort and support those with cancer. She has invested her publicity, time, and generosity in issues she can relate to, rather than adopting a scattergun approach. Today she is a patron of three charities: the National Council for One Parent Families, the MS Society of Scotland, and Maggie's Centre.

To One Parent Families she donated £500,000 and in September 2000 accepted an offer to become their ambassador, a role she has taken to heart. Far more valuable than her money is her time and the attention she can draw to an issue often neglected. An article she wrote for the *Sun* newspaper attacked the public perception of single parents as careless teenagers, pointing out that 60 percent are separated, divorced, or bereaved. "We are all doing two people's jobs single-handed before we even start looking for paid work and, as I found out the hard way, we have to fight twice as hard to get half as far," she wrote.

When Ann Widdecombe had the temerity to suggest that married couples were the norm, Rowling retaliated in a speech at a charities conference attended by Gordon Brown. "We may not be some people's preferred norm but we are here," she declared, before adding: "We should judge how civilised a society is not by what it prefers to call normal but by how it treats its most vulnerable members." The author has continued to support the organisation even though her second marriage means she no longer falls in the category of single parent.

Personal experience of the assistance Edinburgh's Maggie's Centre provided to a friend with breast cancer led her to offer her patronage to the organisation. The aim of Maggie's Centre is to provide cancer sufferers a place where they can receive information and support. Situated close to hospitals that provide treatment, plans are currently afoot to build another six across Scotland. By attending charity functions and organising readings, Rowling has helped raise thousands of pounds for Maggie's. Marie McQuade, the charity's fundraiser, says her backing is invaluable. "Her endorsement has raised awareness and we're delighted with her support." As Rowling declares in the centre's annual report, "I saw with my own eyes the difference that Maggie's Centre made to a very good friend of mine."

The charity to which she has the strongest bond, however, is the Multiple Sclerosis Society of Scotland. It is a cause close to her heart. Rowling's mother was crippled by the disease and it eventually killed her. She donated a large sum to help fund a senior fellowship in multiple sclerosis (MS) research at Aberdeen University, and last year she hosted a Halloween ball at Stirling Castle, which raised £280,000.

Of deep concern to Rowling is the fact that Scotland has the highest MS rate in the world, twice that of England and Wales, for entirely unknown reasons. There is no national standard of care, with treatment varying wildly across the country, and a crucial drug, beta-interferon, is underprescribed. "She's in it for the long haul," says Mark Hazelwood, director of MS Scotland. "She has a deep and personal concern about MS because she has experienced how it affected her mother. She may attract press and publicity when she visits our centres, but when the media have moved on she stays for a few hours just talking to people and I think that says a lot."

Rowling's legacy stretches to the cinema, too. The Harry Potter movies could yet be the most successful series of films in history. If Warner Bros. continue to produce a film for each book, the result could be $5 billion in box office receipts and billions more in merchandise and DVD sales. Daniel Radcliffe, the actor who plays Harry, is set to bow out after the fourth film, but a substitute will be secured and the magic will roll on. The Harry Potter film franchise is a gravy train that will not be derailed.

This level of success in film and literature is unparalleled. J. R. R. Tolkien was dead for decades before the *Lord of the Rings* trilogy was released, and Ian Fleming saw only *Dr. No* before he died, while other best-selling authors such as Stephen King have seen adaptations of their work flop at the box office. In a decade's time a boxed set of all seven films is sure to be a feature in many homes, as traditional at Christmas as *The Wizard of Oz* or *It's A Wonderful Life*.

It now looks likely that Rowling will live to see her net worth surpass £1 billion, the first author ever to do so. But she is grounded enough to know that her most personal legacy remains her two children. Her success in shielding her daughter, Jessica, whom no one has ever legitimately photographed—

those who did so illicitly were rapped by the Press Complaints Council—looks set to be repeated with her son, David. Meanwhile, the incredible wealth the books have generated allows Rowling to focus on what remains her primary purposes, her family and her writing.

The final chapter of Harry Potter's saga lies written, locked in a safety deposit box. For the next few years Rowling will work toward reaching that chapter in adventures that will span two more books. The question remains, what then? There are two things to consider. One is the reaction of children around the globe if the long rumoured climax is true and Harry, as children sometimes do, actually dies. The collective sadness of an entire generation would be palpable and who could judge the consequences of an authorial execution? It is this that spurs fans confidence that she will stay her hand, entwining Harry instead in a romantic ending with Hermione.

Whichever veil she chooses to draw over her multi-book saga, readers will never forget the boy with the lightning-bolt scar.

Bryony Evens on Submitting HARRY POTTER

"Then I started sending the book out. Twelve publishers, including Penguin, turned it down, and then Bloomsbury said yes. They paid Jo about £1,500—very little, but quite normal for a children's book at that time.

"I thought the book would sell, because I was convinced children would love it. It has all the elements of a children's classic—an orphaned child, boarding schools, magic, a secret world. Everything is in there. But I can't say I believed it would be a best-seller."

—Bryony Evens quoted by Tracey Lawson in "Spellbound," News.Scotsman.com (June 14, 2003)

Cover by Gahan Wilson for *Realms of Fantasy*: Gandalf and the Wizard of Oz stand in line to get their Potter books signed

This, in turn, will cast a long shadow over any adult books that flow from her pen. One challenge will be whether she can resist the temptation to return to the ivy-draped cloisters of Hogwarts or to trace Harry's adult adventures. Whether her success will be replicated in the world of adult fiction, something she has expressed an interest in trying when she has finished the Potter canon, remains to be seen.

The ultimate legacy of J. K. Rowling is to create a character that will be read long after she is gone and will sit in the same company as Bilbo Baggins, Peter Pan, and Alice in Wonderland. An immortal wizard is how Harry Potter will be remembered, one who had the power to charm the world.

Stephen McGinty is a senior feature writer with the *Scotsman* newspaper.

Novel Places: The Literary Landscape of J. K. Rowling

In an Internet interview a young American reader asked if there would be any students from the United States attending Hogwarts as a foreign exchange student. No, Rowling answered firmly, Hogwarts is British and will always remain that way.

For non-British readers, that is part of the essential charm of the Rowling novels: a Muggles world similar to our own but with a different culture, and a magical world set against the backdrop of a school for witches and wizards.

For that reason, those in the United States who want to explore the literary landscape of J. K. Rowling, personally and professionally, will have to go across the pond, as they say, to England.

The Guided Tour

Though not officially endorsed by Rowling, Bloomsbury, or Warner Bros., private companies are offering tours themed to Harry Potter, focusing on the film tie-ins. British Tours, for instance, offers tours to several key places that served as film settings:

1. London: The Reptile House at the London Zoo, where Harry speaks Parseltongue to a snake; the Australia House on the Strand served as Gringotts, the Wizard Bank; and King's Cross station, with its dual significance as the place where Rowling's parents first met and the place where Harry Potter begins his journey to Hogwarts.

2. Black Park, Langley, Berkshire, a 600-acre park that served as the setting for the Forbidden Forest skirting Hogwarts.

3. Picket Post Close, Martin's Heron, Bracknell, Berkshire, which served as the fictional Privet Drive where the Dursleys live.

4. Lacock, Wiltshire, the location of Lacock Abbey, a former monastery. Harry's classroom friends were filmed here.

5. Oxford University, Oxfordshire, where the Bodeleian Library served as the Hogwarts library, and where Oxford's hospital served as the Hogwarts hospital. Its Duke Humfrey's Library and its Divinity School also served as locations for interior shots.

6. Gloucester Cathedral, Gloucester, the cloisters of which served as the setting for ghost scenes.

7. Alnwick Castle, Northumberland, used for the exterior of Hogwarts, for the Quidditch games, and the broomstick lesson from the first film. (The second largest occupied castle in England—the first is Windsor—it has been the home of the Percy family's earls and dukes of Northumberland since 1309.)

8. Durham Cathedral, in which can be found one of the classrooms at Hogwarts. Also, its cloisters served as hallways for Hogwarts students.

9. Goathland Station, North Yorkshire, which served as the train station for Hogwarts.

For more information, go to http://london-tour.conciergedesk.co.uk/private-guide-tour-harry-potter.htm.

For those with a more adventurous bent, a self-tour using maps provided by the British Tourist Authority offer more flexibility, allowing you to linger at favorite places instead of being on a forced march with a planned itinerary. This also allows stops at non-film-related sites and personal sites as well, if you know where to look, which is important because Rowling's novels draw heavily on a sense of place.

A good place to start is the British Tourist Authority (www.visit england.com), which is the official government office that provides both Web and print-based resources. Though incomplete—owing to restrictions placed on the number of places Warner Bros. would allow to be cited—a free map, "Discovering the Magic of Britain," with Harry Potter on the front, is available. The map has been hugely successful, with 340,000 copies in print, in six languages, in all 26 countries where the British Tourist Authority maintains offices. (The U.S. office can be reached by telephone at 1-866-4HEDWIG.)

In documentaries filmed for British release, Rowling has gone back to her childhood homes and schools, but understandably the tourism bureau declines to highlight these, since they are not only off the beaten path but, in the cases of the homes, private residences not currently owned by Rowling or her family. Similarly, the schools she attended, all of which have approached her to celebrate the affiliation, are not set up to handle tours.

Here then are the highlights for a personally guided tour, depending on the extent of your interest:

Personal

• Chipping Sodbury, Gloucestershire: Rowling's birthplace.

• 35 Nicholls Lane, Winterbourne: Childhood home.

• 108 Sunridge Park, Yate: Childhood home.

• Tutshill, Gloucestershire: She grew up as a young girl here, in a quaint stone cottage.

• 28 Gardner's Crescent: Temporary quarters until she could get situated, the first apartment she rented after leaving Portugal was in this building.

• 7 South Lorne Place in Leith, Edinburgh, Scotland: She rented an unfurnished one-bedroom apartment in this building after borrowing money from Séan Harris to afford the move.

• 19 Hazelbank Terrace in Edinburgh, Scotland: Her first home, purchased with the proceeds of the U.S. sale of the first Harry Potter book.

• Edinburgh, Scotland: After returning from Portugal, she rented an apartment here; after Scholastic bought the U.S. rights to the first Harry Potter novel, she bought her first house here, which she subsequently gave away to a single mother who befriended her in those early years; and after becoming successful on a big scale, she bought a larger house, her current residence. She maintains two other residences: a Georgian mansion in London's Kensington, and a Georgian mansion (Killiechassie House, Aberfeldy, Scotland).

Educational

- Tutshill Church of England Primary School: This was her childhood school in Tutshill, Gloucestershire.

- Wyedean Comprehensive: She attended this school in Sedbury after primary school.

- University of Exeter: She graduated with a degree in French.

- Moray House: She obtained her postgraduate Certificate of Education here.

- St. David's Roman Catholic High School in Dalkeith: She student-taught here.

- Leith Academy: She taught French here to get her teaching certification, and was subsequently posted here.

- Porto, Portugal: She taught English as a Second Language at Encounter English Schools.

Miscellaneous Sites

- Nicolson's in Edinburgh, Scotland: The café is no more—it's now King's Buffet, a Chinese restaurant. This was where, at a corner table overlooking the street, Rowling nursed cups of coffee while she wrote in longhand and her daughter Jessica slept in a baby carriage.

- A train ride from Manchester to London. On such a train ride, during an unexpected prolonged stop at an undisclosed location, Rowling dreamed up the beginnings of the Harry Potter universe. (Who knows what *you* might dream up on such a ride? There could be magic in the air!)

- Bloomsbury Publishing in London. Obviously, there are no tours of Rowling's publishing house, but the city's many bookstores, new and used, make it a delight for any bibliophile.

- Severn Bridge in Tutshill, Gloucestershire, a favorite hangout of Rowling and Séan Harris, a model for Ron Weasley, Harry Potter's best friend.

Making Your Way Around Jolly Old England

The first stop any traveler should make is a Web visit to the official U.K. tourism website (www.visitbritain.com) where you'll find a wealth of information enabling you to start planning a trip.

It helps, too, to have a photo-illustrated, information-packed travel guidebook to read *before* making the trip. My recommendation: *Great Britain* (DK: Eyewitness Travel Guide). Its 672 pages feature outstanding photographs (over 2,000 photos, illustrations, and maps), succinct writing, and, most important, updated information.

Another book worth your time and money is *The Essence of England, Scotland, Wales and Ireland,* which is published annually by Heritage Handbook Company (www.heritagebritain.com).

To find your way around London, get a fold-out, laminated map. Measuring four by nine inches, National Geographic's *Destination Map: London* is a handy guide. On the front, a color-coded map of London proper, with an inset of the London Underground, the subway system; on the back, general information, a regional map, a close-up map of Hyde Park and Kensington, and a street index (in *very* tiny type, unfortunately).

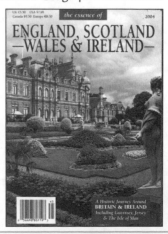

- Platforms 4 and 5 at King's Cross station, where Harry Potter catches the train to Hogwarts in the film version.

- Waterloo and City line at King's Cross station, which served as backdrops in the first two Harry Potter films.

- The North Yorkshire Moors Railway at the moorland village of Goathland, North Yorkshire: This served as the terminus for the train line from King's Cross station to Hogwarts—Hogsmeade Station in the Harry Potter films.

- The Dining Hall at Christ Church College in Oxford, which was used as the Hogwarts Great Hall.

In the United States, there are no specific sites of interest; however, the New York bookstore of Scholastic is worth a visit, since it is the best place to see a wide array of Potter products, from books to toys for girls and boys. Its address: 557 Broadway, New York, NY 10012; 212-343-6166.

Frequently Asked Questions (FAQs): General Things People Need to Know about J. K. Rowling

Most authors' websites have a FAQs (Frequently Asked Questions) page because it saves them the trouble of answering general questions their readers are likely to ask. Because Rowling does not have a FAQs section on any websites with which she's affiliated, I have answered the questions most commonly asked by her readers and the media, drawn from interviews.

Why does she use initials instead of her full name on her novels?

Because her British publisher was concerned that boys would not read a children's book written by a woman—an ungrounded fear, as it turned out.

What does J. K. Rowling stand for?

Joanne Kathleen Rowling. Her middle name comes from her grandmother on her mother's side.

Is there an official J. K. Rowling fan club?

No. Nor is one in the works. Sometimes, as with *The Lord of the Rings*, the film studio licenses an official fan club, mostly to promote the film and tie-in merchandising. But Warner Bros. has not done so, and is not likely to do so.

How can I get a signed copy of one of Rowling's novels?

Unfortunately, there are no inexpensive sources for signed copies of her books. Your best bet is to tap into the network of antiquarian booksellers, accessible through www.abebooks.com.

What's the best way to reach J. K. Rowling?

By regular mail sent to her U.S. or U.K. publishers. Despite the volume of mail, she does read what she can and, occasionally, even answers mail. Obviously, with millions of readers, it's impossible for her to be your pen pal, so be forewarned that a response is unlikely.

Her U.S. publisher: J. K. Rowling, c/o Scholastic, 557 Broadway, New York, NY 10012, USA.

Her U.K. publisher: J. K. Rowling, c/o Bloomsbury Publishing, 38 Soho Square, London, W1V 5DF, UK.

Does she have an e-mail address?

Yes, but even if I knew it—and I don't—I wouldn't share it with anyone. In fact, it's a secret more closely guarded than what's in vault #713 at Gringotts, so if you know what's good for you, you won't even ask.

What are the official websites?

The principal sites include: (1) www.harrypotter.com, the Warner Bros. site; (2) www.scholastic.com, her U.S. publisher's general book site; (3) www.blooms bury.com, her U.K. publisher's website; and (4) www.jkrowling.com, her literary agent's website.

What's the title of book six and when is it due out?

Despite any rumors you may read about on the Internet, the title is not generally known, and won't be known until Rowling gets a little farther down the road. Her agent has confirmed that she's currently writing the sixth book, but no projected publication date has been set. Though she has said that she expects it to be shorter in length than book five (250,000 words), we won't really know until it's finished, and I'd rather not guess.

When do you think the final book will be out?

I wish I had a crystal ball like Professor Trelawney, but since I don't, I'd rather not make a prediction.

Will Rowling write any more books about Harry Potter?

No. She has repeatedly said that she planned a seven-book series. Though readers would love to read about Harry Potter after he graduates from Hogwarts and (presumably) becomes an Auror (a wizard from the Ministry of Magic who goes after dark wizards), Rowling has no intention of writing more Potter novels. If you absolutely *cannot live* without stories about a post-Hogwarts Harry, then check out the fan fiction on the Internet—a wide body of work, running the gamut from bad to pretty good.

What does Rowling plan to write after she finishes the seventh book?

In at least one interview, she's stated that book eight would most likely be a detailed Harry Potter encyclopedia, in which she can tell us more about Harry Potter and Hogwarts than she's been able to put into the novels. As she has repeatedly pointed out in interviews, because she's the creator she needs to know more about Harry Potter and his universe than what she's imparted in the books. In fact, she has reams of material written that has never seen the light of day. Such an encyclopedia would be the perfect place to publish some of that material.

How do I become an extra in one of the Harry Potter movies?

With great difficulty. For one thing, Rowling is adamant about keeping Harry Potter true to form, which means (among other things) that the film director and casting director draw from the talent pool in the United Kingdom. Typically, a general announcement is made in the media, since it's not always a requirement that one be a professional actor; Rupert Grint (playing Ron Weasley), after all, had no prior acting experience. But be warned that the turnout will be large and the chances of actually landing a character role are *very* slim. Recently, for instance, an open casting call went out for twin Asian sisters, to fill the role of the Patil sisters, Pavarti and Padma, and thousands of hopefuls showed up.

Can J. K. Rowling recommend a literary agent to me?

No. If you want to write and get published, do what she did and go to the library to consult the standard writers' directories, which provide detailed information on what publishers and literary agencies are looking for and how to contact them. Then put together a first-class presentation for an agent. Remember, you won't get a second chance to make a first impression.

Also, if you can't, or won't, do your own research, writing is probably not the vocation for you: it's all paperwork.

Can J. K. Rowling read my work and tell me what she thinks?

No. Best-selling authors are frequently asked to do this, but as any attorney will tell you, it inevitably leads to unwanted lawsuits. It's always an amateur who claims his idea was stolen by the pro. It's insulting because Rowling doesn't *need* to steal ideas from anyone, since she comes up with some pretty good ones on her own.

Can J. K. Rowling make an appearance at my house/store/business/school?

No. Again, one writer cannot personally serve the needs of millions of people, all of whom want a personal connection. She's had requests to attend children's birthday parties, charity functions, school events—you name it. Rowling can best serve everyone by producing more work, instead of spending valuable time meeting far fewer people at private functions.

Is it possible to become a writer if you're not a reader?

No. End of discussion.

I've written a screenplay. Can she help me get it in front of a major film studio?

No. Film agents exist for that purpose, and can be reached via addresses published in standard directories. Without exception, film studios return, unopened, any unsolicited submission to its sender, because they want to avoid even the suspicion of theft.

I've read about J. K. Rowling or her representatives suing to protect their interests. What are justifiable grounds for her lawsuits?

Rowling, like most creators, prefers spending her valuable and irreplaceable time writing, not suing. But sue she must if she wants to protect what is unarguably the most valuable literary franchise of our time. In addition to defending herself against charges of theft (e.g., the case brought against her by Nancy Stouffer), she's had to bring suit twice, against a Chinese publisher and a Russian publisher; they both issued books that constituted literary plundering, with the Harry Potter characters stolen outright or minimally changed. Unfortunately, Rowling had no option but to sue because if she as a creator does not protect her copyrights, she runs the real risk of losing them forever.

Don't I have the right to take pictures of Rowling in public or ask her for an autograph? After all, as a reader, I'm the reason she's successful. Without me, she'd be nowhere.

Being rich, famous, and a public figure means that Rowling gives up some of her privacy in public, but common sense must prevail. Unless she's in a public venue like a bookstore signing or at a public appearance, she should be considered a private person and treated accordingly. She has the right, for instance, to shop at her favorite stores without being interrupted by well-intentioned fans who want a personal moment or memento in the form of an autograph. She has the right to sit in a café and write without interruptions and not have to endure press stories in which someone gleefully reports a "Rowling sighting." As to her success and its relationship to you: She writes a book, you buy it, and it's a fair exchange.

A Concordance: The People, Places, and Things in Joanne Rowling's Life

7, South Lorne Place, Leith, in Edinburgh, Scotland: An unfurnished, ground-floor apartment Rowling rented while on social welfare.

£2800: The total amount in royalties Rowling received from her first year's worth of sales. (Note: A book advance is in essence a loan from the publisher to the author on contract signing; it's an advance against future royalties.)

Amnesty International: A human rights organization for which Rowling worked as a research assistant after graduating from college.

Arantes, Jorge: Rowling's first husband, a Portuguese journalist with whom she had their daughter, Jessica. After a heated argument between Rowling and Arantes in November 1993, he threw her out of the house, but she later returned to get her daughter; two weeks later, mother and daughter left Porto, Portugal behind and headed to Edinburgh, Scotland. Subsequently, when Arantes traveled to Edinburgh to see her, she obtained a temporary restraining order; on the day the order became permanent, she also obtained a divorce from him. Arantes later attempted to sell his story to the British

tabloids, which ran stories headlined "Lost Love Who First Saw Harry Potter" and "Why I threw my wife out of our home five months after our baby was born and waved goodbye forever to our marriage and my daughter."

Austen, Jane: Rowling's favorite novelist (1775–1817) who wrote six novels, including *Emma* and *Pride and Prejudice,* set in the English countryside.

Bloomsbury Publishing: Rowling's publisher in the United Kingdom, who was the first to take a chance on her work.

Book eight: Since the Harry Potter series are chronologically published, they are often referred to as book one, book two, and so forth. If she were to write book eight, Rowling said in an interview, it would not be a novel but a work of nonfiction, *The Harry Potter Encyclopedia,* which would be a concordance of people, places, and things, with all proceeds going to charity. Like most authors, she knows more about her fictional universe than the readers do, because she has to. If published, this eighth book is where the history of Hogwarts and other miscellany might eventually see the light of day.

Brewer's Dictionary of Phrase and Fable: Originally published in 1989, this dictionary contains 18,000 words with "tales to tell." Rowling uses it as a sourcebook for ideas and names.

Cartoonist: Rowling is a skilled cartoonist who enjoys doodling. A preview of her artwork, shown on a BBC documentary, makes one wish she had illustrated her own books. (Like another British author, J. R. R. Tolkien, Rowling downplays her skill as an illustrator.)

Chipping Sodbury, England: Birthplace of Rowling.

Columbus, Chris: Film director whose credits include *Home Alone, Mrs. Doubtfire, The Goonies, The Young Sherlock Holmes,* and *Gremlins.* He directed the first two film adaptations: *Harry Potter and the Sorcerer's Stone* and *Harry Potter and the Chamber of Secrets.*

Comic Relief: A charitable organization established in 1985 to end poverty and social injustice in the United Kingdom. At the behest of U.S. literary agent Richard Curtis, Rowling agreed to write two books (*Fantastic Beasts and Where to Find Them,* and *Quidditch Through the Ages*), with all royalties going to this organization. He originally asked for a short story for an anthology, but she offered the books as an alternative. "You will do real magic by buying these books," she later told a child interviewer, in a video clip posted on the Comic Relief website, at www.comicrelief/harrysbooks. The two books raised an estimated $27 million for the charity.

Cuarón, Alfonso: Director of the third Harry Potter movie, *Harry Potter and the Prisoner of Azkaban.*

Department of Social Security: The social welfare system, to which Rowling applied for benefits after leaving Portugal. It was a humiliating and demeaning experience for Rowling, through which she received approximately $100 a week in benefits.

Doctor of Letters: Rowling was honored by her alma mater, the University of Exeter, with an honorary doctorate degree 13 years after her graduation.

Dunn, Alfred: The headmaster at St. Michael's Church of England School when Rowling attended its junior school.

Edinburgh, Scotland: After a failed marriage in Portugal, Rowling and her daughter moved to this city, because her sister lived there. Rowling's principal residence is in this town; she has two other homes, in Kensington and in the Scottish Highlands.

Elephant House: Like Nicolson's, a café where Rowling sought refuge to write fiction.

Evens, Bryony: A "first reader" of unsolicited manuscripts at the Christopher Little Literary Agency, Evens championed Rowling's submission, the first Harry Potter novel, accompanied by her illustrations. (Mindful of Evens's role in Rowling's career, in a copy of *Harry Potter and the Goblet of Fire*, Rowling wrote, "To Bryony—who really did discover Harry Potter.")

Fraser, Lindsey: The executive director of Scottish Book Trust, Fraser interviewed Rowling for *Conversations with J. K. Rowling* (Scholastic, 2001). It's not a biography, despite what Scholastic or Rowling has stated. Yes, it *does* have biographical information, but it's an interview followed by an overview and not (as one might be led to believe) a full-fledged biography.

Gallivan, Janet: Pete Rowling's second wife, whom he married less than two and a half years after Anne Rowling's death. Some believe this marriage created a temporary rift between Rowling and her father, since the dedication of the first Harry Potter novel acknowledges everyone in her family except him—a curious but understandable omission.

Goudge, Elizabeth: Author of *The Little White Horse*, Rowling's favorite book, which she credits as a big influence on the Harry Potter novels.

Gray, Francesca: Author of the first fan letter Rowling ever received. Like most others at that time, Gray had no idea Rowling was a woman, and addressed the letter with the salutation "Dear Sir."

Guinea pig: Rowling owns one, named Jasmine (the name given by her previous owner).

Harris, Séan: One of Rowling's best friends. He owned a turquoise Ford Anglia which they used to get away from the rural community of Tutshill. He is generally considered to be an inspiration for the fictional character Ron Weasley, Harry Potter's best friend.

Hazelbank Terrace: After the sale of her first novel through Little's agency to Scholastic, Rowling left South Lorne Place and bought an apartment here, near her sister's apartment. After she became wealthy, she gave this apartment to a single mother who befriended her in those early years.

Heyman, David: Formerly with Warner Bros., he moved to England and set up Heyday Films to act as a talent scout for Warner Bros. for potential film properties from the United Kingdom. This association eventually resulted in Rowling signing with Warner Bros., whose first two Potter films grossed $1.9 billion worldwide.

Howle, Fleur: A freelance reader who screened unsolicited manuscripts at the Christopher Little Literary Agency. With Bryony Evens, Howle championed Rowling's submission, the first Harry Potter novel.

June 26, 1997: The official publication date of *Harry Potter and the Philosopher's Stone* in England.

Kensington (London, England): The location of one of three homes owned by Rowling, in a suburb of London. A Georgian-style house costing nearly $7 million, this is her home away from home when she goes to see her publisher or literary agent on business. (Previously, she would have to stay in hotels when in town.)

Killiechassie: A residence of Rowling's, this house, within two hours of Edinburgh, is two miles from the nearest town, Aberfeldy. Originally constructed in 1864, this stone house has among its virtues not only the square footage necessary to accommodate a growing family but, more importantly, the seclusion necessary to shield Rowling from prying eyes—journalists, of whom she is not fond, and the general public, which treats her as if she's a public commodity.

Leith Academy: Rowling student-taught here in preparation for her teaching certificate; after obtaining her Postgraduate Certificate of Education, she subsequently taught at this school.

Levine, Arthur A.: An editorial director at Scholastic (U.S.), who secured the U.S. publishing rights for the Potter novels.

Little, Christopher: Literary agent who represents Rowling.

The Little White Horse: Novel by Elizabeth Goudge, which Rowling admired. "I absolutely adored *The Little White Horse,*" blurbed Rowling for an edition reprinted in 2000. A careful reading of the book shows it to be an influence on the Harry Potter novels.

Matthewson, Emma: The editor of all the Harry Potter novels.

McDonald, Natalie (Gryffindor): A nine-year-old girl who is mentioned on page 159 of the U.S. edition of *Harry Potter and the Goblet of Fire,* she is the only real person whose name appears in any of the Potter novels. A big Harry Potter fan, the child died before Rowling could respond to family correspondence about her, so Rowling gave her literary immortality by making her a student at Hogwarts; and as long as there are Potter fans reading the books, her name will live in print.

Merchiston (Edinburgh, Scotland): A residence of Rowling's, this Georgian mansion features enhanced security measures—a nine-foot-high wall with a security panel—to ward off journalists and the general public, to the dismay of her neighbors, who felt it was not in keeping with the "look" of the neighborhood.

Misty: Family dog when Rowling was in her mid-teens.

Mitford, Jessica: American writer whom Rowling credits as the most influential on her work. Jessica, Rowling's daughter, is named after Mitford.

Moray House: The postgraduate school that Rowling attended to obtain a teaching certificate, which she got in July 1996.

Murray, David Gordon Rowling: The son of Joanne Rowling and Dr. Neil Murray, born March 23, 2003.

Murray, Dr. Neil: Rowling's second husband, whom she married in a ceremony at her Perthshire home in Scotland on December 26, 2002. Only 15 guests, mostly members of the immediate family, were invited.

Newell, Mike: Director (*Mona Lisa Smile, Donnie Brasco,* and *Enchanted April*) set to helm the fourth Harry Potter movie, *Harry Potter and the Goblet of Fire,* scheduled for release in 2005.

Nicolson's: A restaurant in Edinburgh, where Rowling, nursing coffee, wrote fiction. The family connection: It was half-owned by her brother-in-law, Roger Moore.

Porto, Portugal: After graduation from the University of Exeter, Rowling moved here to teach at Encounter English School. While in Porto, she met Jorge Arantes, whom she married and subsequently divorced.

Postgraduate Certificate in Education: Obtained by Rowling so she could teach school.

Rabbit: Rowling's first attempt at fiction at age six, a novel influenced by the fiction of Richard Scarry. She later got a large black rabbit, which her daughter named Jemima.

Rowling, Anne: Rowling's mother who died in December 1990 at age 45 from complications resulting from multiple sclerosis.

Rowling, Dianne: Rowling's only sibling, born at home on June 28, 1967, at 109 Sundridge Park. Her family nickname is "Di."

Rowling, Jessica: Daughter of Joanne Rowling and Jorge Arantes, born July 27, 1993.

Rowling, Kathleen: Rowling's grandmother on her father's side, who died from a heart attack at age 52. After her death, Joanne Rowling adopted her grandmother's first name as her middle name, thus: Joanne Kathleen Rowling.

Rowling, Pete: Rowling's father who met his first wife-to-be, Anne Volant, at King's Cross station in London.

Scamander, Newt: Pen name Rowling used as the author of *Fantastic Beasts and Where to Find Them,* the proceeds of which went to charity.

Scottish Arts Council: Organization that supported the arts with grants. After submitting her proposal, which discussed her plans for the Harry Potter novels, Rowling obtained a grant for £8,000, the council's maximum allowable amount to a single person.

Second Tidenham (St. Mary's) Brownie Pack: In September 1975, Rowling became a Brownie scout.

Shepherd, Lucy: Secondary school teacher who taught English; Rowling credits her as an early, lasting influence.

Spiders: Rowling has arachnophobia, a fear of spiders.

St. David's Roman Catholic High School (Dalkeith, Scotland): Rowling student-taught here in preparation for a teaching certificate.

St. Michael's Church of England Primary School: The first school she attended, at age five.

Stouffer, Nancy: American writer who unsuccessfully sued Rowling for copyright infringement, claiming that her 1984 book, *The Legend of Rah and the Muggles,* was ripped off by Rowling, an assertion that, predictably, drew a lot of media attention to Stouffer and her books. In the end Rowling

prevailed and Stouffer not only lost the suit, but was also fined $50,000. According to U.S. District Judge Allen G. Schwartz, "the court finds, by clear and convincing evidence, that Stouffer has perpetuated a fraud . . . through her submission of fraudulent documents as well as through her untruthful testimony." End of case, end of story.

Though Rowling emerged triumphant in the courts, she found herself distracted by the legal brouhaha, one of several matters that may have had a bearing on the three-year interval between book four *(Harry Potter and the Goblet of Fire)* and book five *(Harry Potter and the Order of the Phoenix* published in 2003).

Thumper: Family dog when Rowling was a small child.

Tutshill: Rural community in South Wales where Rowling grew up.

Tutshill Church of England Primary School: Rowling attended this school beginning in 1974.

University of Exeter: After failing to get into Oxford, Rowling applied for and was accepted to this university.

Warner Bros.: Film studio that wooed Rowling and secured the film and merchandising rights to the Harry Potter franchise.

Whisp, Kennilworthy: Pen name Rowling used as the author of *Quidditch Through the Ages,* the proceeds of which went to charity.

Wyedean Comprehensive: Rowling was a head girl at this school, which she attended after Tutshill School. (A head girl or boy is a senior student assigned to monitor duties.)

Give a Hoot! No Owls for Pets!

If you give a hoot about real owls, here's my advice, echoed by animal trainers and animal conservancy groups: *Don't give your child a snowy owl for a pet.*

Not surprisingly, when children read the Harry Potter novels and, especially, see the film adaptations, the mistaken impression they get is that owls are wonderful pets: beautiful to look at, cuddly (especially the snowy owl), and responsive to human interaction.

Nothing could be further from the truth.

In a BBC news story (December 18, 2001), Lucy Clark, a spokesperson for the Royal Society for the Prevention of Cruelty to Animals, stated, "We are concerned by the surge in demand for owls because we don't think they make suitable pets. By their nature they are shy and reclusive birds, preferring to spend time in secluded places."

Here are a few facts about the owl that you probably didn't know, according to Clark, as quoted by the BBC:

Pepe Lulu, an adult Barn Owl

Nick Derene, courtesy of Raptor Education Group

1. It is large. Up to two feet tall with a six-foot wingspan, it can weigh up to eight pounds.

2. It is noisy, especially at night.

3. It is expensive, if you can find one. (In Europe, you can buy one, but there are strict laws governing their ownership. In the United States, you *cannot* own one, unless you have a special license.)

4. It has very sharp talons and can inflict deep wounds.

5. It requires a regular supply of food.

6. It requires a flight aviary and specialist veterinary care.

7. It lives up to 20 years, which means owning one is a commitment. (When children tire of their pet cats and dogs, it's off to the animal shelter with the pets.)

The BBC story also quoted Campbell Murn, of the Hawk Conservancy in England: "Unless they are trained properly they are not going to sit on a perch or a fist."

An article in the *Washington Post* (November 28, 2001) pointed out that the gentle hooting associated with owls isn't necessarily the sound emitted by *all* owls. As *Post* staff writer Don Oldenburg humorously observed, "[N]ot all owls give a hoot. Instead of the resonant muffled 'whoot' associated with the great horned owl, the screech owl makes a quavering down-scale whistle and the barn owl lets out a chilling hissing scream. . . ." Oldenburg added that during mating season female snowy owls "make odd guttural noises and doglike barks, cackles, shrieks, and hissing. Hey, it's a jungle out there."

In other words, the image of a cuddly, affectionate owl who is going to hoot appreciatively and give you a gentle nip with its beak is a fantasy, which belongs, properly, in the pages of the Harry Potter novels and not in your child's life.

If that's not enough to discourage you, the prospects of owning an owl in the United States are slim to none, for it requires a wildlife or falconry permit, which most people can't get. The same article in the *Washington Post* quoted Patricia Fisher, a spokeswoman for the U.S. Fish and Wildlife Service, who bluntly said, "The deal is, you are not going to get one. You are not going to find one for sale by a legitimate pet dealer."

If you're a parent, chances are good that after every popular movie featuring potential pets—Dalmatians *(101 Dalmatians)*, clown fish *(Finding*

Nemo), and more horses than you can whinny at—your child will clamor for one "just like the one in the movie." Be thankful, perhaps, that your child doesn't want a shark (Bruce, in *Finding Nemo*); but after all is said and done, if your child still cannot live without an owl, two recommendations come to mind.

First, adopt an owl being protected by an organization. Raptor Education Group will gladly accept your donation to adopt a bird. An owl, for instance, costs $100 to adopt. And what, you ask, do you get for your money? You get a chance to make a real difference and help protect a species, some of which are on endangered lists. On its website, the Raptor Education Group encourages contributions:

> Wildlife does not have health insurance. Expenses, i.e., veterinary and pharmacy costs, can add up to many hundreds of dollars for treatments for a single bird. Food and housing costs significantly increase these numbers. By joining our adopt a bird program, you can contribute financially to the annual support of one of our avian residents.
>
> Please choose the level at which you would like to contribute and send this form, along with your adoption donation to: Raptor Education Group, Inc., P.O. Box 481, Antigo, WI 54409. (Special adoption requests may be submitted.) In return, we will send you a photo of the bird you are supporting, as well as information about that bird's history and a certificate suitable for framing. Your involvement is priceless to the future of these wild birds. We truly appreciate your support of the Raptor Education Group.

The other alternative—and one that will fit your budget and be cute and cuddly—is to buy the licensed plush doll, a replica of Harry's owl, Hedwig, which costs $14.95, available in toy stores nationwide.

Hedwig plush doll

Footprints on the Heart:
Catie Hoch and Joanne Rowling

T his is all TOP SECRET, so you are allowed to tell [some close friends] and your Mum, but no one else or you'll be getting an owl from the Ministry of Magic. It is clear to me . . . that you are an extremely brave person and a true Gryffindor. With lots of love, J. K. Rowling (Jo to anybody in Gryffindor).
> —*in an e-mail (January 2000) from Rowling to Catie Hoch*

Joanne Rowling has, through her novels, touched millions of lives, most of whom she can never, and will never, meet.

One reader in particular—a brave little girl named Catie Hoch—counted herself among those millions, but with a difference: Rowling had planned to meet her because of a special bond that existed between them. Sadly, the two never met because Hoch, who had suffered from a malignant form of cancer that afflicts children, died at the age of nine.

Her death, as Rowling so poignantly put it, left "footprints on my heart."

With Catie having so much to live for but so little time, her parents tried to give her everything they could, to make her last few years as comfortable as possible under the circumstances. Like other children, she was a big Harry Potter fan and asked that all the Potter novels be read to her.

Her mother, Gina Peca, sat down to do just that, and in due course finished reading aloud the first three, which were in print; the fourth, unfortunately, could not be read because it was still being written. So her mother did what any other parent would do. She sent an e-mail to Rowling's pub-

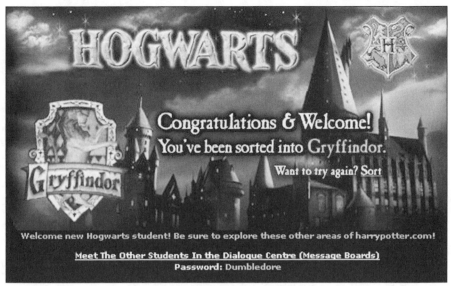

Screenshot of Warner Bros. website

lisher to ask when the fourth book would be released, and spoke of the joy the Potter novels had brought into her daughter's life, a life that would not likely see the publication of the fourth Potter novel.

Rowling's fan mail is, as you might expect, voluminous. I'm sure Catie's mother would have understood, though she would have been disappointed, if no response was forthcoming. Realistically, her mother probably thought the best she could hope for was a firm publication date, so she could, in a race against time, buy the book and read it to her dying daughter.

Rowling's publisher realized the uniqueness of the letter and forwarded it to Rowling, who, to the surprise and delight of mother and daughter, replied with news about the next novel, *Harry Potter and the Goblet of Fire*.

And so began an extraordinary, special friendship.

Rowling followed up with a toy owl, Pigwidgeon. Putting on a brave face, Rowling likely wrote through her tears as she wrote the note that accompanied it: "I'm so glad Pigwidgeon got there all right because (as you find out in book four) he's not a very reliable owl—a bit overenthusiastic."

Rowling has often said that she writes for an audience of one—herself. But in this special circumstance, she also wrote for one other—a brave child who, facing a certain and premature death, was determined to fight until the end.

As Catie and Rowling exchanged e-mails, their friendship blossomed, but there would be no fairy tale ending in this real-life story.

Rowling was there for Catie, with encouragement, by e-mail; and when Catie was too ill to answer e-mail, the author was there with phone calls,

The Catie Hoch Foundation

The Foundation gratefully accepts donations. (Foreign donors are urged to buy an international bank check.) The address to mail checks:

The Catie Hoch Foundation
27 Southwood Drive
Ballston Lake, NY 12019
Phone: 518-877-7539
e-mail:
gina@catiehochfoundation.org

reading the work in progress, knowing—like Catie's mother—that it was a losing race against time.

Even toward the end, the child was a tiny figure of strength. "Catie never complained or asked 'Why me?' She was a ray of sunshine," her mother quietly affirmed.

Catie Hoch died on May 18, 2000. The long-planned get-together between Hoch and Rowling would never happen. But what did happen was that, as Rowling put it, the brave little girl touched her deeply. As Rowling wrote to Catie's parents, "I consider myself privileged to have had contact with Catie. I can only aspire to being the sort of parents both of you have been to Catie during her illness. I am crying so hard as I type. She left footprints on my heart. With much love, Jo."

After her daughter passed away, Catie's mother agreed to give an interview to a British newspaper to publicize a memorial fund that she had set up to help other ill children, and the process of asking for donations began.

Out of the blue, Rowling, who had read of the foundation, sent a $100,000 check accompanied by a heartfelt letter as well. Her unselfish actions speak volumes about her generous heart, about the power of the written word to touch and inspire us, and, most of all, about what Rowling considers *real* magic—the enduring power of love and the human heart.

NOTE: Several newspapers and magazines have run stories about Catie Hoch, most drawing on articles published in the *London Sunday Telegraph* and the *Times Union.* These two newspapers, *Newsweek,* and the official Catie Hoch website (www.catiehochfoundation.org) are my sources for this article.

One-Parent Families and
J. K. Rowling

A single parent herself, Rowling went through an all-too familiar and painful experience that many other women face every day. Knowing full well the difficulties involved, Rowling became an Ambassador for One Parent Families (a registered charity in England; website: www.oneparentfamilies.org.uk), using her visibility to bring attention to this worthy cause. She has also made a sizable donation to assist the organization, which actively solicits contributions through its website or through the mail.

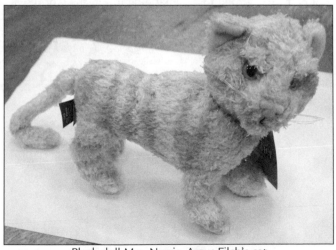

Plush doll Mrs. Norris, Argus Filch's cat

On October 4, 2000, the organization launched its official website and at a press conference to publicize the event Joanne Rowling not only showed up but spoke eloquently, demolishing the myths of single parenting and hammering home the facts that most people don't know, or don't care to know.

At the press conference, Rowling concluded:

> I am very proud to be the new Ambassador for the National Council for One Parent Families, proud to help work toward a fairer deal for a group of people who need to be supported, not stigmatized. Seven years after becoming a lone parent myself, I feel qualified to look anyone in the eye and say that bringing up children single-handedly deserves congratulation, not condemnation. We do two people's jobs single-handedly even before we take on paid work. I would like to think that the day will come when the phrase "single mother" and the word "penniless" do not go together quite as easily as they do now and that there will be much less surprise the next time one of us turns up in the newspapers as a success story.

J. K. Rowling on Being a Single Parent

Do you have any advice for struggling single mothers?

Rowling: "I am never very comfortable giving other single mothers 'words of advice.' Nobody knows better than I do that I was very lucky—I didn't need money to exercise the talent I had—all I needed was a [pen] and some paper. Nor do other single mothers need to be reminded that they are already doing the most demanding job in the world, which isn't sufficiently recognized for my liking."

—*quoted by Margaret Weir in*
"Of Magic and Single Motherhood,"
Salon.com (March 31, 1999)

Multiple Sclerosis and J. K. Rowling

Beyond the obvious, there are two good things about being wealthy and famous: The former allows you the financial freedom to give back to the community, and the latter allows you to lend your name to publicize any cause you endorse.

For Rowling, that cause is the Multiple Sclerosis Society of Scotland, for which she is a patron, currently spearheading a nationwide effort to fight the

Plush doll Fluffy, Hagrid's pet

disease on several fronts: by educating the public, by pushing for much-needed and long overdue legislation, and by soliciting tax-deductible donations.

Like most people, the disease was the furthest thing from Rowling's mind until it hit home. Her mother, diagnosed with it at age 35, lived a scant ten more years. Then, on December 31, 1990, for Rowling, what is normally a time of celebration became a time forever fixed in pain. Her father called and said her mother had died the night before. Multiple sclerosis (MS) finally took its toll and claimed another victim, this time striking at her heart's center.

If you have never lost a parent suddenly, unexpectedly, you cannot begin to understand the extent of the pain. For the parent who has passed away, the suffering has ended; but for you, it has just begun, and you will carry it to the end of your days.

As you go through life and celebrate its most poignant moments, you want to share them with those closest to you, but you can't: Your mother or father is gone, and your heart breaks, time and again.

Rowling's infinite regret is underscored by her sure knowledge that if a national standard of care had existed in Scotland for those afflicted with MS, her mother might still be here, or would have suffered less.

Love, of course, and infinite regret.

In *Harry Potter and the Sorcerer's Stone,* Harry Potter looks into the Mirror of Erised (*desire* spelled backwards) and sees what he wants the most. He sees his parents and reaches out to try and touch them, but he can't. He feels happiness and profound sadness at the same time, for seeing them brings joy, but knowing he will never know them brings a profound sadness.

This one brief scene of Harry Potter reaching out to his parents is Rowling the writer at her most poignant. She can write about it with such clarity because she knows what Harry Potter is going through. She knows all too well what the young wizard-to-be feels because she's been there.

Rowling, like everyone else, looks back and tortures herself with "what if" questions, the kind you ask yourself regarding a frustrating situation.

Back then Rowling could do nothing but rage against the darkness of the night. Now she can use her visibility to draw attention to the disease, and as a patron of the MS Society of Scotland she has become its most visible spokesperson, championing its cause.

Way too much has been written about Rowling and the essentially inconsequential: the number of books sold, the dollars earned in merchandised Potter products, the box-office receipts of her movies, and her personal holdings and wealth, which put her in a financial position that exceeds that of English royalty.

Far less has been written about her advocacy of the Multiple Sclerosis

Society of Scotland. Though newsworthy, it's a depressing subject that journalists would rather gloss over or ignore. More's the shame, since Rowling has worked and will continue to work tirelessly to promote the organization, to bring the disease to public awareness, even as journalists trip over themselves to report every little upward tick in her personal fortune.

When basketball star Michael Jordan's grandmother died, he carried the grief privately, and no one knew just how much she meant to him until he put it in terms everyone could understand. When asked if he had any regrets in life, he said that he'd give anything just to have five more minutes to spend with his grandmother. Tragically, a few years later, his father would be senselessly murdered and Jordan would grieve again. Being rich and famous, as Rowling would readily admit, doesn't insulate you from the kind of never-ending sorrow that visits when you lose someone close to you. Your life is irrevocably changed and all you can do is pick up the pieces and move forward.

> ## J. K. Rowling on Multiple Sclerosis
>
> "Would a national standard of care have made much difference to my mother? I am convinced that it would have done. Visits from a specialist nurse, proper support from social services, physiotherapy when appropriate: all would have improved her quality of life dramatically. . . . I cannot give her my time anymore, but I see being patron of the MS Society as my continuing tribute to her, to all she did for me and my sister, Di, and to how much we loved her. I know she would have cared deeply that nothing much has improved for people with MS in over a decade. It now remains to be seen whether the people in Scotland with the power to change that situation care enough to make the difference."
>
> —*from an op-ed piece in the* Sunday Herald *(November 16, 2003)*

Rowling has done just that. By being involved in a prominent way with the Multiple Sclerosis Society of Scotland, she does her most important work. Her books may entertain, but her work for that organization illuminates a greater cause.

J. K. Rowling at the Royal Albert Hall in London: One Author and 4,000 Children

Rowling has a cold place in her heart for journalists, but a warm one for children. In an increasingly media-centric world, the press is courted by book publishers anxious to get the word out. What the press wants, the press usually gets, unless it's an audience with Rowling, who acknowledges that its members have a job to do but often pursue it too vigorously. No wonder she parodied the press in her caricature of a pushy newspaper reporter, Rita Skeeter, whose insectlike name is rather apt. (A "skeeter" is a "mosquito," about which *The American Heritage Dictionary* notes that "the female of most species is distinguished by a long proboscis for sucking blood." That certainly sums Rita up, doesn't it?)

Instead of the media onslaught of interviews that usually presages the appearance of a new book, Rowling's interviews for book five were restricted to a handful. Notably, one with U.S. television anchorwoman Katie Couric and, in Rowling's own backyard, a long interview with the BBC. All other requests for interviews were politely declined.

Journalists, though, were invited to cover what turned out to be the media event of the year in the book trade. On June 26, 2003, Rowling appeared at the Royal Albert Hall, her only major public appearance.

Most of the 4,000 tickets sold were available on a school lottery basis to teachers in Britain and Ireland. (Ten were set aside for children from the United States, who were encouraged to write short essays on the question: "If you could have one special power taught at Hogwarts, what would it be and why?")

For the rest of the world, the event seemed off-limits, until a real-time webcast was set up so that everyone could enjoy what promised to be a unique event.

For those lucky enough to attend, it turned out to be a picture perfect day, sunny and warm. Thousands of excited schoolchildren converged on the grounds of the Royal Albert Hall. Considering the crush of the crowd, no one would have faulted Rowling for slipping in unseen through a back entrance, but she obviously didn't want to disappoint her young fans who wanted to see her, not from a distance, but up close and personal, and close enough to get a book signed, if possible.

When Rowling arrived in the late afternoon, pandemonium ensued. The press immediately surged forward, shouting to get her attention. She made a beeline for the American children, however, the contest winners who waited with books in hand for signing.

She stopped to make a brief statement to the press, but it wasn't enough. The media shouted even

Scholastic Essay Contest Winners

Initially, American students had no hope of getting a ticket to the Royal Albert Hall appearance of Rowling, until Scholastic arranged for a group of handpicked schoolchildren to get tickets by writing a 300-word essay on "If you could have one special power taught at Hogwarts, what would it be and why?" Students put on their thinking caps and took pen to paper, writing a total of 12,000 entries, from which ten were chosen.

Those lucky ten not only got to see the event, but were able to attend free of cost, with an all-expenses-paid trip courtesy of Scholastic. On top of that, Rowling signed copies of their books as well.

According to one of the contest judges, Scholastic's Editorial Director Arthur A. Levine, "Reading these essays was a wonderful reminder of the deep connection Rowling's books make with her readers, how her stories tweak the imagination, and speak to our deep yearning for the power to make our lives better and to leave an impact on this world."

The children ranged in age from 8 to 16:

Sudipta Bandyopadhyay (Somerset, NJ)

Daniel Boyce (Camarillo, CA)

Marty Cain (Marlboro, VT)

Nancy Chen (Tulsa, OK)

David Dawson (St. Petersburg, FL)

Louisa George (Rexburg, ID)

Brittany Hawkrigg (Bohemia, NY)

Emily Grayson (Brownsburg, IN)

Thomas Pardee (Modesto, CA)

Angela Wyse (Tecumseh, MI)

more loudly to get her attention, but she turned away from them and refocused her attention on the kids, signed more books, and then went inside.

No expense was spared to make this a special event for the attendees. The Royal Albert Hall was transformed into Hogwarts, with everyone involved playing a part, including the ushers dressed as Hogwarts students. On stage, a set recalled the common room of a Hogwarts house, complete with an overstuffed sofa, framed portraits on the wall, and a crackling fireplace.

With the audience divided into four sections—one for each Hogwarts house—students felt as if, for those few hours, they *were* at Hogwarts, trappings and all, with two special guests: Rowling herself and Stephen Fry, who reads her Potter novels on audiotape for the books-on-tape market.

Fry made his grand entrance via Floo Powder in the fireplace and wasted no time in making it clear why he was present. "Can I introduce J. K. Rowling, the most famous and most popular author in the whole wide world?"

He could and did, and the hall rocked with the collective enthusiasm of thousands of young Harry Potter fans who surely had counted down the days to this special event, just as they had done for the appearance of the fifth Potter novel, which had appeared only five days previous.

After a conversational interview conducted by Fry, a precarious dangling Ford Anglia descended from the ceiling and took a position behind Rowling. It was time for Rowling to read, which she does with considerable skill. (Clearly, she could, if she wanted, read her own books instead of relying on others.) She read from page 583 of the British edition of *Harry Potter and the Order of the Phoenix*, encouraging those who had brought a copy of the book to read along.

She finished the reading and closed the book. The children gave her a standing ovation. She thanked the crowd and—poof!—she was gone, leaving behind an auditorium filled with excited children.

The Art of Illustration:
Mary GrandPré and Cliff Wright

Alice was beginning to get very tired of sitting by her sister on the bank and of having nothing to do: once or twice she had peeped into the book her sister was reading, but it had no pictures or conversations in it, "and what is the use of a book," thought Alice, "without pictures or conversations?"

—*Lewis Carroll,* Alice's Adventures in Wonderland

Mary GrandPré

Painting vivid word pictures in our collective minds' eye, Rowling's prose hardly needs illustrations—or so I thought,

Welcome to the visionary world of Mary GrandPre. The portfolio is divided into two sections; Gallery and Children's books to simplify your browsing. Please take your time and enjoy!

Screenshot of marygrandpre.com

until I bought American editions of the Potter novels with art by Mary GrandPré. Unlike the British editions, the American editions are wonderfully,

It's about TIME: Harry Potter's Cover Story

The best portrait ever done of Harry Potter, drawn by Mary GrandPré for a *Time* magazine cover story on Harry Potter ("The Magic of Harry Potter," September 20, 1999) is available as an inexpensive miniposter from Time, Inc. The print (alas, with type overlaid) is available in two sizes. It is available online from the webstore Barewalls (www.barewalls.com). Type "Harry Potter" in its search engine, which will yield movie posters and two versions of the *Time* cover: an 8 x 10-inch print for $15.95, and the 11 x 14-inch print for $19.95 (plus a $6.50 flat rate for shipping).

Time magazine cover
with art by Mary GrandPré

delightfully, and appropriately illustrated with her charming work. In fact, I can't imagine reading a Potter novel without her delightful illustrations that adorn the chapter heads.

With deft skill and the right humorous touch, GrandPré's illustrations are perfect examples of how the right art can serve not as mere decoration but can also illuminate the text. Take, for instance, the illustration for chapter one from the first novel: Swaddled in blankets, the infant Harry Potter is asleep under a sky of stars. All looks normal, but looks can be deceiving. What, one asks, is that curious mark on Harry's forehead? Another example: the illustration for chapter two from the same book shows Dudley Dursley surrounded by a mountain of birthday gifts. The look on his face suggests his sense of entitlement and an air of disdain for his cousin, Harry Potter.

I could go on for pages, pointing out one delightful illustration after another, from all five of the Potter novels, but I won't. After all, you are best advised to go to the source and see for yourself—GrandPré's art is magical.

Mary GrandPré's involvement with Scholastic began with an unexpected phone call when its art director asked if she'd be interested in illustrating the first Harry Potter book, of which she knew nothing.

"It sounded like a nice job," reflected GrandPré in a profile for *Communication Arts*, "so I said 'sure.' I presented three cover sketches, they chose one, and I was pretty happy with

everything. They were great to work with, and I think I remember them saying there might be more. At the time, it just seemed like another job."

It was anything *but* just another job. As with Cliff Alexander (the British cover artist for the first Potter novel), Mary GrandPré suddenly found herself in the limelight, principally because of her high visibility Harry Potter-related assignments, including book covers and interior illustrations for the subsequent four books, a portrait of Harry Potter for a *Time* magazine cover story, and art for the official Rowling websites.

So, you ask, how good is Mary GrandPré? She is, simply, the best. In fact, Rowling herself has in several interviews stated that although many artists have illustrated her work, she ranks GrandPré's art first—no small compliment from a writer who is a talented cartoonist in her own right.

Unfortunately, fans who want posters of GrandPré's art are bound to be disappointed because Scholastic has not seen fit to publish them. No posters, no signed art prints, nothing. It's a curious omission that many hope Scholastic corrects, since GrandPré's art deserves to be seen the way the artist intended, as a color poster or art print without the distractions of overlaid type found on the Potter book covers.

As GrandPré discovered, being an integral part of the Harry Potter book world translates to instant fame. In demand at schools and bookstores, GrandPré is probably a bit surprised at the overwhelming response to her art. After all, although she's got an impressive resume, all that most people see is her Harry Potter art, the most visible of her output.

As GrandPré told *Communication Art,* "Harry

British edition of *Harry Potter and the Philosopher's Stone*

Potter is the most popular part of my work. But it's a very small part."

It may be a small part of her output, but it's a big deal to millions of

American readers who take delight not only in the Harry Potter stories but in their illustrations from the talented pen of Mary GrandPré.

Cliff Wright

The world got its first look at Harry Potter when Cliff Wright drew the cover art for the British edition of *Harry Potter and the Philosopher's Stone.* The illustration showed Harry Potter in ordinary street clothes; he's carrying a school backpack and standing in front of the Hogwarts Express. An overhead sign bears an odd number, "9³/₄."

Wright's visual interpretation of Harry Potter defined the look of the young boy wizard to Brits. The cover itself soon became one of the most recognizable covers in book publishing history.

Like Mary GrandPré, who would subsequently illustrate the U.S. editions of the Potter novels, Cliff Wright had no inkling that his association with Rowling would become his most popular work. He told the BBC, "When I began work on these illustrations in 1997, I had no idea how Harry Potter would grip the world's imagination. . . . Seeing my creative work spread across the U.K. and beyond was really quite unbelievable. It now seems a fitting time to offer my original illustrations for sale and allow fans to share in the works that have brought me such artistic reward."

As it turned out, only well-heeled fans could even dream of affording the original art. Wright, who also drew the cover art for the British edition of *Harry Potter and the Chamber of Secrets,* had no idea his watercolor for *Philosopher's Stone* would go on to sell at Christie's in London for an eye-popping £85,000.

Hoping to reap a king's ransom in Galleons, Christie's followed up that sale with an auction of three watercolors by Wright from the second Potter book. This time, however, sales expectations were not met. The BBC reported that the cover art remained unsold; two other pieces of art from the book fetched minimum prices—£12,000 for an illustration of Harry and Ron in the flying Ford Anglia, and £4,000 for one of Hogwarts.

The second auction proved to be a general disappointment, but perhaps the historic price fetched by the first cover illustration inflated sales expectations of the second to unrealistic heights.

Unlike the U.S. editions with the work of a sole artist, the U.K. editions sport work by several artists.

For British fans of Harry Potter, though, there will always be a special spot in their hearts for the first ever Harry Potter book cover, a charming illustration of Harry that proved Cliff was the right artist for the job.

The Harry Potter Symposiums

Hermione Granger, Witch

Named after a top-ranked broom, Nimbus 2003 was the first international Harry Potter symposium, held July 17–20 at the Swan and Dolphin hotel at Walt Disney World in Orlando, Florida.

An unofficial symposium sponsored by HP Education Fanon, a nonprofit corporation, Nimbus 2003 attracted a crowd of 600 people who gathered to immerse themselves in the world of Harry Potter. According to the Nimbus website, the weekend was marked by "dozens of hours of discussions of the books, as well as a feast, two showings of both Harry Potter films, [and] an amazing auction. . . ."

What made this get-together memorable was that it was not, as you might expect, purely a fan convention, nor was it purely a symposium, which would have been understandable considering the roster of academicians who attended to present papers, but a combination of the two: in short, something for everyone.

Unlike a convention that draws thousands and can charge correspondingly less for admission, Nimbus 2003 charged $179.75 per person, of which the three-quarters (75¢) is an in-joke for Pottermaniacs, who will recognize its significance. You see, in the Harry Potter novels, the passageway to Hogwarts is a train station that is numbered platform nine and three-quarters.

Nimbus 2005: The Witching Hour

Rather appropriately, the second symposium will be held in Salem, Massachusetts, October 6–10, 2005. Here is a preview from the symposium website (www.witchinghour.org):

> No town in the world celebrates Halloween in quite the same way as Salem, Massachusetts. Festooned with trappings of the season, the town comes alive with events throughout the month of October—nighttime terror trails, educational costume parades, a city-wide Halloween ball, tours exploring witchcraft and dark arts histories, live tellings of local ghost stories, fortune telling and psychic gatherings, and live music with traditional dancing, among others.
>
> But in October of 2005, there will be a new event in Salem Village. Harry Potter fans from across the globe will be invited to descend upon a community waiting to welcome them. To don their cloaks, grasp their wands, tote their magical texts, and Apparate to the Historical District for five days of magic and merrymaking, text and context, craft and criticism, canon and fanon.
>
> We have planned several tracks of formal academic programming, a concert, a ball, a fall festival, and Quidditch! In addition, we have included several nontraditional ways to explore your Harry Potter writing and art—a beta booth, fic readings and workshops, to name a few. The Sorting Hat will be ready, the Prefects badges pinned on, and our Minister of Magic dressed in his purple cloak of office!
>
> So be prepared! Get ready to dissect the canon and analyze the fanon. Get ready to explore our themes of choice, moral ambiguity, and the darkness within all of us. Get ready to workshop your favorite character or attend a keynote dinner discussing treatments of morality in young adult literature.

Collecting Autographs

A friend of mine, a professional autograph dealer, decided to collect the signatures of everyone connected to Stephen King, including the author himself, people with whom he has associated professionally, and television and movie directors, stars,

J. K. Rowling's autograph

and writers. He did it for his own enjoyment, collecting a scrapbook of signed photographs, playbills, movie tickets, posters, and so forth.

He had no intention of selling it, since this was done for his own amusement, but when the time came to sell, the scrapbook sold to the first buyer for over $3,000—not a bad return for his well-spent time! (When the buyer resold the collection, it went for over $5,000.)

I should point out that this prime collection took years to assemble, so please don't think you can get rich quick by collecting autographs.

For most fans, selling autographs is not a primary consideration; owning an original autograph from a favorite writer or film star is its own reward. A case in point is Bryony Evens, who approached Rowling for a signature at a 1998 book signing at the Cheltenham Literary Festival and got a warmly inscribed copy of *Harry Potter and the Goblet of Fire*. And no wonder: Evens, who worked at the Christopher Little Literary Agency, pulled the manuscript of *Harry Potter and the Philosopher's Stone* out of the slush pile and championed it. When Rowling, who had never met Evens, realized who had presented the book, she hugged Evens and on the title page signed her copy: "To Bryony—who really did discover Harry Potter."

It's unlikely Evens would part with her inscribed copy, nor should she. An important part of Harry Potter publishing history, Evens was there *before* Pottermania struck.

First, a caveat: Beware of items purportedly signed and offered for sale by online auction houses. Without a documented history of ownership, authenticity is questionable. Obviously, there *are* legitimately signed collectibles for which no provenance will be offered, but do you want to take that risk?

Buying Tips

1. Buy from a reputable autograph dealer, who buys and sells from other reputable sources.

2. Don't expect to get a bargain. If the offer looks too good to be true, it is. You may end up buying a bogus signature.

3. Antiquarian book dealers offer signed copies of books that are most likely authentic. Because these people make their living buying Rowling collectibles, usually from trusted sources, the likelihood that a reputable dealer will sell you a bogus collectible is slim.

Rowling's Signature

Obviously, the most desirable signature is Rowling's, on the title page of one of her books.

Unfortunately, because of Rowling's popularity, book signings are out of the question. For *Harry Potter and the Order of the Phoenix,* there were no book signings scheduled, though she did in fact sign copies at a bookstore in her hometown of Edinburgh. As the witching hour approached, the all-kids audience was told to count down the last few seconds; and at the stroke of midnight, Rowling herself appeared, to the surprise and delight of all.

Reported the BBC, "J. K. had with her a huge wooden chest full of copies of *Harry Potter and the Order of the Phoenix,*" which were handed out as kids lined up to get copies signed.

Gushed one young fan, a nine-year-old girl named Sidra, "I shook her hand—I'm never going to wash it again."

That was the only book signing for *Order of the Phoenix,* which means that signed copies of that book are scarce indeed—rare as a dragon's egg.

At some point, Rowling may simply stop signing books, like best-selling author Stephen King, who recently announced an end to his own signings. Since 1974 King has signed tens of thousands books, posters, photographs, playbills, and other memorabilia. He even allowed fans to mail in copies of books for signatures, though only three copies per person. (To ensure fairness, King's secretaries set up a computerized database of names and addresses to track requests.) Recently, King said "no more," he's done enough and had enough, and so those seeking an autograph will have to buy one from a book dealer.

Getting J. K. Rowling's signature has become increasingly difficult and expensive. What, then, should you do?

Depending on your budget:

1. Buy a book signed by Rowling from an antiquarian book dealer. Go to www.abebooks.com and type Rowling's name and the book title in the search engine. (Be prepared for sticker shock!)

2. Buy a book from eBay, if the provenance is established; in other words, buy only if you have a reasonable assurance that the signature is the genuine article. (Her signature, large and loopy, is relatively easy to forge.)

3. Contact her directly through one of her publishers, who will forward the mail, but don't be surprised if you get no response. She gets more mail than any other author on the planet.

J. K. Rowling
c/o Scholastic
557 Broadway
New York, NY 10012
USA

J. K. Rowling
c/o Bloomsbury Publishing
38 Soho Square
London W1V 5DF
UK
Note: For best results, use this address.

Though Rowling has not, to my knowledge, spoken directly on the subject of fan mail, any professional writer will tell you that trying to respond personally with even a postcard is like trying to sweep the ocean back with a broom—it's an impossible task.

As for getting an autograph at one of her public events, it's logistically impossible. The crowds have become too large and, as I've said before, it's a case of pleasing a minority of fans at the cost of disappointing the majority. At that point, it's better for her not to sign books at all.

Film Celebrity Signatures

As for signatures from anyone other than Rowling, several options are available:

1. If the celebrity in question has an official website, signed memorabilia may be available for direct purchase. This is your best bet.

2. If the celebrity in question attends public functions to meet the public, you should show up early with pen and autograph book in hand and try to make your way to the front of the crowd.

3. Check conventions in your area—comic, science fiction, and film/media— since many film celebrities attend them to promote their latest projects. Though most celebrities will sign on the spur of the moment, planned signing events at these shows offer everyone the opportunity to get photos or memorabilia signed.

4. Send a personal letter to the celebrity directly, who typically has his or her mail handled by a professional agency. A heartfelt, handwritten letter will stand out, whereas a form letter will be ignored. In the autograph trade, "graphers"—people who send 3 x 5-inch index cards for signatures—send out hundreds, if not thousands, of requests, using directories, mailing lists, and other reference sources. The reason they send out an index card is because it can then be matted and framed with a picture or other memorabilia for resale. In short, don't present yourself as a greedy "grapher." Instead, present yourself as a genuinely interested fan. Keep in mind that the average celebrity gets thousands of similar requests, so what makes *your* request/letter stand out from the pack?

Getting the Autograph by Mail

For most fans, the following procedure will be the easiest and most fruitful way to secure a genuine autograph:

1. Get the right address. Either subscribe to a celebrity address database service or send correspondence to a production company that can forward mail to the actors. In the case of Harry Potter films, one address suffices: Harry Potter Production in Leavesdon Studio.

Serious autograph collectors should consider subscribing to the Star Archive (www.stararchive.com), which has in its database 45,531 celebrities and their current addresses. A small subscription fee allows you to log on

and search the site. It's more efficient than relying on printed directories, which may have outdated information.

2. Draft a personalized letter and read it over carefully several times to ensure that it says exactly what you want it to say. Ask for an autograph and be polite, not demanding. You are, after all, asking the celebrity for a freebie.

3. If you enclose anything for signing, keep in mind that the celebrity may take weeks, possibly months, to return it, *if* you get it back. In other words, there's *no guarantee* that what you send will be returned, so don't send anything you aren't willing to lose.

4. Provide a self-addressed, stamped envelope for the return of anything you submit (such as a photo or card), so the celebrity doesn't have to mail your freebie at his own expense.

5. Be prepared to wait as long as necessary, and realize that there's no guarantee you will get a response. But if you do, *keep the return envelope,* which is proof of delivery, with a postmark to help establish the provenance of the signed item.

6. After three to six months, if you hear nothing, send another request. If it's worth a first effort, it's worth a second one. After all, you have nothing to lose but a signed collectible!

7. Be suspicious of anyone who posts on an Internet message board, purporting to be a celebrity. *You can't be sure you're communicating with the celebrity.* More often, it's just a fan who likes to have some fun at your expense.

Most celebrities surf the Internet and post anonymously, though actor Rupert Grint, who plays Ron Weasley, does post to the BBC message board under the name of "permlessboy." He is, however, a notable exception.

Actor Names and Addresses

Although numerous Harry Potter fan websites provide mailing addresses, accuracy is suspect, especially since some simply repeat what has been posted elsewhere on the World Wide Web. Your best bet is to send your letter to the Leavesden Studios; in turn, the studio will forward your letter to the designated actor.

All of the actors and actresses in the Harry Potter films can be reached at:

[Insert here the name of the actor/actress]
c/o Harry Potter Production
Leavesden Studios
P.O. Box 3000
Leavesden, Hertfordshire
WD2 7LT
UK

Tim Kirk

Notable and Quotable:
The Real World of J. K. Rowling

Early in her career, Rowling gave hundreds of interviews, principally to newspapers, resulting in a bounty of quotes that provide snapshots on how she views the world.

Antichrist: "There's a lot about witchcraft and evil and spells and magic. I was taught at church that that was not good."

—a young Christian boy, Eric Poliner, quoted by Jodi Wilgoren in "Don't Give Us Little Wizards, the Anti-Potter Parents Cry," *New York Times* (November 1, 1999)

Being alone: "I can be very outgoing with the right people, but I have always liked to spend time alone. I have got the perfect temperament for a writer because I don't need to be surrounded by people all the time."

—Rowling in a Barnes & Noble interview (March 1999)

Best-sellerdom: "She is a money-making machine. The temptation to keep writing after the last of her seven planned Potter adventures must be irresistible. She could be the first billionaire author in history."

—Philip Beresford in "Harry Potter Sales Reach 250 Million," Reuters (November 17, 2002)

Booksigning at Borders gone bad: "'It was a total fiasco, really ugly,' said Matthew Demakos, another attendee. 'Irate parents were screaming; people who had bought books were demanding their money back. . . .' Young Allison Zimmer decided to express her disappointment in a letter she sent to the local newspapers. In part she wrote: 'A dark cloud fell over the parking lot. Lots of little kids were screaming and crying. If Borders could only see how many customers were upset they would be amazed.'"

—Shannon Maughan in "Keeping Up with Harry," *Publishers Weekly* (November 1, 1999)

Censorship: "For generations, we have had books based on fairies, witches, goblins, magic, all with differing views. We cannot remove something from this world because of fear and ignorance. These are children's books, and as long as they are not nasty, cruel, ridiculous in any way or show witches as evil, obscene creatures, then there is no cause for mudslinging or legal retaliation."

—Arch Priestess Tamara Forslun of the Church of Wicca (Australia) in "Look Out, Harry Potter!," *Education World* (April 10, 2000)

"If this subject offends people, that isn't what I want to do, but I don't believe in censorship for any age group, and this is what I wanted to write about. The book is really about the power of the imagination. What Harry is learning to do is to develop his full potential. Wizardry is just the analogy I use. If anyone expects it to be a book that seriously advocates learning magic, they will be disappointed. Not least because the author does not believe in magic in that way. What I'm saying is that children have power and can use it, which may in itself be more threatening to some people than the idea that they would actually learn spells from my book."

—Rowling in "Talking with J. K. Rowling," *Book Links* (July 1999)

Charity: "One day a week is spent doing 'charity stuff.' She has a charitable trust and is the patron of several groups, including one for single parents and the MS (Multiple Sclerosis) Society Scotland (her mother died of the disease in 1990 at the age of 45). I say that I believe she gives quite a lot of money away anonymously and she stares at the carpet, lips pressed."

—Ann Treneman in "J. K. Rowling: The Interview," Timesonline.co.uk (June 20, 2003)

Childhood books: "If it's a good book, anyone will read it. I'm totally unashamed about still reading things I loved in my childhood."

—Rowling quoted by Elizabeth Gleick in "The Wizard of Hogwarts," *Time* (April 12, 1999)

Daydreamer: "I lived a lot in a fantasy world when I was younger and spent a lot of time daydreaming—to my parent's frustration."

—Rowling from a transcript of an online chat on BN.com (September 8, 1999)

Empowerment: "When I was younger, I think my greatest fantasy would have been to find out that I had powers that I'd never dreamt of, that I was special, that 'these people couldn't be my parents, I'm far more interesting than that.' I think a lot of children might secretly think that sometimes. So I just took that one stage further and I thought, 'What's the best way of breaking free of that?' Okay, you're magic."

—Rowling in response to a question from Skyler, an eight-year-old, who asked, "How did you get the idea of writing about magic?" during an interview by Margot Adler, *All Things Considered* (October 2000)

Fallout: "There's a lot of halo effect from Harry Potter that's positive and negative. Harry Potter is getting many people to read who wouldn't pick up a book. But what's happening is that it's eclipsing some of the literature. Kids don't want to read about animals, or they don't want to read fabulous things for their own age, or they're reading Harry too young. So we're spending a lot of time reminding parents that their kids are too young for 'Harry.'"

—Diane Garrett, owner of Diane's Books, quoted by Doreen Carvajal in "Booksellers Grab a Young Wizard's Cloaktails," *New York Times* (February 28, 2000)

Fantasy books: "More can be learned from them about the inner problems of human beings, and of the right solutions to their predicaments in any society than from any other type of story within a child's comprehension."

—Bruno Bettelheim, *The Uses of Enchantment* (1975)

Grief: "I know, of course, that these feelings are not unique to me, I know that guilt goes hand in hand with grief, as does its close relative, anger. I was very angry indeed: angry at myself, angry that my mother had died so young, angry at the illness that killed her, but also, and increasingly, angry at the care, or lack of it, that she had received."

—Rowling in "Multiple Sclerosis Killed My Mother," *Sunday Herald* (November 16, 2003)

Halloween: "Halloween, you'd not be surprised to know, is my favorite holiday."

—Rowling in *Time* magazine (October 30, 2000)

Heart's desire: "I was conscious that when I looked in the Mirror [of Erised], I would see exactly what Harry saw. But it was only when I'd written it that I fully realised where it had all come from. It is an enormous regret to me that my mother never knew about any of this, second only to the fact that she never met my daughter."

—Rowling quoted by Helena de Bertodano in "Harry Potter Charms a Nation," *Electronic Telegraph* (July 25, 1998)

Invisibility: "When asked what magical power she would like to possess and what she would do with it, Rowling replied, 'Invisibility. I would sneak off to a café and write all day.'"

—Rowling, quoted by Shannon Maughan, *PW Daily for Booksellers* (June 27, 2003), publishersweekly.com

Legal victory: "The court found 'clear and convincing evidence' that there was no infringement and that Stouffer had made false claims in presenting material to the court for characters that she neither created nor sold when she claimed she did. Stouffer, the judge wrote, 'engaged in a pattern of intentional bad faith conduct and failed to correct her fraudulent submissions,' and ordered her to pay $50,000 in attorney's fees and court costs."

—Jim Milliot and Steven Zeitchik in "Scholastic Rebuffs Potter Infringement Charges," *Publishers Weekly* (September 23, 2002)

Lightning bolt scar: "Shay Corrie almost died trying to save his friend, but was thrilled when he woke up in the hospital with a Harry Potteresque lightning bolt scar on his forehead."

—from the *Hogwarts Wire* online (October 30, 2003)

Literacy: "She is of outstanding distinction and has an international impact in her own field. She had an impact in reversing the worldwide trend in decreasing literacy. Her writing has attracted a huge number of children who previously had difficulties in beginning to read, and the society sees that her work has dispelled the myth that children lack the attention span to engage with longer books."

—Rowling lauded as an honorary fellow of the Royal Society of Edinburgh, as reported by Frank O'Donnell in "Rowling Joins Academic Elite," *Scotsman* (March 5, 2002)

Make-believe: "Come on, Jerry. It's just a story. The kids know it's make-believe; that's what novels are all about. Have you ever read one?"

—Jack Moseley in "Kids Have the Right to Read Harry Potter," *Arkansas News Bureau* (March 14, 2003)

Merchandising: "The magic is going. Soon there will be nothing special about Harry Potter. He'll be just another face on a cereal box. And a Coke can. And a toy. And candy."

—Matthew Flitton in "Harry Potter Merchandising Will Make the Magic Go Away," HardNewsCafe.usu.edu (November 28, 2001)

Merchandising, a kid's perspective: "J. K. Rowling created a feeling of magic when she wrote Harry Potter but all this merchandising and filmmaking is taking away that special feeling."

—Mark Luney, aged 14, quoted in "Harry Potter and Potty Ulster," childrens-express.org (January 1, 2002)

Merchandising nightmares: "I knew about the alarm clock. How do I feel about it? Honestly, I think it's pretty well known, if I could have stopped all merchandising I would have done so. And twice a year I sit down with Warner Bros. and we have conversations about merchandising and I can only say you should have seen some of the stuff that was stopped: Moaning Myrtle lavatory seat alarms and worse."

—Rowling in an interview conducted by Jeremy Paxman that aired on BBC Two (June 19, 2003), quoted in BBC News online

Money: "'But,' I ask, 'aren't you going to buy something, like a yacht perhaps?' This makes her bark with laughter."

—Ann Treneman in "J. K. Rowling: The Interview," *Times* (June 30, 2000)

Moviegoers: "In our world, not everyone is a reader first. There are people who go to movies and then realize there is a book."

—Barbara Marcus, President at Scholastic, quoted by David D. Kirkpatrick in "New Sign on Harry Potter's Forehead: For Sale," reprinted from the *New York Times* in the *Atlanta-Journal Constitution* (June 16, 2003)

Muggle: "Am I a Muggle? Yes, I am definitely a Muggle—a Muggle with an abnormal amount of knowledge about the wizarding world."

—Rowling interviewed in the *Connection* (October 12, 1999)

Parenting: "And I wouldn't mind being remembered as a good parent. But we won't know whether I've achieved that until my daughter writes *J. K. Dearest*."

—Rowling quoted by J. F. O. McAllister in "The Shy Sorceress," a sidebar to "The Real Magic of Harry Potter," *Time* (June 23, 2003)

Parody: "'If Warner sues, we might as well roll up literary parody right now,' he said. Gerber said the book, which features an attempt to prevent a movie about the School of Hogwash from being made, is meant not only as entertainment, but as a serious comment on media conglomerates."

—on Michael Gerber's *Barry Trotter and the Unauthorized Parody*, from a story by Steve Zeitchik in *Publishers Weekly* (December 24, 2001)

Pet owls: "We are concerned by the surge in demand for owls because we don't think they make suitable pets. By their nature they are shy and reclusive birds, preferring to spend time in secluded places."

—Lucy Clark, spokesperson for the Royal Society for the Prevention of Cruelty to Animals, quoted in "Potter Sparks Pet Owl Demand," BBC online (December 18, 2001)

Poverty: "I remember reaching the supermarket checkout, counting out the money in coppers, finding out I was two pence short of a tin of baked beans and feeling I had to pretend I had mislaid a ten pound note for the benefit of the bored girl at the till. Similarly unappreciated acting skills were required for my forays into Mother care, where I would pretend to be examining clothes I could not afford for my daughter. All the time I would be edging ever closer to the baby-changing room where they offered a small supply of free nappies [diapers]."

—Rowling quoted by Clare Goldwin in "J. K. Rowling on her Days of Poverty," mirror.co.uk (May 20, 2002)

Privacy gone: "In fact, Rowling has tried to throw a cloak of invisibility around her family so they can live almost normal lives. But simple pleasures like strolling to the supermarket at home in Edinburgh or attending Jessica's Christmas pageant require constant vigilance against an army of tabloid reporters and the occasional stalker."

—J. F. O. McAllister in "The Shy Sorceress," a sidebar to "The Real Magic of Harry Potter," *Time* (June 23, 2003)

Proprietary fans: "In one sense, the boy wizard has slipped beyond her control; he is out there, everywhere, and legions of people feel a sense of ownership. But in the most important way, Harry still belongs to her. His future is in her head, as is that of the entire fictional universe she has set in motion."

—Paul Gray, "The Magic of Potter," *Time* (December 17, 2000)

Public relations nightmare: "It's really horrible. . . . So 10-year-old kids there have been told by a local paper that I'm getting out to sign. And then you have the police on the platform saying, 'Don't get out. It'll cause trouble.' So it's torturous as I'm just sitting there staring at crying children."

—Rowling commenting on a publicity tour nightmare, a train stop at which the local paper erroneously reported that she was there to sign books, quoted by Evan Solomon in "J. K. Rowling Interview," Canadian Broadcasting Company (July 2000)

Putin parodied: "The Russian radio station Ekho Moskvy reported that a group of Russian lawyers is preparing to take legal action against the film's producers. The lawyers apparently claim that the artists who created Dobby intentionally based him on Putin [president of Russia]. And that, naturally, shouldn't be allowed."

—Kathleen Knox in "Harry Potter and the Putin Imputation," atimes.com (January 29, 2003)

Quirky book: "I never expected to make money. I always saw Harry Potter as this quirky little book. I liked it and I worked hard at it, but never in my wildest dreams did I imagine large advances."

—Rowling quoted by Eddie Gibb in "Tales from a Single Mother," *Herald* (June 29, 1997)

Reclusiveness: "It makes me laugh, it really makes me laugh. It makes friends of mine laugh. I'm not reclusive. There are two reasons why I haven't done a lot of interviews recently. One, as I say, is I wanted to be working. An interview knocks out half a working day for me, and I was working ten-hour days on this book. I could not afford the time. To me, it was a waste of energy. I would rather be writing the book. And the other thing, which in my experience people tend to forget, is I'm still a single parent."

—Rowling quoted by Evan Solomon in "J. K. Rowling Interview," Canadian Broadcasting Company (July 2000)

Serendipity: "An interview with Rowling ran in the *Seattle Times* two days before she arrived in that city, and while the author was signing copies of *Harry Potter* in a bookstore in Seattle, a woman arrived, waving the newspaper clipping. When she asked if the store stocked the book, Rowling said, 'She had no idea I was there, and was quite pleased when the bookseller responded that not only did they have the book, but its author was sitting just behind her and would sign it for her. That was one of the most wonderful moments during my trip.'"

—Sally Lodge, from "Children's Authors and Illustrators Share Memorable Moments from Recent Book Tours," *Publishers Weekly* (January 4, 1999)

Nancy Stouffer: "It was as if some strange woman had come out of nowhere saying she was my children's mother . . . It was like a punch in the stomach. People think that if you have been successful, you are insulated from normal feelings of hurt, but you aren't."

—Rowling quoted by J. F. O. McAllister in "The Shy Sorceress," a sidebar to "The Real Magic of Harry Potter," *Time* (June 23, 2003)

Transition: "I don't know what I'll do now. I'm very nervous of just packing in my part-time teaching and becoming a full-time author, even though that is something I have always wanted to do."

—Rowling in "Book Written in Edinburgh Café Sells for $100,000," *Herald* (July 8, 1997)

Unauthorized books: "Rowling's legal team took exception to *The Irresistible Rise of Harry Potter* on the grounds that the colour scheme, typography and use of star symbols created the impression it was officially endorsed. . . . They objected to the purple colour scheme, the spiky typeface and the use of stars, and asked for a prominent disclaimer making it clear the book was not officially endorsed."

—Annabel House in "Potter Spin-off Spellbound by Legal Guardians," *Scotland on Sunday* (November 17, 2002)

Unfit literary fare: "These are not, however, books for adults. Unlike

Huckleberry Finn or *Alice in Wonderland,* the Potter series is not written on two levels, entertaining one generation while instructing another. Rather, it is in the category of Tom Swift and Dr. Dolittle; I was hooked on reading by them, but have laid aside my electric rifle and no longer talk to horses."

—William Safire, in an op-ed piece, *New York Times* (January 27, 2000)

Wands: "I drop in on two wand manufacturers. Allivan's is run by Dave Wedzik, whose prices range from $35 for a basic model and up to $65 for a customised ebony version. 'We have had the occasional person ringing to say: My wand does not work,' says Wedzik. As for phoenix feathers: 'It has been difficult to find them lately. But we get calls about those, too.'"

—Roger Highfield at the Nimbus 2003 Harry Potter convention, reported in "All This Magic Makes My Brain Ache," Telegraph.co.uk (July 22, 2003)

Warner Bros. website: "The official Harry Potter website looks like it's had an awful lot of time and money invested in it. Given the amount of money JK's Harry has made everyone, though, they can probably afford it."

—From "Harry Potter Official Website," News.scotsman.com (June 5, 2003)

Welfare: "I had no intention, no desire, to remain on benefits. It's the most soul-destroying thing. I don't want to dramatise, but there were nights when, though Jessica ate, I didn't."

—Rowling quoted by Elisabeth Dunn in "From the Dole to Hollywood," *Electronic Herald* (August 2, 1997)

Witchcraft: "I have met thousands of children now, and not even one time has a child come up to me and said, 'Ms. Rowling, I'm so glad I've read these books because now I want to be a witch.' They see it for what it is. It is a fantasy world and they understand that completely. I don't believe in magic, either."

—Rowling in "Success of Harry Potter Bowls Author Over," CNN.com: Book News (October 21, 1999)

Part Two:
A Writer's Life

Tim Kirk

To understand and appreciate Rowling's life and work, it's essential not only to understand why she does what she does, but how she does it. Rowling's success has inspired countless people of all ages to pick up a pen and start writing. Some of those dreamers simply want to hold a finished book in their hands, but others have loftier goals—not only to publish, but also to become a best-selling author.

The Magic of Words: A Storyteller's World

I'm not writing for the money: It's for me and out of loyalty to fans.
—Rowling, in an interview conducted by Ann Treneman for the Times

Mike and Sully (*Monsters, Inc.*) play charades. The clue: Harry Potter.

To most the act of creative writing is a mystery—almost magic. To demystify the process, writer Harlan Ellison, best known for his essays, short fiction, and screenplays, has on numerous occasions set up his manual typewriter and typed out a short story from start to finish in one sitting, which is then photocopied, autographed, and given to customers who buy copies of his books from that store.

To counter the occasional charge from the nonbelievers that he's rigged the event—that he's a ringer—he'll ask someone to name specific story elements, which he'll then use to build a story. In other words, he's staking his reputation on the fact that he can write about anything, anywhere, and at any time. It's not magic, he says, it's hard work, imagination, creativity, and a lifetime of reading, writing, observing, and living life.

For nonwriters, the idea for a piece of writing can be likened to oyster grit. For nonwriters, who lack the imagination to create something from nothing, the grit will forever remain just a piece of dirt that irritates the oyster. But for writers, the grit may over time produce a pearl, a gem of a story.

In the world of creative fiction, the oyster bed of ideas realized by Rowling has yielded a rich bounty indeed. Journalists, who work on impossibly tight deadlines and want to catch the reader's attention, are quick to point out that she's richer than the Queen of England, that she owns three magnificent houses, that she's a rag-to-riches story. It's all part of Rowling's life story, but in the end, as Shakespeare reminds us, the play's the thing.

Rowling's early years before she finally hit it big sound similar to that of other successful writers. Like Stephen King, Rowling has always written for an audience of one (herself), never expected to make a fortune, taught school to support herself, and was finally freed to do what she felt was her life's work when a major subsidiary sale allowed her to quit teaching.

In Rowling's case, the odds certainly seemed stacked against her, because the captains of the book industry, especially children's book publishers, tend to look backward.

Unable to afford the cost of photocopying, Rowling typed out two copies of the first Harry Potter novel on a typewriter she bought for $80. Though there are conflicting reports in the media as to whom she sent the fledgling manuscript, the fact remains that the first publisher who saw the over-80,000-word manuscript rejected it on the grounds that it was too long for a children's book. (Imagine trying to convince a child who compulsively read the first book in one unbroken reading session that it was too long; if anything, readers complain that her books are, like *The Lord of the Rings* books, too short.) Frankly, I'd hate to be the acquisitions editor or agent who rejected Rowling, since it's a mistake one can't afford to make twice. Writers like Rowling are so rare, you can count them on one hand, with four fingers hidden from view.

Fortunately for Rowling, she happened to send her manuscript to the Christopher Little Literary Agency in London, which remains her agency to this day—a rare enough circumstance in these times when writers are quick to leave at the first sign of a better offer. But no, Rowling is fiercely loyal to those who were there when she was a no-name author; and in turn, they are fiercely loyal to her.

To me the enduring genius of Rowling's Harry Potter novels is that, having invested seven years working on the first novel, and having meticulously mapped out the remaining six novels, using gridded paper that now occupies several boxes in her office, she was able to write an interlocking series instead of episodic novels. The result is that each book keeps the reader interested, always alert, picking up clues that will pay off in later books.

Currently, Rowling is working on book six, but we know nothing about it. As with book five, she's writing without the burden of facing a deadline, so when it's completed, she'll turn it in, and the publisher will crank up a publicity and marketing campaign to ensure that excitement reaches fever pitch.

Given that numerous fantasy novels revolve around the adventures (and misadventures) of boy wizards, what, one asks, makes Rowling's novels about Harry Potter so compelling and, judging from the dozens of editions published worldwide, so universally appealing?

Entire books have been written on that subject, for the world of academia has pounced on Rowling's fiction as virgin territory for theses; but the long and short of it is that Rowling is a world-builder whose fully imagined fictional universe harbors a sense of verisimilitude, a world we recognize and with which we are familiar, since it is anchored in the real world that coexists with the magical world.

It helps, too, that the characters are archetypal and immensely appealing—the orphaned wizard boy empowered beyond his imagining, and his loyal friends who stand by him through fair weather and foul, as the saying goes. It's an accessible story of good and evil, which is a theme that allows a writer to paint on a wide canvas. For Rowling, all the world's a stage and she's got the necessary space to create a fictional universe where, as in the real world, bad things can happen to good people—even death.

Often sudden and without warning, the fictional deaths are real to her. The characters are her literary creations to which she gave birth and when they die, she can feel their acute pain. (Imagine how you'd feel if, in a perverse mood, Rowling killed off Harry Potter—you get the idea.)

When it was announced that an important character dies in book five, young readers wrote in to beg her to spare Ron Weasley because in their experience it's always the hero's best friend who gets killed.

There *is* a death in book five, but it's not someone you'd expect; and if you want to find out who it is, go read the book because I'm not telling.

But what I will tell you is that to Rowling the death was real, as she explained to BBC interviewer Jeremy Paxton in a June 19, 2003, broadcast. After writing the death scene, she was distraught and went into her kitchen to compose herself. As she recounted to Paxton:

Well, I had rewritten the death, rewritten it and that was it. It was definitive. And the person was definitely dead. And I walked into the kitchen crying and Neil said to me, "What on earth is wrong?" and I said, "Well, I've just killed the person." Neil doesn't know who the person is. But I said, "I've just killed the person." And he said, "Well, don't do it then." I thought, a doctor you know . . . and I said, "Well, it just doesn't work like that. You are writing children's books, you need to be a ruthless killer."

In other words, her husband, an anesthesiologist who sees life and death played out at the hospital and in the operating room, didn't intuit that his wife *had no choice.* The story is boss and the writer must be true to the book. Rowling did what *had* to be done, and just because it's fiction doesn't mean that the writer has a choice in the matter.

Vocationally, Rowling and her husband, Dr. Neil Murray, live in two different worlds: She's a dreamer, an imagineer, given to flights of fancy, with the power to make her imaginary stories real—so substantial that, as you're reading her novels, the world she's created seems real. Samuel Taylor Coleridge termed this the "willing suspension of disbelief" because as you fall through the pages of a book, the reality of the fictional universe—if it's consistent and true and resonates with verisimilitude—*seems* real to you. That's the power of Rowling's imagination at work, for *she* believes and therefore she can make *you* believe.

Vocationally, Rowling's husband lives in a Muggles world, whereas she lives in a wizarding world. When Dr. Murray witnesses a death in the course of his work, he's been trained to be clinically detached to keep him from being emotionally overwhelmed. Rowling, however, has to be a human receptor and live the lives of her characters to know them, to understand them, and to bring them to life, to make them ring true. So, understandably, when her characters die—and die they must, if she is true to the story—she feels their loss, she suffers their pain. To her and, by extension, her readers, fictional bereavement is *real.*

Rowling has expressed surprise that, because her books are so very British in setting and tone, the audience for them extends far beyond the borders of the United Kingdom. Indeed, part of the charm of the novels is precisely because of their setting. The British language, geography, and history are not only familiar but loved by readers who treasure the literature of the fantastic: Kenneth Grahame's *The Wind in the Willows,* J. M. Barrie's *Peter Pan,* A. A. Milne's *Winnie-the-Pooh,* Lewis Carroll's *Alice in Wonderland,* C. S. Lewis's *The Chronicles of Narnia,* Philip Pullman's *His Dark Materials* trilogy, and of course, J. R. R. Tolkien's *The Hobbit* and *The Lord of the Rings.* It's a literary landscape with which we are already familiar, and one we love.

Give us a world we can lose ourselves in, we ask; give us a story well-told; and most of all, give us characters we believe in and root for, as well as those we boo loudly. In short, give us a fully contained imaginary world where, for a brief period, we can leave our mundane world behind.

In C. S. Lewis's classic *The Lion, the Witch, and the Wardrobe,* Lucy goes into a closet and passes through a snow-filled world; so, too, we wish to get away from our world and leave our troubles behind.

Escapist fiction? Yes, for some, but in addition to that, it's fiction that illuminates. At its heart, the Potter novels are not about witchcraft and wizardry but about human values like honesty, loyalty, courage, sacrifice, and the enduring power of love.

Rowling's stories are so compelling that readers worldwide—young and old, of all races, creeds, colors, and nationalities—empathize with Harry Potter, the boy wizard who spent most of his early years thinking he was a Muggle, "just" Harry, as he put it, though those in the magical community know of him as "the boy who lived," the only one to survive a direct attack from Lord Voldemort.

At its core, the Harry Potter novels are about imagination, about self-empowerment, which is an appealing message no matter one's age or nationality. We want to believe in Harry Potter and, by doing so, harness the power of believing in ourselves. And we want to believe, if only for a few hours, in lions and tigers and bears. Oh my.

Though Rowling has yet to write an autobiography (I, for one, wish she would do so, or at least publish her memoirs, like Stephen King's *On Writing*) in the (mostly) speculative biographies on her and in numerous interviews, we've all heard the oft-repeated story of how she conceived of Harry Potter during a stalled train ride in England. Lacking paper, she was forced to remember everything and commit it to memory, starting with a fundamental question: Why doesn't Harry Potter know who he is? Because he's not what he seems—he's not an ordinary boy, he's a wizard. From that came the idea of Hogwarts, a school for young wizards, and from that the question of who else would be found at such a place—ghosts such as Nearly Headless Nick.

Of course, part of the fun is in trying to determine the linkages between her real life and imaginative fiction. And although such linkages obviously exist, as she's explained in interviews, the real magic is in how she's filtered these life experiences through her imagination and transmuted them into a fictional reality with substance and shape.

The bare bones, then: Ron Weasley is modeled after one of her best friends whom she met in high school, Séan Harris; Hermione Granger is a caricature of Rowling herself, a self-termed "swot" (a person who studies

---

Which Potter Book Is Best?
A BBC Poll

In a BBC online poll (June 23, 2003), 8,676 online viewers cast their votes for their favorite Potter novel:

Harry Potter and the Philosopher's Stone: 2%
Harry Potter and the Chamber of Secrets: 4%
Harry Potter and the Prisoner of Azkaban: 40%
Harry Potter and the Goblet of Fire: 19%
Harry Potter and the Order of the Phoenix: 36%

---

excessively); several professors at Hogwarts are drawn from those she knew when she was growing up; and Harry . . . well, he's the mystery. Harry Potter, as any writer might tell you, came from nowhere . . . and came from everywhere. To my mind, however, Harry Potter is very much a writer's construct, meaning he is at the heart of his novels and serves a purpose beyond that of the protagonist; he is in fact a metaphor for any writer who is initially unsure of herself and her talent, but then subsequently seeks to develop that talent to its fullest.

Let me explain: To a creative writer, most of the world *is* populated with Muggles (non-magic folk). A Muggle, as Rowling points out, is not necessarily a derogatory word; after all, Hermione Granger's parents are Muggles, yet wizards like Lucius Malfoy and his kind hold them in contempt. This is Rowling's way to write about bigotry, but without a preachy tone.

Regarding creative writing, you can either do it, or you can't. And if you can't, it means you can never understand what it's like to live in an imaginary world you've created and be constantly at war with a world that can't understand. As a writer, it's not that you *think* you're better but that you *know* you are different. Put simply, as a creative writer, you do think differently. Imagination, Nabokov once wrote, is an African dreaming up snow.

To put it in perspective, you may think up a story about a boy wizard, but that's just the bare shell of an idea; Rowling, on the other hand, dreamed up and fully imagined a boy wizard and his world that coexists (admittedly uncomfortably) with the real world, and then populated it with things like Quidditch, Diagon Alley, Hogwarts, the Ministry of Magic, and Aurors. It's the *execution* of the idea and not the idea itself that's valuable. Or to put it in terms of the currency to be found at Gringotts, the wizards' bank in the Harry Potter novels, the idea is worth a Sickle, but the proper execution of that idea is worth a Galleon.

Stephen King was not joking when he suggested, in an *Entertainment Weekly* book review of the fifth Potter novel, that Rowling should have her imagination insured by "Lloyd's of London (or perhaps the Incubus Insurance Company) for the two or three billion dollars it will ultimately be worth over the span of her creative lifetime. . . ."

Rowling's books become, over the years, more imaginative, more substantial: The first novel (*Harry Potter and the Sorcerer's Stone*) is a straightforward narrative; the second novel (*Harry Potter and the Chamber of Secrets*) offers a compulsively readable narrative against the backdrop of the familiar school for wizards, Hogwarts, and adds a mystery; the third novel (*Harry Potter and the Prisoner of Azkaban*) offers the narrative, a mystery, and a wholly satisfying conclusion that lends depth to the story itself; the fourth novel (*Harry Potter and the Goblet of Fire*) is a braided, complex story with multiple storylines; and the most recent novel (*Harry Potter and the Order of the Phoenix*) delivers all of these previous elements, with the complexity of Harry Potter as he struggles with adolescence, as the story becomes increasingly darker in tone. In other words, the books are—unlike some of their paler imitations in the field—deeper, richer, more imaginative, and more fully developed with each successive installment.

Obviously, boy wizards grow in power as they master their craft . . . and so, too, has Rowling.

Harlan Ellison once pointed out that there are only a handful of fictional characters that are known around the world: Tarzan, Superman, and Sherlock Holmes, for example.

To that list we can safely add Harry Potter, but please don't take my word for it. Listen to Rowling's fans, who have bought millions of copies of her novels; listen to the critics who initially approached her work with a jaundiced eye and came away with appreciation; and listen to the millions who have discovered Harry, not through the books but through the films, which in turn brings them to the books, where they, too, become converts.

Come close and listen carefully as I whisper in your ear: *Harry Potter is one for the ages.*

Don't take *my* word for it, but you can safely take the word of master storyteller Stephen King, who reviewed *Harry Potter and the Order of the Phoenix* in *Entertainment Weekly* (July 11, 2003). After a thorough explication on why the novel is, as he put it, "a slam dunk," he poses the eternal question that every writer's work must face, the question of time's verdict on the work. On that note, King reassures us, we need not worry. As for whether or not Harry will be around a century from now—long after we have become dust—King concludes that Rowling's "is one series not just for the decade, but for the ages."

King, a former high school English teacher, then gives the novel a well-deserved grade of A.

Coffee and Cafés Fuel Rowling's Creativity

Invisibility. I would like to sneak off to a café and write all day.
—*Rowling, when asked what magical power she'd most like to have,
in response to a question posed to her at a public
appearance at London's Royal Albert Hall in July 2003*

Imagine walking past your favorite bookstore and seeing a man banging away on a manual typewriter. You'd do a double-take, wondering if your eyes were deceiving you.

If it's Harlan Ellison, it's no joke: He is probably one of the few writers in the world who would ever *want* to write in such a setting and, more to the point, could pull it off. He's done this numerous times in the past, drawing large crowds, some of which pour into the bookstore to find out what's going on.

Stephen King is a frequent attendee at Red Sox baseball games in Boston; he carries a composition book and writes longhand between innings, oblivious to the curious who wouldn't mind sneaking a peek over his shoulder to see what he is writing.

Insofar as writing in public goes, Ellison and King are exceptions. Both

of these demon-driven writers have shown a propensity for writing under any circumstances because they're hardwired that way.

As for Rowling, I think she'd react with predictable horror at the mere prospect of writing in a bookstore's display window with passersby gawking at her. She does, however, love to write at cafés, if the coffee is hot, her cup is periodically refilled, and the other customers leave her alone, so words can pour out of her pen.

Unfortunately, the days when she'd park herself at a window table at Nicolson's in Edinburgh are history, as is the restaurant itself. Half-owned by her brother-in-law, the café made world-famous by her presence was sold to a restaurateur who transformed it into a Chinese buffet restaurant. (I think he missed a sure bet by not incorporating the word "dragon" into its title, for the obvious linkages to the Harry Potter universe, especially Rubeus Hagrid, who covets dragons.)

Even a change in venue to a café in a local museum in Edinburgh provided no refuge. Everything was fine, until a reader wrote a letter to the local paper to report with unbridled glee his Rowling sighting, after which she simply never returned. It wasn't enough for him to have seen her; he had to announce it to the world, as if to bask, for a few seconds, in the limelight that she so assiduously avoids. (If he had to live perpetually in that limelight as she does, he would have understood the rules; namely, we both know I'm here, but please respect my privacy. Don't bother me and don't go out and tell the world, because then you'll force me to leave, you selfish git!)

These days, Rowling is forced to write at home because the public has permanently driven her away from cafés.

In an essay for a book of autographs published by a small press, Stephen King noted that writers do their best work when they are observers and not the observed. The anonymity of the writer—the chronicler, the compulsive observer—is at the heart of all writers. But when a writer out in public is recognized, she can no longer do her job. Formerly invisible, she's now visible, exposed to naked scrutiny.

In Ernest Hemingway's *A Moveable Feast*, one sketch limns the problem Rowling and other writers who seek refuge in a café must face—the unwanted intrusion of others. As Hemingway wrote:

> The blue-backed notebooks, the two pencils and the pencil sharpener, . . . the marble-topped tables, the smell of early morning, sweeping out and mopping, and luck were all you needed. . . .
>
> Then you would hear someone say, "Hi, Hem. What are you trying to do? Write in a café?"

Your luck had run out and you shut the notebook. This was the worst thing that could happen. . . .

Now you could get out and hope it was an accidental visit and that the visitor had only come in by choice and there was not going to be an infestation. There were other good cafés to work in but they were a long walk away and this was my home café. It was bad to be driven out of the Closerie des Lilas. I had to make a stand or move.

Rowling would empathize with Hemingway, who was the first celebrity writer of modern times whose nonliterary exploits got as much press as his prose. The curious sought him out, just as they do Rowling. (In one instance, a fan traveled all the way from Japan with the hope that he'd meet Rowling in Edinburgh as she went her appointed rounds. Disappointed that he never did, he reluctantly left for home.)

It would be nice, Rowling told an interviewer, if she could surrender some of her fortune to buy enough privacy to sit again at a café and blend in with the crowd. Unfortunately, Rowling is far too recognizable around the world, especially in Scotland and England, and even her wealth can't buy her that which she had when she was an unknown writer—the luxury of writing away from home, free of its distractions, with a bottomless cup of coffee on hand as she fills narrow-lined sheets of paper with magical words.

She now writes in the privacy of her home office, ensconced behind a nine-foot-high wall that encircles her property in Edinburgh, far from the crush of the common man and the madding crowd, where she dreams up her uncommon stories.

Tim Kirk

Harold Bloom, Stephen King, and Harry Potter: Strange Bedfellows Indeed

After Yale professor Harold Bloom attacked both Stephen King and J. K. Rowling—the former in the *Los Angeles Times*, the latter in the *Wall Street Journal*—a question arises: Is Harold a blooming idiot, as some might think, or does he know whereof he speaks?

Bloom has written or edited numerous well-regarded books: *Genius: A Mosaic of One Hundred Exemplary Creative Minds*, *The Western Canon: The Books and School of the Ages*, *Shakespeare: The Invention of the Human*, *How to Read and Why*, and—particularly pertinent to this discussion—*Stories and Poems for Extremely Intelligent Children of All Ages*.

Despite an impressive literary pedigree, Bloom's thesis—that King and Potter are, simply, popular literary trash—is suspect.

Upset that King was the 2003 recipient of the National Book Foundation's annual award, Bloom sneeringly wrote in the *Boston Globe* (Sept. 13, 2003), "By awarding it to King they recognize nothing but the commercial value of his books, which sell in the millions but do little more for humanity than keep the publishing world afloat." He suggested that if sales are the barometer of whether or not the award is justified, "perhaps next year the committee should give its award for distinguished contribution to Danielle Steel, and surely the Nobel Prize for literature should go to J. K. Rowling."

Bloom's observed, "Our society and our literature and our culture are being dumbed down. . . ."

Citing other writers whom he feels are deserving of the National Book Foundation's award—Thomas Pynchon, Cormac McCarthy, and Don DeLillo—Bloom concluded that honoring King is, in the end, "a terrible mistake."

In a separate op-ed piece for the *Wall Street Journal*, he took up arms against Rowling, while lambasting J. R. R. Tolkien as well. "The Harry Potter epiphenomenon will go on, doubtless for some time, as J. R. R. Tolkien did, and then wane."

Of Rowling's work Bloom had nothing good to say. One could almost hear him sighing loudly as he complained that readers of Harry Potter will not go on to read Lewis Carroll's adventures with Alice or Kenneth Grahame's *The Wind in the Willows*—an assertion that simply doesn't make sense, since devotees of children's literature do indeed cherish Carroll and Grahame, Baum (the Oz books), Tolkien, and a score of other writers who laid the groundwork for Ursula K. LeGuin, Philip Pullman, and Rowling.

Bloom concluded his op-ed piece by consigning Rowling to literary oblivion, dismissing the Potter books, based solely on a reading of the first book of the series and no more.

Bloom is way off his mark.

Unlike all other forms of mass entertainment—movies, plays, concerts, videogames, and toys of every shape and description—reading is participatory and active; the others are passive.

At a time when parents are astonished that their kids will read anything at all, no wonder they are surprised when their children hungered to read the fifth Potter novel, a fact so unusual that numerous editorial cartoonists have drawn identical scenes: A stack of expensive, bulky electronic toys sit neglected, gathering dust, as a child is mesmerized by the latest Potter novel.

Citing Grahame's utterly delightful *The Wind in the Willows* as worthy reading, Bloom fails to recognize that what makes that book so memorable is *exactly* what makes the Potter books similarly enjoyable. It's the story of three friends—the boastful Toad who learns humility, the wise, fatherly Badger, and the steadfast Rat—celebrating their relationship and showing us very human values: hubris, loyalty, friendship, and sacrifice. Not coincidentally, these are the same values that are found (and celebrated) in the Potter novels. In other words, Grahame's book and the Harry Potter books have more in common than they do not, for Grahame and Rowling are of like minds.

Stephen King at the National Book Awards

For the highbrow literary community, it was a moment of unimaginable horror. Stephen King, whom they regard as little more than a hack, had beat out scores of other writers to win a lifetime achievement award in American letters. The literary community immediately divided itself into two groups. Those who, like Harold Bloom, felt the award was not deserved; and those who felt it was long overdue. That debate will rage on for years, but here's what King had to say:

> For far too long the so-called popular writers of this country and the so-called literary writers have stared at each other with animosity and a willful lack of understanding. This is the way it has always been. . . . But giving an award like this to a guy like me suggests that in the future, things don't have to be the way they've always been. Bridges can be built between the so-called popular fiction and the so-called literary fiction.
>
> Tokenism is not allowed. You can't sit back, give a self-satisfied sigh and say, "Ah, that takes care of the troublesome pop lit question. In another 20 years or perhaps 30, we'll give this award to another writer who sells enough books to make the best-seller lists." It's not good enough. Nor do I have any patience with or use for those who make a point of pride in saying they've never read anything by John Grisham, Tom Clancy, Mary Higgins Clark, or any other popular writer. What do you think? You get social or academic Brownie points for deliberately staying out of touch with your own culture?

Grahame's novel delights us for the same reasons that the Potter books delight us. We read these novels not simply because we want diversion and escape—though the books provide those qualities in abundance—but because we want to know more about ourselves. The situations in which these fictional characters become embroiled and how they achieve ultimate resolution resonate in our lives.

Put differently, if Grahame's novel and the Harry Potter novels were nothing more than entertaining reads, neither Grahame nor Rowling would stand the test of time.

What Bloom has failed to recognize, much less acknowledge, is that what the books are about eclipses all other considerations. If the Potter novels were modest successes, hand-sold by independent booksellers, Bloom would still criticize them; but because the Potter novels sell so phenomenally well, they are suspect.

This is literary elitism of the worst sort. Though such elitism dismisses Rowling's novels for their supposed lack of cerebration, the fact remains that Rowling's novels are a matter of celebration. Bloom feels that children are better off reading other novels instead of Potter's and King's. Mind you, this is the considered opinion of an educated man who has thought and written extensively on the subject of literary merit, so how can he be so obtuse?

Yes, one can fault Rowling for her excessive use of adjectives, a minor fault that Stephen King noticed and chided her for in his review of *Harry Potter and the Order of the Phoenix*. But taken on the whole, beyond the obvious storytelling engine that propels the reader from first to last page at a galloping pace, Rowling's books offer more, not less, as Bloom suggests. Far from being the literary equivalent of a McBook (A QUARTER MILLION SOLD!), Rowling's Potter novels speak to children in a vocabulary they understand, talking *to* them instead of down *at* them, and highlighting moral concerns—making the right choice as opposed to the easy choice—while affirming human values, especially loyalty and friendship and sacrifice. This raises the question: Does Bloom not see these attributes or does he choose to ignore them?

More the latter, I think. In Bloom's op-ed piece one can almost hear another sigh as he sees the ivory towers of academe crashing around him, a wasted literary landscape dotted not with the Grahames and Carrolls of the world but the Kings and Rowlings. He perceives a diminution of values and tastes, a dumbing-down of America, as he puts it.

I think the reading public is smarter than Bloom would admit, because there's plenty of room in bookstores for the Pynchons and DeLillos and McCarthys of the world, just as there's room for the Kings and Rowlings of the world.

Perhaps Bloom should worry less about whether Rowling's and King's books are the literary equivalent of McDonalds meals and think more about what worlds of imagination their books offer.

Harry Potter, Censorship, and Book Banning

You don't have to burn books to destroy a culture. Just get people to stop reading them.

—*Ray Bradbury, author of* Fahrenheit 451

Rowling finds herself in good literary company these days: Nobel prize-winning author Maya Angelou, America's best humorist and national treasure, Mark Twain, Nobel prize-winning author John Steinbeck, children's book author Judy Blume, and the celebrated recluse J. D. Salinger. They are all authors of some of the "100 Most Frequently Challenged Books of 1990–2000," according to the American Library Association. Rowling, of course, is high on the list.

At first glance, especially if one knows nothing about Rowling or her Harry Potter novels, it might seem appropriate until you crack open the covers of her books and realize that she's writing fantasy and not a how-to manual on ritual animal sacrifices. At second glance, one realizes that there's a world of difference between the fun, make-believe magic she writes about and the very real world of Satan worshippers. It's the critical difference between fantasy and reality, a distinction some choose not to make. Case in point: Reverend George Bender, the pastor of the Harvest Assembly of God Church in Penn Township, Butler County, in Pennsylvania.

Gathering at night in the parking lot behind his church, Rev. Bender expressed regret that attendance at his March 2001 book-burning was sparse. In a story by Carmen J. Lee of the *Post-Gazette,* she quotes him as saying: "I would have liked to have seen more visitors. But I think it worked out well. It made us pay attention to what we're doing. It makes us think about how to focus on the Lord as we should. I hope people understand our intentions, though I know some won't."

Most won't.

Like most censors quick to preach, quick to condemn, and too quick to burn anything that offends him, Rev. Bender never bothered to *read* the Harry Potter books he tossed in the bonfire, nor did he need to: He simply knew the books were the devil's work. "[He] was firm in describing the Potter books, specifically, and Disney productions, in general, as containing sorcery and witchcraft," wrote reporter Lee.

The problem, as pointed out in an article on the Education World website, is that because the Potter books have the trappings of witchcraft, that's more than enough for some people to damn them outright. Mark West, a college professor and author of *Trust Your Children: Voices Against Censorship in Children's Literature,* observed, "They don't see it as fantasy. They see it as real. A small group of Americans can't accept fantasy that way. They really do care [about the book's impact], so they go against others' legal rights."

More than legal rights, such people are asserting their "superior" moral rights. They know what's best for them—and best for *you,* as well; they know what offends them—and want to make sure it won't offend anyone. They are smug in their ignorance, usually citing the Bible, that they are doing the Lord's work for the betterment of all by condemning, burning, and challenging the presence of Rowling's novels in public libraries and, especially, school libraries.

Christian author Berit Kjos, quoted in an article on the Education World website, explains the concerns of the Christian community:

> Christianity clashes with a love for witchcraft. . . . It is a religion that is very real and is spreading throughout the country. It makes me very uncomfortable when [children] are immersed in topics that make witchcraft very exciting. It can be very confusing for them.

It's not *children* that seem to be confused, for most children seem to understand the important distinction between fantasy and reality, between a world of make-believe and the real world.

Unfortunately, you can't argue with such paralogia, because it boils down to a matter of belief, of bedrock faith. The fossilized mindset of those

who would want to censor Harry Potter cannot be changed. As Beverly Green, a Sunday school teacher from Eastman, Georgia, explained to Wired.com reporter Julia Scheeres, "*Harry Potter* is saying you can dabble in witchcraft as long as it's entertaining. If it's not good, it's evil. There ain't no in-between. When you start dabbling in demonic spirits, that's dangerous ground. You're opening up your home, yourself, to all kinds of attacks from the Devil."

The American Library Association

For anyone interested in knowing more about the ongoing and never-ending battle against censors, go to the ALA website (www.ala.org). It provides information and printed resources for readers and educators interested in free expression.

Well, maybe not necessarily from the Devil but from religious zealots who are supremely confident that they know best—and want *you* to know it, too, even if it means filing challenge after challenge, burning books, and putting their best efforts into banning books for *your own good!*

Echoing Green's comments, Reverend Jack D. Brock, citing Acts 19:19–20 of the Bible, encouraged members of his congregation to join him in a book-burning. The Harry Potter books, he explained, are "examples of our society's growing preoccupation with the occult. The Potter books present witchcraft as a generally positive practice, while the Bible expressly condemns all occult practices."

It's worth noting that, according to the online article from children-books.about.com, Rev. Brock had never *read* the Potter novels but "had researched their contents."

Apparently, he didn't read closely enough, because if he had, he'd have found out that the books espouse qualities worth celebrating, as opposed to the "burn them all!" mindset of book-burners like Rev. Brock, who ardently believes that "stories like Harry Potter that glorify wizardry and sorcery will lead people to accept and believe in Satan."

Judy Blume, author of *Are You There, God? It's Me, Margaret, Superfudge,* and other children's books, is one of the most censored authors of our time. She wrote an op-ed piece for the *New York Times* (October 22, 1999) in which she observed that the backlash from religious fundamentalists against Rowling was only a matter of time: "I knew this was coming. The only surprise is that it took so long—as long as it took for the zealots who claim they're protecting children from evil . . . to discover that children actually liked these books. If children are excited about a book, it must be suspect."

Perhaps Blume's eight-year-old grandson said it best. After Blume tried to explain why some adults wanted to keep their children from reading

Harry Potter novels, he exclaimed, "But that doesn't make any sense!" No, it doesn't, but religious zealots will continue to condemn, criticize, and challenge Rowling's imaginative fiction because they prefer to curse the darkness and light bonfires, not candles.

Harry Potter Ripped Off

As Rowling fans worldwide waited anxiously for the publication of the fifth novel (*Harry Potter and the Order of the Phoenix*), an enterprising Chinese book publisher, aided and abetted by an anonymous Chinese author, published what appeared to be a Harry Potter novel. The cover, after all, bore a familiar name, and the names of translators and editors were likewise familiar. The icing on the cake was a photograph of Rowling.

Despite the photo, the byline, and the editorial credits, the book was bogus, from cover to cover. Published by the Bashu Publishing House in Chengdu, *Harry Potter and the Leopard Walk Up to Dragon* sold on the streets for $1.50.

Understandably, when the Christopher Little Literary Agency got word of its publication, the response was swift. According to the BBC News ("Fake Harry Potter Novel Hits China," July 4, 2002), Neil Blair of the Christopher Little Literary Agency stated, "As with all piracy matters throughout the world, we take this issue extremely seriously and are looking into the matter urgently." For the Chinese publisher who had legitimately bought book rights to the fifth novel, it was also a matter of urgency, since the sales of the under-priced bogus books would undercut the market for the legitimate editions.

In the interim, the success of *Harry Potter and the Leopard Walk Up to Dragon* inspired the plundering Chinese publisher to rush into print two more titles: *Harry Potter and the Golden Turtle* and *Harry Potter and the Crystal Vase*.

When the law finally caught up with the Bashu Publishing House in Chengdu, the publishers apologized in print in a Chinese newspaper and got off with a small fine.

In a somewhat similar case, which Rowling also pursued vigorously and won, a Russian author named Dmitry Yemets copied the character of Harry

Harry Potter and the Leopard Walk Up to Dragon

From the bogus novel, here's an unappetizing sample from the first chapter, "A Sweet and Sour Rainfall."

> Harry did not know how long this bath would take, when he would finally scrub off that oily, sticky layer of cake icing. For someone who had grown into a cultured, polite young man, a layer of sticky filth really made him feel sick. He lay in the high quality porcelain tub ceaselessly wiping his face. In his thoughts there was nothing but Dudley's fat face, fat as his Aunt Petunia's fat rear end.
>
> Harry was a fifth-year student at Hogwarts School of Witchcraft and Wizardry. At that heavenly amusement park his grades were the highest of all the students in his class. Because of this, when summer approached he was named the Head Student in his class. But for some reason Harry did not understand, Professor Dumbledore firmly insisted that his summer practice be at his aunt's house at 4 Privet Drive.
>
> His objections to this were overruled by the Headmaster on the last day before leaving school. Because of this Harry had been unhappy the whole day. Four Privet Drive to him was his childhood heaven, but also his childhood hell.
>
> His first day back, his cousin Dudley also returned home from school. This was his nightmare. From the depths of his heart he was not willing to pass summer vacation with his fat cousin, but there was absolutely no way to change the fact. At the magic school he was a young celebrity, but at Privet Drive he was still a protected object.

Potter and incorporated elements into his own novel, *Tanya Grotter: The Magic Double Bass,* which sold 100,000 copies before Rowling's lawyers swooped down like fire-breathing dragons to stop its publication, but not before a second book in the series (*Tanya Grotter and the Disappearing Floor*) saw print.

Tanya Grotter is an orphan with a distinctive mark on her head. The teenaged girl Tanya attends a school for witches to develop her magical powers, which she needs to fight an evil villain so terrible that he cannot be named. She doesn't ride a broom but, instead, prefers a magic double bass. She also wears eyeglasses.

In his own defense, Yemets told the BBC in a phone interview that Tanya Grotter "is a cultural reply rather than plagiarism." Yemets, in the same phone conversation, added that his book was a parody. Quick to defend their author, Dutch publisher Byblos added, "Tanya Grotter doesn't harm Harry Potter in any way; rather, she is his burlesque sister."

Well, perhaps Byblos should get a dictionary and look up "burlesque," "parody," "plagiarism," and "lawsuit," in that order.

Unlike the two Barry Trotter novels, Tanya Grotter is clearly *not* a parody. In fact, Tanya is unquestionably a rip-off of the worst sort, an out-and-out misappropriation, which is how a Dutch court saw it, to Rowling's relief.

In all of this, one begins to ponder where copyrights (and wrongs) begin and end. In the case of the Chinese publisher, the defense mounted was ludicrous. In the Tanya Grotter case, the Dutch publisher's position was indefensible, since the plot similarities are virtually identical.

So You Want to Be a Novelist? Advice for Budding Writers about Writing and Publishing

Though her critics complain she is churning out literary pap, Rowling is beloved by parents worldwide who are flabbergasted to see their children pick up a thick novel instead of a television remote. Similarly, she's celebrated by booksellers who haven't seen this much excitement over a book series in years, not to mention a jaded book industry that has seen all the conventional rules of publishing wisdom demolished by the Harry Potter phenomenon.

Sparking the imagination of a worldwide audience, Rowling's novels have been published in 55 languages in 200 countries in only a few short years.

What's happened is nothing short of magic. With the release of book five (*Harry Potter and the Order of the Phoenix*), Rowling's position as *the* best-selling author of all time is firmly established, and it's not likely anyone will soon challenge her dominance.

With such success, it's inevitable that a certain number of readers will be inspired to become writers. From children with stardust in their eyes to teenagers and the middle-aged (or older), readers are inspired by her example and some want to try their hand at what is arguably the oldest profession in the world, the art of telling stories.

Just as Woodward and Bernstein inspired generations of journalists who wanted to be investigative reporters to break stories like Watergate, Rowling has had a similar effect on aspiring writers. The recent bumper crop of first-time novelists—notably a British teen named Helen Oyeyemi who scored a record-breaking £400,000 advance from Bloomsbury for her novel *The Icarus Girl*—owe Rowling thanks for the public resurgence of interest in fantasy, which Tom Shippey (a Tolkien scholar) asserts is the dominant form of literature in our time, due in no small part to Tolkien and, more recently, Rowling.

Over the years, in media interviews, Rowling has commented on the process of writing, on editing, and on book publishing. I've culled her observations and added my notes (Lesson Learned) to put things in context.

Rowling's Time-Tested Words of Publishing Wisdom

"I don't think there's any subject matter that can't be explored in literature." (*Time*, October 30, 2000)

Lesson Learned: Don't be afraid to write about anything. Don't worry about what your friends, neighbors, parents, or critics think. Let your imagination run free.

"This is not vanity or arrogance, but if you look at the facts, very, very few people manage to write anything that might be a best-seller." (*Time*, September 20, 1999)

Lesson Learned: Because best-selling authors are all that we hear about in the media, and because most people have no idea that most professional writers are part-timers, the fantasy cherished by unpublished writers is that their work will be critical and financial successes. As Rowling points out, the odds are against making a fortune writing. It happens, but when it does, it's rare enough to make the news.

"Those five years really went into creating a whole world." Rowling speaking of the time spent in plotting the Harry Potter novels (*Time*, September 20, 1999)

Lesson Learned: Rowling is a master at plotting, but it takes time to get the details right, especially in a series in which key clues that will bear fruit later are planted early on. Writing such an airtight plot means that the imaginary world must be fully realized. If *you* believe, so, too, will the reader. Case in point, J. R. R. Tolkien's *The Lord of the Rings*, which took 13 years to write.

A Dozen Tips for Publishing Success

1. Read omnivorously.

2. Write, write, write!

3. Learn how to properly format a manuscript for submission.

4. Finish the work.

5. Get constructive criticism from several impartial sources.

6. Consult directories to research the best agent to represent you.

7. Write a one-page query letter and send it to several agents.

8. Be prepared to send in the finished manuscript *only* if invited to do so.

9. If rejected by the agent, go on to the next one.

10. Repeat until you have representation.

11. Start your next book immediately.

12. Don't quit your day job.

"If it's a good book, anyone will read it. I'm totally unashamed about still reading things I loved in my childhood." (*Time*, April 12, 1999)

Lesson Learned: Read anything and everything and don't develop a snobbish idea as to what constitutes "literature" and what does not. Readers don't care. They want, simply, the best story you can tell. It's what they've paid for and it's what they deserve.

"I had been very realistic about the likelihood of making a living out of writing children's books . . . and that didn't worry me. I prayed that I would make just enough money to justify continuing to write. . . ." (Salon.com, 1999)

Lesson Learned: In terms of what to expect of a writing career, keep your income expectations low. Editors at book publishing houses tell first-time writers not to quit their day jobs. Even Stephen King didn't quit his day job until he sold his first novel, *Carrie*. He wisely waited until he had gotten a major subsidiary sale, which allowed him to quit teaching.

"I always advise children who ask me for tips on being a writer to read as much as they possibly can." (Salon.com, 1999)

Lesson Learned: Writers are readers who read anything and everything they can get their hands on. They cannot *not* read. (A writer will read the text on a cereal box if nothing else is on hand.) If you don't enjoy reading, and reading a lot, you'll never be a writer.

"I didn't know anything about agents but I went to the library and looked up some addresses in the Artists' and Writers' Yearbook." (*Telegraph,* Spring 1997)

Lesson Learned: Do your research. Go to the standard references in the field and look up who may be interested in buying your book. Write a polite, short, to-the-point query letter; if interested, the agent will contact you to ask for a completed manuscript.

"I was about six and I haven't stopped scribbling since, but this is the first time I'd tried to get anything published." On submitting a book titled *Rabbit* to Penguin, which later reportedly turned down the first Harry Potter novel. (*Telegraph,* June 24, 1997)

Lesson Learned: At any early age, Rowling submitted work professionally. Though she submitted prematurely, it was an indication as to where her true interests and talents resided.

"I never expected to make any money." (*Sunday Times,* June 29, 1997)

Lesson Learned: A new writer isn't the next Charles Dickens and shouldn't have great expectations. If you're fortunate enough to get published, consider that its own reward. And if you make any money at it, consider that a bonus.

"I thought I am the luckiest person in the world. I am now being paid to do what I have been doing my whole life for nothing." (*Independent,* November 21, 1997)

Lesson Learned: Follow your bliss. It's the central thesis of Joseph Campbell's books. As Campbell explains, if you follow your bliss, you'll be happy, even if you don't make any money in the process.

But if you're lucky enough to write *and* make money, you should realize your good fortune.

"Yes, I've wanted to be an author as long as I can remember. English was always my favorite subject at school. . . ." (Amazon.com UK, 1999)

Lesson Learned: Writers discover early on that their great passion is writing. Understandably, their best subject in school is English. Pay attention to these early signs because they are indicators of where your true interests reside.

"I never really think in terms of ingredients, but I suppose if I had to name some I'd say humor, strong characters, and a watertight plot." (Amazon.com UK, 1999)

Lesson Learned: A work of fiction is not made by slavishly following a recipe. Think in terms of what makes a story a compelling read.

"Whenever someone younger asks me for advice in writing, I always say 'Read!', because that will teach you what good writing is like, and you will recognize bad writing too." (Barnes & Noble, March 1999)

Lesson Learned: Read, read, and then read some more. Reading will be an integral part of your life. If you read carefully and read enough, you may learn to recognize the good from the bad writing.

"I have got the perfect temperament for a writer, because I don't need to be surrounded by people all the time." (Barnes & Noble, March 1999)

Lesson Learned: Writing is a solitary act between you and a blank sheet of paper. Fill it with your best work. But if you are the kind of person who craves and needs an audience, consider an alternate career as a stand-up comedian or an actor.

"I just never really spoke about it, because I was embarrassed. And because my parents were the kind of parents who would have thought, 'Ah yes, that's very nice, dear. But where is the pension plan?'" (*School Library Journal,* September 1, 1999)

Lesson Learned: Budding word wizards and story sorceresses won't get much encouragement from their Muggle-thinking parents. In a list of jobs parents would prefer their children to consider—doctor, lawyer, teacher, or businessman—a career as a writer would definitely not be one of them.

"Here's the recipe for life: find what you do best and figure out a way to make it pay for you." (*Star-Ledger,* Newark, NJ, October 16, 1999)

Lesson Learned: This gets back to what Joseph Campbell affirmed. If you are good at something and it makes money, then you will have found your bliss. The hours of your life are short, so do you *really* want to spend the bulk of them doing work you hate with a passion?

"First you must read, then practice, and always plan." (*Boston Globe,* October 18, 1999)

Lesson Learned: This sounds simple, but it's not; it's a lifelong plan. Read extensively, in and out of the field you've chosen, to give your writing depth; write a lot, since you're going to have to get rid of the rubbish before you write narratives that shine like polished gems; and plan your work in depth because you don't need any rude surprises, and neither do your readers.

"And for their parents, don't tell them it's unrealistic. Never say that. Because even if they're not published, writing, well, writing is the passion of my life, so it's an important thing to do." (National Press Club, October 20, 1999)

Lesson Learned: Parents, don't discourage the dreamer. I wonder how many writers of talent never pursued their dreams because their parents kept telling them that it was stupid to even *dream* of being a writer. Life's full of disappointments, which your children will find out in due course, so why not let them believe in their dreams? Don't take that from them.

"I sat down to write something I knew I would enjoy reading. I do not try to analyse it and I don't write to a formula." (National Council for One Parent Families, September 29, 2001)

Lesson Learned: Write to please yourself. Don't write for any preconceived market.

"I doubt a writer who has got what it takes will need me to tell them this, but persevere!" (Scholastic, Fall 2000)

Lesson Learned: A truism: if you're an unpublished writer and *can* be discouraged, you *should* be discouraged, because real writers *never* give up!

"Persevere, but if everyone's turned you down, then it's time to try writing something else. And if that doesn't succeed, it *might* be time to think about a different career. But some great writers had lots of books rejected before they got published, so don't lose heart." (Yahooligans, October 20, 2000)

Lesson Learned: There comes a point when you have to accept your natural limitations and recognize that writing, despite your great passion for it, isn't one of your talents. It's one thing to persist, but another to waste the precious years of your life nurturing false hope, harboring an unrealizable dream.

"I enjoy the editing process, but I edit fairly extensively myself before my editors get to see the book. . . ." (Scholastic.com, 2000)

Lesson Learned: Good writing is rewriting. A first draft is the fun part; the second and subsequent drafts are where you polish the prose until the manuscript is letter-perfect. A good sentence, a good paragraph, a good chapter—all combine to make a good book.

The Next J. K. Rowling

When Tom Clancy wrote *The Hunt for Red October* in 1984 and thereby invented the military technothriller, the hunt was on by book publishers for the "next" Tom Clancy. Now, two decades later, it's clear that the "next" Tom Clancy has not been found, though many writers came forward to grind out their technothrillers.

Currently, the hunt is on for the next J. K. Rowling.

At least seven writers are currently being hyped as the "next" Rowling. Their respective publishers are hoping to replicate the Harry Potter phenomenon by promoting the books heavily, selling film rights to bring the books to a wider audience, and planning extensive merchandising campaigns to provide an additional boost.

Will book publishers and motion picture executives in Hollywood "discover" the next Harry Potter-like franchise? Or will we see a repeat of what happened in Clancy's genre? A wide variety of books, of varying quality, by writers who have been able to get a piece of the action but not enough to eclipse the writer who started it all.

Here are some of the writers to watch:

• Philip Pullman (U.K.). My money's on this guy. *The Golden Compass, The*

Subtle Knife, and *The Amber Spyglass* comprise a trilogy awkwardly titled *His Dark Materials,* drawn from Milton's *Paradise Lost.* Unlike most of his contemporaries, Pullman already has an enviable track record in children's fiction, which gives him an advantage. But more than his previous credits, the sheer breadth and imagination of this trilogy will win new readers and, when it reaches the silver screen, will present challenges to the special effects wizards that will make or break the movies. New Line Cinema, flush with money from the success of its Tolkien film trilogy, has begun filming all three books back-to-back as two films.

- Cornelia Funke (Germany). With *The Thief Lord* and *Inkheart,* she has captured the imagination of the reading public hungering for contemporary fantasy. "Discovered" by Barry Cunningham—formerly with the Christopher Little Literary Agency who plucked Rowling out of the submissions stack—Funke's *The Thief Lord* has already been bought by Hollywood. *Inkheart* is another fantasy trilogy, which perhaps should be one word, fantasytrilogy, since few contemporary fantasists can envision a series as anything but three of a kind. (Wunderkind Christopher Paolini's *Eragon,* yet another Tolkien-inspired tale, is—you guessed it—the first of three in his series.)

- Jonathan Stroud (U.K.). A former children's book editor, Stroud follows the tried-and-true formula of writing yet another fantasy trilogy, this one chronicling the adventures (and misadventures) of a smart-talking, somewhat jaded djinn (or genie, to most of us), who locks horns with a fledgling boy wizard. Film rights for the Bartimaeus trilogy, of which only the first book has appeared *(The Amulet of Samarkand),* have already been snatched up by Miramax.

- Steve Voake (U.K.). His first book, *The Dreamwalker's Child,* sold to British book publisher Faber and Faber for $160,000, after a ferocious tooth-and-nail battle with two other publishers. Not surprisingly, a movie may be in the works, since four major Hollywood studios have expressed an interest.

- Louisa Young (U.K.), pen name Zizou Corder. She's young, blonde, has a daughter, and writes fantasy. Sounds like Rowling, don't you think? *Lion Boy,* written with her daughter Isabel (aged ten), is the first book in a new trilogy, with film rights sold to Steven Spielberg.

- G. P. Taylor (U.K.). Reverend Graham Taylor, a Vicar who wrote a story set in the seventeenth century, chronicles a battle between good and evil in *Shadowmancer,* originally a self-published book, most copies of which sold to his parishioners, who are undoubtedly overjoyed that their first editions are now selling for £4,000.

- Helen Oyeyemi (U.K.). She's only 18, but her first novel, *The Icarus Girl*, demanded attention. Her book editor noted, "The prose sings immediately right from the first page." In a two-book deal, the 18-year-old first-year college student commanded a £400,000 advance from Bloomsbury.

Tim Kirk

Notable and Quotable:
On Writing and Publishing

Anticipation: "'I can't wait! I can't wait!' cries ten-year-old Alula Greenberg-White, hugging herself in expectation. It's 9 A.M. outside a large bookshop in north London and Alula is at the head of a queue of 100 excited children and parents. They peer through the windows at stacks of a 640-page novel, eyes searching for the small strawberry-blonde Pied Piper who has brought them here—and to bookshops round the globe—and who is somewhere inside nursing a coffee."

—Tim Boquet from "J. K. Rowling: The Wizard Behind Harry Potter," *Reader's Digest* (December 2000)

Awards: "This business shouldn't be about awards but it's a vote of confidence and if there's the slimmest chance of winning I get terribly nervous."

—Rowling quoted by Anne Johnstone in "We Are Wild about Harry," *Herald* (January 26, 1999)

Being published: "The purest, most unalloyed joy was when I finally knew it was going to be a book, a real book you could see sitting on the shelf of a bookshop."

—Rowling quoted by Judith Woods in "Coffee in One Hand, Baby in Another—A Recipe for Success," *Scotsman* (November 20, 1997)

Books recommended: "Anything by Philip Pullman. Of modern writers there's a book called *Skellig* by an English author, David Almond, which I think is absolutely magnificent. Stuff I enjoyed when I was a child—I loved E. Nesbitt. I think she was a genius. Paul Gallico. He's out of print now. I really love his work, too."

—Rowling interviewed by Sean Bowler at a public talk at the National Press Club (October 20, 1999)

Booksigning: "The first time I ever had to do a reading which was to about four people, in fact so few people turned up at this bookshop that the staff felt really sorry for me and came and stood around and listened as well. I was shaking so badly I kept missing my line. I was terrified. But since then, I have found readings to be the most fantastic experience."

—Rowling quoted by Caroline Davies in "The Queen Meets Two of Britain's Best Loved Best-Sellers," *Daily Telegraph* (March 23, 2001)

Cafés: "I do still write longhand, and I do write away from the house whenever possible because it's very easy to get distracted when you're home. I use cafés as offices, really, with the added bonus that there's normally good music and someone to bring me coffee all the time, which is great."

—Rowling quoted by Jeff Baker in "Harry Potter: Need She Say More?" *Oregonian* (October 22, 2000)

Dreams: "I never, ever dreamt this would happen. My realistic side had allowed myself to think that I might get one good review in a national newspaper. That was my idea of a peak. So everything else really has been like stepping into Wonderland for me."

—Rowling quoted by Ann Treneman in "Joanne Rowling's Secret Is Out," *Independent* (November 21, 1997)

Editing: "Carving the books out of all her notes was a case of editing and condensing and sculpting it so the story moulded into shape. She had a mass of stuff on Harry that she had to edit down quite a bit. She figured Harry Potter would be a book for the obsessives. She figured it was a book for people who enjoyed every little detail that a story like Harry offers."

—from a BBC Special on Rowling (Christmas 2001)

Expectations: "I was totally realistic about what children's books involved. And that involves really no money at all. I mean, a lot of really great children's writers I know also do other work—they have to."

—Rowling quoted by Mark Phillips, CBSNews.com (July 9, 2000)

Fan fiction: "The author is 'flattered by genuine fan fiction,' said Neil Blair, an attorney for the Christopher Little Literary Agency, which represents Rowling. But she has been alarmed by 'pornographic or sexually explicit

material [based on her characters] clearly not meant for kids.' Christopher Little began sending out letters last year because it feared 'the dangers of, say, seven-year-olds stumbling on the material as they searched for genuine [Harry Potter] material,' Blair said in an e-mail response to questions."

—Ariana Eunjung Cha in "Harry Potter and the Copyright Lawyer," *Washington Post* (June 18, 2003)

Fan mail: "'I could have been my own full-time secretary.' Now the American fan mail is diverted to and dealt with in America."

—Rowling quote, followed by statement by journalist Elizabeth Grice in "Harry's On Fire Again, Casting a Spell His Creator Can No Longer Ignore," *Daily Telegraph* (July 10, 2000)

Fantasy fiction: "I don't really like fantasy. It's not so much that I don't like it, I haven't really read a lot of it. I have read *The Lord of the Rings*, though. I read that when I was about 14. I didn't read *The Hobbit* until much later, when I was in my 20s. I'd started *Harry Potter* by then, and someone gave it to me, and I thought, yeah, I really should read this because people kept saying, 'You've read *The Hobbit*, obviously.' And I was saying, 'Um, no.' So I thought, well, I will, and I did, and it was wonderful."

—Rowling from an interview in *Newsweek* (July 10, 2000)

Favorite books: When asked if any one child stood out in her mind: "My favourite was the girl who came to the Edinburgh Book Festival to see me. When she reached the signing table she said, 'I didn't want so many people to be here—this is MY book.' That really resonated with me, because that's how I feel about my own favourite books."

—Rowling in an interview on Scholastic.com (October 16, 2000)

Finis: "I'm not going to say I'll never write anything to do with the world of Hogwarts ever again. Because I have often thought that (if I wrote) book eight, I think it would be right and proper that it should be a book whose royalties go to charity entirely. It could be the encyclopedia of the world (of Hogwarts) and then I could rid myself of every last lurking detail, but no: not a novel."

—Rowling in "Potter Author Knows How It Will All End," *Ananova* (December 2001)

Harry Potter: "He feels so real to me, I think it's going to break my heart to stop writing about him."

—Rowling quoted by Rosemary Goring in "Harry's Fame," *Scotland on Sunday* (January 17, 1999)

"The funny thing is that Harry came into my head almost completely formed. I saw him very, very clearly. I could see this skinny little boy with black hair, this weird scar on his forehead. I knew instantly that he was a wizard, but he didn't know that yet. Then I began to work out his background. That was the basic idea. He's a boy who is magic but doesn't yet know. So I'm thinking, well, how can he not know? So I worked backwards from that point. It was almost like the story was already there waiting for me to find it. It seemed to me [that] the most watertight explanation for him not knowing that he was a wizard was that his parents had been a witch and a wizard who had died and that he had been raised by Muggles, non-magic people."

—Rowling in an interview, *Connection* (October 12, 1999)

Job change: "Rowling also revealed that, when she decided to quit her teaching job and write full time, she announced her departure to her students, who were mainly from working-class backgrounds. She said one student asked her, 'Miss, are you going on the dole?' 'No,' she replied. 'I've got another career.' There was a pause, and then another student asked, 'Miss, are you going to be a stripper?' Rather than give the boy detention on her last day there, she thanked him for the compliment."

—Mark McGarrity from his profile on Rowling in "Harry Potter's Creator Meets Her Public," *Star-Ledger* (October 16, 1999)

Literature: "There are two books whose final lines make me cry without fail, irrespective of how many times I read them, and one is *Lolita*. There is so much I could say about this book. There just isn't enough time to discuss how a plot that could have been the most worthless pornography becomes, in Nabokov's hands, a great and tragic love story, and I could exhaust my reservoir of superlatives trying to describe the quality of the writing."

—Rowling quoted by Sarah-Kate Templeton in "How Lolita inspired Harry Potter," *Sunday Herald* (May 21, 2000)

Magic rules: "There is legislation about what you can conjure and what you can't. Something that you can conjure out of thin air will not last. This is a rule I set down for myself early on. I love these logical questions!"

—Rowling quoted on swns.com

Jessica Mitford: "My most influential writer, without a doubt, is Jessica Mitford. When my great-aunt gave me *Hons and Rebels* when I was 14, Mitford instantly became my heroine. She ran away from home to fight in the Spanish Civil War, taking with her a camera that she had charged to her father's account. I wished I'd had the nerve to do something like that. . . . I think I've read everything she wrote. I even called my daughter after her."

—Rowling, quoted by Lindsey Fraser in "Harry and Me," *Scotsman* (November 9, 2002)

Muggle: "I think I derived 'Muggle' from the word 'mug,' which in Britain means a stupid person or a fellow who's easy to dupe."

—Rowling quoted by Roxanne Feldman in "The Truth about Harry," *School Library Journal* (September 1, 1999)

Names: "I used to collect names of plants that sounded witchy, and then I found this, *Culpepper's Complete Herbal,* and it was the answer to my every prayer: flaxweed, toadflax, fleewort, goutwort, grommel, knot grass, mugwort."

—Rowling quoted by Ed Bradley and Lesley Stahl in "Harry Potter Book Sales Skyrocket Around the World," CBS' *60 Minutes* (September 12, 1999)

Nicolson's café: "It is an escapist book and by writing it I was escaping into it. I would go to Nicolson's café, because the staff were so nice and so patient there and allowed me to order one expresso and sit there for hours, writing until Jessica woke up. You can get a hell of a lot of writing done in two hours if you know that's the only chance you are going to get."

—Rowling quoted by Judith Woods in "Coffee in One Hand, Baby in Another—A Recipe for Success," *Scotsman* (November 20, 1997)

Practice: "I know this sounds like a teacher, but remember, I was a teacher before I began the Harry books. This is what works for me: First you must read, then practice, and always plan. Read as much as you can, because that teaches you what good writing is. Then, when you write, you will find yourself imitating your favorite writers, but that's OK, because it is part of the learning process. You will go on to find your own personal voice and style. Writing is like learning an instrument. When you are learning guitar, you expect to hit bum notes. And when you practice writing, you are going to write rubbish before you hit your stride. I know this sounds terribly boring, but it is much more productive to plan out exactly where you want to go when you sit down to write about something."

—Rowling quoted by Stephanie Loer in "All about Harry Potter, from Quidditch to the Future of the Sorting Hat," *Boston Globe* (October 18, 1999)

Romanticized: "Some articles written about me have come close to romanticising the time I spent on Income Support. The well-worn cliché of the writer starving in the garret is so much more picturesque than the bitter reality of living in poverty with a child."

—Rowling quoted in "Harry Potter Author: I Was Humiliated by Poverty," *Ananova* (May 20, 2002)

Sequels: "My terror when I first met the publisher after they'd taken the book was that they wouldn't ask for sequels. Because I had seven mapped, and I had boxloads of stuff on Harry."

—Rowling quoted by Rosemary Goring in "Harry's Fame," *Scotland on Sunday* (January 17, 1999)

Serendipity: "I don't know. It really is the weirdest thing. I was on a train journey in 1990 and the idea just came to me out of nowhere. It was really as though it just fell into my head. I have no idea where it came from."

—Rowling quoted in "Rowling Discusses the Adventures of Harry Potter," *CBS News: This Morning* (June 28, 1999)

Shameful secret: "It was a secret. People at the office used to ask me if I was coming down to the pub and I would say that I was going shopping. And then they would ask me what I had bought! I just felt embarrassed about saying, well, actually I'm writing a book. I've met so many people in bars who say they are writing a book and it means that they've written down a few ideas in a notebook. . . . I thought, I am the luckiest person in the world. I am now being paid to do what I have been doing my whole life for nothing. I can sit here and know that this book is actually going to be published. Then I suddenly realised: I am a writer. I'm being paid for it now. This is now my secret shameful habit that I don't tell anyone about any longer."

—Rowling quoted by Ann Treneman in "Joanne Rowling's Secret Is Out," *Independent* (November 21, 1997)

Slush pile: "These things can sit in a pile for ages. They're known as the slush pile. They're the unsolicited and, you know, it's the also-rans usually. And just by chance, two days afterwards, I picked up this pile and went to a lunch because somebody was turning up late. And inside, I started reading about Harry Potter and, you know, my toes curled."

—Christopher Little quoted in "The Magic Behind Harry Potter," CBSNEWS.com (June 15, 2003)

Smarties prize: "It's a particularly wonderful award to win from my point of view, because the final judging is done by children, and they are obviously the people whose opinion matters to me most."

—Rowling quoted in "Children Pick Winner of $2,500 Literary Prize," *Herald* (November 19, 1997)

Stereotyping: "I was portrayed as a penniless, divorced, single mother, pushing a buggy round Edinburgh, on income support, and writing in play parks and cafés while the baby slept. Yes, of course I realise it was good copy—and yes, it was true; but I resented the reporter's implication that I should have gone out and got a proper job instead of sitting around writing. It wasn't a soft option. Not many people would have put up with those conditions. And then, just as I was able to feel secure for the very first time since my daughter was born, I was defined by what was in many ways the saddest part of my life. It was hard enough at the time, without having to relive it. It was dreadful—for a long time it stopped me writing. But don't get me started on that."

—Rowling quoted by Joanna Carey in "Who Hasn't Met Harry?" *Guardian Unlimited* (February 16, 1999)

Unauthorized biography by Sean Smith: "J. K. Rowling, the notoriously private author of the Harry Potter children's books, has reacted furiously to

the publication of a new biography which rakes over her failed marriage, her miscarriage and claims she fell out with her father when he remarried."

—From "Rowling Mad About Biography Published in September 2001," *Scotland on Sunday* (September 2001)

Writer?: "One of her pupils eventually discovered she was writing a book. The girl had turned up without pen or paper; Rowling gave her the obligatory telling off and sent her to get some from the notepad on her desk. 'She was ages at the desk, and I turned round and said, "Maggie, will you come back and sit down," and she went (putting on a Jean Brodie voice) "Miss, are you a writer?"' Rowling felt embarrassed, exposed. 'I think I said, "No, it's just a hobby."'"

—Rowling quoted by Simon Hattenstone in "Harry, Jessie and Me," *Guardian* (July 8, 2000)

Writing: "My ideal writing space is a large café with a small corner table near a window overlooking an interesting street (for gazing out of in search of inspiration). It would serve very strong coffee and be non-smoking (because I've now given up for two years and don't want to be tempted) and nobody would notice me at all. But I can't write in cafés any more because I would get recognized a lot."

—Rowling quoted by Brian Ferguson in "JK Rowling's Fame Spoils Her Café Culture," *Edinburgh Evening News* (February 6, 2003)

Writing as career: "You've got to persevere, because it's a career with a lot of knock-backs, but the rewards are huge. It's the best thing in the world. Very rewarding. But it's not a career for people who are easily discouraged, that's for sure. And for their parents, don't tell them it's unrealistic. Never say that."

—Rowling interviewed by Sean Bowler at a public talk at the National Press Club (October 20, 1999)

Writing fame: "I am rarely recognized and I am very happy about that, because I like being an anonymous person! It usually happens when I'm writing in cafés, because the connection between me and cafés is strongly imprinted in Edinburgh people's minds. Occasionally I have handed over my credit card and people have recognised the name, which is a very comfortable level of recognisability. One shop assistant told me she had taken the second *Harry* book to read on her honeymoon! The most embarrassing occasion was when I took my daughter to see *A Bug's Life* with some friends, and a woman with a party of a dozen little girls asked me if she could take a picture of me with all her charges."

—Rowling quoted in "Harry Potter: An Interview with J. K. Rowling," Scholastic website (Fall 2000)

Writing for children: "If at the end of my life I had only ever published for children, I would in no way see that as second best. Not at all. I feel no need to write my Serious Adult Book."

—Rowling quoted by Emily Gordon in "The Magic of Harry Potter," *Newsday* (October 19, 1999)

Part Three:
Harry Potter–
Screen Magic

Tim Kirk

It is every writer's worst dream come true, a nightmarish situation: Hollywood beckons, siren-like, with buckets of money and honeyed words. Sell us your novel, they say, and we'll take you to the next level of success. Just sign on the dotted line and we'll make all your dreams comes true.

The reality, as far too many novelists have found out, is far different, and more sobering. A novel that took years to write must be compressed into a film script of 120 double-spaced pages. It takes a craftsman to distill the novel's essence and translate it into a screenplay, a dedicated director to translate it faithfully to the big screen, and an army of people behind the scenes to bring it all together.

For a few years Rowling resisted the blandishments of Hollywood. Rather than see her novels twisted out of shape, beyond all recognition, she tenaciously held onto the film and merchandising rights, until Warner Bros. finally won her hard-earned confidence.

Thus far three of the movies have appeared—careful translations of the wonderful texts, with casting perfection. Warner Bros. has pulled it off. They've delivered on their promise to Rowling to remain faithful to the books, and they've delivered on their promise to the fans, to give them the best movie-going experience money can buy and talent can assemble.

The Power of Imagination:
The Reality of Fantasy in Harry Potter

Cover story in *Vanity Fair*

In the wake of the huge success of *The Lord of the Rings: The Return of the King*, the final installment of Peter Jackson's film trilogy based on J.R.R. Tolkien's novel, Hollywood and jaded critics alike have expressed surprise that fantasy is suddenly hot.

In truth, it isn't "suddenly" hot, it's *always* been hot. Of the 13 top-grossing movies of all time, an astonishing 12 are fantasy; the sole exception is *Titanic*. The others are: *Harry Potter and the Sorcerer's Stone; Star Wars: The Phantom Menace; The Lord of the Rings: The Two Towers; Jurassic Park; Harry Potter and the Chamber of Secrets; The Lord of the Rings: The Fellowship of the Ring; Independence Day; Spider-Man; Star Wars; The Lion King; E.T.: The Extra-Terrestrial;* and *The Matrix Reloaded.*

In 2004 two more were added to the list of top-grossing films: *The Lord of the Rings: The Return of the King* and *Harry Potter and the Prisoner of Azkaban.*

In terms of a film franchise, Harry Potter will ultimately eclipse *The Lord of the Rings* for the simple reason that *Rings* is comprised of three films, whereas the Potter novels will, when completed, comprise seven films, each building on the success of its predecessors. Simply put, Rowling's Harry Potter novels will likely be the most successful film franchise in motion picture history, which is why executives at major film studios ardently wooed Rowling. Unlike most authors, she was initially cool to all overtures, including those from Warner Bros., the studio that eventually secured the Potter film franchise. At stake: not millions but *billions* of dollars.

Like other writers, Rowling had seen too many bad movies adapted from good books and was adamant that her novels not suffer the same fate. Better not to have a movie at all, she decided, than to have a bad one. The money was not an issue, but fidelity to the source material would be the key to unlocking the door to the Potter film franchise.

When Warner Bros. finally secured the rights, which included the lucrative merchandising rights estimated to be worth a billion dollars alone, the studio faced a situation in the marketplace similar to that faced by another studio, New Line Cinema, when it announced its film trilogy *The Lord of the Rings.*

The established base of readers, numbering in the millions, was protective of the author and the works, and if the early buzz on the Internet from the hard-core fans was unenthusiastic or, worse, condemnatory, it would prove to be a major obstacle. Again, as with *The Lord of the Rings,* the Harry Potter film franchise wasn't merely a gamble with one film but with several. The upside gain, however attractive, was soberly balanced by the downside risk. The studio could stand to make, or lose, a fortune.

As soon as the first Potter film was announced, fans chimed in on the Internet with the usual concerns. Who would be the director? Who would be cast? How close would the film hew to the book? Harry Potter fans were anxious to see a film adaptation, but only if it served the source material.

To make the first Harry Potter film a success, it would require a faithful screenplay, a committed director, state-of-the-art special effects, and, most important of all, a hand-picked cast that would forever be imprinted in the imaginations of Potter fans worldwide.

The common bond shared by all was a desire to meet, or exceed, the expectations of a hard-to-please worldwide fan base.

The screenwriter, Steve Kloves, worked hand-in-hand with Rowling to ensure that the book would be faithfully translated to the screen. It would

be a real challenge, since the first Harry Potter book necessarily gets off to a slow start, establishing its back story and laying the groundwork for the six books to follow.

As with *The Lord of the Rings*, state-of-the-art special effects were necessary to give a realistic "look" to the first Potter film. With the $126 million budget for the film, however, that wouldn't be a problem. But even with a first-rate script and a big budget, the principal component to success would be the casting. Early on, when Steven Spielberg expressed an interest in helming the project, his choice for the pivotal role of Harry Potter was an American child actor, Haley Joel Osment, a fine actor but not who Rowling had envisioned. To be true to the book, the film, she insisted, would not only have to be shot on location in England but have an all-British cast.

In hindsight, the casting was perfect. In fact, two of the crucial roles were filled by children with little or no prior acting experience: Emma Watson in the role of Hermione Granger and Rupert Grint in the role of Ron Weasley.

The key role of Harry Potter was, as one would expect, the most difficult to fill. The casting director screened 16,000 child actors, but none of them fit the bill. Then, two months before principal shooting was scheduled to begin, Steve Kloves (screenwriter) and David Heyman (producer) were in a movie theatre and saw Daniel Radcliffe in the audience. They knew they had found the right boy to play Harry Potter—a conviction reinforced when the screen test showed Radcliffe's considerable acting strengths.

The casting for the supporting roles of the faculty members at Hogwarts was relatively easy, since there was a large pool of adult talent from which to draw. Among them, the late Richard Harris as Dumbledore, Alan Rickman as Professor Snape, Maggie Smith as Professor McGonagall, and Robbie Coltrane as gameskeeper Rubeus Hagrid.

Throughout the entire process of filming, the common ingredient found among all—the actors, screenwriter, producers, and director—was a passion to get everything right, to translate Rowling's words faithfully to the big screen in a way that would satisfy not only the hard-core fans but the larger body of general filmgoers who would be new to Rowling's world.

When the trailer was finally released, the response was positive. Fans enthusiastically endorsed director Chris Columbus, who would go on to direct the second Harry Potter film, as well. (He declined to helm the third movie, citing the enormous strain and commitment required. It was time, he affirmed, for someone else to carry the torch.)

Any fears harbored by Warner Bros. over its substantial investment evaporated when the early reviews, mostly positive, came in. Early box-office receipts were also impressive, with a worldwide gross of $975 million dollars, second only to the box-office take of *Titanic*.

Barnes & Noble store display
of Harry Potter books

Supported by a well-orchestrated marketing and promotion campaign, and backed up with a selective merchandising line to complement the movie, *Harry Potter and the Sorcerer's Stone* convincingly recreated Rowling's fictional universe with remarkable fidelity.

Rowling's magical world coexists with our own, populated with characters who, though able to draw on magic to help them get through life, deal with the usual problems of being human that magic cannot solve—the ache of losing one's parents, the sacrifices one makes for friends, the bonds of respect found in the student-teacher relationship, the difficulty in confronting one's fears, and the realization that in life hard choices must be made and their consequences accepted.

All of these are underscored by a scene in the movie when Harry, for the first time, sees his parents in the Mirror of Erised, which shows him that which he wants more than anything. Since his parents died when he was an infant, Harry has no memory of them.

As Rowling fans know, that scene came from the heart, for Rowling had lost her own mother, who never lived to see her daughter become the world's best-selling author, or to see her two grandchildren.

At the heart of Rowling's wonderful first novel is a heartfelt story of a boy who discovers his potential and is destined to take his rightful place in the wizarding world.

In book seven, Harry Potter will graduate from Hogwarts. It will be a moment of mixed emotions: a happy moment for readers who will have waited many years for that pivotal event, tempered by sadness because of the realization that there will be no more tales of the boy wizard. Though it's fun to contemplate the prospects of Harry Potter as an Auror, a professor or a headmaster at Hogwarts, or the Minister of Magic—imagine how that would infuriate Draco Malfoy!—the fact remains that Rowling is not likely to change her mind, to the infinite regret of her millions of readers worldwide.

Notable and Quotable: Film Quips

Films live and die on their casting.
—*Director Peter Jackson, who helmed the Tolkien film trilogy*
(from the appendices of the extended DVD of The Two Towers*)*

Acting is an interpretive art in which the best actors not only step into the roles and become the characters they portray, but also bring something of themselves to help bring the character to life.

The casting is key, as director Peter Jackson affirms: Pick the right person for the right role and the film will come alive.

All of the Potter films to date have benefited from superb casting choices.

To promote the films, the actors have collectively given hundreds of interviews, from which I've drawn the quotes that appear here, with my comments on the casting.

Sean Biggerstaff as Oliver Wood. The Quidditch team captain, Wood, an upperclassman, is confident and exudes a take-charge air as befitting his position. Sean Biggerstaff is a natural, giving a novice Harry Potter the benefit of his experience in Quidditch. A good performance with just the right touch of humor.

Biggerstaff got his first break when veteran actor Alan Rickman saw him in a production of *Macbeth* and recommended him to the casting director of the Harry Potter films.

Biggerstaff on his film character: "He's very sporty, slightly eccentric, and very passionate about Quidditch. Wanting to win the Quidditch House Cup is like the Holy Grail for him." (Quoted in *16 Magazine*, November 2001.)

David Bradley as Argus Filch. The caretaker of Hogwarts, Filch is a rather nasty man. He longs for the good old days when he could mete out positively medieval discipline—hanging students by their thumbs in the dungeon (or so he says). Less concerned with the student body, he seems more concerned about the welfare of his cat, Mrs. Norris. When someone puts a petrifying spell on her, it pushes him over the edge emotionally. He angrily names Harry Potter as the culprit and demands immediate justice. Ever so patiently, Dumbledore explains that the petrification is only temporary; besides, Madam Pomfrey, the school nurse, will be able to administer the potion necessary to restore Mrs. Norris to her former state.

Bradley is a delightfully cantankerous caretaker, who brings his obnoxious characteristics to life.

Bradley on book five: "I heard that writer J. K. Rowling had killed off one of the characters in her last book and that she had cried afterwards, and I thought, 'Well, it can't be Filch—no one would cry over him.'" (Quoted by Marion McMullen in "Potter Villain Is Out for Blood," online at: http://icCoventry.co.uk, September 12, 2003.)

Kenneth Branagh portraying Professor Gilderoy Lockhart. Although Lockhart only briefly appears in book five, he steals the show in book two, *Harry Potter and the Chamber of Secrets.*

The first choice was Hugh Grant, who no doubt would have given a fine performance, but Branagh is now indelibly imprinted in our collective minds' eye, with his over-the-top performance. Flamboyantly dressed—he's quite the natty dresser—and full of himself, Branagh hams it up and hogs the limelight.

Branagh plays the role to the hilt and lends a much-needed humorous touch to an increasingly dark series of books.

Branagh on his film character: "Gilderoy Lockhart is a fantastically successful wizard and writer of many famous books which are now being used as textbooks at Hogwarts School. He is very much admired by the female students, which is very irritating to the boys. He is a narcissus, a gadfly, very full of himself and faintly idiotic. But he can be rather touching at times. He amuses and intrigues us. Is he or isn't he a good guy? He is certainly a strange peacock of a man. (From "Interview with Kenneth Branagh" at countingdown.com, September 15, 2002.)

John Cleese as Nearly Headless Nick. Funnyman Cleese is perhaps best known for his work as part of the comedy troupe Monty Python, so it's no surprise that Cleese plays with brio the part of one of the ghosts that delightfully haunts Hogwarts. A haughty ghost whose head literally hangs by a thread, Cleese plays the role with the right touch of nobility, as befitting the ghost's lineage—Sir Nicholas de Mimsy Porpington.

Robbie Coltrane as groundskeeper and keykeeper Rubeus Hagrid. Standing eight feet, six inches tall in the novels (according to Rowling), Hagrid is a giant among men, physically and literally. In the film Coltrane must portray the gentle giant who can simultaneously show his strength and his compassion—two sides of a man of seeming contradictions. Coltrane brings a presence to this critical role, one that Rowling reportedly considered to be a crucial one in terms of casting. Larger than life, Coltrane plays the role of Hagrid to the hilt, and convinces us that he's just an overgrown kid who dotes on Albus Dumbledore, whom he looks upon as a father figure.

Coltrane on his role: "I've seen the movie and, believe me, it looks fantastic and is so true and honest to the book." (Quoted by Louis B. Hobson in "Magic Monsters Set Loose" in the *Calgary Sun,* November 5, 2001.)

Christian Coulson as student Tom Riddle (Lord Voldemort). Coulson portrays the diabolical Lord Voldemort, whose given name was abandoned because of his Muggle heritage on his father's side. Coulson appears at the end of book two, when he announces that he is the true heir of Salazar Slytherin—not Harry Potter, which most students mistakenly believed.

Coulson provides a solid performance as an angry young man who has patiently bided his time to bedevil the wizarding world.

Coulson on his new fame: "It hasn't really changed me. People don't recognise me. Not long ago I walked past a group of people who had just seen the film, and were talking about Tom Riddle. They clocked me but had no idea who I was. That was kind of nice in a way. I can't imagine what life would be like if you couldn't take a bus or ride on the tube." (Quoted from a press conference for the first film in London prior to its release, from BBCi Films: Interviews on www.bbc.co.uk, undated.)

Warwick Davis as Professor Filius Flitwick and a goblin bank teller. Although the roles are quite different—a charming, diminutive professor who teaches charms at Hogwarts, and a goblin of serious mien at Gringotts, the wizard bank—Davis plays both well. A solid, creditable performance by an underappreciated actor, Davis's sympathetic portrayal of Professor Flitwick is delightful to see.

Davis on his role: "We were filming the Great Hall scene. I looked to my left, and I saw Maggie Smith, Alan Rickman, and Richard Harris; and then, on my right, I saw Robbie Coltrane. I thought to myself, 'It doesn't get any better than this.'" (Quoted from "Exclusive Interview with Professor Flitwick" on the website entertainment-rewired.com, November 15, 2001.)

Tom Felton as Draco Malfoy. The arch-nemesis of Harry Potter, Draco Malfoy is not only a rich snob of the worst sort, but also prejudiced to the extreme. Proud of his heritage as a pureblood, Malfoy is a supercilious boy whose chief goal in life is to act as a foil to Harry Potter. After Harry becomes the Seeker for Gryffindor, it is no great surprise when Draco becomes the Seeker for Slytherin, so the two are pitted once again, not on the ground but in aerial combat.

Felton, as a actor, has a difficult challenge in portraying Malfoy because the character is essentially "flat." That is to say, the character is one-dimensional fictionally. He is always the bad egg, the one who insults Harry at every opportunity, and sneers at Hermione Granger and anyone else he considers inferior. (It's worth noting that it is Granger, not Malfoy, who shines academically.)

Felton plays the role with a delicious evilness, a biting sneer, and a look of unrivaled contempt on his face at Potty and the Weasel, his nicknames for Harry Potter and Ron Weasley.

More a caricature than a fully developed character, Malfoy serves his purpose all too well, but one would wish for a more rounded character, so we can see Felton stretch himself as an actor in a role that, despite its one-note tone, is a fan favorite.

Felton on his role: "Inevitably, people have the impression that I'm as mean and nasty as Malfoy. The worst is the reaction of little kids. When five- or six-year-old fans see me, they often start to cry. They're terrified because they think I'm really Malfoy. They don't make the distinction between the actor and the character. One time, Chris Columbus's kids ran away when they saw me! [laughs] These reactions make me a little angry, but at least it proves I was convincing in my role. That's gratifying enough." (Quoted from an interview posted on an HP fan website, original source: *One Magazine*, November 2003.)

Michael Gambon as Albus Dumbledore. The late Richard Harris had committed to the film series but passed on before the third began principal photography.

Gambon on his new, challenging role: "My friends' children come round and see me now, which they never did before. I'm getting letters from all over the world and kids knock on my front door, which is a bit of a nuisance, but you have to keep smiling and be nice. Being Dumbledore is a big responsibility." (Quoted by John Hiscock in "Dumbledore Makes Gambon Kids' Favourite" from News.Scotsman.com, as cited in *Showbiz Digest*, September 29, 2003.)

Richard Griffiths as Vernon Dursley, Harry Potter's uncle. Griffiths is convincing in this role. The books portray Vernon as an unimaginative man who has never liked, and will never accept, Harry Potter in his life. Though he begrudgingly accepts Harry into his home, it's clear in book one that Uncle Vernon wants to keep Harry in his place. Harry's place, of course, is in the cupboard under the stairs, which is symbolic of Vernon's feelings: the cupboard is where you store things to keep them out of sight.

Griffiths portrays the blustery Vernon Dursley to perfection. We, as viewers, are absolutely convinced this is Vernon Dursley, the uncle from Hell.

Griffiths on the books: "The stories are becoming more dark and I think that's what makes them more attractive. Because the people that saw the first movie were 13- and 14-year-olds, they're growing along with the story. So it's natural of movies to also grow, and become more complex and mature. Of course there will always be new children of ten years, to see the first movie and repeat the cycle. They wouldn't be able to use the same people and repeat the stories changing just a little. It wouldn't be fun." (Quoted on a HP fan website, zanzaro.com, from Omelete.com during a launch party for the second film, undated.)

Rupert Grint as Ron Weasley. Among the cast of characters, three are critical: Harry Potter, Ron Weasley, and Hermione Granger. Of the three, only Rupert Grint has no prior film experience, which makes his standout status all the more remarkable. In the books, Ron is Harry's best friend. The youngest in a wizard family long on love but short on money, Ron gets the family hand-me-downs and is used to a life of genteel poverty. Actor Rupert Grint plays Ron Weasley to perfection. By turns self-effacing, incredulous, fearful, or angry as the occasion requires, Grint's nuanced performance brings Ron Weasley from page to film screen with astonishing fidelity. Unaffected, unabashedly normal in every way, with the right touch of regret at having been born in a poor wizarding family, Grint as Weasley is picture-perfect. He is my favorite among all the child actors in the Potter films. In short, bloody brilliant!

Grint on his role: "It all started when I was watching this English children's television programme called *Newsround*. The show told you how to audition for a part in Harry Potter and so I sent in a letter because I really wanted to play the part of Ron. But, for weeks I heard nothing. So, I was looking on the *Newsround* website one day and saw how another kid had sent a video of himself. So, my mum helped me to make an audition tape with me doing a rap of how much I wanted to be in the film, reading some lines as Ron which I wrote myself and also dressing up as my drama teacher. That was the most embarrassing part as she's a woman! I sent it in and the next thing I knew I was being called by the casting director. And then I was doing screen tests! And then I got the part!" (From a fan website, rupertgrint.net, undated.)

Richard Harris as Albus Dumbledore. The late Richard Harris defined the character on screen. The book takes great pains to establish the character as one of worldly wisdom and restraint. We know, for instance, that he's held in wide regard among the wizarding community and considered the only one who could face, and best, Lord Voldemort in a wizards' duel. (Who, one wonders, would be Dumbledore's second?)

Harris fits his role like a hand in a racing glove. It's hard to imagine anyone filling his considerable shoes, but Michael Gambon is likely up to the challenge. Even still, everyone will fondly remember Harris as Dumbledore from the first two Potter films as the wise wizard and father figure for Harry Potter, a role he brought to life.

Harris on the child actors in the film series: "They're very good, actually. They were terrific. What amazed me about them was that they were so confident. They weren't intimidated by anything, like Maggie Smith or myself, or Robbie Coltrane, or anybody. I was kind of enamoured by it." (Quoted in a profile by Claire Bickley in the *Toronto Sun,* November 13, 2001.)

Harris's commitment to the film series: "That huge commitment caused him to turn the role down at first, but the production had a secret agent close to him to change his mind. The books were the favourites of Harris' then 11-year-old granddaughter Ella.

"She called me up and she said to me, 'If you don't do it, I'll never speak to you again.' So I said, 'Okay, I'll do it.'

"Ella spent two days on the film's set and has a background role as a student in a Hogwarts dining hall scene." (Profile by Claire Bickley in the *Toronto Sun,* November 13, 2001.)

Ian Hart as Professor Quirrell. People are sometimes not w-w-w-what they s-s-s-seem. Case in point: The stuttering Professor Quirrell, the new Defense Against the Dark Arts teacher in the first year Harry Potter attends Hogwarts. Quirrell first meets Harry at the Leaky Cauldron, where the young boy wizard is surprised that everyone there not only knows his name but respects him—a hitherto unique experience, since he's used to being ignored or mistreated. Hart delivers a noteworthy performance as a disarming admirer of Harry Potter and one who, when faced with the prospect of a troll on the loose in Hogwarts, faints in fear.

At the end of the first film, he shows himself as he actually is: Far from being a stuttering, squeamish professor, he's actually someone far more powerful, allied to the dark side.

Hart on his audition: "Even before my audition, there were several pages missing from my script because those bits were so unbelievably secret not

even I was allowed to see them. I'm not usually attracted to big-budget American films. . . . I only decided to do this one because it's a different kind of role. There are a lot of special effects in the film so, from a technical point of view, it was a challenge." (From "Wild at Heart" in *Nova* magazine, June 2001.)

Shirley Henderson as Moaning Myrtle (a student-turned-ghost). Although ghosts haunt Hogwarts, most roam throughout the entire building—all except one: Moaning Myrtle, who hangs out in the girl's bathroom, where she died under suspicious circumstances. Myrtle's nickname is apt, since she bemoans her fate and laments her early, and unforseen, passage into the spirit world. (She is, in fact, the only student-turned-ghost.)

Actress Shirley Henderson steps perfectly into the role of Moaning Myrtle, with the right tone of indignation and sorrow, balanced by righteous anger at her lamentable circumstances. She didn't choose death—it chose her.

Sweet on Harry but harsh on Ron, Moaning Myrtle, stuck in limbo, has made her troubled peace with her life as a ghost.

Henderson (aged 37) on her role: "I loved Harry Potter, but I thought it was crazy me getting a part in it. I didn't think I'd get it because she's a schoolgirl. It was great fun: When you're a ghost, you're flying through the air in a harness and it's quite physical. I'd never done any special effects before." (Quoted from the newspaper website scotsman.com, August 19, 2003.)

Joshua Herdman as Gregory Goyle. A crony of Draco Malfoy, Goyle is an appendage of Draco.

John Hurt as Mr. Ollivander. The proprietor of Ollivander's Wand Shop, which is a store frozen in time, has a remarkable memory. Remembering every wand he's ever sold, he tells Harry Potter that he distinctly remembers selling wands to his parents, and wondered when the son would show up to get his wand.

Hurt plays the part as if he's been in the business of selling wands for a long time. Picking among the many boxes of wands in his store, he finally finds the *only* wand for Harry—a wand he was destined to own.

Though only on the screen briefly, Hurt more than fits the bill: He is tailor-made as a storekeeper in Diagon Alley.

Hurt on acting: "Well, yes, pretending to be other people is my game and that to me is the essence of the whole business of acting." (Quoted by Geoff Andrew in the *Guardian*, April 27, 2000.)

Jason Isaacs as Lucius Malfoy. A confident wizard with supercilious manners, Lucius is the father of Draco Malfoy—not surprisingly, like father, like son. The father is contemptuous of any witch or wizard not born in a wizarding family; purebloods like himself, he believes, are the only ones worthy of being taught magic. Non-magic witches and wizards shouldn't even be allowed to enroll at Hogwarts—"mudbloods," he derisively calls them.

Jason Isaacs is memorable as Lucius Malfoy. Fearsome when angry, placating when necessary, politically suave as the situation dictates, he exhibits a range of emotion that we don't see in his son, Draco, who walks around Hogwarts with a perpetual sneer and an insulting manner whenever he sees Harry Potter or his friends.

Knowing what will happen in book five, all one can say about Jason Isaacs is that we expect a great performance from him, and he will surely deliver.

Isaacs on his role: "I probably shouldn't mention this in public, but [Rowling] has actually sent me an early draft of the next book, which is called *Harry Potter and the Chronicles of Lucius,* which is all about Lucius's early romantic adventures. She's warned me it might change before publication, so I'll wait and see." (Quoted by Alec Cawthorne in "Harry Potter and the Chamber of Secrets" from BBCi Films Interviews, November 2002.)

Toby Jones as the voice of Dobby the house-elf. A wonderfully realized character, Dobby appears on the scene as a hand-wringing, deeply concerned elf who will stop at nothing to prevent Harry Potter from returning to school for his second year—an attempt that is doomed to failure, but not before Dobby uses all the powers at his command to dissuade, then physically bar, Harry, even at the risk of injury.

Though CGI technology can create a computerized person, it cannot create that person's voice. In this regard, Toby Jones's voice blends seamlessly with Dobby, a downtrodden house-elf who is overly emotional when Harry Potter simply recognizes his existence and is minimally polite—a stark contrast to Dobby's usual condition of servitude, in which he's used, abused, and misused by the Malfoy family.

Toby Jones's voice ranges from contrite to adamant as the occasion dictates.

I'm looking forward to seeing more of Dobby and hearing more of Jones.

Matthew Lewis as Neville Longbottom. Pertually put-upon, Longbottom, in the second movie, laments, "Why is it always me?" Unsure of himself and bedeviled by Slytherins, especially their head, Professor Snape, Longbottom's role is more than aptly filled by Matthew Lewis, who plays the part so convincingly that one wonders if the young actor had similar experiences in school. I suspect, though, that he's simply a good actor, and one whose role in the upcoming films will become increasingly visible and more important as he assumes his rightful place in the wizarding world.

Lewis on the scene in which Hermione Granger temporarily immobilizes him with a petrification spell: "I kept doing it and doing it—I even practised at

home with my brother—but eventually they had to get a stunt man in because my legs kept flying up at the ends." (Quoted by Clare Youell in "Potter Boys Reveal COS Acting Secrets" from BBC Newsround, Novembers 15, 2002.)

Miriam Margolyes as Professor Sprout. The professor of Herbology, Sprout is jovial and down to earth. Margolyes fittingly plays the part and makes us wish she had been given a bigger supporting role in the book and, therefore, the films. A delightful visual interpretation, Margolyes has certainly got at the root of the character.

Marygoyles on her role: "It's a very friendly set. Chris Columbus, the director, has a sweet personality—he only looks about 12, actually. And the kids are delightful: they like each other very much. . . . I enjoyed myself a lot. . . . I was delighted with it: I was terribly good, and I think the film is terribly good." (From "Harry Potter Exclusive: Interview with Professor Sprout," a RealAudio interview conducted by Dominic King from www.bbc.co.uk, Radio Kent film, January 16, 2000.)

Harry Melling as Dudley Dursley. In real life Harry Melling is undoubtedly a prince of a fellow, a fine young lad, which is a stark contrast to the character he plays—a bullying git named Dudley Dursley, who enjoys bedeviling Harry Potter and making his life as miserable as possible. Dudley is a whining, obnoxious, self-centered brat of a boy, which Melling portrays to perfection. Given a choice of roles, Melling might prefer a more winsome role, but somebody's got to play the bad guy, and in this case Melling is very good as the very bad Dudley.

On his role: "It was fun playing the baddie, though—more challenging." (Quoted on an online site, www.thisisheartfordshire.co.uk, September 18, 2001.)

Gary Oldman as Sirius Black. I am twitching, I tell you, twitching with anticipation to see Oldman as Sirius Black. Though we only have a brief teaser to give us a taste of what is to come in June 2004, the snippets of footage with Oldman are delightful. I especially love the "WANTED" poster with Oldman laughing maniacally—the perfect touch—and the shot of him in Azkaban, as he turns his gaze toward the viewer.

In the third Potter film, Sirius Black is on center stage and in the spotlight, and I'm telling you now, even without the benefit of Professor Trelawney's crystal ball, I feel confident in saying that Oldman is going to steal the show. Something wicked—though not in an evil sense: think British slang—this way comes!

James and Oliver Phelps as Fred and George Weasley. Twin brothers (obviously), they are perfectly cast as the Weasley twins, magical pranksters whose career goals are nontraditional. They want to make a living as full-time inventors and vendors of magical novelties.

Think of what a discussion around the Weasley dinner table must be like around O.W.L. time—Molly stressing the need to do well on the exams, Arthur automatically endorsing his wife's view, and Fred and George exchanging knowing glances, since they have no intention of following in their father's footsteps by joining the rank-and-file at the Ministry of Magic.

James and Oliver Phelps are a pure delight and, knowing what comes in book five, I'm very much looking forward to seeing them in that film, from the first practical joke on poor Dudley Dursley to their grand joke on Professor/High Inquisitor/Headmaster Dolores Umbridge.

On their roles. James: "It was a once in a lifetime experience, to see how it's created." Oliver: "Working alongside such big name actors was fantastic; it hasn't really sunk in yet." (From an interview on www.oliver-phelps.com, undated.)

Daniel Radcliffe as Harry Potter. All the king's horses and all the king's men couldn't put this film franchise together again if the casting for Harry Potter wasn't dead-on. A casting challenge on the scale of Everest, Harry Potter is so well-defined in one's imagination, due in large part to the visual interpretations by Mary GrandPré, that it seemed nearly impossible to find a child actor who could fit the bill.

In fact, even after interviewing thousands of young boys, with principal shooting scheduled to begin in a few weeks, the key role remain unfulfilled, a casting director's nightmare.

By luck, Daniel Radcliffe showed up on the radar, though not in a way anyone had envisioned. He was sitting in the audience at a movie theater and providentially spotted.

Radcliffe is superb as Harry Potter. Perfect casting, Radcliffe—no matter what else he does in the film community—will be forever remembered for his role as Harry Potter.

To watch Harry Potter in the books grow up is a reader's delight; and to watch Radcliffe's interpretation of the character in the film versions is a corresponding delight.

Daniel Radcliffe is an extraordinarily talented young actor who has carried the awesome (a word I use sparingly) responsibility of carrying the film series to date. These are films that gross nearly a billion dollars each!

If, as Rowling writes, the wand chooses the wizard, then it's not too far-fetched—especially under the circumstances under which the actor was discovered—to assume that the film picks the actor. In this case, it was an inspired choice and a wonderful performance by an indisputably gifted young man.

Rowling may have given us Harry Potter, but Radcliffe has *shown* us Harry, and done so brilliantly.

Radcliffe on Emma and Rupert: "We get along really well because we're all quite like our characters and Rupert's very funny, Emma's very intelligent and I'm in between because that's how Harry is, I think." (Quoted from "Daniel Radcliffe: Full Interview," conducted by Lizo Mzimba, from BBC Newsround on: http://News.bbc.co.uk, October 24, 2002.)

Chris Rankin as Percy Weasley. The character of Percy Weasley is a good example of how Rowling has very carefully thought out how fictional characters should grow. The straight-laced, by-the-book Percy Weasley is professionally interpreted by Chris Rankin, who delivers a solid performance. Walking a thin line between being fussy and too stiff, Rankin has the right touch. For instance, in a scene from the first film, Percy encounters Draco Malfoy, who spies what he thinks are his cronies Crabbe and Goyle, who are in fact not. Percy walks up and puts Malfoy in his right place—a small but memorable moment.

A young man whose life is defined by rules, Percy is wonderfully brought to life by Chris Rankin.

Rankin on his role: "I feel very happy that people appreciate the work I do and who I am. I still think that I'm the same guy I was before Potter came along. I'm no celebrity, and I don't want to be. I like doing the work I do, it's just a job at the end of the day, and if people get enjoyment out of it—I've done the job well. Percy's a great character, so I'm not suprised there's websites about him!" (Quoted from "My Interview with Chris Rankin" by an uncredited staffer of a fan website, www.percyweasley.com, January 25, 2003.)

Alan Rickman as Professor Severus Snape. Rickman is best known for his film roles as a bad guy—the Sheriff of Nottingham in *Robin Hood* and the terrorist mastermind in *Die Hard,* to name two that come immediately to mind.

Professor Snape is portrayed by Rowling as a very skilled potions master at Hogwarts, but his career aim is to teach Defense Against the Dark Arts, which tells us much about the character and his nature.

Rickman plays this role in a controlled, understated manner. The word *precision* comes to mind when I think of how he portrays Snape. He is in total control of his lines and delivers them exactly.

In the first book, Snape tells his first-year class about the beauty of potion-making, a subtle scene in which we begin to understand why he harbors such love for this difficult, exacting craft. In the film (scene 14 on the DVD), Rickman bursts in on his class and carefully, deliberately, performs this scene with understated control. He is clearly in command and as an actor delivers his lines with confidence, with the students hanging on his every word.

Rickman brings his considerable acting talents to bear in his interpretation of Snape—one that's a standout in a film series filled with memorable characters played by good and great actors.

Rickman on the first Harry Potter film: "It looked tremendous to me. I think the thing is that whenever . . . I was on the set and children were coming in and visiting, the endless refrain was, 'Wow! It's just like the book!' And I think that was certainly Chris Columbus's and the producers' aim: to be faithful to J. K. Rowling's imagination. And I think, given the fact that at the end of the screening last night the entire cinema stood up and cheered, I guess they've done it!" (Quoted by Tim Sebastian on BBC Hardtalk, November 7, 2001.)

Fiona Shaw as Petunia Dursley. The perfect wife for Vernon Dursley—she is similarly unimaginative and excessively concerned with appearances, though blinded to the shortcomings of their obnoxious son. Aunt Petunia is pure caricature: the class-conscious housewife who dotes excessively on her son and whose job is to support her husband blindly.

Fiona Shaw steps into this role and becomes Petunia Dursley, convincing us that, like her husband, all is not right in the world unless she finds continual fault with nephew Harry Potter, whom she resents.

A first-class, professional performance by Shaw complements the performances by actors Richard Griffiths and Harry Melling.

Shaw on her role: "Bad? Me? No, but I am very honoured to be Aunt Petunia. It is great to be part of a cultural touchstone, the film's very exciting and beautifully directed by Christopher Columbus." (Quoted from "Harry Potter's Wicked Aunt" in www.empireonline.co.uk, November 28, 2000.)

Maggie Smith as Professor Minerva McGonagall. As Rowling has pointed out in interviews, McGonagall is a powerful witch. The head of Gryffindor house, she is a key figure at Hogwarts.

The role is demanding—in fact, crucial, according to Rowling, who was concerned about its casting—but Maggie Smith is more than capable of filling the role. One of England's most celebrated actresses, Dame Maggie Smith is a consummate professional, a pro's pro. She delivers a carefully nuanced role, which she seems to fill without exertion.

In one film scene, she confronts Harry and Ron, who have just barely escaped a direct attack by the aptly named Whomping Willow. A miserable Ron sighs, resigned to his fate, and says he'll get his things now and leave Hogwarts, because he's been expelled. Maggie Smith, in her role as the head of Gryffindor, delivers the line, "Not today, Mr. Weasley." How she delivers that line with dry wit and precision makes her a joy to watch. In the vernacular of Harry Potter-aged kids, Smith RULES.

Smith on why she committed to the film series: "It's very simple really.

Harry Potter is my pension." (Quoted by Chloe Fox in "Spellbinding" on www.telegraph.co.uk, January 14, 2004.)

Verne Troyer as Griphook the Goblin. Best known for his role as "Mini Me" in the Austin Powers films, Troyer has only a brief appearance in one scene, when Harry Potter and Rubeus Hagrid go to Gringotts to make withdrawals. Harry needs cash for school supplies and Hagrid needs to pick up a special package on the instruction of Albus Dumbledore.

Troyer's walk-through is all too brief (more, please, about the Gringotts' goblins). Though Troyer is diminutive in real life, he's a giant of an actor.

Julie Walters as Molly Weasley. The mother that Harry Potter never had, Molly Weasley is the wife of Arthur Weasley and the mother of six boys and one daughter, all of whom have gone to or are currently enrolled in Hogwarts. As longtime readers know, there's more to her than meets the eye—particularly obvious in book five—and her role becomes increasingly more visible in each book.

Julie Walters plays well the part of Molly Weasley. She steps into the role and becomes the character. An endearing interpretation, Walters portrays Molly exactly as Rowling has written her—she runs the Weasley household, lays down the law with her own children, dotes on Harry Potter, and can still be like a giddy schoolgirl when in the presence of someone famous and flamboyant like Gilderoy Lockhart. (Ron is right: She fancies Lockhart, but of course downplays that notion.)

Hers is a solid performance that in the films to come will require rising to the occasion and reaching new heights of character interpretation.

Walters on her role: "Since playing Mrs. Weasley in *Harry Potter,* I've had a lot of children asking me for autographs. But usually it is women who say, 'I did an Open University course after seeing *Educating Rita.*' . . . Anyway, we live a very ordinary life so we don't come into contact with the starry thing. We live in a small community where everyone knows us and I'm just the local actress who opens the fetes. . . ." (Quoted from "The Actress Next Door" by an uncredited staff writer on www.theage.com.au, October 11, 2003.)

Emma Watson as Hermione Granger. The only character that Rowling has admitted is drawn from a real person, Hermione is a "swot," a brainy girl who uses her intelligence to mask her insecurities. It's a portrait of Rowling herself, who in high school was a head girl, as is Hermione in book five.

The danger for any young actress attempting this role is striking the right balance, achieving the right tone. If played too tightly, Granger would appear as unsympathetic and such a know-it-all that we as viewers would find her off-putting, like Ron Weasley does in his initial meetings with her. But in time a grudging friendship between them develops into a bona fide friendship, and she, Ron, and Harry become inseparable.

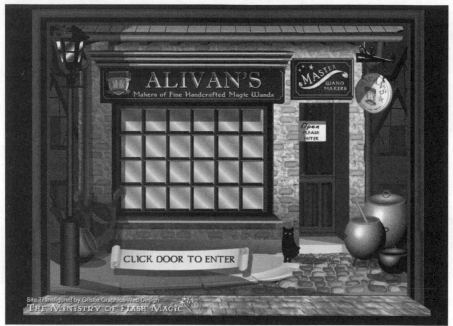

Screenshot of Alivans.com, a webstore that sells wands

Emma Watson is brilliant as Hermione Granger. The initial scene with her on the train as she first meets Harry and Ron tells us everything we need to know about her interpretation of the character. We are in good hands. Watson *is* an endearing know-it-all, who is initially an aggravation, subsequently an annoyance that borders on grating, and finally one who realizes when to obey the rules and when to break them (Percy Weasley, take note!).

Watson is an accomplished young actress who has to display a wide range of acting skills to pull off this challenging role. Fortunately for the film series, she is not only up to the challenge but throws herself into her role with unbridled enthusiasm.

Watson on what she doesn't like about her character: "She's a bit too [concerned with] rules. She overdoes it when Harry gets the Firebolt and she seeks out Professor McGonagall. She was obviously worried, but I probably would've had a talk with my friend before I sought out a teacher." (Quoted from "Emma Watson: Hermione" in *Nickolodeon Magazine,* October 30, 2001.)

Mark Williams as Arthur Weasley. The husband of Molly Weasley, Arthur is an employee at the Ministry of Magic, which gives us glimpses into its inner workings. Williams plays the role to perfection, whether it's showing delight and surprise when discovering that his sons have brought Harry Potter to his home as they all gather around the kitchen table for a hearty breakfast, or his childlike curiosity when he discovers that Ron, George, and Fred took his enchanted Ford Anglia for an unauthorized flight; he excitedly asks them how it went, and then assumes a mock-angry tone after being chided by his wife, who really runs the house and rules the roost.

Williams on his role: "It's a great film to work on. It's like all your favorite actors. Julie Walters is my wife, which is fantastic!" (Quoted from the Johnny Vaughan Show on BBC 1, September 23, 2002.)

Bonnie Wright as Ginny Weasley. The only daughter of Arthur and Molly Weasley, Ginny is initially awestruck when first encountering Harry up close, when she sees him at the family breakfast table. It turns out that she had been talking about Harry all summer to her bemused brother Ron, who says a little talk about Harry is okay, but she had become tedious, going on endlessly about poor Harry.

As with other secondary characters in the series, Ginny grows up. The speechless schoolgirl in the first film becomes a key figure in the second film, as she becomes more confident in herself—a difficult thing to do when you've been raised in a family of boys with no older sister to confide in.

Bonnie Wright strikes no wrong tones in her interpretation of Ginny Weasley. A loyal Gryffindor to the core, as are her brothers and Harry Potter, Ginny is a character to watch—as is the talented Bonnie Wright.

Wright on stardom: "I have had a few people recognise me in public. But I wouldn't like everybody to recognise me. I can still walk across the street and not be noticed. If I was Daniel Radcliffe I think I would find it much harder to deal with." (Quoted from "BBCi Films: Bonnie Wright. *Harry Potter and the Chamber of Secrets*," an interview conducted by Jamie Russell, undated.)

HARRY POTTER AND THE SORCERER'S STONE

Warner Bros., 2001. Running time: 153 minutes. November 16, 2001. (DVD issue: May 28, 2002.) Budget: $130 million. Worldwide Gross: $975 million.

Awards: Best Live Action in the category of Family Film from the Broadcast Film Critics Association.

Credits

Source: novel by Joanne Rowling
Screenwriter: Steve Kloves
Director: Chris Columbus
Producer: David Heyman, Mark Radcliffe (no relation to actor Daniel Radcliffe)
Cinematographer: John Seale
Composer: John Williams
Costume Designer: Judianna Makovsky
Editor: Richard Francis-Bruce
Executive Producers: Chris Columbus, Michael Barnathan, Duncan Henderson, Mark Radcliffe

Production Designer: Stuart Craig
Visual Effects Supervisor: Rob Legato

Cast (Actor: Fictional Character)
Bayler, Terence: The Bloody Baron, Slytherin ghost
Biggerstaff, Sean: Oliver Wood, Gryffindor Quidditch captain
Bradley, David: Mr. Argus Filch, caretaker
Cleese, John: Nearly Headless Nick, Gryffindor ghost
Coltrane, Robbie: Rubeus Hagrid, groundskeeper
Dale, Emily: Katie Bell
Davis, Warwick: Professor Flitwick and Goblin bank teller
Fearon, Ray: Firenze, centaur
Felton, Tom: Draco Malfoy
Fisher-Becker, Simon: The Fat Friar, ghost
Griffiths, Richard: Uncle Vernon Dursley
Grint, Rupert: Ronald "Ron" Weasley
Harris, Richard: Headmaster Albus Dumbledore
Hart, Ian: Professor Quirrell
Herdman, Joshua: Gregory Goyle
Holmes, David: Adrian Pucey
Hurt, John: Mr. Ollivander
Lewis, Matthew: Neville Longbottom
Melling, Harry: Dudley Dursley
Murray, Devon: Seamus Finnigan
Phelps, James: Fred Weasley
Phelps, Oliver: George Weasley
Radcliffe, Daniel: Harry Potter
Rankin, Chris: Percy Weasley
Rickman, Alan: Professor Severus Snape
Shaw, Fiona: Aunt Petunia Dursley
Smith, Maggie: Professor Minerva McGonagall
Spriggs, Elizabeth: The Fat Lady, Gryffindor
Sutherland, Leilah: Alicia Spinnet
Taylor, Danielle: Angelina Johnson
Troyer, Verne: Griphook the Goblin
Walters, Julie: Molly Weasley
Wanamaker, Zoe: Madam Hooch
Watson, Emma: Hermione Granger
Waylett, Jamie: Vincent Crabbe
Wright, Bonnie: Ginny Weasley
Youngblood, Luke: Lee Jordan

Selected Reviews

Daily Mail (U.K.): "I am happy to report that it truly is a wizard show. I suspect that fans of all ages will want to see it again and again. . . . Shooting the movie in British locations with a mostly British crew and all-British cast helped ensure that the film has been mostly free of the saccharine gloss that has choked the life out of many a Hollywood film.

"And the controlling hands of author J. K. Rowling and producer David Heyman have kept the picture true to the novel."

Daily Telegraph (U.K.): "When Steven Spielberg turned down the director's job to make *A.I.*, the choice of *Home Alone* filmmaker Columbus over the other candidates such as Ivan Reitman, Brad Siberling, and Terry Gilliam initially came in for criticism from Harry Potter fans. Many felt Columbus's tendency toward sentimentality—as demonstrated in *Stepmom* and *Bicentennial Man*—would be highly unsuitable for the weird and wonderful world of Harry Potter. But he has managed to keep the saccharine to a minimum, and instead allows Rowling's story to unfold almost exactly as she wrote it. . . . Screenwriter Steven Kloves has managed to retain all the essential elements of the book, while, by necessity, paring down and omitting a few of the minor characters. . . . [But] the stars of the film are its three children, on whose shoulders its credibility rests.

"Daniel Radcliffe . . . is in almost every frame and is a wonderful Harry, often bemused but always determined to do the right thing. . . ."

Jack Gardner for the Rochester *Democrat and Chronicle*: "There's magic galore in *Harry Potter and the Sorcerer's Stone*—even a Muggle like me can see it. The most eagerly anticipated movie adaptation of a novel since *Gone with the Wind* is a rousing success. . . . All told, the film propels the filmmaker into rarefied Spielberg and Lucas territory. *The Sorcerer's Stone* is the first of what will almost certainly be the most popular series of fantasy films since *Star Wars*."

E-Wired: "The cast could not have been more perfectly assembled. Rupert Grint was 'bloody brilliant.' Emma Watson shined as the almost-goody-goody Hermione, and Daniel Radcliffe, well, he *is* Harry Potter—the boy we have been awaiting so very long to see. . . . I thank the cast all kindly for bringing these characters to life, characters that have meant so much to myself, and millions of others."

Hollywood Reporter: "Fortunately, all hands involved in the production have faithfully observed the mantra 'It's the book, stupid.' Taking only a few shortcuts and hewing as close to the spirit of a literary work as any movie can, *Harry Potter* vividly imagines the world of wizards, magic school, and mystical creatures found in Rowling's series of children's adventure books. Clearly, the sky's the limit, not only for worldwide boxoffice but video, DVD, television, and merchandising."

Jonathan Foreman for the *New York Post:* "Adapting books for the screen is not easy to do well. It's even harder if fidelity to the original material is a major priority—and with *Harry Potter and the Sorcerer's Stone* it was more of a priority than in any of Hollywood's biblical epics."

James Berardinelli for *ReelViews:* "Viewed exclusively as a piece of cinema—something extraordinarily difficult to do with this property, *Harry Potter and the Sorcerer's Stone* stands out as a solid piece of entertainment. The film's spell may not be as potent as that of the book, but there's still some magic in what Columbus and his crew have wrought."

Joe Baltake for the *Sacramento Bee:* "If every movie that's greedily earmarked as a cinematic franchise could be as immaculately conceived as Chris Columbus's *Harry Potter and the Sorcerer's Stone,* there would be no reason to complain about the crass commercialization of films."

Jeff Strickler for the *Star Tribune:* "This is not a great movie, but it is a very good one. That's quite an accomplishment in light of the parameters forced upon him: He had to make a movie that works on its own terms for viewers who aren't familiar with the book, while appeasing the legion of Harry devotees who consider the source material the Holy Grail of kid lit."

Richard Corliss for *Time:* "How to make a film out of such a cinematic experience that 100 million readers have seen in their minds' eyes? Either by transferring it, like a lavishly illustrated volume of Dickens, or transforming it with a new vision. Columbus, along with screenwriter Steve Kloves and the Potter production team, chose Column A and made a handsomely faithful version, with actors smartly cast to type."

TV Guide: "Based on the first of Rowling's mind-bogglingly popular novels, Chris Columbus's lavishly appointed film aims for fidelity to the source in all things. And if it's a little airless, in the manner of certain *Masterpiece Theater* adaptations of literary masterworks, no matter. Fans will be so relieved to find the world they love transplanted to the screen intact that they won't mind a bit."

HARRY POTTER AND THE CHAMBER OF SECRETS

Warner Bros., 2002. Running time: 161 minutes. November 2002. (DVD issue: April 11, 2003.) Budget: $100 million. Worldwide Gross: $869 million.

Credits

Source: novel by Joanne Rowling
Screenwriter: Steve Kloves, Rowling
Director: Chris Columbus
Producers: David Heyman, Chris Columbus
Cinematographer: Roger Pratt
Composers: John Williams, William Ross
Executive Producers: Michael Barnathan, David Barron, Chris Columbus, Mark Radcliffe
Production Designer: Stuart Craig
Special Effects Supervisor: John Richardson

Cast (Actor: Fictional Character)
Biggerstaff, Sean: Oliver Wood, Captain of the Quidditch team for Gryffindor
Bradley, David: Mr. Argus Filch, caretaker of Hogwarts
Branagh, Kenneth: Professor Gilderoy Lockhart, Hogwarts teacher of
    Defense Against the Dark Arts
Burke, Alfred: Armando Dippet
Cleese, John: Nearly Headless Nick
Coltrane, Robbie: Rubeus Hagrid, groundskeeper
Columbus, Eleanor (Chris Columbus's daughter): Susan Bones
Coulson, Christian: Tom Riddle
Dale, Emily: Katie Bell
Davis, Warwick: Professor Filius Flitwick
Enoch, Alfred: Dean Thomas
Felton, Tom: Draco Malfoy
Glover, Julian: voice of Aragog the Spider
Griffiths, Richard: Harry Potter's uncle, Vernon Dursley
Grint, Rupert: Harry Potter's best friend, Ronald "Ron" Weasley
Hardy, Robert: Minister of Magic, Cornelius Fudge
Harris, Richard: Albus Dumbledore, headmaster at Hogwarts
Henderson, Shirley: ghost student, Moaning Myrtle
Herdman, Joshua: Gregory Goyle
Isaacs, Jason: Lucius Malfoy, father of Draco Malfoy
Jones, Toby: voice of Dobby the house-elf (for the Malfoys)
Lewis, Matt: Neville Longbottom
Margolyes, Miriam: Professor Sprout, Hogwarts teacher of Herbology
Mayall, Rik: Peeves the Poltergeist
Mitchell, Hugh: Colin Creevey
Murray, Devon: Seamus Finnigan
Padley, Gemma: Penelope Clearwater
Phelps, James: Fred Weasley
Phelps, Oliver: George Weasley
Radcliffe, Daniel: Harry Potter
Randell, Edward: Justin Finch-Fletchley
Rankin, Chris: Percy Weasley
Rickman, Alan: Professor Severus Snape, Hogwarts teacher of Potions
Shaw, Fiona: Harry Potter's aunt, Petunia Dursley
Smith, Maggie: Professor Minerva McGonagall
Sutherland, Leilah: Alicia Spinnet
Walters, Julie: Molly Weasley
Watson, Emma: Hermione Granger
Waylett, Jamie: Vincent Crabbe
Williams, Mark: Arthur Weasley

Selected Reviews

Roger Ebert for the *Chicago Sun-Times:* "What's developing here, it's clear, is one of the most important franchises in movie history, a series of films that consolidate all of the advances in computer-aided animation, linked to the extraordinary creative work of Rowling, who has created a mythological world as grand as *Star Wars,* but filled with more wit and humanity. Although the young wizard Harry Potter is nominally the hero, the film remembers the golden age of moviemaking, when vivid supporting characters crowded the canvas. The story is about personalities, personal histories and eccentricity, not about a superstar superman crushing the narrative with his egotistical weight."

Kirk Honeycutt for TheHollywoodReporter.com: "More than ever, the film must rely on its technical crew. Nick Dudman's imaginative creature and makeup effects, Roger Pratt's painterly cinematography, Lindy Hemming's flamboyant costumes and Stuart Craig's labyrinthine sets that melt into many visual and special effects all convincingly usher us into the realm of the fantastic."

Kenneth Turan for latimes.com: "Perhaps as an acting choice, perhaps because of the effects of the illness that eventually took his life, Harris plays Dumbledore with a quavering but resolute frailty that gives the character an effective gravity. His speech about the life span of his beloved phoenix, Fawkes, one of those creatures that 'burst into flames when it is time for them to die,' provides an unintentional valedictory to an impressive career."

Lou Lumenick for nypost.com: *"Harry Potter and the Chamber of Secrets* proves that sometimes you can have too much of a good thing. Crammed full of labyrinthine plot twists, this second installment will delight Potter-crazy kids even as their parents grow restless at the 2-hour-and-41-minute running time."

A. O. Scott for nytimes.com: "Mr. Columbus, once again working with the screenwriter Steve Kloves and a cast of talented children (especially Emma Watson, who plays the brainy and intrepid Hermione) and grown-up British luminaries, has acquitted himself honorably. . . . My fellow critics and I may occasionally fault a movie for departing, in detail or in spirit, from its literary source, but the grousing of a few adult pedants is nothing compared to the wrath of several million bookish ten-year-olds."

William Arnold for seattlepi.com: "Best of all, the second Potter movie

reunites its adult cast: Richard Harris, Maggie Smith, Robbie Coltrane, John Cleese, Alan Rickman, Julie Walters, and others—a veritable Who's Who of British actors that single-handedly elevates the proceedings out of the kid's movie genre into something special."

HARRY POTTER AND THE
PRISONER OF AZKABAN

Warner Bros., May 4, 2004. Running time: 142 minutes. Budget: $130 million. Opening weekend gross: $93.7 million.

Screenshot of the movie trailer; Gary Oldman as Sirius Black

Screenshot of the movie trailer; Michael Gambon
as Hogwarts Headmaster Albus Dumbledore

Credits

Source: novel by Joanne Rowling
Screenwriter: Steven Kloves
Director: Alfonso Cuarón
Producers: David Heyman, Chris Columbus, Mark Radcliffe
Executive producers: Michael Barnathan, Callum McDougall, Tanya
    Seghatchian
Associate producers: Chris Carreras, Paula DuPré Pesman
Art Director: Alan Gilmore
Cinematographer: Michael Seresin
Composer: John Williams
Costume Designer: Jany Termime
Film Editor: Steven Weisberg
Production Designer: Stuart Craig

Cast (Actor: Fictional Character)

Best, Peter: Buckbeak's executioner
Bradley, David: Caregiver Argus Filch
Christie, Julie: Madame Rosmerta
Coltrane, Robbie: Rubeus Hagrid, Keeper of Keys and Grounds
Dale, Emily: Katie Bell

Davis, Warwick: Wizard (in previous films, he played Professor Flitwick)
Enoch, Alfred: Dean Thomas
Felton, Tom: Draco Malfoy
Ferris, Pam: Aunt Marge
French, Dawn: The Fat Lady (in painting)
Gambon, Michael: Headmaster Albus Dumbledore (after the late Richard
    Harris)
Gardner, Jimmy: Ernie (driver of the Knight Bus)
Gaunt, Genevieve: Pansy Parkinson
Griffiths, Richard: Uncle Vernon Dursley
Grint, Rupert: Ron Weasley
Hardy, Robert: Cornelius Fudge
Henry, Lenny: voice of Shrunken Head on the Knight Bus
Herdman, Joshua: Gregory Goyle
Ingleby, Lee: Stan Shunpike
Lewis, Matthew: Neville Longbottom
Margolyes, Miriam: Professor Sprout
Melling, Harry: Dudley Dursley
Murray, Devon: Seamus Finnigan
Oldman, Gary: Sirius Black
Phelps, James: Fred Weasley
Radcliffe, Daniel: Harry Potter
Rankin, Chris: Percy Weasley
Rawlins, Adrian: James Potter
Rickman, Alan: Professor Severus Snape
Shah, Sitara: Parvati Patel
Shaw, Fiona: Aunt Petunia Dursley
Smith, Jennifer: Lavender Brown
Smith, Maggie: Professor Minerva McGonagall
Somerville, Geraldine: Lily Potter
Spall, Timothy: Peter Pettigrew
Sutherland, Leilah: Alicia Spinnet
Tavaré, Jim: Tom, an innkeeper
Taylor, Danielle: Angelina Johnson
Thewlis, David: Professor Remus Lupin, Defense Against the Dark Arts
    professor
Thompson, Emma: Professor Sybill Trelawney
Walters, Julie: Molly Weasley
Watson, Emma: Hermione Granger
Waylett, Jamie: Vincent Crabbe
Whitehouse, Paul: Sir Cadogan (in painting)
Williams, Mark: Arthur Weasley

Wright, Bonnie: Ginny Weasley
Youngblood, Luke: Lee Jordan

Perspectives

Joanne Rowling in *USA Today*: "For the very obvious reason that books and films are such different media, to do a very literal adaptation maybe wouldn't serve the material best, and I think [Cuarón] has done exactly what I hoped he would do. He's put a lot of humor in there, and I think it's fantastic. I'd be very, very surprised if most people didn't find their favorite parts of the book in that film."

Claudia Puig for *USA Today*: "Though *Potter* is set in a magical realm with an ethereal beauty, there is an honest and grounded quality to the human interactions. To paraphrase one of Harry's spells, this third Potter film has managed mischief brilliantly."

Paul Clinton for cnn.com: "It's safe to say that the mythology of Harry Potter is creating one of the most successful film franchises in Hollywood history, and *Harry Potter and the Prisoner of Azkaban* is a top-notch entry. Indeed, if they're all this good, I'd be happy to see a Harry Potter movie come out every year until he's collecting retirement."

Caroline Westbrook for bbc.co.uk: "Radcliffe has never been better, and it is a pleasure to see the central trio growing into their roles, as much as the characters are growing with them. All of which adds up to one of the best films of the summer so far, and one that bodes well for Harry Potter's future on film."

Reviewer for aint-it-cool-news.com: "In the end, this film is what all the Harry Potter films should aspire to be. The magic is captured, the characters are faithfully realized and the acting is top notch. The script is as tight as it could be without losing important threads from the books."

Tim Kirk

Notable and Quotable: Film Clips

Book to script: "The challenge always for me is keeping it from being four hours. What I honestly think is magical about what Jo does is the details. And so my first drafts are always chockful of details."

— Steve Kloves, screenwriter, quoted on Disc 2 of *Harry Potter and the Chamber of Secrets* DVD

Casting Harry: "Dan is great. It was a very difficult process. Finding Harry was very hard. It was like trying to find Scarlett O'Hara, this one. And I think everyone was getting slightly desperate. And I was walking down the streets of Edinburgh and London and looking at boys who passed me in a very suspicious-looking way. You know, I was thinking, could it be him? And then the producer and director walked into a theater one night and found Dan, an actor, who is just perfect. I saw his [screen] tests and I really had everything crossed that Dan would be the one, and he is."

— Rowling on Dan Radcliffe, from "J. K. Rowling Discusses Surprising Success of *Harry Potter*," an interview on *Larry King Live* (October 20, 2000)

Chris Columbus: "At last it can be told: despite the $900 million it made at the global box office, despite its ranking as the highest-grossing film of

2001, director Chris Columbus was not entirely happy with *Harry Potter and the Sorcerer's Stone.* 'I always thought we could have gotten the visual effects better,' he says. The pacing of the film, he admits, was a bit sluggish. 'The first 40 minutes of the first Harry Potter film were introductions.'"

—Jess Cagle from "When Harry Meets SCARY," *Time* (November 11, 2002)

"Not all the news is good. Harry Potter will soon be appearing at a multiplex near you. The initial project is being helmed by Chris Columbus, a filmmaker of no demonstrable ingenuity; one doubts if the director of *The Goonies,* one of the loudest, dumbest, and most shriekingly annoying children's movies ever made, is up to bringing Rowling's scatty wit and vibrant imagination to the screen. (I hope, on behalf of the millions of children who love Harry, Hermione, and Ron Weasley, that Columbus will prove me wrong.)"

—Stephen King in the *New York Times* (July 23, 2000)

Disappointed viewer: "I must regretfully admit I am disappointed in both of the film versions of Harry so far. They have first-rate casts and a number of really nice scenes here and there, but they somehow always fail to come together."

—Cartoonist/writer Gahan Wilson in "Harry Potter and the Amazing Success Story," *Realms of Fantasy* (August 2003)

Emotional connection to characters: "It is what the characters say, not how they look, that enables us to make an emotional connection with them. Though some of the excellent cast manage to act their way beyond the special effects (notably Alan Rickman's Snape, Robbie Coltrane's Hagrid, and Emma Watson's Hermione), many characters get lost in the dazzle of light and sound that filmmakers feel compelled to throw at us. If characters, and not scenery, had the starring role, viewers could become as involved with the film as they were with the novel."

—Author Philip Nel in "Bewitched, Bothered, and Bored: Harry Potter, the Movie," *Journal of Adolescent and Adult Literacy* (October 2002)

Fidelity to the novels: "As I recently said to my biographer, when I first started to get offers from film companies, I initially said 'no' to all of them. I am not against cinema—I actually love good movies. However, the vital thing for me was that the studio which eventually got the production contract, Warners, promised to be true to the book, and I have great faith in their commitment to that."

—Rowling quoted in "Exclusive: Writer Rowling Answers Her Readers' Questions," *Toronto Star* (April 22, 2003)

Film rights: "I did not feel I was far enough into the series, I didn't want 'non-author-written-sequels' where a film company could have taken my characters and sent them off to Las Vegas on holiday, or something equally mad. I finally said 'yes' when I knew I was far enough into the books to make it very difficult for the filmmakers to take Harry and company off in directions I didn't want them to go."

—Rowling quoted in "Rowling Despaired of Ever Finishing *Harry*," nzoom.com (May 19, 2003)

Harry Potter #1: "As any reasonable person would have expected, it's a big and often sloppy Hollywood production with some bad computer graphics, a syrupy score from John Williams, and a focus on storybook adventure rather than Rowling's oddball characters."

—Andrew O'Herir in a review of *Harry Potter and the Sorcerer's Stone,* Salon.com (November 16, 2001)

Steve Kloves: "When I first met the screenwriter Steve Kloves, the fact that he was American did indeed make me wary, as I felt that he could very well be careless and insensitive with my creative baby. But as soon as he said his favorite character was Hermione, he completely won me over because she is the character who is closest to me. Steve also won my confidence by saying how protective both he and the production team were about my book, and that they were determined to avoid that usual Hollywood gaucheness."

—Rowling quoted in "Exclusive: Writer J. K. Rowling Answers Her Readers' Questions," *Toronto Star* (April 22, 2003)

Merchandising: "So where, cynical parents sated by *Phantom Menace* merchandise this summer must be wondering, is the movie? Where are the toys? How can this be just a book? Warner Bros. has the film and merchandise rights to the first book, but there will be a lull before American children see their personal image of Harry replaced by a face on a movie screen or have a chance to buy a certified Nimbus 2000 broomstick."

—Eden Ross Lipson in "Book's Quirky Hero and Fantasy Win the Young," *New York Times,* Books (July 12, 1999)

"Warner Bros.' huge marketing juggernaut has been cranking merchandise into the marketplace for more than a year, so you can already 'get' Harry via coffee mug, sweatshirt, lightning-bolt scar stickers, or mantelpiece figurine rather than getting him by reading. Thankfully, the stuff in most cases is so ugly that it helps even the youngest readers separate the wonderfully illustrated books from the movie hype."

—Tracy Mayor in "Kiss Harry Potter Goodbye," Salon.com (November 6, 2001)

Movie as marketing vehicle: "By now we're all used to heavy marketing campaigns for movies. But movies that actually feel like two-hour-plus marketing campaigns are a relatively new phenomenon. Perfunctory, competent,

well-oiled, and yet still stultifyingly dull, *Harry Potter and the Chamber of Secrets* sells itself dutifully minute-by-minute—it's the hardest-working movie in show business."

—Stephanie Zacharek in "The Trouble with Harry," Salon.com (November 15, 2002)

Movie deal: "Ms. Rowling has a deal giving her 1% of box office profits and it is thought she will net five pence for every £1 of Potter merchandise sold. Disney has already paid £49 million for the U.S. TV rights to the film."

—Susan Woods in "Rowling Conjures Up House for Close Friend," *Scotsman* (April 8, 2002)

Movie realism: "Instead of trying to overtake the readers' imagination, we've just given them the best possible version of the book, which means steeping it in reality . . . I wanted kids to feel that if they actually took that train, Hogwarts would be waiting for them."

—Chris Columbus quoted by Jeff Cagle in "The First Look at Harry," *Time* (November 5, 2001)

Protectiveness: "But I sold it to people I trusted, and so far my trust has not been misplaced. We're looking at an all-British cast. At first that looked like an impossibility. There was many a director who couldn't see that working at all. I would say things are going really well at the moment. People have to understand that no one could feel as protective as I do about these characters."

—Rowling quoted by Malcolm Jones in "The Return of Harry Potter," *Newsweek* (July 1, 2000)

Dan Radcliffe: "Having seen Dan Radcliffe's screen test, I don't think Chris Columbus could have found a better Harry."

—Rowling quoted by Laura Miller in "Harry Potter Kids Cast," Salon.com (August 22, 2000)

"It's really funny, but there were a couple of people at school and they had never talked to me before, but as soon as I got the part they started e-mailing me and pretending we were best friends. My close friends have been totally cool about it. At least, I hope they have. And anyway, Mum and Dad keep me leading a normal life. I have some close friends and they are the same now as before I did this. They want to know about it—of course they do—and some of them have come on set to have a look. But nothing's changed."

—Daniel Radcliffe quoted by Tracey Lawson in "Spellbound," News.scotsman.com (June 14, 2003)

Scriptwriter spotlighted: "I've never been involved with a picture that anyone was remotely interested in before I'd handed in the script. Certainly not a picture that people are interested in doing articles on before I'm even finished with the polish on the first draft."

—Screenwriter Steve Kloves quoted by Michael Sragow in "A Wizard of Hollywood," Salon.com (February 24, 2000)

Steven Spielberg: "The Edinburgh-based writer made the aside at the Scottish charity premiere of *Harry Potter and the Philosopher's Stone* at the Ster Century Cinema in Leith. Rowling praised Columbus for remaining true to her book, then added: 'Thank God it wasn't Spielberg.' She then jokingly added: 'Do you think we could be sued for that?'"

—From "Rowling Has a Dig at Spielberg," *Edinburgh Evening News* (November 7, 2001)

Unhappy film fan: "In the Harry Potter Usenet group alt.fan.harry_potter, one potterphiliac entitled her posting 'Nooooooo' and suggested that the film ought to be called *Harry Potter and the Mainstream Inflate-a-Budget Crap.*"

—Laura Miller from "Fans Hate Director Picked for Harry Potter Film," Salon.com (March 30, 2000)

Lacock Abbey (in Lacock, Wiltshire). Its interior was used for interior shots in the Potter films. © WWW.BRITAINONVIEW.COM.

Christ Church Dining Hall at Oxford University (in Oxford, Oxfordshire). Its interior was used as the Hogwarts Great Hall. © WWW.BRITAINONVIEW.COM.

Above: Oxford University (in Oxford, Oxfordshire). Several buildings were used for interior shots in the Potter films. © WWW.BRITAINONVIEW.COM.

Castle (in Edinburgh, Lothian). This prominent castle on a bluff overlooks the city. © WWW.BRITAINONVIEW.COM.

Gloucester Cathedral (in Gloucester, Gloucestershire). Its interior was used for interior shots in the Potter films. © WWW.BRITAINONVIEW.COM.

Durham Cathedral (Durham, County Durham). Its rooms and cloisters were used for interior shots in the Potter films. © WWW.BRITAINONVIEW.COM.

Big Ben (Westminster, London). Ron Weasley and Harry Potter fly past
this prominent landmark in the second film. © www.BRITAINONVIEW.COM.

Alnwick Castle (Alnwick, Northumberland). Its exterior was used for shots in the Potter films. © WWW.BRITAINONVIEW.COM.

The Royal Albert Hall (London). On June 26, 2003, Rowling made a rare public appearance to promote her fifth Potter novel. © WWW.BRITAINONVIEW.COM.

Rowling displays a copy of her latest novel. © The Scotsman Publ. Ltd, Edinburgh/uncredited.

Rowling makes an unannounced appearance at a bookstore in Edinburgh, where she signs copies of her latest novel. © THE SCOTSMAN PUBL. LTD, EDINBURGH/PAMELA GRIGG.

Nicolson's, Rowling's favorite refuge for writing. © THE SCOTSMAN PUBL. LTD, EDINBURGH/PAMELA GRIGG.

Claran Sneddon, 7, waits in the bookshelves of Waterstone's, Edinburgh, to get his copy on publication day. © THE SCOTSMAN PUBL. LTD, EDINBURGH/PHIL WILKINSON.

Rowling and her husband, Dr. Neil Murray. © The Scotsman Publ. Ltd, Edinburgh/Esme Allen.

Baby Saw-whet Owls.
Raptor Education Group/
Nick Derene.

Rowling at a press conference for the Multiple Sclerosis Society of Scotland. © The Scotsman Publ. Ltd, Edinburgh/ Jacky Ghossein.

Only eight days to go until *Harry Potter and the Order of the Phoenix* flies out of stores. © THE SCOTSMAN PUBL. LTD, EDINBURGH/ROBERT PERRY.

Little Bit, a Saw-whet Owl.
RAPTOR EDUCATION GROUP/NICK DERENE.

Yeti (a snowy White Owl) and Little Girl (a Great Horned Owl). RAPTOR EDUCATION GROUP/NICK DERENE.

A steam train out of Goathland, North Yorkshire, used
in the films as Hogsmeade Station. © WWW.BRITAINONVIEW.COM.

Actor Daniel Radcliffe, the boy who was cast as Harry Potter. © *THE GUARDIAN*/FRANK BARON.

A baby Great Horned Own.
RAPTOR EDUCATION GROUP/NICK DERENE.

Watson, a red phase Screech Owl.
RAPTOR EDUCATION GROUP/NICK DERENE.

Pepe Lulu, an adult Barn Owl.
RAPTOR EDUCATION GROUP/NICK DERENE.

Rowling at King's Cross station. © *THE GUARDIAN*/Sean Smith.

A baby Barred Owl.
RAPTOR EDUCATION GROUP/NICK DERENE.

A baby Saw-whet Owl.
RAPTOR EDUCATION GROUP/NICK DERENE.

Part Four:
A Look at the Books

Tim Kirk

ewcomers to Harry Potter's world will likely feel a bit overwhelmed, which is understandable: five books, three movies (and
more on the way), and a wealth of dedicated websites exploring
every nook and cranny of the Harry Potter universe—it all confuses rather
than clarifies.

This section is devoted to a book-by-book look at the five Harry Potter novels in print. By focusing on the principal texts, the newcomer will find negoti-
ating the overwhelming amount of information about Rowling and the Harry
Potter novels much more manageable.

My general recommendations for reading the Potter canon:

1. Read the books in order. Not only are the novels chronological, but Rowling
   plotted them in exquisite detail, which means that each book builds on what
   has gone before. Little details that seem insignificant will, in later books, resonate with meaning and importance.

2. Keep your eyes open for the clues. Rowling employs the literary technique
   of foreshadowing to build anticipation and whet readers' appetites. There
   is nothing superfluous in the novels. Everything has been inserted for a
   reason, even if it's not readily apparent at first glance.

3. Enjoy the movies but realize that they are interpretive, not literal, and thus
   the reader is advised to go to the primary source, the novels, to get the
   story straight.

In this section I'll discuss the story behind the story (the facts surrounding the book's publication), the publishing history of the book, reviews,
awards, and a summation of where the book fits in with the rest of the series.

I will not provide a detailed plot summary, since the first-time reader will
want to discover it in the reading.

Also, because of the large number of people, places, and things in the
novels—all interconnected and of varying importance—I've provided a concordance, to help keep the story elements straight.

HARRY POTTER AND THE
PHILOSOPHER'S/SORCERER'S STONE

I never dreamt this would happen. My realistic side had allowed myself to think that I might get one good review. That was my idea of a peak. So everything else really has been like stepping into Wonderland for me.

—Rowling quoted by
Ann Ireneman in
"The J. K. Rowling Interview,"
Times (June 20, 2003)

The first Potter novel was published in the United States as *Harry Potter and the Sorcerer's Stone* because Scholastic didn't feel American readers would understand the allusion in the British title, *Harry Potter and the Philosopher's Stone.*

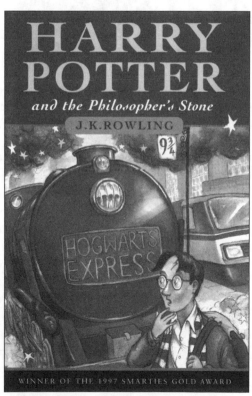

British edition, children's cover version

HARRY POTTER
and the Philosopher's Stone

J. K. ROWLING

'FUNNY, IMAGINATIVE, MAGICAL' - THE TIMES

British edition, adult's cover version (original)

Dedication

"For Jessica, who loves stories,/ For Ann, who loved them too;/And for Di, who heard this one first."

The dedication is for her daughter, Jessica; her late mother, Ann; and her sister, Dianne.

Background

Once upon a time there was a single mother on welfare who became rich and famous by writing her way out of poverty by writing the best-selling series of all time—in other words, an enchanting Cinderella story, in which the handsome prince (the publisher) discovers the beautiful but hitherto ignored blonde heroine.

That's the story journalists writing about Rowling like to tell, since it romanticizes the world of the aspiring writer and offers hope to the millions of others who think that they, too, can go from obscurity to fame with their fiction. (If only it were that easy!)

Rowling undoubtedly rolls her eyes whenever she reads another story that plays up that oft-repeated narrative hook, since it oversimplifies the plain truth. A lifelong writer, she spent most of her adult life working. In fact, she had gotten an £8,000 grant from the Scottish Arts Council to work on the Potter novels *after* she had sold the first book to Bloomsbury. In other words, the journalists showed us a snapshot of a specific moment in her life, but it wasn't representative of the whole.

Like most first-time authors, Rowling faced an uphill battle in getting her first novel published, since she had to confront all the preconceived notions the publishing industry harbors of first-time authors, especially those who want to write children's books.

Though Rowling has a powerful imagination, neither she nor anyone else could have imagined the salutary effect she'd have on the genre. She would go on to transform it permanently, bringing it into the mainstream, like Stephen King did for horror/suspense fiction.

When she submitted her novel to the Christopher Little Literary Agency, two early readers—Bryony Evens and Fleur Howle—championed it in-house and recommended it to their boss, Christopher Little.

After Rowling signed the standard artist-agent contract, Little began submitting the over 80,000-word novel to British publishers, who raised what then seemed quite sensible objections: It is too long for a children's book and, besides, boys won't read a children's book written by a woman.

In hindsight, both objections seem laughable, but at the time they seemed perfectly reasonable; in fact, the latter objection prompted the agency to recommend that Rowling not write under her name but under an abbreviated, gender-free name: J. K. Rowling instead of Joanne Rowling.

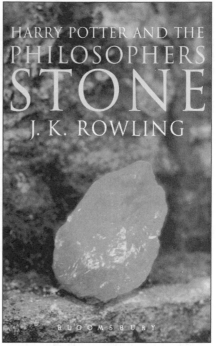

British edition, adult's cover version (for 2004)

Again, in hindsight, the British publishers who passed on what turned out to be the most lucrative literary franchise of our time seem foolish, but this is commonplace in the book industry. Publishing houses rise, and fall, on the wisdom of book acquisitions.

Bloomsbury Publishing wisely decided to take a chance on this unknown but obviously talented writer who, incidentally, was skilled as an illustrator, as well. The offer from Bloomsbury was modest, but Rowling didn't care. She would realize her dream of seeing a book with her name on it in a bookstore.

On June 26, 1997, the book went to press with a modest first printing, most of which sold to libraries and independent booksellers.

Early reviews from newspapers in England were positive, heralding a new voice, but with such modest sales, Rowling could not hope for anything but supplementary income from her writing.

The turning point arrived when the book came to the attention of a publisher in the United States, which would prove to be the world's largest market for Harry Potter books. Janet Hogarth, formerly on the staff at Bloomsbury's children book division, had recently begun working at Scholastic, and championed the book to the firm's editorial director, Arthur A. Levine, who was en route to an international book fair in Germany.

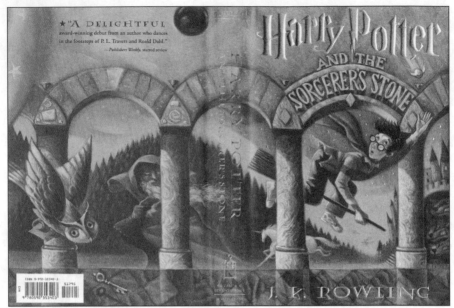

U.S. edition

Levine read the book and loved it, determined to bid whatever was necessary to secure U.S. rights. Soon thereafter, a spirited auction resulted, with Levine bidding furiously, fending off the competition. The result: Levine kept bidding until he had won the U.S. rights for a figure some in the industry felt excessive, especially for a children's book by a first-time novelist.

In sharp contrast to the modest first U.K. printing, Scholastic planned an unprecedented print run of 50,000 copies. The combination of a record advance and a large first printing made news worldwide, and so began the legend of J. K. Rowling. Newspapers ran stories about her as a single parent on the dole who became rich by writing her way to success—a great story, but rather fanciful.

By this time Rowling had finished and turned in the second book in the series, *Harry Potter and the Chamber of Secrets,* and the big question on everyone's mind was whether or not publishing history would repeat itself. Would her second book repeat the success of the first, or was she a one-book wonder?

About the Book

For readers worldwide, this book is pure magic. Though novels about student wizards are (pardon the expression) old hat, Rowling has reinvigorated not only the fantasy field but children's literature, as well.

What makes this book all the more surprising—and make no mistake, the book is *full* of delightful surprises—is that it came not from an established writer with a long publication history but from an unknown writer who didn't even have a short story to her credit.

In short, the odds didn't favor the young author or her fledgling novel, which makes it all the more remarkable that within six years Rowling would sell a record quarter-billion copies of her Harry Potter novels one through five. Greatly exceeding her modest expectations, her books would go on to make book-publishing history.

"A wonderful first novel," wrote a reviewer for the *New York Times,* which certainly sums up the book succinctly. The story of an orphaned boy who lives with his depressingly ordinary relatives—the monstrous Dursley family—Harry Potter is not what he seems. In fact, Harry himself doesn't know who he is, since the Dursleys go to extraordinary lengths to shield his true identity from him and everyone else. As far as Vernon and Petunia Dursley are concerned, and as far as Harry knows, he is just another non-magical boy—a Muggle. But when owl-delivered letters from Hogwarts inexplicably arrive at the Dursley residence for Harry, his uncle intercepts them and, with characteristic glee, burns them in the fireplace.

To his uncle's dismay and mounting frustration, the trickle of letters increases, so he takes the family off to a remote shack by the sea, never realizing that what he's dealing with is beyond his imagination. Indeed, when the letters fail to be delivered, the final letter is hand-delivered, not by an ordinary postman but by a half-giant named Rubeus Hagrid, who is on a mission to deliver an acceptance letter to Harry Potter, inviting him as a first-year student to a magical educational institution, Hogwarts School of Witchcraft and Wizardry.

Kept in the dark about his past and, indeed, his family, Harry Potter had no idea that he was already a legend in the magical community. "You're a wizard, Harry," says Hagrid, to the great surprise of the young boy, who may have had an inkling because strange things happened when he willed them, but he didn't realize why.

Hagrid rescues Harry Potter from his Muggle world and takes him to Diagon Alley, which is his first encounter with the wizarding community. From there, it's on to Hogwarts, along with the other first-year students, on the Hogwarts Express, a train that picks students up at Platform Nine and Three-Quarters in London and transports them to a geographical point far to the north.

At Hogwarts, Harry Potter realizes his place in the universe is in the wizarding world, where great things are expected of him. The son of James and Lily Potter—a wizard and Muggle-born witch—Harry Potter has a singular distinction. He is famous because, as an infant, he survived a direct attack by a powerful dark wizard named Lord Voldemort who failed in killing Harry, despite the employment of the deadliest of all curses, the feared Killing Curse.

Far from being just another fledgling wizard in the magical world, Harry Potter is the only one who has ever survived a Killing Curse and is therefore unique. He is "the boy who lived" when countless others died, including Harry's parents. The attack also sealed his destiny, inextricably linking it to Lord Voldemort's, with the promise that a hellacious showdown is inevitable in the last book in the series.

Will Lord Voldemort finally finish what he failed to do many years ago and kill Harry Potter, or will the boy wizard take his place in the wizarding world by defeating the most feared dark wizard of all time?

In the first chapter of the book, Professor McGonagall makes a prophetic observation about the boy wizard. "He'll be famous—a legend—I wouldn't be surprised if today was known as Harry Potter day in the future—there will be books written about Harry—every child in the world will know his name!"

Professor McGonagall spoke the truth.

Selected Reviews

Booklist: "Rowling's first novel is a brilliantly imagined and beautifully written fantasy that incorporates elements of traditional British school stories without once violating the magical underpinnings of the plot. In fact, Rowling's wonderful ability to put a fantastic spin on sports, student rivalry, and eccentric faculty contributes to the humor, charm, and, well, delight of her utterly captivating story."

New York Times Book Review: "A wonderful first novel. Much like Roald Dahl, J. K. Rowling has a gift for keeping the emotions, fears, and triumphs of her characters on a human scale, even while the supernatural is popping out all over. The book is full of wonderful, sly humor [and] the characters are impressively three-dimensional (occasionally, four-dimensional!) and move along seamlessly through the narrative. *Harry Potter and the Sorcerer's Stone* is as funny, moving, and impressive as the story behind its writing. Like Harry Potter, [Rowling] has wizardry inside, and has soared beyond her modest Muggle surroundings to achieve something quite special."

Publishers Weekly: "Readers are in for a delightful romp with this award-winning debut from a British author who dances in the footsteps of P. L. Travers and Roald Dahl. . . . There is enchantment, suspense and danger galore (as well as enough creepy creatures to satisfy the most bogey-men-loving readers, and even a magical game of soccer-like Quidditch to entertain sports fans) as Harry and his friends Ron and Hermione plumb the secrets of the forbidden third floor at Hogwarts to battle evil and unravel the mystery behind Harry's scar. Rowling leaves the door wide open for a sequel; bedazzled readers will surely clamor for one."

School Library Journal: "After reading this entrancing fantasy, readers will be

convinced that they, too, could take the train to Hogwarts School, if only they could find Platform Nine and Three-Quarters at the King's Cross station."

Awards (U.K. and U.S.)

American Library Association Notable Book
Booklist Editor's Choice
Booksellers Association/Bookseller Author of the Year (1998)
British Book Awards: Children's Book of the Year (1998)
FCBG Children's Book Award: overall winner, and Longer Novel category (1998)
Nestle Smarties Book Prize (1998, Gold Medal)
New York Public Library Best Book of the Year 1998
North East Book Award (1999)
North East Scotland Book Award (1998)
Parenting Book of the Year Award 1998
Publishers Weekly Best Book of 1998
Scottish Arts Council Children's Book Award (1999)
Whitaker's Platinum Book Award 2001

Summation

To categorize *Harry Potter and the Sorcerer's Stone* as a children's novel—that is to say, a novel that only a child would enjoy—is to ignore the enormous appeal that the novel holds for adults, a fact that surprised everyone, especially Bloomsbury, who found adults in England shielding their copies behind newspapers, since they didn't want to be seen in public reading a children's book. As a result, Bloomsbury then issued the novels with two different covers—one for children, and one for adults.

While it's certainly possible for a children's book to sell well on its own, this novel clearly appealed to two sensibilities. Children loved its sense of fantasy and humor, its enormously appealing rite of passage story. They identified with a powerless child who realizes his potential to assume his rightful place in the world.

Adults, who also love a well-told story, appreciated it for the same reasons children did, but realize that the novel offers more. As Rowling pointed out, the book serves as a metaphor to explore the world of imagination. You are either a Muggle or, so to speak, a magician; you either believe in the status quo and a world of rules and order . . . or a world of imagined possibilities, where human potential can be realized.

For children and adults alike, the novel speaks volumes. We empathize with Harry Potter because we can all see a little bit of Potter in ourselves.

HARRY POTTER AND THE CHAMBER OF SECRETS

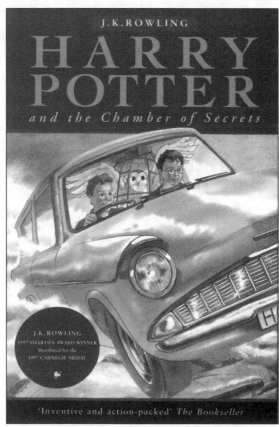

British edition, children's cover version

Dedication

"For Séan P.F. Harris,/ Getaway driver and foul-weather friend."

This refers to her college pal, who is one of her best friends.

Background

Rowling submitted the manuscript for this book to her British publisher in early July 1997, two weeks after the U.K. publication of *Harry Potter and the Philosopher's Stone.*

This second book in the series was published in the U.K. in July 1998, but wouldn't see publication in the U.S. until June 1999. The problem, as Scholastic soon discovered, was that

some eager fans wouldn't wait for the U.S. edition; instead, they ordered the British edition from the U.K. division of Amazon.com, which undercut the sales of the U.S. edition.

To make matters worse, the third book in the series, *Harry Potter and the Prisoner of Azkaban*, would be scheduled for publication in the U.K. on July 8, so the problem was compounded. U.S. fans began ordering significant quantities of the U.K. edition, since the U.S. edition wasn't scheduled for publication until September.

To Bloomsbury's and Scholastic's dismay, Web-savvy U.S. readers upset the delicate order of balance. The appetite for Harry Potter books was so

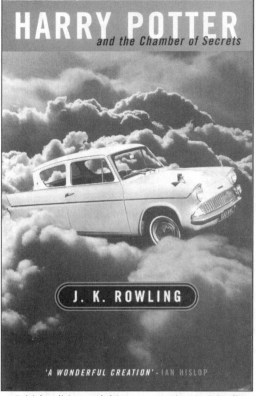

British edition, adult's cover version (original)

great that Scholastic's marketing and sales plan were seriously undercut by the built-in delay in publication between the U.K. and U.S. editions—a problem they would finally correct with the fourth book, *Harry Potter and the Goblet of Fire*.

About Book Two

Contrary to popular belief, lightning *can* strike twice, but it's rare, and especially so in the book field where the promise of a first novel sometimes turns out to be an empty one. The writer, having said all he wanted to say in his first novel, cannot resist the siren call for a second book, which the publisher hopes will be just as, if not more, successful. Far too often, however, the second novel doesn't reach sales, or readers', expectations.

Part of Rowling's great genius in constructing the series was in biding her time. Until she had thoroughly explored her fictional world and knew exactly, book by book, what would happen and when, she refrained from publishing. Consequently, the first book got off to a necessarily slow start, with 113 of its 309 pages just to get Harry to Hogwarts, at which point the real fun begins and the book builds up its momentum, like a train streaking down the tracks at top speed.

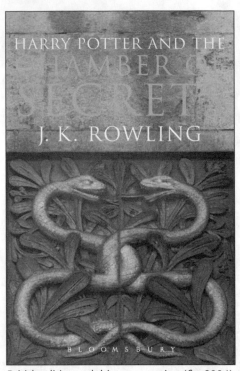

British edition, adult's cover version (for 2004)

In the second book in the series, two facts become obvious. Nothing in the first book is accidental. In other words, there are clues, seemingly innocuous, to what will become important in the books to follow. Also, Rowling dispensed with the back story—telling us who Harry Potter is and why he's so famous in the wizarding community—to get on with the main story. As a reviewer for *Booklist* put it, "The magical foundation so necessary in good fantasy [is] as expertly crafted here as in the first book."

By page 12 of the second novel, we know Harry Potter's got a problem on his hands because Dobby, a house-elf, visits him in his room at the Dursley residence to warn him not to come back to Hogwarts, and does everything in his considerable power to drive the point home.

Having established the main character, the supporting cast (Rubeus Hagrid, Ron Weasley, and Hermione Granger), and the faculty at Hogwarts, Rowling can concentrate on the story at hand. At Hogwarts, the Chamber of Secrets is the stuff of legend. It reportedly resides deep within the bowels of the school, undiscovered despite numerous searches over its more than thousand year history. Though the present faculty is quick to point out that talk of the Chamber of Secrets should be discounted, if not dismissed outright, the talk among the students is animated, especially when things take a somber tone with Hogwarts students turning to stone.

Does the Chamber of Secrets actually exist? And, if so, has someone opened it—presumably, the destined heir of Slytherin—to allow the fabled monster to escape and run amuck at Hogwarts? No one—living or dead—is spared. Animals, students, and even ghosts are all at risk, as pesky poltergeist Peeves warns everyone.

Readers love a good mystery wrapped within a well-told tale, and with her second book, Rowling doesn't disappoint. She, in fact, has written an engaging book series that promises to deliver more with each installment, as Harry Potter learns more about himself and his eventual place in the wizarding world.

In the second novel we also learn much more about the delightful wiz-

U.S. edition

arding world. We are taken to the enchanted home of the Weasleys, where clocks tell more than time, where dishes wash themselves, and the family garden is populated with talking Gnomes, who must periodically be weeded out.

This book adds to the cast of memorable characters Gilderoy Lockhart, a flamboyant and excessively vain braggart who shows up with a flourish at a bookstore to sign copies of his many books, required texts for Hogwarts students, since he's the newest addition to its faculty. (His books are more fiction than fact, however!) We also learn more about Nearly Headless Nick, a ghost at Hogwarts who is certainly the most interesting of the lot. Add to that mix, an engaging assortment of new magical creatures, good and bad, and spiced with a delightful sense of humor throughout, the end result is, as the British would say, a simply smashing read.

Of course, at the heart of the book is the mystery about the Chamber of Secrets, which must be solved by Harry Potter, who is still very much a fledgling student wizard, unsure of himself and his place in the magical world.

By the second book in the series, we know we are in good hands. Rowling has delivered the literary goods once again and whetted our appetite for the third novel, just as any good writer should.

Selected Reviews

Booklist: "Harry Potter's exploits during his second year at Hogwarts completely live up to the bewitching measure of *Harry Potter and the*

Sorcerer's Stone. The magical foundation so necessary in good fantasy [is] as expertly crafted here as in the first book."

Los Angeles Times: "*Harry Potter and the Chamber of Secrets* is a wonderful sequel, as suspenseful, charming, and ultimately satisfying as its predecessor."

A *Publishers Weekly* starred review: "Fans who have been anxiously awaiting the return of young British wizard Harry Potter (and whose clamor caused the Stateside publication date to be moved up three months) will be amazed afresh. And newcomers will likely join Harry's delighted legion of followers, for this tale is perhaps even more inventive than its predecessor, *Harry Potter and the Sorcerer's Stone.* Picking up shortly after his first year at Hogwarts School of Witchcraft and Wizardry, orphan Harry is spending the summer with his detestable Muggle (non-witch) aunt's family. Rowling briskly sets the action rolling with a mysterious warning from an elf named Dobby. The pace accelerates as Harry, now 12, is rescued from his bedroom imprisonment by his best friend Ron Weasley and his irrepressible older twin brothers in a flying car. Their school year gets off to a bad start when Harry and Ron crash-land the car at Hogwarts. More trouble soon follows, first from Harry's old nemesis, supercilious Draco Malfoy, then from a mysterious something that is petrifying Muggle-born students, culminating with Harry and Ron's friend Hermione. And once more, it's up to Harry to save the day. Rowling might be a Hogwarts graduate herself, for her ability to create such an engaging, imaginative, funny, and, above all, heart-poundingly suspenseful yarn is nothing short of magical."

School Library Journal: "Fans of the phenomenally popular *Harry Potter and the Sorcerer's Stone* won't be disappointed when they rejoin Harry, now on break after finishing his first year at Hogwarts. The novel is marked throughout by the same sly and sophisticated humor found in the first book, along with inventive, new, matter-of-fact uses of magic that will once again have readers longing to emulate Harry and his wizard friends."

USA Today: "Those needing a bit of magic, morality, and mystical worlds can do no better than opening *Harry Potter and the Chamber of Secrets.* As she did in *Harry Potter and the Sorcerer's Stone,* Rowling delivers plenty of ghoulish giggles. And in young Potter she has created a hero as resourceful, brave, and loyal as Luke Skywalker himself."

Wall Street Journal: "Harry's enchanted world is a refreshing break from the all-too-familiar settings of many of today's novels."

Awards (U.S. and U.K.)

American Library Association (ALA) Best Book for Young Adults (1999)
American Library Association (ALA) Notable Book

Booklist 1999 Editor's Choice
Booksellers Association/Bookseller Author of the Year 1998
British Book Awards (1998): Children's Book of the Year
FCBC Children's Book Award (1998): Overall winner, and Longer Novel
  Category
Gold Medal Smarties Prize (1999)
National Book Award, U.K. (1999)
North East Book Award (1999)
North East Scotland Book Award (1998)
School Library Journal (1999), Best Book of the Year
Scottish Arts Council Children's Book Award (1999)
Whitaker's Platinum Book Award (2001)

HARRY POTTER AND THE
PRISONER OF AZKABAN

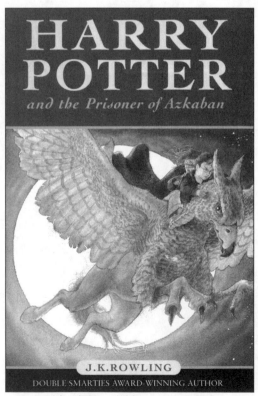

British edition, children's cover version

Dedication

"To Jill Prewett and Aine Kiely, the Godmothers of Swing."

The dedication refers to her two fellow teachers with whom she taught at Encounter English School in Porto, Portugal. She also shared an apartment with them while there.

Background

Of the five Potter novels published to date, this book tops the list of every poll when fans are asked to vote for their most popular book in the series.

Note: With this book the Harry Potter phenomenon

took off in the United States, with impatient fans buying copies of the British editions rather than waiting for the domestic edition.

On June 4, 2004, the third Harry Potter novel debuted as a motion picture, directed by Alfonso Cuarón.

Selected Reviews

Publishers Weekly: "Rowling proves that she has plenty of tricks left up her sleeve in this third Harry Potter adventure, set once again at the Hogwarts School of Witchcraft and Wizardry. Right before the start of term, a supremely dangerous criminal breaks out of a supposedly impregnable wizards' prison; it will come as no surprise to

British edition, adult's cover version (original)

Potter fans that the villain, a henchman of Harry's old enemy Lord Voldemort, appears to have targeted Harry. In many ways this installment seems to serve a transitional role in the seven-volume series: while many of the adventures are breathlessly relayed, they appear to be laying groundwork for even more exciting adventures to come.

"The beauty here lies in the genius of Rowling's plotting. Seemingly minor details established in books one and two unfold to take on unforeseen significance, and the finale, while not airtight in its internal logic, is utterly thrilling. Rowling's wit never flags, whether constructing the workings of the wizard world (just how would a magician be made to stay behind bars?) or tossing off quick jokes (a grandmother wears a hat decorated with a stuffed vulture; the divination classroom looks like a tawdry tea shop). The Potter spell is holding strong."

Booklist: "What results once again is a good story, well told, one that is not only a cut above most fantasies for the age group but is also attractive to readers from beyond both ends of the spectrum. . . . We wait impatiently for the next episode."

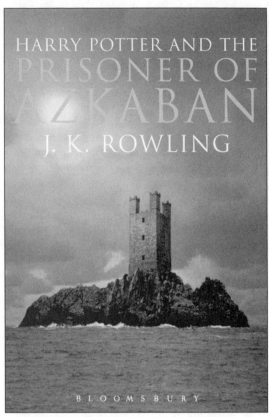

British edition, adult's cover version (for 2004)

New York Review of Books: "The Harry Potter stories belong to an ongoing tradition of Anglo-American fantasy that takes off from Tolkien and C. S. Lewis. . . . What sets Rowling's books apart from their predecessors is partly a lighthearted fertility of invention that recalls L. Frank Baum's Oz books. Even more important is the fact that hers is a fully imagined world, to which she has a deep, ongoing commitment."

School Library Journal: "Isn't it reassuring that some things just get better and better? Harry is back and in fine form in the third installment of his adventures at Hogwarts School of Witchcraft and Wizardry. . . . The pace is nonstop, with thrilling games of Quidditch, terrifying Omens of Death, some skillful time travel, and lots of slimy Slytherins sneaking about causing trouble. This is a fabulously entertaining read that will have Harry Potter fans cheering for more."

USA Today: "It's three for three for British author J. K. Rowling, who scores another home run with *Harry Potter and the Prisoner of Azkaban.*"

Awards (U.S. and U.K.)

American Library Association Notable Book
Booklist 1999 Editor's Choice
Booksellers Association/Bookseller Author of the Year
British Book Awards Author of the Year
FCBC Children's Book Award 1999/Longer Novel category
Gold Medal Smarties Prize (1999)
Los Angeles Times Best Book of 1999
New York Public Library Title for Reading and Sharing

Whitaker's Platinum Book
   Award (2001)
Whitbread Award for
   Children's Literature

U.S. edition

HARRY POTTER AND THE GOBLET OF FIRE

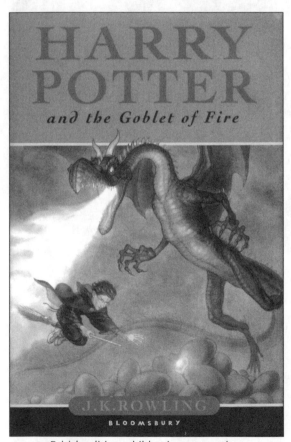

British edition, children's cover version

Dedication

"To Peter Rowling,/In Memory of Mr. Ridley/ And to Susan Sladden,/ Who Helped Harry Out of his Cupboard."

The dedication refers to her father, Peter Rowling; to Mr. Ronald Ridley, who was in part the fictional basis for the character of Ronald Weasley; and to Susan Sladden, whom I haven't been able to identify.

Background

Mindful of U.S. readers who wouldn't wait for the U.S. edition of the Harry Potter book to be published—preferring instead to order from

Amazon.com UK—Bloomsbury and Scholastic wisely decided to release book four simultaneously, thus ensuring that British book sales didn't undercut the U.S. book sales.

By now Rowling was a publishing phenomenon with books that sold in the millions of copies. Good for her publishers, but not necessarily good for the fans, since it meant large crowds turned up for her every public appearance, especially bookstores, at which the demand for signed copies far exceeded supply.

The long and short of it: The publicity tour for this book proved to Rowling and her publishers that such tours were no longer logistically possible in the U.K. or the U.S. At a widely publicized public appearance at King's Cross station, children crowded anxiously to get a glimpse of Rowling, but were disappointed when the press corps forced their way to the front lines, taking photos, and shouting for her. Elsewhere on the tour, in the U.S., a small bookstore was overwhelmed with capacity crowds, for which police were called in as frustrated parents nearly exchanged blows.

For Rowling, the book tour—backed by a multimillion dollar publicity and marketing campaign—made it abundantly clear that, rather than help sell books, her fame and popularity were actually hindrances. A literary superstar, she could not possibly satisfy even a fraction of the demand for her time from the media, from bookstores requesting personal appearances, and from other organizations asking for her presence at their events.

Clearly, decisions would have to be made regarding future promotions, since things—as this book tour amply proved—had gotten way out of hand.

About the Book

Harry Potter and the Goblet of Fire is the midbook in the series, with a count of 734 pages. In this book, Harry Potter grapples not only with the unexpected developments concerning Sirius Black from the previous book, but also with a new challenge. He is, inexplicably, a fourth contender for a Triwizard Tournament for which traditionally only three contenders are selected by the Goblet of Fire. But choose him it does, and so he competes against a fellow Hogwarts student and also top students from the two other wizarding schools in Europe, Durmstrang and Beauxbatons.

The novel opens with a hilarious entry by Arthur Weasley and his sons, Fred and George, who use Floo Powder to arrive at the Dursley residence to pick up Harry Potter, for whom they've bought a ticket to an international Quidditch tournament. What happens at that tournament, however, foreshadows what is to come. The Triwizard Tournament is more than simply a test of will and skill among four contestants; its true purpose is far more sinister.

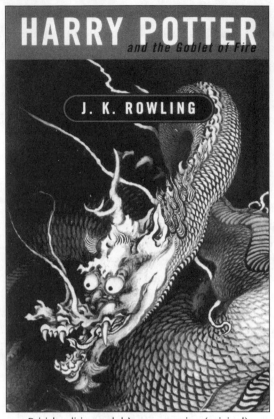

British edition, adult's cover version (original)

A deeper, richer novel than the three previously published novels, carefully textured and painted on a wide canvas, *Harry Potter and the Goblet of Fire* is the kind of book Potter fans willingly lose themselves in, as they explore heretofore unseen aspects of the magical world in which Harry Potter is, for obvious reasons, a focal point.

Rowling points out that far from being children's novels per se, the books will necessarily get more darker in tone and more horrific as the series progresses. Indeed, in this latest installment, a significant character dies. It will be, as Rowling has warned us in several interviews, one of many to come.

Far from being a children's fantasy in which everyone lives happily every after, the Potter novels are imbued with a naturalistic element that gives them a dark touch; a reminder to everyone, even Harry Potter, that we all have to grow up—a painful process in which hard choices must be made, choices that will shape our lives for the years to come.

Selected Reviews

Publishers Weekly: "Even without the unprecedented media attention and popularity her magical series has attracted, it would seem too much to hope that Rowling could sustain the brilliance and wit of her first three novels. Astonishingly, Rowling seems to have the spell-casting powers she assigns her characters: this fourth volume might be her most thrilling yet. The novel opens as a confused Muggle overhears Lord Voldemort and his henchman, Wormtail (the escapee from book three, *Azkaban*) discussing a murder and plotting more deaths (and invoking Harry Potter's name); clues suggest that Voldemort and Wormtail's location will prove highly significant. From here it takes a while (perhaps slightly too long a while) for Harry and his friends to get back to the Hogwarts school, where Rowling is on surest footing. Headmaster Dumbledore appalls everyone by declaring that Quidditch competition has been canceled for the year, then he makes the exciting announcement that the Triwizard Tournament is to be held after a cessation of many hundreds of years (it was discontinued, he explains, because the death toll mounted so high). One representative from each of the three largest wizardry schools of Europe (sinister Durmstrang, luxurious Beauxbatons, and Hogwarts) is to be chosen by the Goblet of Fire; because of the mortal dangers, Dumble-

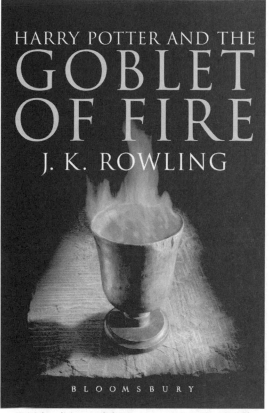

British edition, adult's cover version (for 2004)

dore casts a spell that allows only students who are at least 17 to drop their names into the Goblet. Thus no one foresees that the Goblet will announce a fourth candidate: Harry. Who has put his name into the Goblet, and how is his participation in the tournament linked, as it surely must be, to Voldemort's newest plot? The details are as ingenious and original as ever, and somehow (for catching readers off-guard must certainly get more difficult with each successive volume) Rowling plants the red herrings, the artful clues, and tricky surprises that disarm the most attentive audience. A climax even more spectacular than that of *Azkaban* will leave readers breathless; the muscle-building heft of this volume notwithstanding, the clamor for book five will begin as soon as readers finish installment four."

Booklist: "Harry's fourth challenging experience will more than live up to his myriad fans' expectations. . . . The carefully created world of magic becomes more embellished and layered, while the amazing plotting ties up loose ends, even as it sets in motion more entanglements."

Kirkus Reviews: "Another grand tale of magic and mystery, of wheels within wheels oiled in equal measure by terror and comedy, featuring an

U.S. edition

engaging young hero-in-training who's not above the occasional snit, and clicking along so smoothly that it seems shorter than it is."

Stephen King in the *New York Times Book Review:* "I'm relieved to report that Potter four is every bit as good as Potters one through three. . . . The fantasy writer's job is to conduct the willing reading from mundanity to magic. This is a feat of which only a superior imagination is capable, and Rowling possesses such equipment."

Janet Maslin in the *New York Times:* "As the midpoint in a projected seven-book series, *Goblet of Fire* is exactly the big, clever, vibrant, tremendously assured installment that gives shape and direction to the whole undertaking and still somehow preserves the material's enchanting innocence. . . . This time Rowling offers her clearest proof yet of what should have been wonderfully obvious: What makes the Potter books so popular is the radically simple fact that they're so good."

Awards (U.S. and U.K.)

American Library Association Notable Book
Booklist Editors' Choice (2000)
Children's Book Award in 9–11 category (2001)
New York Public Library Book for the Teen Age
Publishers Weekly Best Children's Book (2000)
Scottish Arts Council Book Award (2001)
Whitaker's Platinum Book Award (2001)
Winner of the Hugo Award, Best Novel category (World Science Fiction
  Convention)

HARRY POTTER AND THE
ORDER OF THE PHOENIX

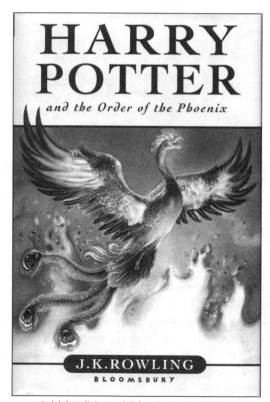

British edition, children's cover version

Dedication

"To Neil, Jessica, and David, who make my world magical."

The dedication refers to her second husband, Neil Murray, her daughter from her first marriage, and her son from her second marriage.

Background

The book industry has a tried-and-true game plan to guarantee as many copies of a book as possible will be sold by its publication date. The plan involves sending out hundreds of galleys well before the book's publication to guarantee early reviews, sending out hundreds of review copies to

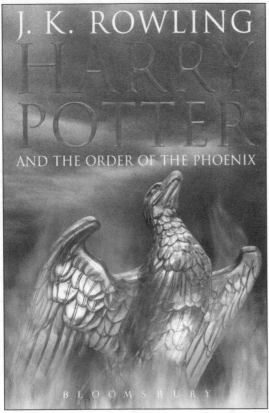

J. K. ROWLING
HARRY POTTER
AND THE ORDER OF THE PHOENIX

BLOOMSBURY

British edition, adult's cover version

newspapers and magazines, and most importantly, scheduling media appearances on television—all designed to snare the attention of a jaded public and get them to buy books.

All of this is predicated, of course, on the completion of the book itself, which in this case became a matter of growing concern to all. The book industry wanted Rowling's latest to help draw attention to books as bestsellers; booksellers wanted it to help their bottom line; and most of all, readers clamored for it because they simply wanted to read it.

This fifth book, however, was plagued with unanticipated delays that dogged it, postponing publication time and again. As a result, the media started running stories about Rowling's presumed writing block. In the absence of truth, speculation ran rampant, but the simple truth was that a confluence of several events delayed the book: She needed to get off the restrictive publishing treadmill that demanded books on demand to suit the publisher's schedule; she wanted to write two short books for Comic Relief, a charity; she was distracted by a meritless lawsuit in which she was later vindicated; but most of all, she needed relief from the overwhelming presence of the media, with reporters showing up at her home in Edinburgh, banging on her door, and demanding interviews.

The biggest problem was the deadline, so Rowling wrote to her publisher and offered to pay back the advance, since she no longer wanted the burden of having to produce on demand. Understandably, Rowling's publisher declined her offer and told her to keep the advance. Write the book on your own schedule, they told her, and when it's done, we'll be happy to publish it. Everyone—the publisher, the booksellers, the media, and the fans—would just have to wait.

As it turned out, the wait would be three years, during which the publisher did not stand idle. Pumping $4 million into promoting the book it

U.S. trade edition

didn't even have on hand, Scholastic embarked on a "stealth" book campaign:

1. No early review copies.

2. No book signings.

3. No media coverage except a BBC interview (in the U.K.) and a profile with Katie Couric (from NBC-TV).

4. A countdown clock on her U.K. publisher's website—a device quickly adopted worldwide by Potter fan websites.

5. Midnight parties scheduled worldwide. Books would go on sale on June 21, 2003, only one minute into the new day.

All, it seemed, was going according to plan, but as poet Robert Burns reminds us, in the affairs of mice and men, things can often go awry. In Rowling's case, an unscrupulous employee smuggled unbound copies out of the printing plant, with the hope of selling chapters to a local newspaper. (His plan failed. The paper cooperated with the police and set up a sting operation.)

On a more serious note, an entire truckload of copies in England was stolen weeks before publication date, which understandably caused grave concern at

U.S. limited collector's edition

Bloomsbury. Where would these copies show up? Would they be sold on the black market as under-the-counter sales? Would copies be shipped immediately to the Pacific Rim, where printing pirates would be quick to manufacture facsimile editions for sale? Would copies show up for sale on the Internet? Nobody knew, but everyone feared the worst.

In the end, the worst that happened was that, in the U.S., a handful of stores mistakenly put copies out a few days early, but when Rowling's publisher explained that if they couldn't observe the embargo this time around, they might not get *any* books the next time around, merchants everywhere got the message: It's one thing to get a Howler, but quite another to be sent to Azkaban. For merchants, not getting books six or seven would be the equivalent of a prison sentence—a form of economic death.

Things settled down as the witching hour approached, when booksellers quietly began opening up specially marked boxes overprinted with text ("Harry Potter and the Order of the Phoenix/J. K. Rowling/DO NOT OPEN BEFORE JUNE 21, 2003"). Meanwhile, the master countdown clock on the website of Bloomsbury Publishing ticked down to its final seconds until its message changed to the declaration everyone had been waiting for: IT'S HERE!

Finally, *Harry Potter and the Order of the Phoenix* saw light—moonlight, as it turned out. At an hour when most families were fast asleep, scores of parents with sleepy-headed kids were at bookstores nationwide, picking up their reserved copies of the biggest Potter novel to date—870 pages.

In my small corner of the world, southeast coastal Virginia, local bookstores stocked up on copies and held midnight parties. The local chain stores, with heavy discounting, got the bulk of the customers. At a Barnes & Noble superstore in nearby Virginia Beach, over a thousand Potter fans (many of them children, and in costume) showed up, as store staffers handed out plastic round-framed eyeglasses, which were eagerly snapped up and donned. It was a curious sight: nearly a thousand children all wearing thick plastic glasses with round frames.

For those who waited until the next day, virtually no copies of the novel were to be had. I checked out two stores and found them sold out. At a local Books-a-Million in Williamsburg, Virginia, I saw dozens of customers, with kids in tow, leaving the store empty-handed; the college bookstore at William and Mary, run by Barnes & Noble, had also sold out but promised copies as soon as possible; and a Barnes & Noble superstore in Newport News, Virginia, which had sold out its allotment, set up a special table near the entrance as staffers queried customers coming in, "Are you here to pick up your reserved copy of *Harry Potter*?"

For those who hadn't reserved copies at local stores or hadn't ordered through Amazon.com, the *only* hope locally was Costco, a warehouse chain with two pallets of books on hand, which is where I bought my own copy.

By the time night fell on publication day, two things were clear: Nobody predicted that the demand for first-day copies would exceed supply, nor did anyone predict that on top of a 6.8 million first printing, a Hagrid-sized second printing of 1.7 million copies would be needed to fill the immediate demand.

The quarter million words that comprised book five proved to be no obstacle for Potter fans who, like Tolkien fans, hungered for more.

As for Rowling, the presumption was that she'd either be far away from Edinburgh, which was the focus of international attention on publication day, or she'd be holed up and inaccessible to all. The least likely scenario—a local appearance—turned out to be Rowling's game plan.

Expecting store clerks to hand out copies of Rowling's latest, customers were astonished when Rowling herself appeared at a Waterstone's to hand them out. One of the customers, an awestruck young girl who excitedly shook Rowling's hand, told a BBC reporter that she'd never wash that hand again.

In short order, millions of Potter fans cracked open their copies to immerse themselves once again in his imaginative universe. The first page began, "The hottest day of the summer so far was drawing to a close and a drowsy silence lay over the large, square houses of Privet Drive." There would be, happily, 869 more pages to go.

The end result, all agreed, was a satisfying novel that delivered on the promise Rowling made to her readers with her first Potter novel: Harry Potter would grow and change with each passing book, and his life experiences would prepare him for the inevitable—a final showdown with the "Lord Voldy-thing," as Vernon Dudley called him.

Scores of reviews began appearing in newspapers, in magazines, and on websites worldwide, but I think Stephen King, writing in *Entertainment Weekly,* said it best: "I think Harry will take his place with Alice, Huck, Frodo, and Dorothy, and this is one series not just for the decade, but for the ages."

When all was said and done, the fifth Harry Potter novel had sold an astonishing 12 million copies worldwide, which will not be eclipsed by any book—until the next Potter novel is published.

The old one-two punch of a best-selling novel, fueled by successful film adaptations, catapulted the camera-shy (read: glum-looking) writer into the limelight. In fact, in an annual assessment of entertainers with clout, Rowling ranks fifth in a list of the top 101 entertainers.

To give you a sense of where she fits on the 2003 year's list, compiled by *Entertainment Weekly,* look at the high-powered names of some of those who preceded her (Steven Spielberg and Tom Hanks) and those who followed her (Oprah Winfrey, Tom Cruise, and Peter Jackson).

As anyone with any experience in Hollywood will tell you, it's a telling ranking. Writers are traditionally considered bottom-feeders in the food chain in that industry. That Rowling would not only make the list but be in the top ten attests to her power position. Rowling—make no mistake—has clout.

About the Book

If Potter fans thought *Harry Potter and the Goblet of Fire,* at 734 pages, was a long read, what would they make of the fifth book in the series? At 870 pages, *Harry Potter and the Order of Phoenix* is the longest Potter novel to date.

As promised by Rowling, Harry Potter is growing up; in fact, his growing pains, as he wrestles with the demons of adolescence, might be off-putting to younger readers, but anyone who is currently going through the pain of adolescence or remembers having gone through it will recognize themselves in Harry Potter.

An admittedly darker novel than its predecessors, it begins with the traditional framing device. We see Harry at the Dursley residence before he leaves for Hogwarts; but unlike the previous books, elements of the magical world come to haunt the Muggles world, and it's up to Harry to defend not only himself but Dudley Dursley, who, like Harry, is no longer a child. Dudley, in fact, has a natural talent for boxing—honed, no doubt, by years of bullying others—but shows his true colors when he's confronted by the unprecedented arrival of the Dementors.

Soon thereafter, events move into high gear as Harry is met by an

Advance Guard that come to the Dursley home to escort him to the head-quarters of the Order of the Phoenix.

The magical world is divided on whether or not Lord Voldemort has in fact returned. The Ministry of Magic's Cornelius Fudge toes the party line and seeks to placate the wizarding community by reassuring them that You-Know-Who has certainly *not* returned, but Albus Dumbledore, Harry Potter, and others know better. They know the truth, that Lord Voldemort *has* returned, which divides the community into those who believe and those who don't.

Cornelius Fudge clamps down on Hogwarts by installing one of his lieu-tenants, a froglike-looking woman named Dolores Jane Umbridge, whose sickly sweet demeanor belies her true nature—she's not honey but, in fact, poison. Umbridge, who joins the faculty as the newest Defense Against the Dark Arts teacher (one new one per school year, thus far), soon becomes the instrument of draconian enforcement by the Ministry of Magic—a High Inquisitor. The position gives her enormous power over the faculty and student body, as well. That power becomes absolute when she is appointed the Headmaster of Hogwarts, replacing Albus Dumbledore. Morale at Hogwarts reaches a new low, but uneasy is the head that wears the crown, so to speak. As a major battle shapes up those at Hogwarts must choose; so, too, must choices be made in the wizarding community when the believers and the nonbelievers must put aside their differences and hang together—or hang separately.

The Order of the Phoenix, the members of which are devoted to Albus Dumbledore, bookends the novel. The Order is prominently featured in the beginning and at the end of the book, though I would have liked to read more about its history and about the members' important role in the battle against Lord Voldemort's followers, the Death Eaters, and Voldemort himself.

By the end of the novel, an endlessly patient and imperturbable Albus Dumbledore explains to an enraged Harry Potter that it's time for frankness. His destiny, Dumbledore tells him, is inextricably linked to Lord Voldemort in ways that cannot be ignored.

It's important for Harry to know because he is destined to meet Lord Voldemort for what will undoubtedly be the battle of his life—a one-on-one fight to the death with Lord Voldemort.

Most frightening of all: Rowling doesn't guarantee that Harry Potter will survive the encounter. She is asked that, of course, by readers and the media at virtually every opportunity, but mum's the word. Don't expect the lock-lipped author to divulge the details because she won't, unless you have some Veritaserum handy—the truth serum that forces someone to talk.

For parents who are concerned about the darkness of this novel, be forewarned. Rowling has made it abundantly clear that the last two novels will be even darker. There will be more preordained deaths because the logic of the story, worked out years ago, requires them. Clearly, books six and seven are not likely to be appropriate reading material for young children. But older teens and adults are likely to find them to be irresistible reads.

Selected Reviews

Publishers Weekly: "Year five at Hogwarts is no fun for Harry. Rowling may be relying upon readers to have solidified their liking for her hero in the first four books, because the 15-year-old Harry Potter they meet here is quite dour after a summer at the Dursleys' house on Privet Drive, with no word from his pals Hermione or Ron. When he reunites with them at last, he learns that the *Daily Prophet* has launched a smear campaign to discredit Harry's and Dumbledore's report of Voldemort's reappearance at the end of book four, *Harry Potter and the Goblet of Fire.*

"Aside from an early skirmish with a pair of dementors, in which Harry finds himself in the position of defending not only himself but his dreaded cousin, Dudley, there is little action until the end of these nearly 900 pages. A hateful woman from the Ministry of Magic, Dolores Umbridge (who, along with minister Cornelius Fudge, nearly succeeds in expelling Harry from Hogwarts before the start of the school year) overtakes Hogwarts—GrandPré's toadlike portrait of her is priceless—and makes life even more miserable for him. She bans him from the Quidditch team (resulting in minimal action on the pitch) and keeps a tight watch on him. And Harry's romance when his crush from the last book, Cho Chang, turns out to be a major waterworks (she cries when she's happy, she cries when she's sad). Readers get to discover the purpose behind the Order of the Phoenix and more is revealed of the connection between Harry and You-Know-Who. But the showdown between Harry and Voldemort feels curiously anticlimactic after the stunning clash at the close of book four.

"Rowling favors psychological development over plot development here, skillfully exploring the effects of Harry's fall from popularity and the often isolating feelings of adolescence. Harry suffers a loss and learns some unpleasant truths about his father, which result in his compassion for some unlikely characters. (The author also draws some insightful parallels between the Ministry's exercise of power and the current political climate.) As hope blooms at story's end, those who have followed Harry thus far will be every bit as eager to discover what happens to him in his sixth and seventh years."

Leslie Rounds for *Children's Literature:* "This is a thrilling read. Those who enjoyed the previous books are not likely to be disappointed, and

Rowling will probably add even more Potter fans with the publication of this volume."

Laura (from Shepshed, Leiceistershire, England), aged 14, who speed-read the book in two hours and 19 minutes after it was officially published: "I'd give it nine out of ten. It was really good. Now I'm going home and read it slowly."

Michael Cart for the *Los Angeles Times*: "In fleshing out her plot, Rowling devotes considerable attention to . . . coming-of-age aspects of Harry's personality, making him a richer and more psychologically complex character than ever before. There's no doubt that Harry is growing up, and the process isn't always pretty, although he remains wonderfully appealing and, when necessary, heroic."

Bethany Schneider, who attended a midnight book release party at her local bookstore, for Newsday.com:

> ### Fan Travels Halfway Around the World for PHOENIX
>
> The *Scotsman* reported that Akira Sadakato, a college student, flew from Japan to Edinburgh, Scotland, to buy a copy of the fifth Potter novel. The paper reported that the young man walked into an Internet café in town and, according to owner Richard Hind, "said it was his dream to meet J. K. Rowling and get his books, which he had in his rucksack, signed. . . . He came in on Thursday and said he was going back to stay in Edinburgh to buy the book when it came out at midnight on Friday."

"What I participated in very early Saturday morning was an international phenomenon, complete with adults in capes and children with scars scrawled across their foreheads. But Rowling is not surfing on her success, nor is she sliding on the childish charm of her characters. She is hauling them and herself forward through troubled and changing waters."

Eva Mitnick, Los Angeles Public Library, for *School Library Journal*: "Children will enjoy the magic and the Hogwarts mystique, and young adult readers will find a rich and compelling coming-of-age story as well."

Lev Grossman for *Time* magazine: "Just when we might have expected author J. K. Rowling's considerable imagination to flag . . . she has hit peak form and is gaining speed."

Deirdre Donahue for *USA Today*: "The book richly deserves the hype. All the qualities that marred the fourth book . . . have evaporated. Indeed, the faux gothic horror of the fourth has been replaced by a return to the wonderful, textured writing of the three earlier novels. . . . *Order of the Phoenix* allows the reader to savor Rowling's remarkably fertile imagination."

Robin Videmos for the *Denver Post*: "The [Potter] legend has grown with each succeeding volume, not because she's written to a formula but because she continues to deliver the same combination of enticing elements without allowing them to become predictable."

Emma Pollack-Pelzner for the *Yale Review of Books:* "Although the *Harry Potter* series' intricately worked-out moral content, fun character relationships, and vividly imagined world make them rewarding reading for anyone, don't let these books elbow aside ones that you loved as a child; just add them to your list."

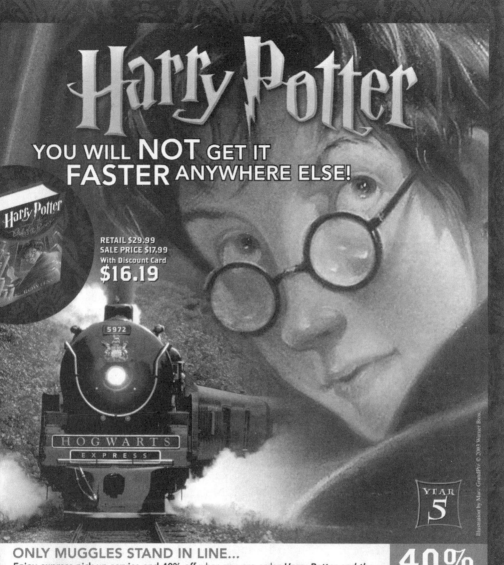

Books-A-Million promotion on Harry Potter

HARRY POTTER AND THE
ORDER OF THE PHOENIX:
A Brit's View of Its Book Publication

by Allan Harvey

Screenshot of the Ford Anglia from the official Harry Potter website

June 20, 2003, turned out to be bright and sunny, the perfect kind of day for a trip around London's West End on the eve of the launch of the fifth Harry Potter novel, *Harry Potter and the Order of the Phoenix*.

I caught the tube into London and alighted at Oxford Circus—right at the heart of the West End—on the corner of Oxford Street and Regent Street. I took the opportunity to wander along Regent Street passing the large toy store Hamleys. A poster in the window enticed shoppers to come in and view the large display of Harry Potter toys they had on sale, and they appeared to be doing brisk business. As I continued my journey a familiar red double-decker bus glided past, but this one was a little different: the whole side of the bus was a colourful advertisement announcing the coming publication of *The Order of the Phoenix*.

HARRY POTTER
BOOKS FROM BLOOMSBURY

BUY THE BOOKS

ROYAL ALBERT HALL EVENT

WITCHES & WIZARDS

0 hours, 0 mins, 56 secs to go...

MUGGLES

HOWLERS AND OWLERS • ENQUIRIES • BLOOMSBURY

Screenshot of Bloomsbury Publishing's website, showing
the countdown to the publication of the fifth Harry Potter novel

Arriving at Piccadilly Circus, I turned right into Piccadilly itself and made my way to Hachards, which—as its sign informs the shopper—has been a bookseller since 1797. A poster in the window revealed that the shop would be opening early the following morning to sell the new Potter volume. Inside, directly facing the main door, shelf space lay empty awaiting the time it would be filled with copies of the book. Upstairs, in the children's department, a vivid display of the previous four Potter novels greeted me and, again, space had been set aside for *The Order of the Phoenix.*

An assistant explained that staff had spent much of the previous few days unpacking the books in advance of the launch date. The unmarked boxes had contained both the regular cover and the alternate "adult" cover versions, and these had taken a long time to sort out. The shop has five

Almost £308 a Word: Rowling's Outline for Book Five

Raising money for charity, Sotheby's generated £28,260 with the sale of a brief outline Rowling wrote that detailed book five. Reportedly purchased by an American who wanted to have a unique gift for his children who love Harry Potter . . . the details of the outline were not revealed by the buyer . . . though a few words were made public, whetting fans' appetites: "Thirty-eight chapters . . . might change . . . longest volume . . . Ron . . . broom . . . sacked . . . house-elf . . . new teacher . . . dies . . . sorry."

floors, so moving everything into place was a major task and it was clear a lot of preparation had gone into getting everything ready.

Just a few yards away from Hachards is the Piccadilly branch of the Waterstones chain. This bookstore was to be the setting for the major press launch for *The Order of the Phoenix* at two minutes past midnight the following morning and preparations were in full swing when I arrived. The windows were decked out with Harry Potter art, posters, and props, while a suit of armour quietly stood guard.

The floor, which normally houses the children's book department, was all but closed as it was being expensively redecorated in a celebration of all things Harry Potter. Part of the floor was to be given over to a recreation of Platform Nine and Three-Quarters, while themed alcoves welcomed the shoppers. Various props adorned the walls and floors.

The midnight opening promised to be a major event involving actors dressed as Potter characters; a countdown to the book's launch for the children; a champagne reception for the grownups; and a signing by Rowling herself. As I was there the press were being briefed on the evening's schedule, and being given a guided tour of the as yet unfinished scenery. Everything was a rush, and there was a real buzz of excitement and anticipation in the air. I asked the person serving at one of the checkouts whether they were really expecting so many people to attend the launch, which was, after all, at midnight, an hour when most people are happily tucked up in bed. "Ooh, just one or two . . ." he replied with a wry smile.

Most of the larger bookshops in the West End were due to open at midnight to make the new book available to fans as soon as possible. This was repeated on a more local level as well, with many provincial stores around the country making the effort to open so as not to keep Potter's young fans waiting.

From Waterstones I crossed over Piccadilly Circus. It was very busy in town by now and moving about was difficult. As I moved through the crowds in Leicester Square, my ears were assaulted at every turn by the sound of the Harry Potter movie theme being piped out of various shops and establishments along the way. It seemed as though the whole of London was just waiting for midnight!

Charing Cross Road is *the* place in London to get books, as much of its length is dominated by specialist bookshops of all varieties. I visited the branch of Borders; their window was dominated by posters announcing the imminent arrival of the new Potter book. As an added incentive to the casual shopper, the store was offering a 20 percent discount off any other book purchased along with *Harry Potter and the Order of the Phoenix* as well as offering a chance to enter a prize draw for a signed copy of the new book. As I entered, a friendly voice filled the air, counting down the time in exact hours and minutes until the midnight launch!

Again there were empty shelves in preparation and the children's department downstairs was in a bit of a disarray as shelves were being rearranged. The assistant was busy but seemed in good spirits about the forthcoming events; in fact she was expecting something of a shopping frenzy come midnight. "There's so much interest; it's an amazing phenomenon," she said, an opinion with which I agreed. I added that I thought it a very good thing that children—and indeed adults—were being brought back into bookshops by the strength of Rowling's creation. The assistant generally agreed, but opined that she felt sorry that earlier authors such as Tolkien had struggled in relative obscurity.

Not all shop assistants were as excited, however. In the final shop I visited on my tour, the staff were involved in some rather heavy discussions about the Potter phenomenon and were less than enthusiastic, branding the books "derivative" and "boring." They also seemed to be attempting to start a conspiracy theory by claiming that publisher Bloomsbury was "too scared" of Rowling to edit her, and that, anyway, the publisher didn't mind as the larger books generated more revenue! I quietly left them to it and headed for home.

The next day the book launched and proved wildly successful for all concerned. Most stores offering the book were selling it with a range of discounts, which varied from shop to shop—some were selling it for as much as 50 percent off the cover price! Even some shops which didn't normally sell books were getting involved, offering attractive Potter displays to entice the casual shopper. Surely no one in London could have failed to know what day it was. Indeed, as I came home from picking up my morning newspaper I almost bumped into a young Potter fan coming in the opposite direction, oblivious to the world, her nose buried in her new purchase: *Harry Potter and the Order of the Phoenix.*

She seemed very happy indeed.

Londoner Allan Harvey is a lifelong fantasy fan and an aspiring artist.

QUIDDITCH THROUGH THE AGES, FANTASTIC BEASTS AND WHERE TO FIND THEM, and CONVERSATIONS WITH J. K. ROWLING

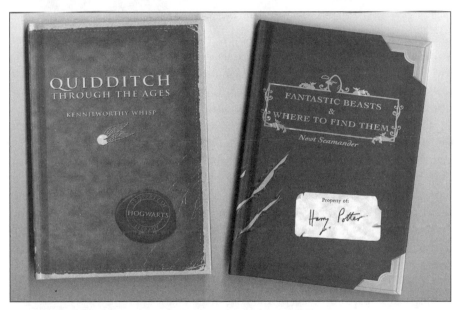

Quidditch Through the Ages, by Kennilworthy Whisp. Whizz Hard Books, 56 pages (September 2001).

Fantastic Beasts and Where to Find Them, by Newt Scamander. Obscurus Books, 42 pages (September 2001).

During the prolonged—and for some, unendurable—wait for *Harry Potter and the Order of the Phoenix,* Rowling published two books under two different pen names: Kennilworthy Whisp and Newt Scamander. Though fans preferred the feast of words promised in the eagerly anticipated *Order of the Phoenix,* these two literary appetizers more than fit the bill.

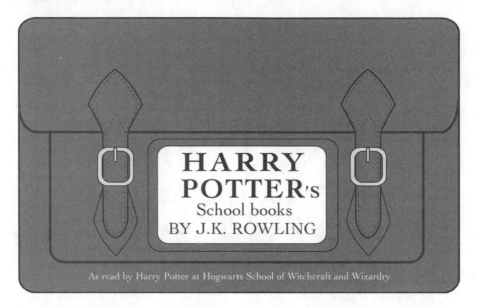

HARRY
POTTER's
School books
BY J.K. ROWLING

As read by Harry Potter at Hogwarts School of Witchcraft and Wizardry

Sold as a boxed set for $12.95, these two books belong on the shelf of any Harry Potter fan. Written as fundraisers for Comic Relief, a charity based in England, these books provide information on two topics of great interest to Potter fans: the sport that all wizards love (Quidditch), and the beasts that populate Rowling's imaginative fictional universe.

Quidditch Through the Ages is packaged as a book from the Hogwarts library. On the first page, a dire warning from Hogwarts librarian Irma Pince virtually guarantees that borrowers will return the book in good condition. Albus Dumbledore, in his introduction to the book, knows all too well the hidden hazards thereof. Even after removing the protective spells on the book, he cautions readers that Madam Pince is known to add jinxes to them as well, as the Professor found out when he "doodled absentmindedly" in a library book and, to his surprise, found himself under attack. The book, he said, beat him "fiercely about the head."

Not surprisingly, *Quidditch Through the Ages* is free of the usual doodlings, markings, and defacements that often mark student texts.

As for the text itself, its "reviews," printed in the front of the book, run from the straightforward ("The definitive work on the origins and history of Quidditch," says Brutus Scrimgeour, author of *The Beaters' Bible*) to the whimsical ("I've read worse," from reporter Rita Skeeter in the *Daily Prophet*). We also find out that the book's author, Kennilworthy Whisp, has penned other books, including (as you'd expect) more books on Quidditch.

In ten short but informative chapters, Quidditch is thoroughly covered, with art illuminating the text. Required reading for all Hogwarts students, magically minded Muggles everywhere will find much of interest in Whisp's

Comic Relief

Poverty, as Rowling found out, is no laughing matter. Unfortunately, far too many people around the world find themselves in dire circumstances and must rely on the charity of strangers to survive.

To support Comic Relief, Rowling wrote two books, both published under pen names, that were published in the U.K., the U.S., Canada, Australia, New Zealand, and Germany. These books (*Quidditch Through the Ages* and *Fantastic Beasts and Where to Find Them*) have raised £15.7 million, with money going all over the world.

In her native England, the money raised by Comic Relief goes to help a broad spectrum of people—disabled people, young people living in the streets, troubled teens, older people, people living in deprived communities, and immigrants experiencing discrimination.

Regarding Comic Relief, Rowling points out in an interview published online at the scholastic.com website that all those involved in printing, selling, and distributing her two charity books have donated their time and services, just as she has. The result is that the lion's share of the cover price (80 percent) goes to the charity, and not for overhead. In other words, at this charity, your money will go further than with some others, and both Comic Relief and Rowling are grateful for all the support.

Harry Potter fans have shown, time and again, that when it's time to give back to the community, they do so without hesitation. Why not, then, extend the effort internationally and reach beyond your backyard?

"There is something wonderful about the idea that laughter should be used to combat real tragedy and poverty and suffering and it is just the most wonderful thing," Rowling observed in the online interview published on the Scholastic website, which promotes the two charity books.

"You will be doing real magic by buying these books," she told a young boy who interviewed her for Scholastic, and she's right: Buy the books and know that the money is going to a great cause. Like Hedwig, give a hoot! Go to www.comicrelief.com and make a donation online today. As Rowling has said, every dollar (or pound) will help.

explication of the wizarding sport that Rowling says most closely resembles basketball in our world.

Fantastic Beasts and Where to Find Them, unlike *Quidditch Through the Ages,* is a student text, and so is defaced, torn, illustrated, and annotated by Harry Potter, Ron Weasley, and Hermione Granger. In fact, this facsimile is Potter's own copy, as evidenced by the sticker on the front cover.

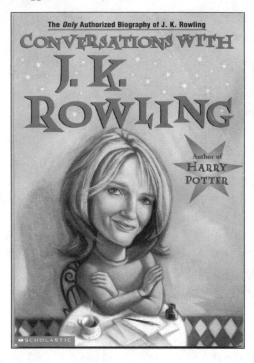

The *Only* Authorized Biography of J. K. Rowling

CONVERSATIONS WITH

J. K. ROWLING

Author of
HARRY
POTTER

SCHOLASTIC

As with *Quidditch Through the Ages,* Professor Albus Dumbledore contributes an introduction, in which he writes: "Newt's masterpiece has been an approved textbook at Hogwarts School of Witchcraft and Wizardry ever since its publication and must take a substantial amount of credit for our students' consistently high results in Care of Magical Creatures examinations— yet it is not a book to be confined to the classroom."

Found in every magical household, *Fantastic Beasts* is a delightful text, filled with fabulous beasts of all kinds; the first entry tells the specifics about the dreaded Acromantula, which earns the highest Ministry of Magic classification of five Xs, to which Potter (or Weasley) has added nine more Xs, for good reason. The book, arranged from A to Z, ends with Y for "Yeti" (also known as Bigfoot, the Abominable Snowman).

The two books are conveniently packaged in a sturdy slipcase bearing the legend, "J. K. Rowling: Classic Books from the Library of Hogwarts School of Witchcraft and Wizardry."

Conversations with J. K. Rowling, by Lindsay Fraser. Trade paperback, 96 pages, $4.99, Scholastic, October 2001. Cover art by Mary GrandPré.

This is billed on the cover as "The *Only* Authorized Biography of J. K. Rowling," but the billing is somewhat misleading. It's not a biography. It is more accurate to say this is a short interview supplemented by an overview of Rowling's books, a distinction made clear when it was originally published in England by Mammoth, an imprint of Egmont Children's Books, as *Telling Tales: An Interview with J. K. Rowling.*

The book is set in large type with wide margins. The first half is an interview with Rowling, a traditional one-on-one sit-down chat; the second half is comprised of an overview of the books, supplemented with previously published interview material from *Entertainment Weekly, O, The Oprah Magazine, Larry King Live,* and *Newsweek.*

The cover art by Mary GrandPré, who is the artist (cover and interior) for the U.S. editions of the Potter novels, is a portrait of Rowling.

Bottom line: Recommended, with reservations—this short interview of 46 pages is padded with filler material to bulk out the book to its 96 pages.

Readers wanting a full-fledged biography are better served by Sean Smith's book, *J. K. Rowling: A Biography.* Albeit unauthorized, it does cover her life more thoroughly than any other biography currently on the market.

Harry Potter and the SparkNotes

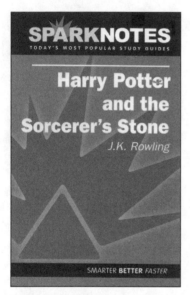

What does Rowling have in common with Shakespeare, Dante, and other literary greats?

Her novels about Harry Potter are explicated in SparkNotes' study guides, online and in book form, for students wanting to write papers for school. (SparkNotes publishes more than a thousand study guides, not only on literature but on other disciplines as well.)

The bane of teachers everywhere, study guides have become literary substitutes. Rather than read an assigned book, students can turn to its study guide for a plot summary, analysis, key facts about the work, analyses of major characters, an explication of themes, motifs, and symbols, and an historical context for the author. For students, it's an easy and painless way to "know" the book without reading it—enough, they hope, to bluff the teacher into thinking they *have* read it.

SparkNotes is hardly the groundbreaker: Cliff Hillegass published 16 study guides, which he called CliffsNotes, in August 1958, after a conversation with a Canadian bookseller, Jack Cole, whose own chain (Cole's, The Book People) published a line of study guides called Cole's Notes.

It's hard for me to imagine why anyone would prefer the slim SparkNotes (or their equivalent) to an actual reading, but for those who want a shortcut, SparkNotes (a Barnes & Noble publication) provides the first four Potter novels online, with Web-based discussions; the first Potter novel is available in book form, as well.

For more information, go to: www.sparknotes.com.

Harry Potter Parodied: The Barry Trotter Novels by Michael Gerber

A lready overrun by brawling, fetid fans of the best-selling Barry Trotter books, Hogwash is certain to be pulled down brick by brick after Barry's new big-budget biopic debuts. So Barry Trotter, Ermine Cringer, and Lon Measly are hauled out of retirement to face their toughest challenge yet. Not only do the 22-year-olds have to elude packs of rabid fans, outwit Barry's sponging godfather Serious, and vanquish their old foe Lord Valumart, they have to face the most powerful enemy of all: Hollywood!

> *—back cover plot summary of* Barry Trotter and the Unauthorized Parody *from the publisher, Simon and Schuster*

Barry Trotter and the Unauthorized Parody, by Michael Gerber, illustrated by Rodger Roundy. Trade paperback, 176 pages, $11, Simon and Schuster/Fireside. (Also available as an unabridged audiocassette, read by Christopher Cazenove; New Millennium Audio, $25.)

The only non-parodistic text to be found on this book is on its back cover, where it states: "Note: This book has not been authorized by J. K. Rowling or the publishers of the Harry Potter books. 'Harry Potter' is a registered trademark of Warner Bros."

Any other text on or in this book cannot and should not be taken seriously, because it's a parody, a send-up of the Harry Potter novels.

The cover itself should be enough of a clue: A demonic-looking Harry Potter look-alike bears a scar on his forehead—a question mark and an exclamation mark that, on first glance, might be misconstrued as a dollar sign; over his right shoulder, a clownish, drooling red-haired boy wearing a belled clown cap; over his left shoulder, a demonic-looking blonde girl, eyes wide open, tongue out. Above the demented-looking trio is a white owl smoking a cigar and, seen framed in the open window, the demonic figure that suggests Lord Voldemort.

Make no mistake, author Michael Gerber intends to have a lot of fun lampooning Harry Potter.

For those who want a sample of what is in store, the chapter headings are suggestive: "The Right Snuff," "A Breaking Windfall," and in a nod to Disneyland's ride inspired by Toad (from *The Wind in the Willows*), "Mr. Barry's Wild Ride."

Just so there's no misunderstanding, on the copyright page, the publisher makes no bones about the reason this book saw print: "This book exists solely to make a quick buck."

The book begins with a chapter titled "The Trouble with Muddles":

> The Hogwash School for Wizards was the most famous school in the wizarding world, and Barry Trotter was its most famous student. His mere presence made sure that each year, 20 candidates applied for every open spot, no matter how rapacious Hogwash's tuition became.

Like *Bored of the Rings* (a send-up of J. R. R. Tolkien's great fantasy novel *The Lord of the Rings*), this book will likely not appeal to purists who take Rowling and Harry Potter seriously—too seriously, it seems, at times, since Potter fans are defensive to a fault. (When Nancy Stouffer sued Rowling for copyright infringement, loyal Potter fans bombarded her with hate mail.) But if you don't mind having a good laugh at Rowling's expense—a parody is protected by copyright—then buy this book and help Gerber make a few quick bucks.

Barry Trotter and the Unnecessary Sequel. Trade hardback, 288 pages, $9.95, Gollancz.

Just when you thought it was safe to go back into the bookstore, Michael Gerber has penned another Potter parody—not surprising, since his first one sold 100,000 copies.

Obviously, Gerber's books will mean nothing to you unless you've read the Harry Potter novels. You won't get the jokes. But if you have, and you do, then here's all you need to know about its plot, provided by a staff writer at Amazon.com: "[Barry Trotter] has married Ermine Cringer and they now have two relatively delightful children. The eldest is a skilled magician, but the youngest just seems to lack that conjurer's touch. Have Barry and Ermine given birth to . . . a MUDDLE?"

This is Gerber's second parody book on Harry Potter, which makes me wonder if he's planning a seven-book series. If so, the mind boggles.

Tim Kirk

Notable and Quotable:
The World of Book Publishing

Artist on writer: "I don't talk to J. K. We're not buddies or anything. I met her about four years ago in Chicago, and she's a great lady, but I don't speak with her, really. The publisher often doesn't want the author and illustrator [of children's books] to speak."

    —Mary GrandPré quoted by Dan Nailen in "Harry Potter Artist Speaks at Library," *Salt Lake Tribune* (November 16, 2003)

Audiobooks: "So, in *Order of the Phoenix* there are 134 characters, but more than 60 of them are brand new. The challenge was trying to find new voices and accents. I thought I'd explored them all when I invented five, let alone 100. I have to go instinctively now; the first voice I think of, I go with that. Nobody's complained yet, including J. K. Rowling. She's the one we try to please."

    —Audiobook reader Jim Dale, quoted by Shannon Maughan in "The Voices of Harry Potter's World," *Publishers Weekly* (July 14, 2003)

Book contracts: "[Christopher] Little may even consider offers from other publishers for the next three books. Although reports have long suggested that

Bloomsbury and Scholastic have a contract for the whole series, Little says this is not the case: 'I negotiate on a book-by-book basis,' he says."
—Sheryle Bagwell, *Australian Financial Review* (July 19, 2000)

Book sales: "Over decades or centuries, Shakespeare and Dickens, Keats and Wordsworth, or Agatha Christie and P. G. Wodehouse may have sold more books, but no one within living memory can match the phenomenal number sold by J. K. Rowling over the past six years."
—Brian MacArthur, "Sales of Harry Potter Books Speak Volumes," Timesonline.co.uk (June 20, 2003)

Boys reading: "The most phenomenal thing is that boys who didn't read are devouring this book. And the book seems to have awakened in children a realization that reading is entertainment."
—Margot Sage-El of Watchung Booksellers, quoted by Bernard Weintraub in "New Harry Potter Book Becoming a Publishing Phenomenon," *New York Times* (July 3, 2000)

British to American English: "But although there are many legitimate reasons for praising the series—the exciting plots, the new young readers being drawn to books, the quality of the writing—I am disappointed about one thing: the decision by Scholastic, publisher of the American edition, to translate the books from 'English' into 'American.' . . . By insisting that everything be Americanized, we dumb down our own society rather than enrich it."
—Peter H. Gleick in an op-ed piece, "Harry Potter, Minus a Certain Flavour," *New York Times* (July 10, 2000)

Censorship: "I don't think there's any subject matter that can't be explored in literature. Any subject matter at all. I really hate censorship. People have the right to decide what they want their children to read, but in my opinion they do not have the right to tell other people's children what they should read."
—Rowling quoted in *Time* (October 2000)

"With Harry Potter, the perceived danger is fantasy. . . . According to certain adults, these stories teach witchcraft, sorcery, and satanism. But hey, if it's not one 'ism,' it's another."
—Judy Bloom, *New York Times* (October 22, 1999)

Child's view of licensing: "None of the kids are crazy about it. Some people say how stupid it is that they are coming out with Harry Potter toothbrushes and things like that. I think they should just stop with the books and movies, otherwise it just goes sort of overboard into a more Disney thing."
—Nine-year-old Emma Bradford quoted by David D. Kirkpatrick in "New Sign on Harry Potter's Forehead: For Sale," *New York Times* (June 16, 2003)

Children's books as cool: "There's not a particle of me that's troubled by the idea that adults might be reading children's books. They jolly well should be. Thank you, J. K. Rowling, for making it cool to read children's books."

—Brenda Bowen, executive vice president and publisher of Simon and Schuster Children's Publishing, quoted in "The Trouble with Harry," *Book* magazine (May/June 2003)

Christian fundamentalists: "When fundamentalists look at Harry Potter, they see a seething Hieronymous Bosch painting, a grotesque and frightening world rife with sin and temptation and devilry. . . . It's odd, though, that when one looks at a child reading a Harry Potter book, lost in a private world, one senses something entirely different. Just a child, secure in a place that is impenetrable to adults and their interpretations. Children read for the same reasons adults do: to escape. Why is it that some adults want to drag them back to their own world of fears and discord? Perhaps because if a book is selling like Harry Potter sells, you can't very well leave it to children."

—Philip Kenicott in "A Scholar Who Gives 'Harry' the Evil Eye," *Washington Post* (November 23, 2003)

Collectibles: "Meanwhile, a hard-backed version of a Harry Potter book bought by a woman from Swindon for £10.99 five years ago was sold at auction yesterday for £13,000. Dominic Winter Book Auction in Swindon, which sold the book, said it was one of just 300 printed. Only a few are privately owned. It was bought by a book dealer from Bristol."

—David Lister in "Bidder Pays £28,000 for Harry Potter Secrets," www.independent.co.uk (December 13, 2002)

Exasperating adult: "In the last tour, in the U.K., I finally lost my temper. And I have a fairly long fuse for my readers, but halfway down a queue of about a thousand people, I had to make a train. This was a train to see my daughter, so this was not a thing I wanted to miss. Halfway down the line, I've got this guy with every bit of Harry Potter paraphernalia he could get his paws on and he wanted them all personalized. And I said to him, 'If I do this for you, that means 12 children at the end of this queue won't get their books signed.' And he argued, and I lost my temper. But eBay . . . explains a lot of it."

—Rowling quoted by Frank Garcia in "Harry Pottermania in Vancouver," *Dateline* (November 16, 2000)

Glasses: "Potter was drawn with spectacles because, Ms. Rowling said, she had worn thick glasses as a child and was frustrated that 'speccies were swots but never heroes.'"

—Rhys Williams in "The Spotty Schoolboy and Single Mother Taking the Mantle from Roald Dahl," *Independent* (January 29, 1999)

Harry Potter illustrations: "I love the look of the American books, especially the chapter illustrations."

—Rowling quoted on Scholastic.com (October 16, 2000)

Hogwarts headaches: "A pediatrician says he had three otherwise healthy children complain of headaches for two or three days last summer. It turns out all had been reading the 870-page *Harry Potter and the Order of the Phoenix* in marathon sessions."

—Stephanie Nano, Salon.com (October 29, 2003)

HP1: "A four-year-old American girl is in critical condition in the hospital after apparently trying to fly on a broomstick, like the characters in *Harry Potter and the Philosopher's Stone,* it was reported today. . . . Police in Shelby, North Carolina, told TV reporters the girl crawled onto a kitchen counter, straddled a broom, and then jumped off shortly after watching the film."

—From "Girl, 4, Critical after Harry Potter Broomstick Stunt," *Edinburgh Evening News* (July 22, 2002)

"Of all the questions that children asked me, the most memorable was from a boy in San Francisco, who asked me why Harry's aunt and uncle don't send him to an orphanage if they hate him so much. This is a very important question and it has an answer, but I can't give it without ruining the plot of the fifth Harry Potter book. I have been waiting a long time for someone to ask me that question and I was stunned that I had to travel across the Atlantic to hear someone put his finger on it."

—Rowling quoted by Sally Lodge in "Children's Authors and Illustrators Share Memorable Moments from Recent Book Tours," *Publishers Weekly* (January 4, 1999)

"On the whole *Harry Potter and the Sorcerer's Stone* is as funny, moving, and impressive as the story behind its writing. . . . But like Harry Potter, she has wizardry inside, and has soared beyond her modest Muggle surroundings to achieve something special."

—Michael Winerip in a review of the book, *New York Times* (February 14, 1999)

"So much of *Harry Potter and the Sorcerer's Stone* was written and planned before I found myself a single mother that I don't think my experiences at that time directly influenced the plots or characters. I think the only event in my own life that changed the direction of 'Harry Potter' was the death of my mother. I only fully realized upon rereading the book how many of my own feelings about losing my mother I had given Harry."

—Rowling quoted by Margaret Weir in "Of Magic and Single Motherhood," Salon.com (March 31, 1999)

"This book [*Philosopher's Stone*] saved my sanity. Apart from my sister I knew nobody. I've never been more broke and the little I had saved went on baby gear. In the wake of my marriage, having worked all my life, I was suddenly an unemployed single parent in a grotty little flat. The manuscript was the only thing I had going for me."

—Rowling quoted by Anne Johnstone in "Happy Ending, and That's for Beginners," *Herald* (June 24, 1997)

"When I got that first phone call, we had no idea this little kid was going to be on everyone's shelves and be a phenomenon. When that first call came, the publisher was saying, 'It might be part of a series, but we'll probably do just one.'"

—Harry Potter artist Mary GrandPré quoted by Dan Nailen in "Harry Potter Artist Speaks at Library," *Salt Lake Tribune* (November 16, 2003)

HP3: "Rowling took time to say a cheery 'hello' to each of the 100 children who waited in line to have Rowling sign her latest book, *Harry Potter and the Prisoner of Azkaban*. She told one child who said proudly that she, too, was a writer: 'You keep writing, and one day when you're famous, we'll meet again.'"

—Karen McPherson in "'Harry Potter' Goes to Hollywood," *Post-Gazette National Bureau* (October 21, 1999)

"We can't know where J. K. Rowling will take our Harry. But if her series goes on the way it's started, Harry will be 17 by the last installment. . . . Maybe by then J. K. Rowling will have achieved what people who love the best children's books have long labored after: breaking the spell of adult condescension that brands as merely cute, insignificant, second-rate the heartiest and best of children's literature."

—Fantasy author Gregory Maguire in a review of the novel *Lord of the Golden Snitch, New York Times,* Books (September 5, 1999)

HP4: "416. That is how many times I respond in a reasonable tone [to my daughter], explaining patiently that we will have to wait until July 8, the worldwide publication date for all English language versions [of *Harry Potter and the Goblet of Fire*]."

—Michelle Slatalla in "Waiting for Harry Potter in Long Lines on the Net," *New York Times* (April 27, 2000)

"A few seconds past the wizarding hour of midnight Saturday, the most annoying and unnecessary marketing campaign in publishing history finally delivered the goods. J. K. Rowling's *Harry Potter and the Goblet of Fire* would have sold millions of copies had its U.S. and British publishers simply dumped them in bookstores, unannounced, and then got out of the way as word of mouth spread among stampeding Pottermaniacs."

—Paul Gray in "The Wait Was Worth It," *Time* (July 8, 2000)

"For all its frenzy of publicity, this book has arrived like a midsummer night's dream. Enter it and you find a place where the enemies are obsessed with racial purity and the heroes are the ones who have to learn tolerance, community, and reaching across boundaries of fear. If children learn and adults re-learn that lesson in this season of reading, they will find the book very rewarding indeed."

—Steven R. Weisman in "A Novel That Is a Midsummer Night's Dream," *New York Times*, Editorial (July 11, 2000)

"It is worth remembering right about here, that *Harry Potter and the Goblet of Fire* is not a Hollywood summer blockbuster, although its weekend grosses will probably be announced in a breathless press release. It is a book, a really long book, with no moving images, sound track, or joysticks. Reading it or listening to someone else read it aloud requires a modicum of silence, the exact antithesis of all the bells and whistles and clarions that heralded its arrival."

—Paul Gray in "Harry Is Back Again," *Time* (July 17, 2000)

"It was the knowledge, unprecedented in a life devoted to the solitary practice of reading, that last night and throughout this weekend, I and millions of other people, young and old, will all be reading the very same book."

—Laura Miller in "Pottermania at Midnight," Salon.com (July 8, 2000)

"It's the end of an era in the context of the whole series of books. For Harry his innocence is gone."

—Rowling quoted by Alan Cowell in "All Aboard the Potter Express," *New York Times* (July 10, 2000)

"The first Harry Potter book was the best. It went into such vivid detail. I really wanted to go to King's Cross and find Platform Nine and Three-Quarters. The first book was the base, the second built the characters, and the third gave the background. So I was excited about the fourth book. Unfortunately, there were too many subplots—like Harry falling in love and the House-elves—that took away from the main Voldemort plot. I enjoyed reading *Harry Potter and the Goblet of Fire*, but *Harry Potter and the Philosopher's Stone* is still my favourite."

—Lucy Barton, aged 14, quoted by Fiona Barton and Lesley Yarranton in "Fear Stalks the Hogwarts Express," *Mail on Sunday* (July 9, 2000)

"The working title had got out—*Harry Potter and the Doomspell Tournament*. Then I changed *Doomspell* to *Triwizard Tournament*. Then I was teetering between *Goblet of Fire* and *Triwizard Tournament*. In the end, I preferred *Goblet of Fire* because it's got that kind of 'cup of destiny' feel about it, which is the theme of the book."

—Rowling quoted by Jeff Jensen in "Rowling Thunder," *Entertainment Weekly* (August 4, 2000)

"There has never been anything like this in the history of book selling. I think this could be the most profitable book we ever sold. If we can get kids hooked on a seven-book series, hopefully we could get them hooked on reading for life."

—Vice Chairman of Barnes & Noble, Steve Riggio, quoted by David D. Kirkpatrick in "Harry Potter Magic Halts Bedtime for Youngsters," *New York Times* (July 9, 2000)

HP4 book tour and the media: "I'd really love to talk to some children, if I ever manage to finish with you lot."

—Rowling quoted by T. R. Reid in "All Aboard the Publicity Train," *Washington Post* (July 9, 2000)

HP5: "Ms. Rowling has imagined this universe in such minute and clever detail that we feel that we've been admitted to a looking-glass world as palpable as Tolkien's Middle-earth or L. Frank Baum's Oz. The wizards, witches, and Muggles who live there share complicated, generations-old relationships with one another and inhabit a place with traditions, beliefs, and a history all its own—a Grimm place where the fantastic and fabulous are routine, but also a place subject to all the limitations and losses of our own mortal world."

—Michiko Kakutani in *"Harry Potter and the Order of the Phoenix,"* *New York Times* (June 21, 2003)

"But what really makes the Harry Potter series great is its dual nature. It's a fantasy wrapped around a nightmare, an unreal, escapist fiction with an icy core of emotional pain that is very real."

—Lev Grossman in "That Old Black Magic," *Time* (June 30, 2003)

"I'd spend £1,000 on it if I had to."

—Sinead Miller, aged 13, on what she'd pay for the fifth Harry Potter novel, quoted by Chris Heard in "Potter Mania Sweeps Nation," BBC News: UK Edition (June 21, 2003)

"If you were simply craving a megadose of the old Hogwarts magic, along with the promised twists and surprises (a romance, the death of a key character), then the new book is worth every Potter-deprived minute. J. K. Rowling's great gift—her ability to conjure a rich, teeming, utterly believable alternative world—hasn't failed her."

—Elizabeth Ward in "Harry Potter, Still Quite the Charmer," *Washington Post*'s Book World "For Young Readers" column (June 24, 2003)

"In the U.S., the president of the New York Public Library donned white gloves to accept a signed first edition delivered by armoured car. 'We put the white gloves on only for the most special books,' the library head, Paul LeCler, told the Associated Press news agency."

—From "World Greets New Harry Potter," BBC News (June 21, 2003)

"It is written for people whose imaginative lives are confined to TV cartoons, and the exaggerated (more exciting, not threatening) mirror-worlds of soap, reality TV, and celebrity gossip."

—Author A. S. Byatt in "Harry Potter and the Childish Adult," *New York Times* (July 7, 2003)

"The nation's children are up in arms. Where is their annual fix of the young magician? At this rate they will have to compensate—shock, horror—by reading other—do they know there are any?—books for children by the likes of Philip Pullman, Jacqueline Wilson, Anne Fine, Lemony Snicket, Joan Lingard, and Teresa Breslin."

—Giles Gordon in "Publish or Be Damned," *Scotsman* (September 20, 2002)

"The publisher already has distributed 3 million bumper stickers, 400,000 buttons, 50,000 window displays, and 24,000 stand-up posters with countdown clocks. . . . Scholastic has also sent out more than 15,000 'event kits' to bookstores and other retail outlets, where parties are planned all over the country."

—From "Publisher Preps for Potter," MSN Entertainment News (June 5, 2003)

"Thus a multiethnic multiculture of warlocks, mermaids, mugawumps, trolls, vampires, fairies, dwarfs, ghouls, mummies, pixies, gnomes, banshees, wood nymphs, dementors, boggarts, veelas, animagi, and parselmouths."

—John Leonard in *"Harry Potter and the Order of the Phoenix:* Nobody Expects the Inquisition," *New York Times Book Review* (July 13, 2003)

"We knew it was big—the massive first printing, the media hype, the midnight release parties, the assured instant-best-seller status. But perhaps nobody knew *Harry Potter and the Order of the Phoenix* would be this big, this fast. According to reports from Scholastic, an estimated five million copies of the book were sold on Saturday, its first day of release."

—PW staff in *"Harry* Makes History—Again," *Publishers Weekly* (June 23, 2003)

Licensing: "I would do anything to prevent Harry from turning up in fast-food boxes everywhere. I would do my utmost. That would be my worst nightmare."

—Rowling quoted by David D. Kirkpatrick in "New Sign on Harry Potter's Forehead: For Sale," *New York Times* (June 16, 2003)

"In 1998, Rowling sold worldwide licensing rights to Warner for about $500,000 (a price now considered insanely low), although she does receive unspecified royalties based on licensing revenues. For example, she gets an estimated $1 to $1.50 for each Harry video game that is sold. About 75 products have been licensed so far. Hard as it is to believe, that's not so many for

a brand of this visibility, part of a strategy by Warner to sell a modest number of licenses for a massive number of dollars."

—Gordon T. Anderson in "Harry Potter and the Big Wad of Cash," CNNMoney.com (June 20, 2003)

"I've had some very weird offers. A margarine company wanted to put Harry on its margarine, if you can believe it."

—Rowling quoted by Katy Abel in "Harry Potter Author Works Her Magic," *Family Education* (summer 1999)

"Ms. Rowling created the characters, and she has the right to kill them off . . . or turn them into Happy Meal action figures, if that's where her heart lies. But the sentimentalists among us are going to mourn the days when Harry existed only in books, which were smaller than breadboxes."

—Gail Collins in an op-ed piece, "Moby Dick on a Broom," *New York Times* (July 7, 2000)

"We're getting over 100 inquiries a day, whether it's the Sony Corporation or Microsoft or Boeing, to people that make cups and saucers."

—Christopher Little quoted by Ed Bradley on *60 Minutes* (September 12, 1999)

Literary power of Potter: "Parents report reading levels jumping four grades in two years. They cannot quite believe this gift, that for an entire generation of children, the most powerful entertainment experience of their lives comes not on a screen or a monitor or a disc but on a page."

—Nancy Gibbs in "The Real Magic of Harry Potter," *Time* (June 23, 2003)

Magical book: "One little girl said her books were 'magic.' Rowling told her that that was the nicest compliment she had ever received. Eventually more than 1,000 fans filed through."

—Linton Weeks in "Charmed, I'm Sure," *Washington Post* (October 20, 1999)

Magical reality: "What makes the Harry Potter books fly, so to speak, is not so much their otherworldliness as their fidelity to the way things really are (or were, at least, when quills and parchment were still more common than computers): wizards, Harry Potter's world suggests, are only regular Muggles who've been to the right school."

—Pico Iyer in "The Playing Fields of Hogwarts," *New York Times,* Books (October 10, 1999)

Master plan: "I want to finish these seven books and look back and think that whatever happened to me—however much this hurricane whirled around me—I stayed true to what I wanted to write. This is my Holy Grail: that when I finish writing book seven, I can say—hand on heart—I didn't

change a thing. I wrote the story I meant to write. If I lost readers along the way, so be it, but I still told my story. The one I wanted. Without permitting it to sound too corny, that's what I owe to my characters. That we won't be deflected, either by adoration or by criticism."

—Rowling quoted by Linda Richards in "January Profile: J. K. Rowling," januarymagazine.com (October 2000)

Model for Hermione Granger: "She is a caricature of me: I was neither as bright nor as annoying as Hermione. At least, I hope I wasn't, because I would have deserved drowning at birth. But she, like me, lightens up. As I went through my teens, things actually got better. I began to realize that there was more to me than just someone who got everything right."

—Rowling quoted by Helena de Bertodano in "Harry Potter Charms a Nation," *Electronic Telegraph* (July 25, 1998)

Muggle technology: "But one of the interesting things about Hogwarts in the Potter books is that it contains no technology at all. Light is provided by torches and heat by massive fireplaces. Who needs electricity when you have plenty of wizards and magic wands? . . . Technology is for Muggles, who rely on contraptions because they cannot imagine the conveniences of magic. Who wouldn't choose a wizard's life?"

—Paul Gray in "Wild About Harry," *Time* (September 20, 1999)

Occult: "The books are written in a very amusing way, but those underlying tones of death, murder, and the occult is what scares us. Especially here in the States with all the violence we've had in our schools. A lot of that has been linked to kids getting involved in the occult. . . . It's too violent. There were parts that really scared us, and we didn't want [our son] to lose his innocence."

—David Williamson, a parent protesting the Harry Potter novels, quoted by Celia Farber in "Harry Potter's Toughest Foe," *Sunday Herald* (October 17, 1999)

Panned: "The cultural critics will, soon enough, introduce Harry Potter into their college curriculum, and the *New York Times* will go on celebrating another confirmation of the dumbing-down it leads and exemplifies."

—Harold Bloom in an op-ed piece, "Can 35 Million Book Buyers Be Wrong? Yes," *Wall Street Journal* (July 11, 2000)

"The writing was dreadful; the book was terrible. . . . Rowling's mind is so governed by clichés and dead metaphors that she has no other style of writing. . . . Later I read a lavish, loving review of Harry Potter by the same Stephen King. He wrote something to the effect of, 'If these kids are reading Harry Potter at 11 or 12, then when they get older they will go on to read Stephen King.' And he was quite right. He was not being ironic.

When you read 'Harry Potter' you are, in fact, trained to read Stephen King."

—Harold Bloom, from "Dumbing Down American Readers," *Boston Globe* (September 24, 2003)

Parent-child relationship: "This book has opened up a whole new relationship between my ten-year-old son (who definitely had no passion for reading) and myself (a person who has such a love for reading). We have the best time talking about the characters and the stories! I do believe this has made my son love reading, which is a gift any parent will appreciate! But I think the best part is the quality time we spend reading and talking about the adventures."

—Beth A., in a letter (*Time,* July 11, 2000) responding to "Extra! Extra! Page One of the New 'Harry Potter,'" *Time* (July 7, 2000)

Phenomenon: "Does the word 'miracle' mean anything to you? What we're talking about here is a foreign import with no television show, no movie, and no celebrity. It's a noisy world, and it's hard to get attention for a children's book."

—Nancy Pines, children's book publisher at Simon and Schuster/Pocket Books, quoted by Doreen Carvajal in "Children's Book Casts a Spell Over Adults," *New York Times* (April 1, 1999)

Plotting: "It is a lot of work to create an entire world. It was about five years to finish the first book and to plot the remaining six books, because they were already plotted before the first book was published; and book two was started before book one was finished. Yeah, so I spent an awful lot of time thinking about the details of the world and working it out in depth."

—Rowling quoted in "Interview with J. K. Rowling," *Connection* (October 12, 1999)

Popularity: "We've never had a [children's book] author who has risen as quickly as J. K. I think she might well be regarded as highly as Roald Dahl."

—British book reviewer Julia Eccleshare quoted by William Plummer and Joanna Blonska in "They're Wild about Harry," *Entertainment Weekly* (July 9, 1999)

Private world: "I always find it very hard to talk about the book in these terms because I find it very, very difficult to be objective . . . To me, they remain my private little world—I was writing about Harry for five years before anyone else read a word of him—and it is still an amazing feeling to me to be in a room, as we are today, with people whose heads are also populated with these characters because, as I say, for five years, they were my private secret. From the moment I had the idea for the book, I could just see a lot of comic potential in the idea that wizards walk among us and that we are foolishly blind to the fact that the reason that we keep losing our car keys is that wizards are bewitching them for fun."

—Rowling quoted in "James Naughtie Talks to J. K. Rowling about One of Her Novels," Radio 4's Book Club Programme (August 1, 1999)

Quidditch: "I invented Quidditch while spending the night in a very small room in the Bournville Hotel in Didsbury, Manchester. I wanted a sport for wizards, and I'd always wanted to see a game where there was more than one ball in play at the same time. The idea just amused me. The Muggle sport it most resembles is basketball, which is probably the sport I enjoy watching most. I had a lot of fun making up the rules and I've still got the notebook I did it in, complete with diagrams, and all the names for the balls I tried before I settled on Snitch, Bludgers, and Quaffle."

—Rowling quoted in an interview on Amazon.co.uk (1999)

Rowling's imagination: "The fantasy writer's job is to conduct the willing reader from mundanity to magic. This is a feat of which only a superior imagination is capable, and Rowling possesses such equipment."

—Stephen King in a book review of HP4 for the *New York Times*

Science in Harry Potter's universe: "Irrespective of the specific title of the course, the 'magic' in the fiction is being analyzed by applying concepts of physics, chemistry, biology, and engineering. This honors course creatively packages scientific principles in a contemporary way that will interest today's students."

—Catherine R. Gira, Frostburg State president, on George R. Plitnik's physics course, "The Science of Harry Potter," quoted by David Dishneau in "Harry Potter Gets Some Class at College," Associated Press (September 21, 2003)

Selecting Hogwarts students: "The Ministry of Magic doesn't find out which children are magic. In Hogwarts there's a magical quill which detects the birth of a magical child, and writes his or her name down in a large parchment book. Every year Professor McGonagall checks the book, and sends owls to the people who are turning 11."

—Rowling quoted in "The 24 Most Intriguing People of 1999," *People* (December 31, 1999)

Showing up unannounced at a hometown bookstore: "When *Goblet of Fire* was published, I was desperate to go into a bookshop at midnight and see children's reactions, so this time I'm really pleased I could. Much of the pleasure of being published for me is meeting the children who are reading the books."

—Rowling quoted in "JK in City for Spell at Harry Launch," News.scotsman.com (June 21, 2003)

Tim Kirk

A Muggle's Guide to Harry Potter:
A Fictional Concordance

Rowling's fictional Harry Potter universe is replete with numerous references to people, places, and things. This concordance alphabetically lists them for easy reference.

Notes: My presumption is that most readers of this book will have read the five Potter novels in print. Newer readers should know that there are occasionally spoilers—plot points or information that give key information from the story line—that I've had to discuss because there was no way to avoid them.

2 Sickles: The price of a S.P.E.W. badge, asked by Hermione Granger to support her new cause, the liberation of Hogwarts' house-elves.

10 Galleons: The amount bet between Percy Weasley and Penelope Clearwater on the outcome of a Quidditch match, after Harry Potter gets a Firebolt broom; Weasley collects. Also the cost for an omniocular.

11 to 15 Sickles: The varying fares, depending on amenities provided, from which Harry Potter can choose for his Knight Bus ride from Little Whinging to London.

37 Galleons, 15 Sickles, and 3 Knuts: The amount George and Percy Weasley bet against Ludo Bagman on Viktor Krum getting the Golden Snitch and Ireland winning the international Quidditch match.

170: In an international Quidditch match between the national teams from Bulgaria and Ireland, this is the winning score achieved by Ireland; Bulgaria scored 160.

700 Galleons: The cash prize Arthur Weasley won in the *Daily Prophet's* Grand Prize Galleon Draw. He uses the money to take his family on a trip to Egypt.

1,000 Galleon Reward: The Ministry of Magic posted posters of the ten Death Eaters who escaped from Azkaban and offered this reward for each.

A

Abercrombie, Euan: A Gryffindor student.

Abraxian Horses: Winged horses cited by Hagrid, who has a friend who breeds them.

Abyssinian Shrivelfigs: A plant pruned in Herbology class with Professor Sprout.

Accidental Magical Reversal Department: The "911" department of the Ministry of Magic. Call them when there's an emergency. For example, they deflate Marjorie Dursley (Aunt Marge) and use a memory charm to erase her memory of the event.

Accio: A summoning charm.

Accio Firebolt: Command given by Harry Potter, who calls his Firebolt broom to him during the Triwizard Tournament.

Acid Pops: A candy available at Honeydukes.

Ackerley, Stewart: A Ravenclaw student.

Aconite: A (real) plant, also known as monkshood or wolfsbane.

Advance Guard: Sent to Privet Drive to get Harry Potter and escort him to safety, to the house where the Order of the Phoenix had set up its headquarters. The Guard consists of Alastor "Mad-Eye" Moody, Remus Lupin, Nymphadora Tonks, Kingsley Shacklebolt, Elphias Doge, Dedalus Diggle, Emmeline Vance, Sturgis Podmore, and Hestia Jones.

Adventures of Martin Miggs, the Mad Muggle: A favorite comic book series of Ron Weasley's.

Age Line: Surrounding the Goblet of Fire, it will keep underage students (under 17) from dropping their names in the Goblet for consideration as a champion for the Triwizard Tournament.

Aging Potion: Suggested for use by Fred Weasley to his twin brother, George, since they want to fool the judges into thinking they're older than they are. They want to compete for the Triwizard Cup to get the 1,000 Galleons to finance their joke shop.

All-England Best-Kept Suburban Lawn Competition: Sent by mail, this ruse is used to get the Durlseys out of their home so the Advance Guard can escort Harry Potter to the headquarters of the Order of the Phoenix.

Alohomora: A spell used to unlock doors. Hermione Granger uses it to open a door to escape from Filch after Peeves shouts that they are out of bed after hours.

Ancient Runes: A class Hermione Granger takes as a third-year student.

Ancient Runes Made Easy: A book Hermione Granger reads.

Animagus: A wizard or witch who can change into animal form (the plural is animagi). This is rare and animagi are registered by the Ministry of Magic according to animal species and any specific identification marks. Not all of them, however, have been registered; Peter Pettigrew, Sirius Black, James Potter, and Rita Skeeter have not.

An Anthology of Eighteenth-Century Charms: A library book Harry Potter consults in the hopes that it will help him with his second trial at the Triwizard Tournament.

Anti-Cheating Charms: Placed on the O.W.L. exams to prevent students from cheating.

Anti-Disapparation Jinx: A jinx used by Dumbledore in the Department of Mysteries when fighting the Death Eaters, who tried to escape by Apparation. This jinx prevented them from doing so.

Anti-Umbridge League: A name proposed by Angelina for Harry Potter's unofficial Defense Against the Dark Arts class.

Aparecium: A charm used to reveal writing rendered in invisible ink.

Apparate: The act of appearing. A form of travel used only by experienced witches and wizards, this allows one to disappear and reappear at will. (Underage wizards, i.e., students, cannot use this method of transportation. In fact, in order to be able to use this method, a test must be passed to show competency.)

An Appraisal of Magical Education in Europe: A book Hermione Granger reads for its assessment of various educational institutions for witches and wizards.

Aquavirius Maggots: Another fanciful creature Luna Lovegood believes exists. According to her father, the Ministry of Magic is breeding these.

Aragog: Raised by a young Hagrid who received him as an egg, this giant spider was mistakenly assumed to be the monster in the Chamber of Secrets and blamed for an early killing—Moaning Myrtle. Aragog's mate is Mosag, whom Hagrid also found.

Argyllshire: A map of this on the second floor of Hogwarts which is the hiding place of the Fat Lady after she deserts her picture frame in front of the Gryffindor common room. She is scared into hiding, presumably by the on-the-loose Sirius Black.

Arithmancy: Her favorite subject, it's a course third-year Hermione Granger takes at Hogwarts.

Asiatic Anti-Venoms: A book Harry Potter half-read as he pondered the dilemma of whether or not to take up Hermione Granger's suggestion of forming a secret class to teach Defense Against the Dark Arts.

Astronomy: Taught at the "tallest tower" at Hogwarts; Harry Potter takes this class as a third-year student.

Aunt Petunia's Pudding: A dessert intended for Mr. and Mrs. Mason that does not grace the dinner table but, because of Dobby's intervention, Harry Potter; it crashes down on the floor, splattering the boy wizard from head to toe. As Dobby desperately tries every stratagem to keep Potter safe, Dobby rationalizes that the end justifies the means: Harry must *not* return to Hogwarts!

Auror: A wizard who catches Dark wizards. A Hogwarts student with such a high aspiration must not only be academically outstanding (excellent grades and five NEWTs in his seventh year) but be prepared to spend three additional years of training after graduation. It's not only a highly sought-after and prestigious position, but one for which many are called but few are chosen; in fact, no witches or wizards have been accepted for training for the last several years. However, those who feel they are up to the challenge can apply by owl to Kingsley Shacklebolt at the Auror Headquarters of the Ministry of Magic.

Auto-Answer Quill: Banned from O.W.L. exams, it will automatically answer questions.

Avery: At large, a Death Eater.

Axminster: A carpet that seated 12 people, according to Mr. Crouch, who said his grandfather owned one.

Azkaban Prison: Located out at sea on a tiny island, prisoners are held not by barred doors and walls but within their own crazed minds, driven to that state by its guards, Dementors.

B

Babbling Beverage: A potion that makes the victim talk endlessly and incoherently.

Babbling Curse: A curse that reputedly afflicted a Transylvanian villager, whom Lockhart cured—or so he says.

Baddock, Malcolm: A Slytherin student.

Bagman, Ludovic (Ludo): A wizard who heads the Department of Magical Games and Sports. As Beater for the Wimbourne Wasps, Bagman played Quidditch in an international tournament for England. During his time with them, his team won three consecutive league championships. At the Quidditch World Cup, he's a commentator, broadcasting from the Top Box.

Bagman, Otto: Ludo Bagman's brother, who had a problem with an unnatural lawn mower, which required intervention by Mr. Arthur Weasley.

Bagshot, Bathilda: Author of *A History of Magic,* a standard text; required course book for first-year students at Hogwarts.

Balderdash: Password used for entry to the Gryffindor common room.

Banana Fritters: Another password to gain entry in Gryffindor.

Bandon Banshee: In passing conversation, Gilderoy Lockhart boasts of having got rid of this female creature.

Bane: A centaur who takes centaur Firenze to task for bearing Harry Potter. He later confronts Hagrid in the Forbidden Forest to warn him to stay out and take his half-brother, Grawp, with him.

Bang-Ended Scoots: *Daily Prophet* reporter Rita Skeeter tells Hagrid that the paper runs a zoological column once a week, and suggests a feature on these creatures, which she misnames—they are, as Hagrid corrects her, Blast-Ended Skrewts.

Banishing Charm: A charm used to send an object or person away.

Barrufio's Brain Elixir: A student, Eddie Carmichael, almost closed a sale

of a pint of this for 12 Galleons—a kingly sum, but well worth it to Ron Weasley, who was ready to buy, if Harry Potter would loan him the money. The elixir, according to Carmichael, was the principal reason he received an impressive nine "Outstanding" O.W.L.s in his fifth year. Fortunately, Hermione Granger seizes the bottle and dumps its contents, explaining to a crestfallen Weasley that it is not brain elixir but, in fact, dried doxy droppings.

Bashir, Ali: In a disagreement with Arthur Weasley regarding the import of carpets, Bashir pushes for importation, but Weasley is against it, since they are Muggle Artifacts, according to the Registry of Proscribed Charmable Objects.

Basic Blaze Box: Fireworks sold by Fred and George Weasley, costing five Galleons. Used to disrupt classes at Hogwarts after Umbridge is appointed Headmistress.

Basic Hexes for the Busy and Vexed: A book Harry Potter consults for information, since he must face a dragon in his first Triwizard Tournament challenge.

Basil: Described as a "grumpy-looking" wizard, he is the keeper of Portkeys at the Quidditch World Cup tournament. Dressed as a Muggle, wearing a kilt and poncho, he greets the Weasleys as they arrive on the tournament grounds.

Basilisk: The monster in the Chamber of Secrets at Hogwarts. The basilisk attacks Justin Finch-Fletchley, Colin Creevey, Penelope Clearwater, Hermione Granger, Nearly Headless Nick, and a cat, Mrs. Norris. It has a deadly gaze—it can petrify when seen indirectly—and is susceptible only to the crowing of a rooster, which is fatal to it. This basilisk has venomous foot-long fangs; in a battle with Harry Potter, one of its fangs pierces his arm.

Bat-Bogey Hex: A hex Ginny Weasley is fond of using on her older brothers, George and Fred Weasley. These flapping bogeys are attracted to the victim's face, as Draco Malfoy discovers when Ginny uses it on him.

Battle Helmet: The second gift Hagrid brings to give to Karkus (the chief giant). Made by goblins, the helmet is indestructible.

Bayliss, Hetty: A Muggle woman who lives in Norfolk; she saw the flying Ford Anglia before Ron Weasley pressed the Invisibility Booster, a button on the dashboard, to render it invisible.

Beaters: Quidditch term. Two on each team, they use a small club to swat away two small, fast-moving black balls called Bludgers, that attempt to dislodge players from their brooms. Ideally, the Beaters swat the balls toward their opponents, who must then defend themselves against these dangerous, whizzing balls.

Beauxbatons Academy of Magic: One of three well-regarded schools of magic in Europe.

Belch Powder: An item sold at Zonko's Joke Shop, favored by Hogwarts students.

Bell, Katie: A Chaser for the Gryffindor house Quidditch team.

Bertie Botts' Every Flavor Beans: Wizard candy with an odd assortment of flavors, ranging from the delicious to the inedible, from the ordinary to the extraordinary, from chocolate-flavored to earwax.

Bezoar: A stone that is protection against most poisons. It is found in a goat's stomach.

Binky: A baby rabbit. In a letter from home, Lavender Brown is horrified to read that her pet rabbit was killed by a fox. This reaffirmed to everyone that Professor Trelawney's prediction that something dreadful would happen on October 16 had come true. But always the stickler to detail, Hermione Granger points out that Binky obviously hadn't died on the 16th, since she had just gotten the word via letter, which she received on that date.

Black, Sirius: A classmate and close friend of James Potter and Lily Potter, and godfather to Harry Potter. He is imprisoned in but subsequently escapes from Azkaban, the wizard's prison guarded by the dreaded Dementors. Rumored to have killed 13 people with a single curse in broad daylight, Black is later shown to be innocent. Sirius escapes capture by riding Buckbeak (a hippogriff) to safety to a mountainside cave Dumbledore recommended.

Bladvak: A word in the language of Gobbledegook, which means "pickax."

Blast-Ended Skrewts: Resembling lobsters without shells, these are the subject of a class in Hagrid's Care of Magical Creatures class. Skrewts are the result of a breeding experiment of Hagrid's, in which he crossed manticores with fire-crabs.

Bletchley: A Keeper for the Slytherin house Quidditch team.

Blibbering Humdingers: Luna Lovegood believes these exist, but Hermione Granger sets her straight: they don't.

Blood-Flavored Lollipops: Located in the "Unusual Tastes" section of Honeydukes, they are for vampires, or hard-core goths.

Blood-Sucking Bugbear: A creature cited by Hagrid as a possible explanation for the death of a second rooster on Hogwarts school grounds.

Bloody Baron: House ghost of Slytherin.

Bluebottle: An all-purpose family broom advertised at the Quidditch World Cup Stadium before the game started.

Bludgers: Quidditch term. Two black balls that rocket around the playing field, trying to knock players off their brooms.

Bob: A wizard Arthur Weasley encounters at the Ministry of Magic when escorting Harry Potter to his trial. Bob is holding a chicken that looks normal (a bog-standard chicken), but it's clearly not what it seems to be, since it breathes fire. So Bob thinks it's the result of illegal breeding, despite the Ban on Experimental Breeding.

Bode, Broderick: An Unspeakable who worked for the top-secret Department of Mysteries at the Ministry of Magic, he was found dead at age 49 at the hands of a plant, the Devil's Snare, which was in his hospital room at St. Mungo's Hospital for Magical Maladies and Injuries. He had been bewitched by Lucius Malfoy to remove "the weapon."

Boggart: Preferring sanctuary in dark places, it's a shape-shifter that assumes the shape of whatever you fear the most. It's best to combat it with laughter by using the charm *Riddikulus!* to involuntarily force it to assume a ridiculous appearance. (In Neville's case, he fears Professor Snape, so Professor Lupin suggests he imagine Snape dressed in Neville's grandmother's clothes—a ridiculous image, prompting laughter.) Others in the class see their respective Boggart as a mummy (Parvati), a banshee (Seamus), and a giant spider (Ron Weasley).

Bonaccord, Pierre: Though contested by the wizarding community in Liechtenstein, he was appointed the first Supreme Mugwump of the International Confederation of Wizards.

Bones, Susan: A Hufflepuff student. Her aunt is Amelia Susan Bones.

Boomslang Skin: An ingredient needed to make Polyjuice Potion, it was pilfered by Hermione Granger from Professor Snape's office, though he never knew who took it.

Boot, Terry: A Ravenclaw student.

Borgin, Mr.: An unctuous proprietor at Borgin and Burkes, located in Knockturn Alley. His retail establishment caters to those interested in the Dark Arts. One of his frequent customers is Lucius Malfoy, who goes there to dispose of questionable articles that would prove embarrassing if they were discovered in a Ministry of Magic raid.

Bouillabaisse: A shellfish stew that's on the menu when students from Beauxbatons and Durmstrang visit Hogwarts. It's not usual fare for Hogwarts students, who probably don't care for it.

Bouncing Bulbs: In Herbology class, when Harry Potter was repotting these, one bounced up and hit Harry in the face.

Bounty: The Ministry of Magic put a 10,000 Galleon bounty on Sirius Black, who escaped from Azkaban.

Bowtruckles: Tree-guardians who eat wood lice or fairy eggs; these are vicious creatures that can gouge out eyes.

Brandy: A favorite liquor of Marjorie Dursley, who gets drunk too easily and, in doing so, reveals her true ugly nature.

Branstone, Eleanor: A Hufflepuff student.

Brass Compass: A component of the Broomstick Servicing Kit, used as an in-flight directional aid. (Probably very useful at night, especially if the charm *Lumos* is invoked.)

Break with a Banshee: A book by Gilderoy Lockhart, purportedly non-fiction, but actually fiction, like most of his books, since he tends to boast and exaggerate his exploits. (This is one of several books Lockhart assigns students, since he is Hogwarts' newest Defense Against the Dark Arts teacher.) It was, in truth, a witch, not Lockhart, who banished the Banshee.

Brocklehurst, Mandy: A Ravenclaw student.

Broken Balls: When Fortunes Turn Foul: A book devoted to fortune-telling, found at Flourish and Blotts on a table near a corner of the store.

Broom Compass: Used for directional flying, Ron Weasley gets one as a Christmas gift from Harry Potter.

Broomstick Servicing Kit: A do-it-yourself maintenance kit to keep your broom in prime flying condition. (No magical household should be without one.) Harry Potter received this as a gift from Hermione Granger.

Brown, Lavender: A Gryffindor student.

Bryce, Frank: The Riddles' gardener, he was suspected, but later exonerated, of murdering three members of the Riddle family, who had literally been scared to death. He is killed by Lord Voldemort after eavesdropping on him and his servant, Wormtail, at the supposedly abandoned Riddle house.

Bubble-Head Charm: Used by Fleur Delacour and Cedric Diggory in the second challenge at the Triwizard Tournament, it allows them to stay underwater for an hour.

Bubotubers: An ugly-looking plant resembling black slugs whose pus is effective against acne.

Buckbeak: A hippogriff whom Rubeus Hagrid introduces to his third-year Hogwarts students taking his class, Care of Magical Creatures.

Bulgarian National Quidditch Team: Playing at the 422nd Quidditch World Cup tournament, its members include Dimitrov, Ivanova, Zograf, Levski, Vulchanov, Volkov, and its star, an 18-year-old Seeker, Viktor Krum.

Bulgarian National Team Mascots: Dancing veela, indescribably beautiful women, performing at the 422nd Quidditch World Cup tournament.

Bulstrode, Millicent: A Slytherin student. An unpleasant, and unpleasant-looking, girl.

Bungy the Budgie: In a news report, Bungy, a budgerigar (a species of bird) who lives in Barnsley, has learned to water-ski. Harry Potter, who is monitoring news on TV, realizes when he hears this inconsequential story that it's not likely there will be any stories of interest on that broadcast.

Burning Day: After losing many of its feathers, a phoenix bursts into flame, only to be reborn. This is the day it bursts into flame.

The Burrow: The residence of the Weasley family.

Butterbeer: A foaming beverage available at Three Broomsticks in Hogsmeade. It's not alcoholic, but it can get a house-elf drunk. Winky, a house-elf, drowns her sorrows in six bottles of butterbeer a day.

C

Cadogan, Sir: When this knight is called to temporary duty guarding the entrance to Gryffindor, he shows his wackiness by needlessly challenging, and insulting, students to duels; even worse, he frequently changes the passwords, all of which are complicated and difficult to remember.

Canary Creams: A magical novelty invented by pranksters Fred and George Weasley. Once eaten, the sweet turns the unwitting victim into a molting canary; afterward, the victim turns back to normal, to the merriment of anyone nearby. One cream costs seven Sickles.

Caudwell, Owen: A Hufflepuff student.

Cauldron Cakes: A favorite wizard dessert, these cakes are offered by the witch pushing the food cart on the Hogwarts Express.

Chamber of Secrets: A hidden chamber in Hogwarts harboring a monster that can only be controlled by the heir of Slytherin. It is considered the stuff of legend, since the castle has been searched but the chamber remains undiscovered, until Harry Potter opens its secret entrance.

Champions for Triwizard Tournament: For Durmstrang, Viktor Krum; for Beauxbatons, Fleur Delacour; for Hogwarts, Cedric Diggory. And, to everyone's great surprise—since only three are supposed to be selected—for Hogwarts, Harry Potter, who is underage.

Chang, Cho: A Ravenclaw student and Seeker for her house Quidditch team, she rides an older, less powerful broom, the Comet Two Sixty, which is no match for Draco Malfoy's Nimbus 2001 or Harry Potter's Firebolt broom. She sports a Tornado badge to support her favorite Quidditch team.

"Charm to Cure Reluctant Reversers": A chapter in *Handbook of Do-It-Yourself Broomcare,* on which Harry Potter concentrates to avoid thinking of the gratuitous insults Marjorie Dursley (Aunt Marge) levels against him.

Charm Your Own Cheese: A cookbook found in Mrs. Weasley's kitchen.

Chasers: Quidditch term. On a Quidditch team comprised of seven people, three are Chasers, whose job is to pass the Quaffle to each other and attempt to score by throwing it through one of the hoops, which earns ten points.

Cherry Syrup and Soda: A beverage served at the Three Broomsticks, favored by Professor Flitwick.

Chinese Fireball: The dragon Viktor Krum must face in his first trial at the Triwizard Tournament.

Chipolatas: A food of which Dumbledore is fond.

Chocolate: (1) Hundreds of different kinds are available at Honeydukes; (2) first aid after a Dementor attack.

Chocolate Frogs: Wizard candy. The pack comes with a piece of chocolate in the shape of a frog and a wizard trading card, on which is a brief biography.

Chocolate Gateau: A dessert served in the Great Hall at Hogwarts Castle.

Christmas Gifts to Harry Potter: From Sirius and Lupin, self-defense books; from Tonks, a small, flying Firebolt model; from Ron, a big box of Every Flavor Beans; from Mrs. Weasley, a sweater and mince pies; from Dobby, an unrecognizable portrait of Harry Potter.

Chudley Cannons: Ron Weasley's favorite Quidditch team.

Circe: Found in the card series Famous Witches and Wizards.

Clause Three of the Code of Wand Use: "No non-human creature is permitted to carry or use a wand." Cited when a house-elf, Winky, is found with a wand in her hand, after the Dark Mark of Lord Voldemort appears after the conclusion of the Quidditch World Cup.

Cleansweep Seven: An older model flying broom.

Clearwater, Penelope: A Ravenclaw prefect who is attacked by the basilisk. She is revealed to be Percy Weasley's girlfriend.

Cliodna: A druidess found in the card series Famous Witches and Wizards.

Cockatrice: In a Triwizard Tournament in 1792, three champions were injured when this creature, which they were supposed to catch, went on a rampage.

Cockroach Clusters: A munchy, crunchy candy at Honeydukes.

Coconut Ice: A confectionary found at Honeydukes.

Collectible Figures of Players: Sold at the Quidditch World Cup, these miniature figures are animated and preen themselves.

Colloportus: A door-sealing charm used by Hermione Granger in the Department of Mysteries.

Color-Change: A charm used to change colors. Harry Potter, when he was taking his O.W.L.s, was flustered and used a Growth Charm instead; the result—the rat, which was supposed to turn orange, grew to the size of a badger.

Comet 260: An older flying broom.

Committee for the Disposal of Dangerous Creatures: A committee comprised of Hogwarts School governors that answers to the Ministry of Magic, it decides that after Lucius Malfoy complains about the "attack" of the hippogriff Buckbeak against his son, Draco, the creature must be "tethered and isolated" until a determination is made as to what proper course of action should be taken; the order is signed by the school governors of Hogwarts.

Committee on Experimental Charms: A committee within the Ministry of Magic.

Common Magical Ailments and Afflictions: A standard reference book commonly found in magical households. (The real-world equivalent would likely be the *Physicians' Desk Reference*.)

Common Room: Each house at Hogwarts has its own common room where students from that house mingle.

Common Welsh Green: A dragon used in the first competition at the Triwizard Tournament held at Hogwarts.

A Compendium of Common Curses and Their Counter-Actions: A book Hermione Granger finds in the Room of Requirement.

Confundus Charm: Used to bewitch someone or something. Professor

Snape tells the Minister of Magic that Sirius Black obviously used this charm to confuse Harry Potter, Ron Weasley, and Hermione Granger. It was apparently used by Lord Voldemort (or one of his minions) to confuse the Goblet of Fire, which selected an unheard-of *fourth* champion, and an ineligible one, at that—Harry Potter.

Confusing Concoction: A potion Harry Potter brews, with less than successful results, for Potions class.

Conjunctivitus Curse: Used by Viktor Krum when he had to face a Chinese Fireball dragon in his first trial at the Triwizard Tournament; it's also used to save Hagrid from the giants.

Corned Beef: The sandwiches Molly Weasley usually packs for Ron for his journey on the Hogwarts Express to the school. (Once she surprised him with sandwiches that were *not* made of corned beef.)

Corner, Michael: A Hogwarts student who dates Cho Chang after Harry Potter's relationship with her doesn't work out.

Cornish Pixies: Small (eight inches) blue impish creatures, which soon get out of control and create pandemonium when they are unleashed by Gilderoy Lockhart in his class.

Crabbe, Vincent: A big git of a sidekick of Draco Malfoy, from Slytherin house.

Cragg, Elfrida: Her portrait hangs in Hogwarts. Everard, who has been moving from picture to picture in the school to find news about Arthur Weasley after Harry Potter tells Dumbledore that he had a vision that Weasley was attacked by a snake, reports from Cragg's portrait that Weasley looks in bad shape.

Creevey, Colin: A beamish Gryffindor boy who dotes on and goes out of his way to meet Harry Potter, he's frequently seen with a camera. He has a Muggle father.

Creevey, Dennis: A Gryffindor student, he is Colin Creevey's younger brother.

Croaker: An Unspeakable who works for the top-secret Department of Mysteries at the Ministry of Magic.

Crouch, Bartemius: A wizard who, according to Ludo Bagman, can speak 150 languages. But Percy Weasley corrects him, saying Mr. Crouch can speak over 200, including "Mermish and Gobbledegook and Troll . . ." A former Head of the Department of Magical Law Enforcement and slated to become the Minister of Magic until he became overzealous in his job—authorizing Aurors to kill and using the Unforgivable Curses against suspects—Crouch was the wizard who sentenced Sirius Black to Azkaban, without the benefit of a trial.

Note: His son, Barty Crouch Jr., is condemned to Azkaban, but escapes to Hogwarts and in a devious plot assists Lord Voldemort to deliver Harry Potter to Voldemort and his Death Eaters. Veritaserum is used to get the details of the plot out of Barty Crouch Jr., who is killed when he receives a dreaded Dementor's kiss, which sucks out the victim's soul.

Cruciatus Curse: One of three Unforgivable Curses, it inflicts unbearable pain on a living creature. The command is *Crucio*. Using it against another person rates a life sentence in Azkaban. (See also Imperius Curse and Killing Curse.)

Crumple-Horned Snorkack: Luna Lovegood, whose father edits a tabloid rag, believes these exist, but Hermione Granger sets her straight: they don't.

Crup: A creature resembling a Jack Russell terrier, which Hagrid shows his students in his class, Care of Magical Creatures.

Crystal Gazing: A form of divination Professor Trelawney puts considerable stock in, but one that Hermione Granger does not.

D

Dai Llewellyn Ward: The ward at St. Mungo's Hospital for Magical Maladies and Injuries where Arthur Weasley is being treated, by Healer-in-Charge Hippocrates Smetywyck and Augustus Pye as Trainee Healer.

Daily Prophet: The daily newspaper that serves the wizard community. One of its reporters is Rita Skeeter, who lives up to her namesake (mosquito). Unlike an ordinary newspaper with still photos, this paper's photos move. A photo of the Dursleys in Egypt, for instance, is not static; it shows the whole family waving to the reader.

Dancing Shamrock Hat: Sold at the Quidditch World Cup.

The Dark Arts Outsmarted: A book Hermione Granger finds in the Room of Requirement.

Dark Detectors: Tools used by Aurors to detect the presence of dark magicians. Professor Moody had several of these in his office at Hogwarts.

The Dark Forces: A Guide to Self-Protection: A textbook required for Professor Moody's Defense Against the Dark Arts class.

Death Eaters: Followers of Lord Voldemort.

Death Eaters at Department of Mysteries: Lord Voldemort is present at the Department with his acolytes, including Lucius Malfoy, Nott, Jugson, Bellatrix, Rodolphus, Crabbe, Rabastan, Jogson, Dolohov, Macnair, Avery, Rockwood, and Mulciber.

Death Omens: What to Do When You Know the Worst is Coming: A book found at Flourish and Blotts, which the store manager does not recommend, on the basis that reading it is too suggestive—the reader will tend to see death omens everywhere.

Deathday Party: The opposite of a birthday party, a Deathday party celebrates the anniversary of one's death. Nearly Headless Nick celebrates his 500th anniversary as a ghost, and throws a Deathday party to celebrate in appropriate ghoulish fashion. He died on October 31, 1492.

Decree for the Reasonable Restriction of Underage Sorcery, 1875, Paragraph C: A Decree from the Ministry of Magic that allows expulsion from school if a student (underaged wizard) uses magic outside of school grounds. Harry Potter gets an owl-delivered letter citing this Decree after it appears he's used a levitation charm. The letter is signed by Mafalda Hopkirk, from Improper Use of Magic Office, Ministry of Magic. He accidentally violates it by inflating Aunt Marge; and he deliberately violates it (though in this case it is permissible) and uses a Patronus charm to protect himself and Dudley Dursley from Dementors that, to his surprise, show up in the Muggles neighborhood where the Dursleys live.

Defense Against the Dark Arts: A class at Hogwarts, the faculty staffing of which is transient in nature. Each year this post was occupied by a different person. In order: Professor Quirrell, Gilderoy Lockhart, Professor Lupin (highly qualified), Alastor "Mad Eye" Moody, and, from the Ministry of Magic, Dolores Umbridge.

The Defense Association (DA): A name proposed by Cho Chang for Harry Potter's unofficial Defense Against the Dark Arts class.

Defensive Magical Theory: A textbook by Wilbert Slinkhard, required by Professor Umbridge in her class, Defense Against the Dark Arts.

Deflagration Deluxe: Fireworks sold by Fred and George Weasley, costing 20 Galleons. Used to disrupt classes at Hogwarts after Umbridge is appointed Head of Hogwarts.

Deflating Draft: The antidote to the Swelling Solution.

De-Gnoming the Garden: Once the garden is infested with Gnomes, the only way to get rid of them, albeit temporarily, is to swing them around, dizzying them, and release them so they sail through the air and land, disoriented, unable to find their way back to their Gnome-holes dug in the garden. (The commotion is enough to cause other Gnomes to come out of their holes to see what all the fuss about, resulting in their De-Gnoming.) Not terribly bright, Gnomes are small, leathery, and bald, and have (as Harry Potter found out) razor-sharp teeth.

Delacour, Fleur: The Beauxbatons champion for the Triwizard Tournament, she's tall and beautiful, and part veela. (Her wand has one hair from the head of a veela.) After graduation, she gets a job at Gringotts.

Delacour, Gabrielle: Fleur Delacour's little sister.

Delaney-Podmore, Sir Patrick: Unlike Nearly Headless Nick, Sir Delaney-Podmore was properly decapitated and participates in the Headless Hunt. He writes a rejection letter to Nick, whose head literally hangs by a thread, citing his failure to meet the headless qualification as reason for denial of his request to join the Hunt—to Nick's endless frustration.

Deletrius: A deletion charm.

Dementor: A sightless, wraithlike figure in black recalling the Ring Wraiths in Tolkien's *The Lord of the Rings.* These shadowy figures are the guards at the wizard prison, Azkaban, and are posted on the school grounds at Hogwarts when Sirius Black is on the loose and presumably looking for Harry Potter. Their presence is so dispiriting that you feel cold, chilled to the soul, and as though you'll never be happy again.

Dementor's Kiss: Clamping its jaw on a human mouth, the Dementor sucks the soul out of a person, leaving only a human shell. (The Ministry of Magic has given permission for the Dementors to give Sirius Black such a kiss if he's encountered.)

Densaugeo: A spell cast by Draco Malfoy in an impromptu duel with Harry Potter. The spell ricochets off Harry, though, and hits Hermione, whose front teeth grow to an abnormally large size, past her collar.

Department of International Magical Cooperation: A department within the Ministry of Magic, this is where Percy Weasley works. Its department head is Mr. Bartemius Crouch.

Department of Magical Games and Sports: A department in the Ministry of Magic headed by Ludo Bagman, it is responsible for coordinating the logistics of the Quidditch World Cup.

Department of Mysteries: Located at the Ministry of Magic, it is where Harry, Ron, and Hermione, aided by members of the Order of the Phoenix, confront Lord Voldemort and his Death Eaters. The room contains . . . oops, that's Top Secret!

Dervish and Banges: A wizarding equipment shop in Hogsmeade.

Derwent, Dilys: A famous witch whose framed portrait hangs not only in Dumbledore's office but also in wizarding institutions worldwide. Once a headmistress at Hogwarts, she can move between her portraits there and those at other institutions as well. She tells Dumbledore that Arthur Weasley was taken to St. Mungo's Hospital. She was a healer at St. Mungo's from 1722 to 1741, and a headmistress at Hogwarts from 1741 to 1768.

Detachable Cribbing Cuffs: Another cheating aid banned from use during O.W.L. exams.

Devil's Snare: A plant with living tendrils to ensnare, hold, and squeeze its victim.

Diagon Alley: A narrow street crammed with stores catering to the wizarding community. Among its many stores: an Apothecary, Eeylops Owl Emporium, Gringotts, Madam Malkin's Robes for All Occasions, Ollivanders: Makers of Fine Wands, Quality Quidditch Supplies, Gambol and Japes Wizarding Joke Shop (a favorite of Fred and George Weasley), and Flourish and Blotts. Among those stores' wares: cauldrons, robes, telescopes, owls, and wands.

Diddy: An affectionate name Mrs. Dursley calls her son, Dudley.

Diffindo: A charm Harry Potter uses to split open Cedric Diggory's bag, spilling its contents of books and bottles of ink, since Harry wants to separate Cedric from his friends, who continue on to class at Cedric's urging. This gives Harry an opportunity to share what he knows about the first challenge in the Triwizard Tournament.

Diggle, Dedalus: An excitable wizard whose main attribute is his lack of common sense. (When shooting stars are seen in Kent, Professor McGonagall immediately thinks it's Diggle's doings.) Also a member of the Advance Guard.

Diggory, Amos: A wizard who works at the Ministry of Magic in the Department for the Regulation and Control of Magical Creatures. Cedric Diggory's father.

Diggory, Cedric: In the third book, Hufflepuff's new Quidditch team captain. A handsome boy and a prefect, he's one of four champions at the Triwizard Tournament. Along with Harry Potter, he touches the Triwizard Cup, a Portkey, and is transported to a remote graveyard, where Lord Voldemort and his Death Eaters have been waiting. Diggory gets the full brunt of the killing curse, *Avada Kedavra.*

Dingle's Powdered Dragon Claw: Another reputedly powerful stimulant that promises to help students as they prepare to take their O.W.L.s in their fifth year.

Dinky Diddydums: Another nauseatingly affectionate term Mrs. Dursley calls her son, Dudley.

Dipper, Armando: Headmaster at Hogwarts when Tom Marvolo Riddle (anagram: "I am Lord Voldemort") was a 16-year-old student, 50 years ago.

Disapparate: The act of disappearing. A form of travel used only by experienced witches and wizards, this allows one to disappear and reappear instantly elsewhere at will. (Underage wizards, i.e., students, cannot use this method of transportation since it is risky.)

Disciplinary Hearing: Harry Potter undergoes one at the Ministry of Magic because of alleged offenses. His interrogators: Cornelius Fudge, Amelia Susan Bones, and Dolores Jane Umbridge. The hearing is witnessed by Percy Weasley as court scribe. For the defense: Albus Dumbledore and Arabella Figg.

Disillusionment Charm: Used to make a person or thing blend in with its surroundings, like a chameleon. Used on Harry Potter when the Advance Guard come to get him.

Dissendium: A command Harry Potter uses to open a statue to gain admittance to a secret passage revealed by the Marauder's Map, which allows him to get to Hogsmeade, the wizarding village he is not allowed to visit because he lacks guardian permission.

Dobbs, Emma: A Hufflepuff student.

Dobby: A house-elf belonging to the Malfoy family who shows up unannounced at the Dursley house to beg Harry Potter not to return to Hogwarts, citing grave concerns for his health. Dobby, who has "bat-like ears and bulging green eyes" and is shabbily dressed, will stop at nothing to prevent Potter's return to school. He intercepts and withholds Potter's mail, creates a domestic disturbance at the Dursley home involving a floating dessert, blocks Harry Potter and Ron Weasley from passing through the barrier at King's Cross station when they attempt to catch the Hogwarts Express, and enchants a Bludger during a Quidditch game to injure Harry, all means to Harry's end at Hogwarts. Dobby can only be freed if his master gives him clothes, which Harry tricks Lucius Malfoy into doing—to Malfoy's surprise and extreme displeasure since it costs him his valued (but mistreated) house-elf, who has very powerful magical abilities. Dobby, who always speaks in the third person, must punish himself if he in any way criticizes his master's household, even when it's richly deserved.

Dr. Filibuster's Fabulous Wet-Start: A novelty found at Gambol and Japes Wizarding Joke Shop.

Dr. Ubbly's Oblivious Unction: Used by Madam Pomfrey on Harry Potter after brain tentacles had scarred him in the Department of Mysteries at the Ministry of Magic.

Dolohov, Antonin: A supporter of the Dark Lord, betrayed by Karkaroff, he was convicted of murdering Gideon and Fabian Prewett.

Double Charms: A class taken by fifth-year students.

Double Transfiguration: A class taken by fifth-year students.

Doxycide: A magical pesticide that will paralyze a doxy, a common household pest.

Dragon Breeding for Pleasure and Profit: A reference book, somewhat outdated, from the Hogwarts Library, which Hagrid consults, since he's waiting for a dragon's egg to hatch. The dragon is a Norwegian Ridgeback that Hagrid names Norbert.

Dragon Dung: Fred and George Weasley sent this to bedevil their persnickety brother Percy, who refused to believe it was anything but a sample of fertilizer from Norway.

Dragon Species of Great Britain and Ireland: Reference book about dragons.

Draught of Living Death: A powerful sleeping potion made from asphodel and wormwood.

Draught of Peace: A potion "to calm anxiety and soothe agitation," says Professor Snape.

Dreadful Denizens of the Deep, or Powers You Never Knew You Had and What to Do with Them Now You've Wised Up: A library book Harry Potter consults in hopes that it will help him with his second trial at the Triwizard Tournament.

The Dream Oracle: Written by Inogo Imago, this book discusses dream interpretation. Professor Trelawney uses it in her class.

Droobles Best Blowing Gum: A "special effects" blue-colored gum that won't pop for several days.

Dudders: A nickname of Dudley Dursley used by his excessively doting parents.

Dudley's Gang: Dudley Dursley's friends: Piers, Dennis, Malcolm, and Gordon, all "big and stupid."

Dueling Club: After suspicious events occur at Hogwarts, Dumbledore allows Gilderoy Lockhart to give wand-dueling lessons for self-protection. His "assistant," Professor Snape, is more skilled, obvious to all when both practice a duel at which Lockhart gets the wind (and bluster) knocked out of him.

Dumbledore, Aberforth: Albus Dumbledore's brother, who "was prosecuted for practicing inappropriate charms on a goat."

Dumbledore, Albus Percival Wulfric Brian: The headmaster at Hogwarts, considered to be the most powerful wizard of his time. Wise and benevolent, Dumbledore is the voice of reason, especially at times when things are chaotic. (Rowling says the word "dumbledore" is derived from "bumblebee.") Dumbledore's credits include "Order of Merlin, First Class, Grand Sorc., Chf. Warlock, Supreme Mugwump, International Confed. of Wizards." A famous wizard, he's part of the wizard world's popular culture, with a trading card which summarizes his notable achievements.

Dumbledore's Army (DA): A name proposed by Ginny Weasley for Harry Potter's unofficial Defense Against the Dark Arts class.

Durmstrang: Located in Germany, it is one of three highly regarded magical schools in Europe, though it has a reputation for emphasizing the Dark Arts.

Dursley, Dudley: The only child of Vernon and Petunia Dursley, Dudley is, as his name suggests, a dud of a human being. Excessively indulged as a child, an endless whiner who took every opportunity to bully Harry Potter for years, until he grew to fear his cousin because of his magical skills, Dudley is accurately described by Ron Weasley (Harry's best friend) as a bullying git.

Dursley, Marjorie (Aunt Marge): A monstrous woman, she is Vernon Dursley's sister. This self-inflated, self-righteous woman balloons up in size and floats to the ceiling after Harry Potter accidentally causes her to do so. (When Harry gets angered to the boiling point, he can sometimes make things happen, even without his conscious intent. This incident parallels a similar one in which he makes a glass window disappear at the reptile house at the London Zoo, causing Dudley Dursley to fall into the display.)

Dursley, Petunia: Harry Potter's aunt, described as a horse-faced, bony blonde with an unusually giraffe-like neck, which suits her perfectly, since she enjoys craning it to spy on her neighbors. A busybody who is excessively concerned about appearances and about what her neighbors think, she also knows more about the wizard world than she lets on to her family. Like her husband, she dotes on their son, Dudley, whom they have indulged to excess.

Dursley, Vernon: Harry Potter's uncle. An unimaginative "big, beefy man," he resents having Harry Potter at his home, and takes every opportunity to keep Harry in what he considers to be his proper place.

Dwarves: Employed by Gilderoy Lockhart to deliver valentines at Hogwarts, to everyone's embarrassment. (Harry Potter gets a dwarf-delivered valentine card from Ginny Weasley, which proves to be mutually embarrassing when Draco Malfoy brings it to everyone's attention.)

E

Eagle Owl: The species of owl owned by Draco Malfoy.

Edgecombe, Marietta: A friend of Cho Chang, her mother is Madam Edgecombe, who works at the Ministry of Magic in the Department of Magical Transportation, Floo Network. Marietta betrays Harry Potter and tells Professor Umbridge of the secret class he's been teaching.

Educational Decree 22: It allows the Ministry to appoint a professor at Hogwarts if the headmaster fails to do so.

Educational Decree 23: It creates a new position at Hogwarts, the High Inquisitor, who has broad powers to evaluate its teachers.

Educational Decree 24: It prohibits any student-organized gathering. Three or more students is considered a gathering. Expulsion is the penalty for disobedience.

Educational Decree 25: It gives the High Inquisitor, not the heads of the houses at Hogwarts, the power to punish students for infractions.

Educational Decree 26: It prohibits teachers from discussing with students anything outside their subject matter.

Educational Decree 27: It prohibits students, under pain of expulsion, from having in their possession a copy of the *Quibbler,* after it ran an interview with Harry Potter in which he talks about the return of Lord Voldemort and his Death Eaters. High Inquisitor Umbridge also takes 50 points from Gryffindor and assigns a week's worth of detentions to punish Harry Potter for his transgressions; she does this repeatedly.

Educational Decree 28: It appoints High Inquisitor Umbridge as the Head of Hogwarts after Headmaster Dumbledore is relieved of his duties.

Elderflower Wine: A beverage enjoyed by Percy Weasley.

Elladora, Aunt: A member of the Black family, she instituted the tradition of beheading house-elves when they outlived their usefulness.

Enchanted Windows: Windows that show whatever weather Magical Maintenance (at the Ministry of Magic) wants to show. When Harry Potter and Arthur Weasley go to the Ministry to attend Potter's trial, the magical windows show a bright, sunny day outside, though they are underground.

Enchantment in Baking: A cookbook found in Mrs. Weasley's kitchen.

Encyclopedia of Toadstools: A reference book at Flourish and Blotts that, during a spirited fight between Lucius Malfoy and Arthur Weasley, hits Malfoy's eye.

Engorgement Charm: Used to make objects or things grow. Hagrid uses it to grow extra-large pumpkins. Dudley Dursley is apparently afflicted with it, after eating brightly colored toffee candy deliberately dropped by the inveterate pranksters Fred and George Weasley.

Enlarging Spell: Used to make more room, though outward appearances don't show it. Most often used to make a car larger inside, to accommodate more people than it could normally carry.

Ennervate: A charm used to energize someone hit by a stunner.

Eric: A security wizard at the Ministry of Magic who in-processes Harry Potter and retains his wand for safekeeping. He's fond of reading the *Daily Prophet* when he's not otherwise occupied.

Errol: The Weasleys' family owl known for being somewhat clumsy.

Evanesco: A vanishing charm. Professor Snape uses it to get rid of a badly mixed batch of potion that Harry Potter made.

Evans, Lily: Lily Potter's maiden name.

Evening Prophet: The evening edition of the *Daily Prophet.*

Everard: A renowned wizard and former headmaster whose framed portrait hangs in several locations at Hogwarts, including Dumbledore's office, and also in wizarding institutions worldwide.

Ever-Bashing Boomerang: Caretaker Mr. Filch at Hogwarts Castle has cited this as a banned item for students.

Expecto Patronum: The incantation required to conjure up a Patronus charm. Harry Potter uses it for the first time at a Quidditch match at which he spies what appears to be a group of Dementors but in fact turns out to be Draco Malfoy and his cronies trying to give Potter a scare.

Expelliarmus: A disarming charm that produces a blast of light and a charge that will knock the victim off his or her feet. Professor Snape uses it against Gilderoy Lockhart in a mock duel in front of the student body.

"Explain Why Muggles Need Electricity": An essay Hermione Granger has to write for her class on Muggle Studies.

Exploding Bon-Bons: A "special effects" candy available at Honeydukes.

Exploding Snap: A favorite wizard's game, it is favored by Neville Longbottom.

Extendable Ears: Invented by Fred and George Weasley, this pair of elongated magical ears allows them to snoop from a safe distance.

Extinguishing Spell: Charlie Weasley, on site with other wizards controlling a pen of four dragons to be used in a Triwizard Tournament, says this spell should be at the ready in case things get out of hand with them.

F

Fainting Fancies: Invented by Fred and George Weasley.

Fairy Lights: Password to enter the Gryffindor common room.

Fake Wand: A joke gift invented by Fred and George Weasley. When used, this makes a loud squeaking sound and turns into a "giant rubber mouse." In appearance, fake wands are indistinguishable from real wands, so it's easy to get them confused.

Fang: Hagrid's pet, a black boarhound.

Fanged Frisbees: Caretaker Mr. Filch at Hogwarts Castle has cited these as a banned item for students.

Fanged Geranium: A plant that bit Harry Potter during his Herbology exam for his O.W.L.s.

Fantastic Beasts and Where to Find Them: A standard textbook written by Newt Scamander. (The book's real author is Rowling.)

The Fat Friar: House ghost of Hufflepuff.

The Fat Lady: Her framed portrait bars the round hole that opens to allow passage into the Gryffindor common room, if you know the password. In the first book, the first password used is Caput Draconis, the second is Pig Snout, the third is Wattlebird.

Fawkes: A phoenix that belongs to Dumbledore, Fawkes (like others of his kind) has three main virtues: he is able to carry heavy loads, his tears have

the ability to heal, and he is an extremely faithful pet. Fawkes gave only two feathers for wands—one owned by Lord Voldemort and the other owned by Harry Potter.

Ferret: After Draco Malfoy attacks Harry Potter from behind, Mad-Eye Moody teaches Draco a lesson by turning him into a white ferret, which Moody then bounces up and down until he's stopped by a furious Professor McGonagall.

Ferula: A charm Professor Lupin uses to wind and bind bandages around Ron Weasley's broken leg.

Fever Fudge: Invented by Fred and George Weasley, this unperfected fudge produces fever when eaten, but it has an unexpected side effect: it also produces large boils on the victim's rear end.

Fidelius Charm: A complex spell used to conceal a secret within a person, called the Secret-Keeper. Sirius Black is the Secret-Keeper for James Potter, Harry Potter's father.

Figg, Arabella Doreen: Perceived as a Muggle who is excessively devoted to her cats, this old lady is, in fact, a Squib—she has no magical abilities, though her parents do. She lives on Wisteria Walk near the Dursleys, and has been tasked with a secret mission: Dumbledore has instructed her to keep an eye on Harry Potter.

Filch, Argus: The cranky caretaker at Hogwarts who believes in draconian punishments for relatively minor offenses. He owns a cat, Mrs. Norris, that is petrified by the basilisk, for which he blames Harry Potter. He's a Squib, but doesn't like others to know, so he's taken correspondence courses to learn magic.

Filibuster Fireworks: A joke novelty favored by George Weasley, likely purchased at Gambol and Japes Wizarding Joke Shop. The fireworks throw out "stars and sparks."

Finch-Fletchley, Justin: A Hufflepuff student.

Finite Incantatem: A charm used by Snape to counteract the effects of the *Tarantallegra* charm used by Draco Malfoy against Harry Potter.

Finnigan, Seamus: A Gryffindor student whose best friend is Dean Thomas. Seamus's favorite Quidditch team is the Kenmare Kestrels.

Firebolt: The latest model broom, which can travel up to 150 miles per hour. Displayed in the window of Quality Quidditch Supplies, it has no price tag; customers are invited to inquire. Obviously, owning this state-of-the-art broom gives any Quidditch team an edge, which is why the Irish

International Side, favored for the World Cup, placed an order for seven of them, according to the store owner. After Harry loses his Nimbus 2000 to the Whomping Willow, he receives a Firebolt as a gift from an unknown source, who turns out to be Sirius Black.

Fire-Crab: For their O.W.L. exam in Care of Magical Creatures, students must handle this creature without burning themselves.

Firenze: A centaur who is selected by Dumbledore to replace Professor Trelawney after she's fired by High Inquisitor Umbridge. Firenze lives in the Forbidden Forest but was banished by his tribe after accepting the teaching position at Hogwarts. He tells his students that, unlike Professor Trelawney, who because she's human may be a Seer but cannot see beyond her self-imposed limitations, his kind see the stars and patiently wait, years if necessary, to glean the truth.

Fizzing Whizbees: (1) Levitating sherbet balls, a candy found at Honeydukes. (2) Password used to gain entry to Dumbledore's office, guarded by a stone gargoyle that will come alive and move aside as the wall behind him opens, revealing a staircase that spirals upward.

Flagrate: A charm used to put a flaming mark on an object. Hermione Granger performs this charm in the Department of Mysteries at the Ministry of Magic when, in the dark, revolving doors make it difficult to determine which ones they had already gone through in their search for the right one. By using this charm, she could mark the doors.

Flame Freezing Charm: Used to nullify the effects of fire, it produces a tickling sensation in the "victim" being burned at the stake.

Flamel, Nicholas: A former partner of Albus Dumbledore, Flamel was noted for his work in alchemy and created the Sorcerer's Stone.

Fleet, Angus: A Muggle man who lives in Peebles, he sees the flying Ford Anglia before Ron Weasley renders it invisible by pressing its Invisibility Booster.

Fleetwood's High-Finish Polish: A component of the Broomstick Servicing Kit, it is used to polish a broom's handle.

Flesh-Eating Slug Repellent: Sought by Hagrid, who wants to sprinkle it around the grounds at Hogwarts to ward off the slugs that are eating the school cabbages.

Fletcher, Mundungus: A wizard who was on lookout duty to protect Harry Potter in Little Whinging, but abandons his post to investigate a possible deal with cauldrons, to Mrs. Figg's fury.

Flibbertigibbet: A password used to get into Gryffindor's common room.

Flint, Marcus: A Slytherin student, the Captain of his house Quidditch team.

Flitwick, Professor Filius: A member of the faculty at Hogwarts, he teaches Charms.

Flobberworms: Fond of shredding lettuce, these boring creatures are the subject of a class taught by Rubeus Hagrid.

Floo Powder: A means of traveling from chimney to chimney (Floo = "flew" and chimney "flue"); one takes a handful and throws it on the ground, taking care to speak the destination clearly, lest one arrive at an unexpected destination. (Harry Potter uses it for the first time and, mispronouncing the destination, winds up in nearby Knockturn Alley, the bad part of town.) Note: Brooms, of course, are a favorite form of transportation, but weather can sometimes be a problem. Other methods of self-transportation include Apparating (vanishing and reappearing at will), which requires skill and thus is not used by younger wizards, and using a Portkey, which is a form of mass transportation.

Floo Regulation Panel: A panel at the Ministry of Magic that regulates transportation by Floo powder. In rare instances, it allows connection to a Muggle fireplace, as is the case when the Dursley's fireplace is connected to the Floo network to allow Mr. Weasley and his sons to pick up Harry Potter for the Quidditch World Cup.

Florean Fortescue's Ice Cream Parlor: A store in Diagon Alley, where Harry Potter enjoys free sundaes from its proprietor, Florean Fortescue, who is fortuitously an expert on medieval witch burnings, the topic of an essay Harry Potter was assigned to write for school.

Flourish and Blotts: A wizard bookstore in Diagon Alley, where Gilderoy Lockhart signs his latest book, *Magical Me*.

Fluffy: A large three-headed dog belonging to Hagrid, who bought it from a Greek man he met at a pub. Fluffy guards the Sorcerer's Stone at Hogwarts.

Flying with the Cannons: A book about a Quidditch team, the Chudley Cannons, Ron Weasley's favorite team.

Foe-Glass: A dark detector, a mirror that shows skulkers. Professor Moody had one in his office when he taught at Hogwarts.

Forbidden Forest: The forest that flanks the school grounds at Hogwarts; students are forbidden to enter it.

Ford Anglia: A turquoise car that Mr. Weasley enchanted so it could fly. Ron, George, and Fred Weasley use the car to engineer Harry Potter's escape through the barred window of his bedroom at the Dursleys' house. After failing to get through the brick wall to Platform Nine and Three-Quarters, Ron and Harry fly the car to Hogwarts. Muggles see the car en route, for which the Ministry of Magic fines Mr. Weasley 50 Galleons for illegally bewitching it.

Forests of Albania: Lord Voldemort was thought to be hiding out here, according to sources providing information to Dumbledore.

Fornunculus: A spell Harry Potter casts in an impromptu duel with Draco Malfoy. The spell ricochets off Draco, however, and hits Goyle, who develops large ugly boils on his face.

Fortuna Major: A password required to gain entry to the Gryffindor common room.

Fountain of Magical Brethern: Located in the lobby of the Ministry of Magic, it consists of a circular pool surrounded by golden statues of a wizard, a witch, a centaur, a goblin, and a house-elf. Coins thrown in the pool are retrieved, with all proceeds going to St. Mungo's Hospital for Magical Maladies and Injuries.

Four-Point Spell: Used to make one's wand point to true north.

Fowl or Foul? A Study of Hippogriff Brutality: A book Ron Weasley consults to assist Hagrid in his defense of Buckbeak.

Freezing Charm: Used to immobilize. Hermione Granger uses it to immobilize the Cornish pixies unleashed by Gilderoy Lockhart.

Frog Spawn Soap: A magical joke item sold by Zonko's.

From Egg to Inferno, A Dragon Keeper's Guide: Reference book about dragons.

Fubster, Colonel: A retired military officer who looks after Aunt Marge's 12 dogs when she's not at home.

Fudge, Cornelius: The Minister of Magic. A portly man, he is more a career bureaucrat and clearly not the wizard that Dumbledore is; in fact, Fudge, soon after taking the position, starts sending owls to Hogwarts on a frequent basis, relying excessively on Dumbledore's superior knowledge.

Fuse-Wire and Screwdrivers: Gifts from Harry Potter to Arthur Weasley, who is fond of Muggle artifacts.

G

Gadding with Ghouls: A classroom textbook by Gilderoy Lockhart.

Galleons: Wizard currency. A gold coin, a Galleon is worth 17 silver Sickles (a Sickle, in turn, is worth 29 brass Knuts).

Gambol and Japes Wizarding Joke Shop: A retail store that is very popular among Hogwarts students, especially Fred and George Weasley, who are developing their own line of similar products.

Garroting Gas: A magical joke novelty, it temporarily produces a choking sensation.

Ghoul: The well-off wizard household has a house-elf, but the impoverished Weasley family has a clanking ghoul, an annoying but (to the Weasleys) endearing creature.

Giant Squid: An inhabitant of the lake across the grounds in front of the Hogwarts school.

Giants: Vicious by nature, this race is nearly extinct, hunted down by Aurors. Rubeus Hagrid's mother was a giantess.

Gilderoy Lockhart's Guide to Household Pests: A reference book found in Mrs. Weasley's kitchen.

Gillywater: A beverage served at the Three Broomsticks, favored by Professor McGonagall.

Gillyweed: Eating this allows one to breathe underwater—necessary for Harry Potter to survive the prolonged period underwater for his second trail at the Triwizard Tournament. This is a weed that temporarily transforms Harry into a merman with gills, webbed hands, and webbed feet. Dobby got the weed from Professor Snape's office and gave it to Harry.

Gladrags Wizardwear: A retail store in Hogsmeade where Harry Potter, Ron Weasley, and Hermione Granger go to buy Dobby a pair of ostentatious socks—the kind he favors.

Goblet of Fire: A wooden cup with blue-white flames, it chooses the champions for the Triwizard Tournament. Students who deem themselves worthy write their names and school name on parchment, and drop it in the Goblet of Fire, which will select the competing champions.

Goblins: They run Gringotts, the wizarding bank.

Gobstones: These are made of solid gold, and the closest Muggle equivalent is marbles, but with a difference. In this wizarding game in which one earns

points, the loser receives a nasty-smelling squirt of liquid from the opponent's gobstone.

Godric's Hollow: Lord Voldemort shows up here to find and then kill Harry Potter's parents, James and Lily Potter. He fails, however, to kill their son, "the boy who lived."

Golden Egg: Each champion competing at the Triwizard Tournament is given a golden egg, which has a clue hidden inside.

Golden Snitch: Quidditch term. A small bright-gold ball with silver wings that travels fast and can move erratically. It is the main prize in a Quidditch game, since its capture by a Seeker earns the team 150 points—usually enough to win any game, since it's the equivalent to 15 goals scored with the Quaffle. Catching the Snitch ends the game.

Goldstein, Anthony: A Ravenclaw student selected as a prefect.

Golgomath: This giant killed Karkus and took over his position as Gurg, the chieftain of the giants. Combative by nature, giants often fight one another.

Goshawk, Miranda: Author of *The Standard Book of Spells (Grade 1),* a required course book for first-year students at Hogwarts.

Goyle, Mr.: Father of Gregory Goyle; a Death Eater.

Goyle, Gregory: A large-sized Slytherin sidekick of Draco Malfoy.

Granger, Hermione: The daughter of Muggles (her parents are both dentists), Hermione distinguishes herself as a hard-working student (Gryffindor) who excels in the classroom. Though she gets off to a rocky start with Harry Potter and Ron Weasley, in time she becomes a close friend to both. In the fifth book, she becomes a prefect.

Grawp: Hagrid's half-brother, a giant, though a small one by giants' standards: a mere 16 feet tall. Hagrid hides him in the Forbidden Forest.

Great Hall: The dining hall at Hogwarts where students sit at long tables, the faculty sits at a head table, and the ceiling appears transparent (it is bewitched to show the sky above).

Great Wizarding Events of the Twentieth Century: A book Hermione Granger reads as background study before her first year at Hogwarts. Harry Potter is referenced therein.

Great Wizards of the Twentieth Century: A reference book found in the Hogwarts library.

Gregorovitch: A wand maker who produced the wand used by Viktor Krum. Krum's wand has a hornbeam and dragon heartstring.

The Grim: A death omen, according to Professor Trelawney.

Grindylow: A small, green, horned water demon with very strong fingers. (The best defense, says Professor Lupin, is to break its tenacious grip.)

Gringotts: The wizarding community's bank located in Diagon Alley in London. Guarded by goblins and, reputedly, dragons, its vaults are secured by magic and considered impenetrable. Unlike most banks, Gringotts is mostly subterranean, its vaults accessible only by railcars. Theft at the bank is rare. According to Hagrid, one can get lost wandering around down deep, encounter a dragon, or have to deal with a particularly nasty spell that guards a vault. The goblins warn everyone that it's best not to even try to break in.

Griphook: A goblin at Gringotts who takes Hagrid and Harry Potter to their respective vaults on Harry's first visit.

Growth Charm: Harry Potter mistakenly performs this charm for an O.W.L. exam; he should have used a color-change charm instead.

Grubbly-Plank, Professor: A witch who temporarily substitutes for Hagrid's class, Care of Magical Creatures.

Grunnings: Mr. Vernon Dursley works for this firm as its director. The company makes drills.

Grunnion, Alberic: Found in the card series Famous Witches and Wizards.

Gryffindor: A Hogwarts house founded by Godric Gryffindor; the house trait is bravery.

Gubraithian Fire: A gift from Dumbledore to Karkus, the Gurg (i.e., chieftain) of the giants. The branch was bewitched to produce everlasting fire.

Gudgeon, Davey: A student who nearly lost an eye by playing a favorite student game: trying to touch the trunk of the Whomping Willow.

Gudgeon, Gladys: Cited by Gilderoy Lockhart as one of his biggest fans.

A Guide to Advanced Transfiguration: A book Cedric Diggory was carrying to class when Harry Potter deliberately used a charm to open Cedric's bag.

A Guide to Medieval Sorcery: A library book Harry Potter consulted in the hopes that it would help him with his second trial at the Triwizard Tournament.

Gurg: The title held by the chief of the giants Hagrid visits, bearing gifts.

H

Hagrid, Rubeus: A half-giant, he's a former student at Hogwarts whose wand was broken in half after he was expelled in his third year. He is currently its gamekeeper and keykeeper and also a professor who teaches Care of Magical Creatures. His mother is a giantess named Fridwulfa. He stands, by one estimation, almost eight feet tall.

Hair-Thickening Charm: Professor Snape insisted that Alicia Spinnet, a Quidditch player, had suffered a self-inflicted charm, when in fact she was targeted, along with her other teammates, by Slytherin team members using this charm.

Hand of Glory: A severed hand mounted on a cushion. Harry Potter sees it in a store in Knockturn Alley. Put a candle in its hand and it gives light, but only to the owner. (It's the ideal gift for Draco Malfoy.)

The Handbook of Hippogriff Psychology: A book Ron Weasley consults and studies to assist Hagrid in his defense of Buckbeak.

The Hanged Man: The village pub in Little Hangleton where many debates were held regarding the mystery of what actually happened at the Riddle House—odd deaths took the lives of three members of the Riddle family.

Hannah, Abbott: Hufflepuff student selected as a prefect in her fifth year. As the O.W.L.s loom, she can't take the pressure and Madam Pomfrey has to give her a Calming Draught to soothe her nerves.

Hawkshead Attacking Formation: A Quidditch maneuver involving three players: one up, two back, in a flying wing.

Headless Hat: Fred and George Weasley invent these and are selling them for two Galleons each. Put it on and your head disappears. It incorporates an invisibility spell.

Headquarters of the Order of the Phoenix: Located on a Muggle street in London at number 12, Grimmauld Place.

Healers: The equivalent of doctors in the magical community.

Hedwig: A snowy owl, a gift from Rubeus Hagrid to Harry Potter.

Heir of Slytherin: Reputed to be the one who can open the hidden Chamber of Secrets. The presumption is that Harry Potter is the heir, since he is a Parselmouth (i.e., a person who can speak to snakes; the language itself is called Parseltongue).

Heliopaths: Tall fire spirits, according to Luna Lovegood, who has a propensity to believe in the existence of creatures other people do not.

Hengist of Woodcroft: Found in the card series Famous Witches and Wizards.

Heptomology: Professor Umbridge interrogates Professor Trelawney with questions about this difficult subject to unnerve her.

Hermy: The name Hagrid wants Hermione Granger to use when she's around his half-brother, Grawp, to whom he wants to teach English with her (and Harry Potter's) help.

Hiccup Sweets: A magical joke item sold by Zonko's.

Higgs, Terence: A Seeker for Slytherin. He was subsequently replaced by Draco Malfoy.

A Highly Biased and Selective ***History of Hogwarts, Which Glosses Over the Nastier Aspects of the School:*** A satirical book title Hermione Granger posed as a more accurate one for the book *Hogwarts, A History* because of its omission of information regarding house-elves.

Hinkypunk: Disarmingly nonthreatening in appearance, it's a one-legged creature that lures unwitting people into bogs.

Hippogriff: A magical creature, half-horse, half-bird, known for its pride. (Best not to insult them!) Rubeus Hagrid introduces third-year Hogwarts students to them in his first class as a teacher of Care of Magical Creatures. Unlike unicorns, who consider carrying people an act beneath them, hippogriffs will bear people.

History of Magic: Considered by all to be the most boring class in the curriculum, taught by Professor Binns, who is a spirit; he left his body behind when getting up one morning to teach class.

Hit Wizards: Highly trained wizards from the Magical Law Enforcement Squad.

Hog's Head: A run-down bar in Hogsmeade, it's a sharp contrast to the cleanliness of the Three Broomsticks, which Harry Potter, Ronald Weasley, and Hermione Granger usually patronize.

Hogsmeade: A wizarding village, the only one of its kind in England, which Hogwarts' third-year (and above) students are allowed to attend on weekends.

Hogsmeade Post Office: Two hundred owls, color-coded for speed of delivery, are used for air-mail deliveries.

Hogwarts, A History: The school history of more than a thousand pages. Along with other books, it formed background reading for Hermione Granger, who read it before arriving at Hogwarts.

Hogwarts Express: The train that runs between King's Cross station and Hogsmeade station, carrying students to and from Hogwarts. From King's Cross station, it's accessible only via Platform Nine and Three-Quarters.

Hogwarts School of Witchcraft and Wizardry: The school for witches and wizards that Harry Potter attends. Its headmaster is Albus Dumbledore. According to Rowling, it is physically located north of Scotland. Founded over a thousand years ago, it is only one of three such schools in Europe.

Holidays with Hags: A classroom textbook by Gilderoy Lockhart.

Home Life and Social Habits of British Muggles: A book Hermione Granger studies for her class on Muggle Studies.

Homework Planner: Ron Weasley gets one as a Christmas gift from Hermione Granger. Whenever he opens it, it nags him, urging him to improve his study habits.

Honeydukes: A candy store in Hogsmeade that sells an enchanting (in every sense of the word) selection of delectables; renowned for its great selection.

Honeydukes Chocolates: Candy sold at Honeydukes (a candy shop in Hogsmeade), Harry Potter gets these chocolates as birthday presents from both Ron Weasley and Hermione Granger.

Hooch, Madam: A faculty member at Hogwarts. She teaches broomstick flying and referees Quidditch matches.

Hopkirk, Mafalda: Civil servant, an employee in the Improper Use of Magic Office at the Ministry of Magic; she signs off on letters when violations occur.

Hornby, Olive: A classmate of Moaning Myrtle at Hogwarts who went into the girls' bathroom to inquire about her at the request of Professor Dippet.

House-Elf Liberation Front: Ron Weasley's pejorative term for Hermione Granger's effort to give a voice in the magical community to house-elves.

Hover Charm: A charm used to make an object hover in midair.

Howler: Arriving in a red envelope, it is a piece of enchanted mail that literally shouts its message at top volume. After the message is read, it bursts into flame, disintegrating into pieces, presumably showering the recipient with confetti and, worse, covering him or her in shame. After commandeering the magical Ford Anglia, Ron Weasley receives a Howler from his

mother, delivered in the Great Hall at Hogwarts as the student body and faculty are eating breakfast. Oh, the shame. Neville Longbottom receives one from his grandmother after he compromises security at a trying time by writing down Gryffindor passwords.

Hufflepuff: Founded by Helga Hufflepuff, it is one of four houses at Hogwarts; the house trait is loyalty.

Humongous Bighead: An insulting variation on the abbreviation HB (Head Boy), which Fred Weasley levels at his pompous older brother, Percy, who is an HB and doesn't want anyone to forget it. Predictably, Fred and George Weasley needle him mercilessly about it, to his discomfort and chagrin. (Not surprisingly, when they get hold of Percy's badge, they set about "improving it" to read *Bighead Boy*.)

Hungarian Horntail: A dragon used in the first competition at the Triwizard Tournament held at Hogwarts, it is an exceptionally vicious species. Harry, of course, has to face one for the tournament.

Hurling Hex: A curse that is thought to be afflicting the Firebolt broom given to Harry Potter by Sirius Black, though the broom is free of all curses.

Hut-on-the-Rock: After leaving the Railview Hotel in Cokeworth, the Dursleys take refuge (as it were) in a wretched, smelly shack by the sea, which Vernon Dursley feels is far enough away to discourage mail delivery of letters from Hogwarts. It is here that Rubeus Hagrid shows up, in the middle of a storm, to hand-deliver Harry Potter's acceptance letter to Hogwarts and, afterward, take Harry away from these dreadful premises. The letter bears the address: "Mr. H. Potter, The Floor, Hut-on-the-Rock, The Sea."

I

Ice Mice: A "special effects" squeaking and teeth-chattering candy available at Honeydukes.

Ickle Diddykins: An affectionate term Mrs. Dursley calls her son, Dudley.

Imperius Curse: One of three Unforgivable Curses, it gives the wizard total control over the victim afflicted with it; it can be combated, but as Professor Moody points out, it's better to be vigilant and avoid getting hit with it in the first place. The command is *Imperio*. Using it against another person rates a life sentence in Azkaban. (See also Cruciatus Curse and Killing Curse.)

Imperturbable Charm: Used to keep intruders and intrusions out. Mrs. Weasley uses it to defend against her sons' extendable ears, which they inserted under a door gap at Sirius Black's house to listen in on the conversation.

Impervius: A charm used to repel water. Hermione Granger uses this on Harry Potter's glasses during a rainy Quidditch match against Hufflepuff.

Important Modern Magical Discoveries: Reference book found in the Hogwarts library.

Inanimatus Conjurus: A spell assigned in Professor McGonagall's class to fifth-year students.

Incarcerous: A charm used to entrap the victim with enchanted rope. In the Forbidden Forest, Professor Umbridge uses this charm against a centaur, Magorian.

Incendio: A flame-producing charm. Especially useful for starting fires in fireplaces when setting up to transport through the Floo network.

Inner Eye: The internal, third eye that mystics like Professor Sibyll Trelawney possess that allows them to see all and pierce the veil of the spirit world.

Inquisitorial Squad: Students handpicked by Umbridge, they are supportive of the Ministry of Magic; Draco Malfoy is one of them.

Intermediate Transfiguration: A textbook for third-year students.

International Ban on Dueling: The Ministry of Magic is trying to garner international compliance with this ban.

International Code of Wizarding Secrecy: International agreement to keep all magic secret, intended to keep it from being witnessed by Muggles. Harry Potter would have violated this if he had used a summoning charm (*Accio*) to fetch a Muggles scuba-diving tank, which he felt would be needed to survive a prolonged immersion in the lake outside Hogwarts Castle as part of his second trial for the Triwizard Tournament.

International Federation of Warlocks: A powerful organization within the wizarding community.

Invigoration Draught: A rejuvenation elixir Harry Potter concocts.

Invisible Book of Invisibility: A required school textbook that, according to the manager of Flourish and Blotts, turned out to be a big mistake. Expensive to purchase, this book, being invisible, was impossible to find.

Invisibility Booster: An accessory Arthur Weasley added to the enchanted Ford Anglia. When pressed, it renders the flying car invisible—essential to preventing observation by Muggles.

Invisibility Cloak: A gift from Dumbledore to Harry Potter, it formerly belonged to Harry Potter's father, James; it renders its wearer invisible.

Irish National Quidditch Team: Playing at the 422nd Quidditch World Cup, its members include Connolly, Ryan, Troy, Mullet, Moran, Quigley, and Lynch. Each rides the best broom Galleons can buy, the Firebolt (the same kind Harry Potter rides).

Irish National Team Mascots: Thousands of leprechauns performing at the 422nd Quidditch World Cup.

J

Jelly-Legs Jinx: Used to make someone's legs wobbly.

Jelly Slugs: A candy available at Honeydukes.

Jigger, Arsenius: Author of *Magical Drafts and Potions,* a required course book for first-year students in Professor Snape's class.

Jinxes for the Jinxed: A book Hermione Granger finds in the Room of Requirement.

Johnson, Angelina: A Chaser for the Gryffindor Quidditch team. As a fifth-year student, she became her house's Quidditch Captain. She submits her name to the Goblet of Fire, which accepts it, since she had just turned 17 a week earlier.

Jordan, Lee: A student commentator at Quidditch matches. Jordan is a friend of George and Fred Weasley. As commentator, Jordan often injects personal or technical information for which he's often chided.

Jorkins, Bertha: A witch employed at the Ministry of Magic, presumed lost after traveling to Albania, since she never returned. She has a history of simply getting lost because of her poor sense of direction, but somehow usually manages to find her way back. Unfortunately, on a southbound trip from her second cousin's house to visit her aunt, she was waylaid by Wormtail and was brought by him to Lord Voldemort, who killed her after using magic to extract the information he needed. Most wizards would use a memory charm to erase her memory, but Voldemort points out that it is not foolproof—a powerful wizard can break it.

Junior Assistant to the Minister: Percy Weasley's title at the Ministry of Magic, where he works under Mr. Crouch.

Junior Heavyweight Inter-School Boxing Champion of the Southeast: A title earned by Dudley Dursley for his boxing prowess.

K

Kappas: Resembling scaly monkeys with webbed hands, they live in ponds and seek to strangle anyone who unwittingly comes across them. Professor Lupin teaches basic defense against these creatures in his Defense Against the Dark Arts class. They are, as Snape points out, most commonly found in Mongolia.

Karkaroff, Professor Igor: The head of Durmstrang, whose students arrive by a ship rising out of the lake in front of Hogwarts. Karkaroff, a former Death Eater put in Azkaban by "Mad-Eye" Moody, changed sides and won his release in a deal with the Ministry of Magic by betraying fellow Death Eaters, who were subsequently imprisoned at Azkaban.

Karkus: The name of the Gurg (chief giant) Hagrid visits, bearing gifts. Standing at least 22 feet tall (according to Hagrid's estimation), Karkus weighs as much as two elephants.

Keeper: Quidditch term. This team member tries to stop the other team from scoring by defending the goals.

Kettleburn, Professor: A faculty member at Hogwarts who taught Care of Magical Creatures. His name may be a hint as to why he had to retire prematurely.

Killing Curse: An illegal curse that kills—its signature is a blinding green light and the command is *Avada Kedavra*. There is no defense and, with one exception (Harry Potter), no one has survived this curse. (See also Imperius Curse and Cruciatus Curse.)

King's Cross Station: A train station in London, it has a magical barrier accessible only by wizards that leads to Platform Nine and Three-Quarters. To get to the platform, one runs through a brick column, which is the passageway to the platform. At precisely 11:00 A.M., the Hogwarts Express leaves the station. For the fall term, the train leaves on September 1. (On Harry's first trip to King's Cross station, he can't find the magical Platform Nine and Three-Quarters because he doesn't know how to reach it. Fortunately, the Weasleys assist Harry in finding his way.)

Kirke, Andrew: He replaces one of the Weasley twins on the Gryffindor Quidditch team after Professor Umbridge bans the twins for life from playing.

Knarl: A creature whose quills have "many magical properties." They are also very suspicious beasts. Substitute teacher Grubbly-Plank discusses these creatures because they are likely to show up on the O.W.L.s, which turns out to be true—students are required to find the knarl hidden among hedgehogs.

Kneazle: In Care of Magical Creatures, this creature is studied because substitute teacher Grubbly-Plank notes that it is likely to be encountered on the O.W.L.

The Knight Bus: A wizarding conveyance, a triple-decker bus driven by Ernie Prang; the bus's conductor is Stan Shunpike. Emergency transportation for stranded witches and wizards, the Knight Bus—unlike a conventional bus—can drive on the sidewalk, though without hitting anything. It can take its riders virtually anywhere on land. The bus has a disconcerting habit of startling its riders with a loud BANG when it heads out. Harry Potter catches the bus after leaving the Dursley household, where he accidentally inflates Marjorie Dursley into a human balloon, incurring his uncle's wrath.

Knockturn Alley: A twisting alley in the disreputable part of town, frequented by those with an interest in the Dark Arts; it's located off Diagon Alley.

Knuts: Wizard currency. A brass coin, 29 Knuts equal 1 silver Sickle.

Kreacher: The cantankerous family house-elf of the Black family. He's evasive, malevolent, insulting, and crazy.

Krum, Viktor: The Seeker for the Bulgarian national team who is playing for the Quidditch World Cup. Also Durmstrang's champion for the Triwizard Tournament.

Kwikspell: A correspondence course for beginners' magic, about which Filch had inquired, since he, as a Squib, feels inadequate. The poor man suffers from wand envy.

L

Leaky Cauldron: A famous, albeit grubby-looking pub frequented by the wizarding community. In its backyard Hagrid taps on bricks, which rearrange themselves, opening up to Diagon Alley. While making his way through the pub, Harry meets its elderly bartender, Tom; a witch, Doris Crockford; the excitable Dedalus Diggle, whom Harry recognizes as having met before, to Diggle's delight; and stuttering, turban-wearing Professor Quirrell, the Defense Against the Dark Arts teacher in Harry's first year at Hogwarts.

Legilimency: As Professor Snape explains to Harry Potter, this is "the ability to extract feelings and memories from another person's mind." (See Occlumency—its opposite.)

Leg-Locker Curse: A curse that causes legs to stick together, forcing one to hop. Draco Malfoy tries out this curse on the hapless Neville Longbottom. The command is *Locomotor Mortis*.

Lemon Drop: (1) A Muggles candy that Dumbledore is fond of, which he offers to Professor McGonagall, who politely refuses. (2) It is also a password used to enter Dumbledore's office, superseded by "Cockroach Cluster."

Leprechaun Gold: Fake gold that disappears after a few hours.

Lestrange, Bellatrix and Rodolphus: A married couple who are Death Eaters imprisoned in Azkaban. Bellatrix was convicted of torturing Frank and Alice Longbottom, resulting in their permanent incapacitation and subsequent admission to the wizarding community's hospital, St. Mungo's Hospital for Magical Maladies and Injuries. At her trial, she proclaimed her allegiance to Lord Voldemort. Bellatrix is the sister of Andromeda Tonks.

Lestrange, Rabastan: Brother of Rodolphus Lestrange.

Level 2, Ministry of Magic: This floor houses the Department of Magical Law Enforcement. Its offices include the Improper Use of Magic Office, Auror Headquarters, and Wizengamot Administration Services.

Level 3, Ministry of Magic: This floor houses the Department of Magical Accidents and Catastrophes. Its offices include the Accidental Magic Reversal Squad, Obliviator Headquarters, and the Muggle-Worthy Excuse Committee.

Level 4, Ministry of Magic: This floor houses the Department for the Regulation and Control of Magical Creatures. Its offices include Beast, Being, and Spirit Divisions; Goblin Liaison Office; and the Pest Advisory Bureau.

Level 5, Ministry of Magic: This floor houses the Department of International Magical Cooperation. Its offices include the International Magical Trading Standards Body, International Magical Offices of Law, and the International Confederation of Wizards, British Seats.

Level 6, Ministry of Magic: This floor houses the Department of Magical Transport. Its offices include the Floo Network Authority, Broom Regulatory Control, Portkey Office, and the Apparation Test Center.

Level 7, Ministry of Magic: This floor houses the Department of Magical Games and Sports. Its offices include the British and Irish Quidditch League Headquarters, Official Gobstones Club, and Ludicrous Patents Club.

Lilac: Gilderoy Lockhart's favorite color.

Little Hangleton: The town in which the Riddle House is located. (The Riddle House is the ancestral home of Tom Riddle, AKA Lord Voldemort.)

Little Whinging: The neighborhood the Dursleys live in.

Lockhart, Gilderoy: In the second book, the Defense Against the Dark Arts

professor. A flashy dresser, he's photogenic, which he breathlessly tells the world in his series of autobiographical books that are more fiction than fact. Aside from being skilled in Memory charms—erasing others' minds—he is magically inept, but pretends otherwise. By design he arrives too late to be of any practical assistance in any emergency situation. His resume: Order of Merlin, Third Class; and Honorary Member of the Dark Force Defense League. His signature is as flamboyant (and loopy) as the man himself. At one point, he seizes Ron Weasley's broken wand and attempts to cast a spell, which backfires; as a result, he becomes a long-term resident at St. Mungo's Hospital for Magical Maladies and Injuries, in the Janus Thickey ward, which is where those who suffer permanent spell damage are cared for.

Locomotor Mortis: The command for the leg-locker curse that causes the victim's legs to lock together, forcing the victim to hop. It's used by Draco Malfoy on Neville Lockbottom.

Locomotor Trunk: A charm used by N. Tonks (don't call her by her first name!) to levitate and then move Harry Potter's trunk.

Long White Beards: After using an Aging Potion to fool the Age Line Dumbledore drew around the Goblet of Fire, Fred and George Weasley sport these as temporary punishment (a public embarrassment) for violating the rules. Miss Fawcett of Ravenclaw and Mr. Summers of Hufflepuff were also similarly afflicted.

Longbottom, Frank: The father of Neville Longbottom, he was an Auror tortured by followers of Lord Voldemort for information. His wife was also tortured for information. The torture drove them insane; both are in St. Mungo's Hospital for Magical Maladies and Injuries.

Longbottom, Neville: Lacking self-confidence, Longbottom was brought up by his grandmother (Gran), who is a witch. At eight, he discovered his magical powers after being dangled out of an upstairs window. He fell . . . and bounced down the street. He fears Professor Snape, who torments him as mercilessly as he does Harry Potter. (Harry "borrows" Longbottom's name to hide his identity when he unknowingly summons the Knight Bus.)

Loony, Loopy Lupin: The nickname that Peeves (who more than lives up to his name) gives Professor Lupin.

Lovegood, Luna: Ravenclaw student whose father is the editor of the *Quibbler.*

Luminous Rosettes: Sold at the Quidditch World Cup, these squealed the players' names. They come in two colors: Ireland's is green and Bulgaria's is red.

Lumos: A charm to produce light.

Lupin, Remus J.: A young professor of modest means who assumes the post of Defense Against the Dark Arts in the third book.

M

Macmillan, Ernie: A Hufflepuff student who is selected as a prefect in his fifth year.

Macnair, Walden: He works at the Ministry of Magic, "destroying dangerous beasts." A Death Eater, he is sent by the Ministry to kill Buckbeak.

Madam Puddifoot's: A tea room in Hogsmeade. On Valentine's Day, Harry Potter and Cho Chang go there to discover it is filled with other Hogwarts students—all couples.

Madcap Magic for Wacky Warlocks: A library book Harry Potter consults in hopes that it will help him with his second trial at the Triwizard Tournament.

Madley, Laura: A Hufflepuff student.

Magical Law Enforcement: A division within the Ministry of Magic.

Magical Maintenance: Maintenance workers at the Ministry of Magic decide what kind of weather is exhibited in the underground windows of the Ministry.

Magical Me: A fanciful autobiography of the immodest Gilderoy Lockhart.

Magical Menagerie: A pet shop in Diagon Alley where Ron Weasley takes Scabbers for a once-over, and Hermione Granger buys her orange-colored, odd-looking, rocket-propelled cat, Crookshanks, who shows a great deal of interest in pursuing Scabbers.

Magical Water Plants of the Mediterranean: A book that Professor "Mad-Eye" Moody gives Neville Longbottom, in hopes that Harry will ask him for help to prepare for the Triwizard Tournament.

Magorian: A centaur who lives with his kind in the Forbidden Forest near Hogwarts, he warns Hagrid, who brought his giant half-brother there, to stay out.

Malfoy, Draco: The son of Lucius and Narcissa Malfoy, Draco comes from a pureblood wizard family and, like his father, is contemptuous of anyone who isn't pureblood. Prejudiced to the extreme, he initially offers friendship to Harry Potter, who rebuffs him. Draco then shows his true colors and con-

demns Harry and, guilty by association, Ron Weasley and Hagrid. A Seeker on the Slytherin Quidditch team after his father bought the entire team Nimbus 2001 brooms, Draco becomes a prefect in his fifth year, as do Ron Weasley and Hermione Granger.

Malfoy, Lucius: The father of Draco Malfoy, he lives in a mansion in Wiltshire. A Death Eater, Lucius is well connected with Cornelius Fudge, since he buys favors with large "donations" of Galleons.

Malfoy, Narcissa: Wife of Lucius Malfoy and mother of Draco. She is tall and blonde.

Mandrake: Also known as Mandragora, it's a plant from which an antidote can be made to cure people who have been cursed, transfigured, or petrified. Note: Its high-pitched cry is fatal to people. Administered as Mandrake Juice.

Mandrake Restorative Draught: A potion Gilderoy Lockhart offers to prepare to restore Mrs. Norris from a state of petrification to normalcy, to the displeasure of Professor Severus Snape, who pointedly reminds him that he, and not Lockhart, is the potions master at Hogwarts.

Manticore: A magical creature cited during a research session at the library when Harry, Ron, and Hermione try to find relevant cases to help in Hagrid's defense of Buckbeak against the Committee for the Disposal of Dangerous Creatures.

Marauder's Map: A detailed, enchanted map of Hogwarts with dots to show the exact location of people who are on the move on the school grounds. Each dot is labeled by name, so you know who is on the move. It also displays little-known passages into and out of Hogwarts. The map was created by Moony, Wormtail, Padfoot, and Prongs. After using it, invoke the proper command ("Mischief managed!") and it'll wipe itself clean—a good idea, since it keeps others from reading it. Fred and George Weasley liberated it from a drawer found in Filch's office and gave it to Harry Potter so he could escape to Hogsmeade, since he lacks formal permission to do so; he goes by tunnel and enters Hogsmeade from the cellar in Honeydukes.

Marchbanks, Griselda: The head of the Wizarding Examinations Authority. She's been around so long that she gave Dumbledore his O.W.L. exams. After Educational Degree Twenty-three took effect, she resigned in protest.

Marsh, Madam: A passenger on the Knight Bus when Harry Potter boards it; her destination is Abergavenny.

Mason, Mr. and Mrs: Guests of the Dursleys whom they are trying to impress. Unfortunately, the unexpected (and unwelcome) appearance of

Dobby, a house-elf, occurs during their visit. Dobby is not only noisy, drawing unwanted attention, but uses a levitation charm on a pudding, which he then drops on Harry Potter. The final straw is when an owl appears with a warning message from the Ministry of Magic, to the horror of Mrs. Mason, who has a pathological fear of owls. She and her husband bolt from the house, leaving a very angry Vernon Dursley and an upset Petunia Dursley.

Maxime, Madame: The head of Beauxbatons, she is, like Hagrid, unusually large in size. She and her students arrive in elaborate fashion, in a house-shaped carriage drawn by a dozen elephant-sized winged palomino horses, which will only drink single-malt whiskey.

Maze: The third challenge of the Triwizard Tournament. Not simply a maze, it harbors several formidable obstacles, including creatures provided by Hagrid and spells.

McDonald, Natalie: A Gryffindor student. (This is the only instance in the Potter novels in which the real name of a person is used. Rowling immortalized her in print after the child died of a lingering disease.)

McGonagall, Minerva: A professor at Hogwarts, she teaches Transfiguration. The head of Gryffindor House, she is also the Deputy Headmistress at Hogwarts. She sends acceptance letters to prospective students, which includes a list of what they should bring upon arriving.

The Medieval Assembly of European Wizards: The subject of a report assigned by Professor Binns.

Mediwizards: Medical wizards, especially useful to have on hand during Quidditch matches, since injuries are inevitable.

Mega-Mutilation Part Three: A computer game module that can be played on a PlayStation. One of Dudley Dursely's favorite games.

Meliflua, Araminta: A member of the Black family, she hates Muggles and unsuccessfully attempted to put through a bill to make hunting them legal.

Men Who Love Dragons Too Much: One of many books on dragons Harry Potter consults for information, since he must face a dragon in his first Triwizard Tournament challenge. (The book's title sounds like something Hagrid would enjoy reading.)

Merlin: Found in the card series Famous Witches and Wizards.

Merpeople: Inhabitants of the lake outside Hogwarts Castle, these people have gray skin, green hair, and the traditional fish tail associated with mermaids.

Midgen, Eloise: A Hogwarts student who foolishly tried to rid her face of acne by using a curse instead of bubotuber pus; as a result, her nose fell off.

Mimbulus Mimbletonia: A rare plant given to Neville Longbottom, whose favorite class is Herbology, by his great-uncle Algie. It has, as he discovered, a self-defense mechanism: it can squirt Stinksap, a stinking green liquid, in copious quantities.

Mimsy-Porpington, Sir Nicholas de: Resident ghost of Gryffindor Tower. His nickname is Nearly Headless Nick. Much to his regret, he is denied membership into the Headless Hunt, since he physically doesn't meet its requirements. (Though he received 45 whacks, which caused his death, it wasn't enough to sever his head from body; a thread keeps his head attached.)

Ministry of Magic: The governmental organization that controls and regulates all things in the wizard world, headed by a Minister of Magic.

Ministry of Magic Are Morons Group: A name proposed by Fred Weasley for Harry Potter's unofficial Defense Against the Dark Arts class.

Ministry Witch Still Missing: Headline in the *Daily Prophet* about a witch, Bertha Jorkins, who was in fact not missing but dead, killed by Lord Voldemort.

Mirror of Erised: "Desire" spelled backwards, this mirror shows the viewer's greatest desire. When Harry Potter looks into the mirror, he sees his parents waving at him.

Misuse of Muggles Artifacts Office: The division of the Ministry of Magic where Mr. Weasley works. The office intervenes when a Muggle-made object is bewitched, causing problems in the Muggle world. Memory Charms must then be cast on the involved Muggles to erase their memories of such encounters.

Moaning Myrtle: A student-turned-ghost whose death came suddenly in the girls' bathroom after she stared directly at a basilisk 50 years earlier. Perpetually bemoaning her fate, she is the bathroom's permanent resident.

Mobiliarbus: A charm used to levitate and move an object. Hermione Granger uses it in the Three Broomsticks to distract Cornelius Fudge, Minister of Magic, from noticing that Harry Potter is illegally in Hogsmeade.

Mobilicorpus: A charm that will force an unconscious person to stand up, like a string-controlled marionette. Professor Lupin uses it to make an inanimate Professor Snape stand up.

Mockridge, Cuthbert: The Head of the Goblin Liaison Office at the Ministry of Magic.

Modern Magical History: A book Hermione Granger reads as background study before her first year at Hogwarts. Harry Potter is referenced therein.

The Monster Book of Monsters: A textbook sold at Flourish and Blotts, required for the Care of Magical Creatures class taught at Hogwarts by Rubeus Hagrid. When these ill-tempered books are put together, they tear each other apart. Best to keep it under wraps, or at least very securely bound. To subdue this book, stroke its spine; it will then relax and can be opened normally.

Moody, Alastor ("Mad-Eye"): A retired Auror from the Ministry of Magic, he is personally responsible for incarcerating half the inmates at Azkaban prison; consequently, he has numerous enemies. He comes out of retirement to be the Defense Against the Dark Arts teacher. He has one normal eye and one large, mad-looking eye, hence his name. In the fifth book, he leads an Advance Party from the Order of the Phoenix to fetch Harry Potter and escort him to its headquarters.

Moon: Student (Hogwarts house unknown).

Moony: Professor Lupin's nickname when he was a student at Hogwarts.

Morgana: Found in the card series Famous Witches and Wizards.

Morsmordre: A spell that conjured the Dark Mark, the sign of Lord Voldemort, which appeared at the Quidditch World Cup. It takes the appearance of a large skull.

Mortlake: After a hard day's night, Mr. Weasley cites this person as having been brought in for questioning about ferrets, presumably regarding experimental charms.

Mostafa, Hassan: The referee for the 422nd Quidditch World Cup tournament, he's the Chairwizard of the International Association of Quidditch.

Mountain Troll: Gray-colored creature standing 12 feet high who attacks Hermione Granger.

Mrs. Skower's All-Purpose Magical Mess Remover: A magical cleaner used by caretaker Filch. The Remover, however, fails to clean the interior walls of Hogwarts of the messages left by an anonymous person (or thing) announcing that the Chamber of Secrets has been opened.

Mudblood: A derogatory term often used by pure-blooded magicians to denote a Muggle-born magician. On the Quidditch playing field, Draco Malfoy calls Hermione Granger a "mudblood," which infuriates Ron Weasley; he wields his broken wand to invoke a slug-vomiting curse, which backfires; consequently, he and not Malfoy winds up regurgitating slugs.

Taken literally, the term implies "dirty" or "common" blood, according to Rowling.

Muggle: A non-magic person; not necessarily a pejorative term—Hermione Granger's parents are Muggles. But when it is used in a pejorative sense, it implies ordinariness, conformity, and a lack of imagination, people like the Dursleys. (In 2003 the word made it into the *Oxford English Dictionary*, with attribution to Rowling.)

Muggle Protection Act: Proposed by Arthur Weasley for the protection of Muggles, of whom he is fond—a position not universally in favor in the wizarding world, especially with purebloods like the Malfoy family.

Muggle Repelling Charm: When a Muggle approaches the Quidditch World Cup Stadium, he suddenly recalls he needs to be elsewhere and leaves immediately. This charm is what prompts him to leave.

Muggle Studies: A course taken by Hermione Granger in her third year. Ron thinks that, considering her background, the course is superfluous; however, she cites that it would be interesting to study Muggles from the perspective of the wizarding community.

Mulciber: A supporter of Lord Voldemort, betrayed by Karkaroff.

Mulled Mead: A beverage served at the Three Broomsticks, favored by Rubeus Hagrid.

Murcus: The chief of the merpeople who inhabit the lake outside Hogwarts Castle, this creature witnesses the three champions competing in the Triwizard Tournament and tells the judges what happened underwater, resulting in the highest score going to Harry Potter for bravery.

Murtlap Tentacles: As a solution, when strained and pickled, it is a soothing relief for Harry Potter's bleeding hand.

Musical Box: Found in the Black home, it has a song that makes you sleepy.

Mystery Illness of Bartemius Crouch: Headline in the *Daily Prophet* about Mr. Crouch, the head of the Department of International Magical Cooperation at the Ministry of Magic.

N

Nagini: A 12-foot snake belonging to Lord Voldemort, who orders that it be milked on a regular basis by Wormtail, his servant.

Nargles: According to Luna Lovegood, these infest mistletoe.

Nature's Nobility: A Wizarding Genealogy: A book in the Black family house, which Sirius uses to smash an animated, multilegged tweezer that attempts to puncture Harry Potter.

N.E.W.T.s: Nastily Exhausting Wizarding Tests. Higher level exams at Hogwarts. Percy Weasley got top-grade N.E.W.T.s, as expected. (In the real world, students in England who stay in school for an additional two years take high-level exams, necessary for college entry, in one's major field of study.)

New Theory of Numerology: A book Ron Weasley gives Hermione Granger for Christmas.

Niffler: A long-snouted creature typically found in mines. Nifflers are useful, as Hagrid points out, for finding buried treasure. Professor Umbridge is plagued with these creatures that have been put in her office. She blames Harry Potter but the real culprit is Lee Jordan, a good friend of Fred and George Weasley.

Nigellus, Phineas: A member of the Black family, Sirius's great-great-grandfather. According to Sirius, he had a dubious distinction: he was the least-liked Hogwarts headmaster of all time. His portrait hangs in Dumbledore's office; Phineas has another portrait at Sirius Black's house, at Grimmault Place. Dumbledore instructs him to pass on the word to Sirius that Arthur Weasley was injured in the line of duty for the Order of the Phoenix.

Nimbus Two Thousand: A high-powered, state-of-the-art flying broom that Harry Potter receives after being selected for the Gryffindor Quidditch team. First-year students aren't allowed to have brooms, but an exception was made in Harry Potter's case, to the chagrin of Draco Malfoy. Harry's broom is constructed of mahogany, with a tail of twigs; on the top, in gold, the words "Nimbus Two Thousand." In the third book, the Whomping Willow reduces Harry's broom to kindling.

Nimbus Two Thousand and One: State-of-the-art broom used by the Quidditch players from Slytherin, generously provided by Lucius Malfoy, whose son Draco has now made the team as its newest Seeker.

No-Heat Fireworks: A novelty found at Gambol and Japes Wizarding Joke Shop.

Norbert: A dragon illegally hatched by Hagrid. (At the Warlocks' Convention in 1709, dragon breeding was outlawed.) Since Hagrid can't keep it at Hogwarts, Charlie Weasley, who works in Romania, agrees to take it off his hands.

Norris, Mrs.: Cat owned by Argus Filch, the caretaker at Hogwarts.

Nose-Biting Teacup: A magical joke item sold at Zonko's.

Nosebleed Nougat: Invented by Fred and George Weasley.

Notable Magical Names of Our Time: Reference book found in the Hogwarts library.

Nott, Theodore: A "weedy-looking" student who hangs out with Malfoy, Crabbe, and Goyle after the *Quibbler* appears with Harry Potter's revealing interview.

Nottingham: Lord Voldemort murders a goblin family near this town, a fact cited in conversation by Mr. Weasley during a meal at the headquarters of the Order of the Phoenix.

Nougat: A confectionary found at Honeydukes.

Number 4, Privet Drive, Little Whinging, Surrey, England: The residence of Mr. Vernon Dursley, Mrs. Petunia Dursley (sister of Lily Potter), and their spoiled son, Dudley. It is also the residence of Harry Potter, who initially lives in a cupboard under the stairs; he later moves into a spare room upstairs where Dudley keeps his discarded toys. The Dursleys' two-storied house has four bedrooms. (Real-world fact: The actual house used in the Harry Potter movies went up for auction but failed to sell at its inflated price.)

Number 12, Grimmauld Place, London: The private residence belonging to the Black family, which the Order of the Phoenix uses as its headquarters.

Number 93, Diagon Alley: The address of Weasleys' Wizarding Wheezes, a magical joke shop, the opening of which Fred and George Weasley announce as they make their dramatic escape from Hogwarts.

Numerology and Gramatica: A textbook Hermione Granger uses for one of her classes as a third-year student.

O

Oblansk (Obalonsk), Mr.: The Bulgarian Minister of Magic who is introduced around at the Quidditch World Cup match by Cornelius Fudge, who can't pronounce his name properly.

Obliviate: The command for the Memory charm, used to erase memories. Gilderoy Lockhart interviews others, mining them for their exploits, and then takes credit for their work after performing this charm to cover his tracks.

Obliviator: A witch or wizard who uses Memory charms to erase memories.

Occlumency: Dumbledore assigns Professor Snape to teach Harry Potter this obscure but obviously useful defense technique to guard against Lord

Voldemort. As Professor Snape explains, "this branch of magic seals the mind against magical intrusion and influence."

Oddsbodikins: An odd password Sir Cadogan requires in order to enter the Gryffindor common room. (As usual, a flustered Neville Longbottom forgets it, and is barred entry until Harry Potter shows up to speak it.)

Ogden, Tiberius: A wizard friend of Professor Tofty, who tells him that Harry Potter can produce a Patronus, which is very unusual for someone of Potter's age. To Tofty's delight, Potter produces the silver stag that canters the length of the examination hall, then dissipates. A Wizengamot elder, Tiberius Ogden resigns in protest of Educational Decree 23.

Ogden's Old Firewhiskey: A hard liquor favored by Arthur Weasley and Gilderoy Lockhart.

Ogg: The gamekeeper at Hogwarts when Mrs. Weasley was a student.

Olde and Forgotten Bewitchments and Charms: An old book from Hogwarts library that Hermione consults, which helps Harry Potter prepare for his second trial at the Triwizard Tournament.

Ollivander, Mr.: The proprietor of Ollivanders: Makers of Fine Wands since 382 B.C. He has a prodigious memory and can recall every person to whom he has ever sold a wand. He assists Harry in the selection of his wand and tells him that he remembers selling his parents their wands. As he tells Harry, one does not *choose* the wand—the *wand* chooses the wizard. The wand that chooses Harry is made of holly and is 11.5 inches, with a phoenix feather. It is notable for the fact that the phoenix gave only one other feather for another wand, which belongs to Lord Voldemort. Harry's wand cost seven Galleons.

Omnioculars: Sold at the Quidditch World Cup for 10 Galleons each, they are worth the cost because Quidditch is a fast-moving game and an omniocular enables the viewer to see the action slowed down. It also offers a play-by-play option. Harry buys one for himself, and one each for Ron Weasley and Hermione Granger. He uses the excuse that these are their ten-year Christmas presents.

One Minute Feasts—It's Magic!: A cookbook found in Mrs. Weasley's kitchen.

One Thousand Magical Herbs and Fungi: A required course book for first-year students in the Potions class.

Orb: Professor Trelawney refers to her crystal ball as an orb.

Orchideous: A charm to produce flowers from a wand tip, a way to test its

working condition. Mr. Ollivander uses this charm to ensure that the wands of the champions competing in the Triwizard Tournament are functioning properly.

Order of the Phoenix: An organization founded by Dumbledore composed of witches and wizards who band together in secrecy to combat Lord Voldemort. Dumbledore calls the order into action when he believes that Lord Voldemort is building an army to serve him.

Order of Suspension: Signed by 12 governors who have the authority to appoint or, if necessary, suspend the headmaster at Hogwarts, this document is delivered to Dumbledore to relieve him of his duties after four students are petrified. The chief instigator is Lucius Malfoy, one of the 12 governors. (At the same time, Hagrid is taken to Azkaban.)

Original Order of the Phoenix: The first group consisted of Mad-Eye Moody, Albus Dumbledore, Dedalus Diggle, Marlene McKinnon, Frank and Alice Longbottom, Emmeline Vance, Remus Lupin, Benjoy Fenwick, Edgar Bones, Sturgis Podmore, Caradoc Dearborn, Rubeus Hagrid, Elphias Doge, Gideon Prewett, Fabian Prewett, Aberforth Dumbledore (brother of Albus), Dorcas Meadowes, Sirius Black, Peter Pettigrew, and James and Lily Potter.

Ornithomancy: A method of divination that interprets flight patterns of birds. Professor Umbridge interrogates Professor Trelawney with questions about this difficult subject.

Ottery St. Catchpole: The village nearest to the Weasley home.

Ouagadogou: A town cited by Gilderoy Lockhart, who explains that he prevented the affliction suffered by Mrs. Norris from striking its villagers by providing the necessary amulets. A blow-by-blow account of this, of course, can be found in one of his many autobiographical books.

Owl: Each first-year student at Hogwarts is allowed a pet—an owl, cat, or toad. Owls, Hagrid points out, are the most useful, since they can also deliver mail. With that in mind, Hagrid buys Harry Potter an owl for his birthday on their first outing to Diagon Alley. Harry's snowy white female owl is named Hedwig. (Owls want hard cash for delivery. The going rate is five Knuts, which is what Hagrid instructs Harry to put in a pouch tied to an owl's leg when it delivers a newspaper to Hagrid.)

Owlery: An open-windowed room at Hogwarts that houses all the owls belonging to the school and its students. It is located at the top of the West Tower.

O.W.L.s: Ordinary Wizarding Levels. Lower-level exams at Hogwarts taken when students are 15 years old. (In England, students take O [Ordinary] Level exams at 15 years old, one per subject. When a student says he got seven O levels, it means he's passed seven individual exams. He can then leave school.) The O.W.L. grades at Hogwarts are E (Exceeds Expectations) and A (Acceptable)—both passing grades; and P (Poor) and D (Dreadful).

P

Padfoot: Nickname for Sirius Black when he was a student at Hogwarts, so called because as an animagus he assumed the shape of a large black dog.

Paracelsus: Found in the trading card series Famous Witches and Wizards.

Parchment: Used in lieu of paper at Hogwarts; one uses a quill pen to write on it.

Parkinson, Pansy: Slytherin student who, in her fifth year, becomes a prefect.

Parselmouth: A witch or wizard who can speak to snakes. A rare talent, Harry Potter can speak Parseltongue, as can Lord Voldemort.

Patil, Padma and Parvati: Twin girls, Parvati is in Gryffindor and Padma is in Ravenclaw. Harry Potter reluctantly attends the Yule Ball as part of the social activities supporting the Triwizard Tournament, having asked Parvati, who happily accepts, to be his date for the evening. Ron asks out Padma, who also accepts. (Harry Potter's first choice was Cho Chang, but to their mutual regret, Cedric Diggory had asked her first.) Padma Patil, in her fifth year, is selected as a prefect.

Patronus Charm: A charm of sufficient difficulty that it taxes even experienced wizards, this positive force projection, unique to the conjuror, requires one to focus on a happy memory to produce the physical manifestation of the charm, in Harry Potter's case, a silver stag. Professor Lupin teaches Harry Potter how to cast this charm as a self-defense measure against dementors. The proper incantation is *Expecto patronum.*

Payne, Mr.: The site manager for the area to which Amos Diggory is directed when he arrives on the grounds of the Quidditch World Cup.

Peasegood, Arnold: An Obliviator, he's a member of the Accidental Magic Reversal Squad at the Ministry of Magic.

Peeves the Poltergeist: Not properly a ghost like the other spooky inhabitants at Hogwarts, Peeves is a prankster who can't be controlled by anyone (or anything) except the Bloody Baron, a grim-looking ghost from Slytherin. Peeves more than lives up to his name.

Pennyfeather, Miss: Student (Hogwarts house unknown).

Pensieve: A "shallow stone basin" into which one can empty one's excess thoughts which can then be examined at leisure. Dumbledore has one in his office.

Pepper Imps: A "special effects" fire-breathing candy available at Honeydukes. It makes one "smoke at the mouth."

Peppermint Creams: A "special effects" toad-shaped candy that simulates frog-jumping in the stomach. It's available at Honeydukes. A Peppermint Cream is also called a Peppermint Toad.

Perkins, Mr.: He loans a magical tent to the Weasleys at the Quidditch World Cup. The tent's exterior gives no hint as to its spaciousness inside: a three-room apartment, room enough for its ten occupants (the Weasley family and guests). Perkins, who suffers from lumbago, rarely uses the tent these days, and so he loans it out as needed.

Perks, Sally-Anne: Student (Hogwarts house unknown).

Permanent Sticking Charm: Used to make an object permanently stick to a wall (or other surface). Sirius Black thinks his mother used one on her portrait at the family house; he wants to take the portrait down, but the charm prevents it.

Peskipiksi Pesternomi: An ineffective charm cast by Lockhart, who hoped it would reign in and control the Cornish pixies he unwisely unleashed.

Petrificus Totalus: A curse used to temporarily immobilize someone; a full Body-Bind, it spares only the eyes. Hermione Granger uses it on Neville Longbottom, who protests a repeat night excursion by Harry Potter, Ron Weasley, and herself after their first one took points from their house, Gryffindor.

Pettigrew, Peter: A hanger-on student who attached himself to Sirius Black and James Potter in their school days at Hogwarts. He reportedly died at Black's hand in a wand duel. He received, posthumously, the Order of Merlin, First Class, an undeserved honor. The Potters' Secret-Keeper, Pettigrew betrayed the Potters to Lord Voldemort. Not dead, as it turns out, and needing to hide from Sirius Black, Pettigrew, an animagus, assumed the form of a rat named Scabbers and is a pet in the Weasley household.

Philosopher's/Sorcerer's Stone: Created by Nicholas Flamel, it has two powers: it can turn any metal into gold, and it produces the Elixir of Life, which can make its drinker immortal.

Pig: The nickname given to a small gray owl named Pigwidgeon, a gift from Sirius Black to Ron Weasley.

Pince, Madam: School Librarian at Hogwarts described as thin with an irritable disposition.

PlayStation: A game system favored by Dudley Dursley.

Pocket Sneakoscope: Resembling a glass top, it lights up and spins when a "sneak" (an untrustworthy person) is around. It lights up around the merry pranksters George and Fred Weasley.

Podmore, Sturgis: A member of the Order of the Phoenix and a member of the Advance Guard sent to retrieve Harry Potter, he is charged with trespassing and attempted robbery at the Ministry of Magic; convicted on both counts, he is sentenced to a half-year at Azkaban.

Point Me: A command used to make a wand point true north.

Pointed Green Hats: Sold at the Quidditch World Cup, these have dancing shamrocks to celebrate the Irish national team, favored by Hogwarts student Seamus Finnigan.

Poliakoff: A student from Durmstrang who asks for wine and is admonished by that school's headmaster, Karkaroff, who had only offered it to his star student, Seeker Viktor Krum.

Polkiss, Piers: A rat-faced, scrawny boy, he is Dudley Dursley's best friend. Like Dudley, he is, at heart, a bullying coward, though of course he does not appear to be such to Vernon or Petunia Dursley. (They are as blinded to him as they are to their own son.)

Polyjuice Potion: A potion that temporarily transforms one into someone else. The complicated recipe can be found in *Moste Potente Potions,* a book located in the Restricted Section of the Hogwarts library. Hermione Granger concocts this potion for herself, Harry, and Ron.

Pomfrey, Madam Poppy: The head school nurse at Hogwarts who forever chides students who don't come to her immediately when afflicted with injury, both physical and spell-induced.

Pontner, Roddy: He bet Ludo Bagman that Bulgaria would score first at the Quidditch World Cup.

Popkin: An affectionate term Mrs. Dursley calls her son, Dudley.

Porlock: These shaggy, two-foot high creatures have cloven feet and small arms with only four fingers. They are commonly found in Dorset, England, and southern Ireland. These creatures guard horses. The porlock

is studied in the Care of Magical Creatures class because substitute teacher Grubbly-Plank notes that it is likely to be encountered in the O.W.L. exams.

Porskoff Ploy: A Quidditch maneuver, a diversionary tactic designed to drop off the Quaffle to a player.

Portable Swamp: Invented by Fred and George Weasley, it's their grandest prank, executed when they exit Hogwarts for good.

Portkey: An object, usually commonplace in appearance so as not to draw attention to it, used by wizards for transportation (individual or group) at a prearranged time. It usually takes the form of a boot, newspapers, a deflated football, or empty soda cans—items that Muggles would avoid picking up. For the Quidditch World Cup, 200 were set up throughout the United Kingdom, and an indeterminate quantity were set up on four other continents.

Portus: Command used to make an inanimate object a Portkey, to be used for transportation.

Potter, Harry: The son of James and Lily Potter, Harry was orphaned after Lord Voldemort killed his parents but failed to kill him. Left in the care of his Aunt Petunia (Lily Potter's sister), Harry spends his childhood thinking he's an ordinary boy. But everyone in the wizarding community knows differently. He's a wizard from whom great things are expected, which he finds out to his great surprise, and in due course is invited to attend Hogwarts School of Witchcraft and Wizardry. He is also surprised to discover that everyone in the wizarding community knows who he is—"the boy who lived," the only one to ever survive a direct killing attack from Lord Voldemort. (The attack does, however, leave Harry with a distinctive lightning bolt scar on his forehead.)

Potter, James: Harry Potter's father, a well-regarded wizard in his time who distinguished himself on the Quidditch team when a student at Hogwarts.

Potter, Lily: Harry Potter's mother, Muggle-born, who died protecting her son from Lord Voldemort.

Potty and the Weasel: Draco Malfoy's nicknames for Harry Potter and Ron Weasley.

Potty Wee Potter: Poltergeist Peeves's nickname for Harry Potter.

Practical Defensive Magic and Its Use Against the Dark Arts: A set of books given as Christmas gifts by Black and Lupin to Harry Potter.

Prang, Ernie: The driver of the Knight Bus.

Predicting the Unpredictable: Insulate Yourself Against Shocks: A book, devoted to fortune-telling, found at Flourish and Blotts on a table near a corner of the store.

Prefects Who Gained Power: A book found in a junk shop by Percy Weasley, who studies it carefully. The book is a career retrospective of prefects who graduated from Hogwarts.

Pride of Portree: Cho Chang thinks that the captain of the Gryffindor Quidditch team, Oliver Wood, joined the Quidditch team Pride of Portree, when in fact (as Harry Potter points out) he was taken by the Puddlemere United team.

Pringle, Apollyon: The caretaker at Hogwarts when Mrs. Weasley was a student.

Priori Incantatem: Two opposing wands, bound by a common core. Both Harry Potter and Lord Voldemort's wands share tail feathers from the same phoenix, Fawkes. When their two wands are used in opposition, it creates an unusual effect: one wand will force its brother-wand to expel its spells in reverse order. In the fourth book, Harry Potter and Lord Voldemort duel with brother wands.

Pritchard, Graham: A Slytherin student.

Prongs: Nickname for James Potter when he was a student at Hogwarts; as an animagus he assumed the shape of a silver stag.

Protean Charm: Harry Potter is teaching an unauthorized class, Defense Against the Dark Arts. To alert them as to the next scheduled class, all members carry a fake Galleon. When Harry Potter changes the date on his coin, all the coins held by class members change to reflect Harry's coin. To accomplish this, Hermione Granger put this Protean charm on all the coins.

Pucey, Adrian: A Chaser for the Slytherin Quidditch team.

Puking Pastilles: Found in a skiving snackbox, a two-colored candy; eating the orange half will make you vomit, but eating the purple half will restore your health.

Pumpkin Juice: Usually served chilled, it is a favorite drink of Harry Potter's. Harry had his first taste of this drink on the Hogwarts Express when he bought it from the witch with the food trolley.

Pumpkin Pasties: Wizard candy.

Pureblood: A password invoked by Draco Malfoy to gain entrance into the Slytherin common room. Also a wizard with two non-Muggle parents.

Purge and Dowse Ltd.: Muggles complain that this department store seems perpetually closed for renovations. It's just a façade to fool Muggles because it's actually St. Mungo's Hospital for Magical Maladies and Injuries, which serves the wizarding community.

Purkiss, Doris: She makes the absurd assertion that Sirius Black, an escapee from Azkaban, is a lead singer for a popular band in the magical community. This "fact" is reported in the *Quibbler*.

Put-Outer: A handheld device used to extinguish, or restore, light sources like streetlights. Dumbledore uses one to put out the streetlights on Privett Drive; he, Professor McGonagall (transfigured as a cat), and Rubeus Hagrid (on an airborne motorcycle) meet there to place Harry Potter, then an infant, on the doorstep of the Dursleys' house. Moody, who borrowed it from Dumbledore, uses it to extinguish the lights on a Muggle street to mask the arrival of his Advance Guard.

Q

Quaffle: Quidditch term. A red ball thrown by Chasers. Getting it through the goal posts scores 10 points.

Quality Quidditch Supplies: A retail store in Diagon Alley where one buys supplies for Quidditch.

Quick-Quotes Quill: A magical Quill that transcribes, with great exaggeration, whatever *Daily Prophet* reporter Rita Skeeter dictates. Simply stating her name causes the Quill to write, "Attractive blonde Rita Skeeter . . ."

Quidditch: Wizards' sport resembling basketball in the Muggles world. Six tall goal posts, four balls, and two teams of seven players each. (For detailed information, read *Quidditch Through the Ages*, written by Rowling under a pen name, Kennilworthy Whisp.)

Quidditch Teams of Britain and Ireland: A book Harry Potter takes with him when the Advance Guard shows up at the Dursley home. He received this book as a Christmas gift from Hermione Granger the previous year.

Quidditch Through the Ages: A standard textbook written by Kennilworthy Whisp. (The book's real author is Rowling.)

Quidditch World Cup: Attended by 100,000 wizards from all over the world, this is an international tournament with the teams representing individual countries.

Quidditch World Cup Stadium: Protected by Muggle Repelling charms, this is a 100,000-seat stadium, big enough to hold (by Harry Potter's estimation) ten cathedrals.

Quietus: A charm used by commentator Ludo Bagman to return his voice to normal at the end of the Quidditch World Cup. It is the counter-charm to *Sonorus*.

Quirke, Orla: A Ravenclaw student.

Quirrell, Professor: A faculty member at Hogwarts, he taught Defense Against the Dark Arts. In his travels, he ran across Lord Voldemort, who possessed his body. Quirrell wore a turban to conceal the fact that Voldemort's face was on the back of his head; Voldemort needed the Sorcerer's Stone to regain his strength and become a physical being again.

R

Rabbit Food: Vernon Dursley's pejorative term for salads, fruits, and vegetables, which he's forced to eat when his wife decides that everyone in the family will suffer along with their son, Dudley, whom the school nurse at Smeltings has put on a much-needed and long-delayed diet.

Rackharrow, Urquhart: The inventor of the entrail-expelling curse whose portrait hangs on the wall in the Dai Llewellyn ward at St. Mungo's Hospital for Magical Maladies and Injuries.

Ragnok: A goblin.

Ravenclaw: A house founded by Rowena Ravenclaw; the house trait is wisdom.

Red Caps: Described as goblin-like creatures who lurk and lie in wait to attack in places marked by bloodshed. Professor Lupin teaches basic defense against these creatures (among others) in his class, Defense Against the Dark Arts.

Red Currant Rum: A beverage served at the Three Broomsticks, favored by Cornelius Fudge.

Reducio: A reduction charm.

Regurgitating Public Toilets: Pranksters in the magical community enchant these Muggle toilets to backfire in Bethnal Green, Wimbledon, and Elephant and Castle. The Ministry of Magic dispatches the Magical Law Enforcement Patrol to catch the pranksters and render the toilets normal with an anti-jinx.

Relashio: A charm that typically produces sparks; when used by Harry Potter underwater, it produces a jet of boiling water, repelling the grasping grindylows who unsuccessfully attempt to pull him down. Temporarily transformed into a merman, Harry competes in the Triwizard Tournament.

Remedial Potions: A class Harry Potter tells his classmates he's taking with Professor Snape, when in fact he's taking a one-on-one tutelage with him on Occlumency.

"Remember My Last, Petunia": The verbal message of a Howler Dumbledore sends Mrs. Petunia Dursley.

Remembrall: A device that turns red if you've forgotten something. Neville Longbottom gets one from his Gran.

Reparo: A charm used to repair a broken object.

Reptile House: At the London zoo Harry Potter unknowingly speaks Parseltongue for the first time to a boa constrictor. He liberates the snake by making the glass front to its exhibit disappear. As Harry watches in amazement, the snake sibilantly hisses its thanks and slithers away. Being a Parselmouth (one who can speak Parseltongue) is a rare gift, most commonly associated with those who come from Slytherin House. Lord Voldemort is fluent in Parseltongue.

Restricted Section of the Library: Located in the rear of the Hogwarts library, this area contains forbidden books.

Revealer: An eraser that, when rubbed on a page, reveals the page's contents. Hermione Granger uses it on a page in Tom Riddle's diary without success.

A Revised History of Hogwarts: Hermione Granger's suggestion for a retitling of *Hogwarts, A History*, on the grounds that the original title is not accurate, since it lacks any mention of house-elves.

Rictusempra: A Tickling charm Harry Potter uses in a duel against Draco Malfoy.

Riddikulus!: The charm used to force the shape-shifting boggart to assume a laughable form.

Riddle House: Formerly a majestic manor that belonged to Lord Voldemort's Muggle father, it's now a shambles. Currently occupied by Lord Voldemort and Wormtail, the decrepit house is shunned by the locals in Little Hangleton.

Riddle, Tom Marvolo: AKA Lord Voldemort, born of a Muggle father and witch mother. He writes his name in the air with fiery letters, then rearranges them to spell "I AM LORD VOLDEMORT." Once a head boy and, says Dumbledore, the "most brilliant student" ever to attend Hogwarts, he turned to the Dark Side.

Ripper: Marjorie Dursley's pet dog, on whom she dotes.

The Rise and Fall of the Dark Arts: A book Hermione Granger reads, it has information on how to identify the Dark Mark, the sign of the dark wizard Lord Voldemort.

Roberts, Mr.: The site manager for the area to which Arthur Weasley is directed when he arrives on the grounds of the Quidditch World Cup.

Rock Cakes: A favorite dessert of Hagrid's, formless in shape and dotted with raisins, that lives up to its name. (Once, when faced with starvation rations on a forced family diet at the Dursley residence, Harry Potter sends Hedwig out with letters to his friends, requesting edible rations. Everyone sends edible food except Hagrid, who sends rock cakes.)

Rockwood, Augustus: A supporter of the Dark Lord, he worked in the Department of Mysteries at the Ministry of Magic. He is betrayed by Karkaroff, a traitor convicted of spying on the Ministry for Lord Voldemort.

Ronan: A centaur with his head in the clouds. He is a stargazer like the others of his kind.

Room 11: The temporary lodging Harry Potter takes up at the Leaky Cauldron after being thrown out of the Dursley home because of an incident involving Marjorie Dursley.

Room 17, Railview Hotel, Cokeworth: After the virtual blizzard of owl-delivered mail from Hogwarts addressed to Harry, the Dursleys flee and initially stop at this nondescript hotel, where, to the surprise of Vernon Dursley, the letters (approximately 100) continue to be delivered to Harry, readdressed to him in care of this hotel, forcing the Dursleys to move to a shack by the sea.

Room of Requirement: Also known as the "Come and Go Room," Dobby points this room out to Harry Potter when asked if there's a place at Hogwarts where he can ensure privacy for his unofficial Defense Against the Dark Arts class. The room is such that you can only enter it *if* you really need to do so. Though it's always been there, few people know of its existence.

Rosier, Evan: Betrayed by Karkaroff, this supporter of the Dark Lord was killed by an Auror.

Rosmerta, Madam: She tends the bar at the Three Broomsticks in Hogsmeade.

Ryan, Barry: An Irish International Keeper who made a magnificent save during a Quidditch match against the top-rated Polish Chaser, Ladislaw Zamojski.

S

St. Brutus's Secure Center for Incurably Criminal Boys: Vernon Weasley tells his sister Marge (Marjorie Dursley) that this is the school Harry Potter attends, since he doesn't want anyone to know the truth, that Harry is a wizard attending Hogwarts.

St. Mungo's Hospital for Magical Maladies and Injuries: The wizarding hospital, which consists of five floors: ground floor, artifact accidents; first floor, creature-induced injuries; second floor, magical bugs; third floor, potion and plant poisoning; fourth floor, spell damage; and fifth floor, visitors' tearoom and hospital shop.

The Salem Witches' Institute: A group of American witches camped out on the tournament grounds to attend the Quidditch World Cup.

Saucy Tricks for Tricky Sorts: A library book Harry Potter consults in hopes that it will help him with his second trial at the Triwizard Tournament.

Scabbers: A gray rat that once belonged to Percy Weasley, Scabbers is Ron's pet. What none of the Weasleys realize is that Scabbers is not what he seems.

Scourgify: A charm used to tidy up, to clean.

Scouring Charm: Used for cleaning. Hermione teaches it to Neville Longbottom, who uses it to clean his fingernails, grimed with frog guts after a period of detention under Professor Snape's intimidating gaze.

Screaming Yo-Yos: Caretaker Mr. Filch at Hogwarts Castle has cited these as a banned item for students.

Screechsnap Seedlings: In Herbology, Susan Bones, distracted by the news that ten Death Eaters escaped from Azkaban, puts too much dragon dung on her seedlings, causing them to "wriggle and squeak in discomfort."

Scurvy Cur: The password required by Sir Cadogan to enter the Gryffindor common room.

Secrecy Sensor: A dark detector that looks like a golden TV antenna, it vibrates when it picks up lies and concealment. Professor Moody had one in his office when he taught at Hogwarts.

Secret-Keeper: A person entrusted with the unbreakable Fidelius charm, which is used to conceal another person's secret.

Secret-Keeper for the Order: Dumbledore is the Secret-Keeper for the Order of the Phoenix.

Security Trolls: After the Fat Lady, who guards the entrance to the

Gryffindor common room, is frightened by the prospect of Sirius Black on the loose, these trolls are called to duty to stand in her picture frame.

Seeker: Quidditch term. It is the Seeker's job to catch the Golden Snitch, thereby winning his team 150 points and ending the game.

Self-Correcting Ink: An aid banned from use during O.W.L. exams.

Self-Defensive Spellwork: A book Hermione Granger finds in the Room of Requirement.

Serpensortia: A charm Draco Malfoy uses to produce a black serpent in a duel against Harry Potter.

Severing Charm: A cutting charm, used by Ron Weasley to trim the lace trim from his school robes.

Shacklebolt, Kingsley: An Auror who is part of the Advance Guard who come to take Harry to the Order of the Phoenix. He works at the Ministry of Magic.

Shield Charm: A powerful but temporary force field that deflects "minor curses." Professor Snape states that Harry Potter used this during a session with him when studying Occlumency.

Shooting Star: An antiquated broom, a hand-me-down, owned by Ron Weasley.

Shrieking Shack: Presumed to be the most haunted building in the entire U.K. In fact, even by daylight, it looks forbidding. Its reputation is such that even the Hogwarts ghosts avoid it. The shrieks were not supernatural in nature, however; they were the blood-curling screams coming from wizard-turned-werewolf Professor Lupin, who was housed within.

Shrinking Solution: A potion used to shrink. Professor Snape teaches his class how to brew it.

Shunpike, Stan: The bus conductor of the Knight Bus. Shunpike boasts that he'll be the youngest ever Minister of Magic—an empty claim used to impress three veela of otherworldly beauty at the Quidditch World Cup tournament.

Sickles: Wizard currency. A silver coin, 17 Sickles equal a Galleon.

Silver Snuffbox: An object in a glass cabinet at the Black family house, it can bite and, because of the Wartcap powder it contains, produce a brown crusty cover on flesh.

Silver Stag: The form taken by Harry Potter's Patronus charm.

Sinistra, Professor: A member of the Hogwarts faculty who heads the Astronomy department.

Sites of Historical Sorcery: A travel guidebook Hermione Granger consults.

Skeeter, Rita: A journalist for the daily wizarding newspaper, the *Daily Prophet;* her reportage is more fit for a tabloid rag than a respectable paper, since she enjoys slanting, spinning, and exaggerating the news. She's able to get stories no others can because as an unregistered animagus she can assume the shape of a beetle, allowing her to spy virtually undetected.

Skele-Gro: A potent liquid used by Madam Pomfrey to regrow bones, a painful process. Harry Potter must drink this after he breaks his arm in a Quidditch match, which Gilderoy Lockhart attempts to repair by casting a spell that goes awry. Instead of mending Harry's bones, Lockhart *removes* them, giving Harry a "rubber" arm that dangles uselessly.

Skiving Snackboxes: Invented by Fred and George Weasley, these are sweets deliberately designed to get you temporarily sick; used to get out of class.

Sleekeazy's Hair Potion: Used to straighten out frizzy hair. Hermione Granger uses it on her bushy hair to straighten it out for the Yule Ball.

Sloper, Jack: He replaces one of the Weasley twins on the Gryffindor Quidditch team after they are given a lifetime ban from playing, courtesy of Professor Umbridge.

Slytherin: Founded by Salazar Slytherin and currently headed by Professor Snape, it is one of four houses at Hogwarts. Numerous dark wizards have come from this house. The Sorting Hat wants to put Harry Potter here because it will help him on his path to greatness, but Harry by sheer will asserts his desire to be in Gryffindor, in which he's placed. The house trait of Slytherin is cunning.

Smeltings: A private school Dudley Dursley attends, following in his father's big footsteps. When Vernon and Petunia see their son decked out in the school uniform, they are overcome with emotion, but Harry is silently convulsing in laughter.

Smethley, Veronica: According to Gilderoy Lockhart, she is one of his biggest fans.

Snape, Professor Severus: A member of the faculty at Hogwarts, described as a thin man with shoulder-length black hair, a hooked nose, and sallow skin. The Potions Master at Hogwarts, he has his sights set on Defense Against the Dark Arts. The head of Slytherin House, Snape especially enjoys bedeviling Harry Potter and tormenting Neville Longbottom.

SNEAK: The ever clever Hermione Granger puts a hex on all the students attending Harry Potter's secret Defense Against the Dark Arts class. If a student rats out on Harry, the hex produces purple pustules forming the word "SNEAK" on that person's forehead.

Snuffles: A name Sirius Black tells Harry Potter, Ron Weasley, and Hermione Granger to use when discussing him amongst themselves.

Sock: An article of clothing belonging to Harry Potter; he puts a book inside it and hands it to Lucius Malfoy. Malfoy tosses the sock aside to get at the book, and Dobby, his house-elf, catches it. Malfoy's "gift" of the sock frees Dobby from his lifelong servitude to Malfoy's family. Socks are now Dobby's favorite clothes.

Sonnets of a Sorcerer: A bewitched book found by Arthur Weasley; after reading it, the reader forever speaks in limericks.

Sonorus: A charm used to amplify your voice. To use it, point your wand at your own throat and speak the charm. As commentator, Ludo Bagman uses it to speak to the 100,000 witches and wizards who have filled the seats of the Quidditch World Cup Stadium for its 422nd tournament.

Sorting Ceremony: New students at Hogwarts must be sorted into one of its four houses: Gryffindor, Hufflepuff, Ravenclaw, and Slytherin. This is accomplished by a ceremony at which a Sorting Hat is placed on each student; the cogitating, talking hat then decides where the student should be placed. The hat customarily belts out a rhyming sorting hat song to explain what it does.

Sorting Hat: Kept in Dumbledore's office when not in use at the beginning of each school term, this ancient and wise hat sings a song before beginning its principal duty, which is to choose the appropriate house for each student.

Spattergroit: A skin affliction that leaves the victim pockmarked.

Spellotape: Used by Ron Weasley to repair his damaged wand.

S.P.E.W.: An acronym invented by Hermione Granger, which stands for Society for the Promotion of Elfish Welfare. (Her original title was "Stop the Outrageous Abuse of Our Fellow Magical Creatures and Campaign for a Change in Their Legal Status.") Granger becomes a passionate advocate of house-elf rights after seeing Winky badgered by Ministry of Magic officials at the Quidditch World Cup tournament.

Spinnet, Alicia: A Gryffindor student and a member of the Quidditch team.

Splinch: The unfortunate result of apparating ineptly, which results in leaving half of oneself behind; the only remedy for the victim, who is physically stuck between two places, is to call the magical equivalent of 911 (the Accidental Magic Reversal Squad) for assistance. For this reason, even some experienced witches and wizards prefer to use other methods of locomotion.

Spore, Phyllida: Author of *One Thousand Magical Herbs and Fungi,* a required first-year course book for the Herbology class taught by Professor Sprout.

Spotted Dick: A dessert served in the Great Hall at Hogwarts Castle.

Sprout, Professor: A member of the faculty at Hogwarts who teaches Herbology.

S.P.U.G.: Society for the Protection of Ugly Goblins, an acronym Ron Weasley makes up to mock Hermione Granger's S.P.E.W.

Staircases: Hogwarts has 142 staircases, which move without warning, shifting position of their own volition.

The Standard Book of Spells: By Miranda Goshawk, this is a standard textbook required at Hogwarts.

Stealth Sensoring Spells: Placed by Professor Umbridge around her office door after Lee Jordan deposited nifflers inside.

Stinging Hex: A spell that causes a painful red welt. Harry Potter produces one against Professor Snape during a personal tutelage on Occlumency. When Potter recalls an intensely personal moment—he and Cho Chang under the mistletoe—he accidentally produces this hex.

Stink Pellets: A joke toy favored by Fred and George Weasley, stink pellets are sold at Zonko's Joke Shop, a retail store specializing in such things, which is why it's one of the Weasley twins' favorite stores.

Stoatshead Hill: For the Quidditch World Cup, 200 Portkeys were set up around England. The one nearest to the Weasley family, in the form of an old boot, was located on this hill.

Stonewall High: The public school Harry Potter attended before Hogwarts.

Strengthening Solution: A potion fifth-year students are taught in Professor Snape's class.

Strout, Miriam: A Healer at St. Mungo's Hospital for Magical Maladies and Injuries, she's the one who discovered the body of Broderick Bode. She had mistaken the plant near his bedside for a harmless Flitterboom, but it was actually a deadly Devil's Snare.

Study of Ancient Runes: A course taken by Hermione Granger in her third year at Hogwarts.

A Study of Recent Developments in Wizardry: Reference book found in the Hogwarts library.

Stupefy: A stunning spell that takes the form of fiery red light. Dragon keepers used it to rein in four dragons at the Triwizard Tournament.

Substantive Charm: In preparation for their O.W.L.s, Seamus Finnigan studies this charm, while Dean Thomas checks its definition against a standard textbook, *The Standard Book of Spells*.

Sugar-Spun Quills: A "special effects" candy available at Honeydukes.

Summoning Charm: A charm used to bring an object to you—a broom, for instance.

Swedish Short-Snout: A dragon Cedric Diggory faced in the first competition at the Triwizard Tournament held at Hogwarts.

Swelling Solution: A potion that induces immediate swelling.

Switch, Emeric: Author of *A Beginner's Guide to Transfiguration,* a required course book for first-year students in Professor McGonagall's Transfiguration class.

T

Tail-Twig Clippers: A component of the Broomstick Servicing Kit.

Tarantallegra: A charm used to make someone dance uncontrollably, Draco Malfoy uses it on Harry Potter in a wizards' duel.

Tawny Owl: The owl owned by Neville Longbottom.

Theory of Charms: The first O.W.L. exam faced by Harry Potter and his classmates.

Thestrals: Winged horses that can only be seen by those who have seen death firsthand. Hogwarts has a small herd of thestrals used to pull carriages. Dumbledore occasionally uses one for personal transportation in lieu of Apparating.

Thomas, Dean: Gryffindor student who dates Ginny Weasley. Seamus Finnigan's best friend.

Three Broomsticks: In Hogsmeade, this is the place to get hot, foaming butterbeer.

Tibbles, Mr.: Put on the lookout by Mrs. Figg to protect Harry Potter.

Time-Turner: A "tiny, sparkling hourglass," it turns back time. Hermione Granger uses it to give her more time for studying. She also uses it for a

highly illegal purpose: to change the future, a risky proposition. (She wants to save Buckbeak from execution.)

Timms, Agatha: She bets Ludo Bagman on the outcome of the Quidditch World Cup by putting up half her share in her eel farm.

Tiny Firebolts: Sold at the Quidditch World Cup, these are miniature flying models.

Toffee: A confectionary found at Honeydukes.

Tofty, Professor: An O.W.L. examiner who looks to be the oldest among those who show up from the Ministry of Magic.

Tonks, Andromeda: Mother of Nymphadora Tonks, she married Ted Tonks.

Tonks, Nymphadora: A very young and clumsy Auror, she is part of the Advance Guard who take Harry from the Dursleys' house.

Ton-Tongue Toffee: A joke candy invented by Fred and George Weasley, it comes in a brightly colored wrapper and, if eaten, will enlarge one's tongue to a length of at least four feet, possibly more. Fred and George Weasley deliberately drop this candy in easy reach of Dudley Dursley, who eats one and discovers that his tongue is inexplicably growing to an extraordinary length. Fortunately, Mr. Weasley is on hand and restores Dudley to normalcy.

Toothflossing Stringmints: A "special effects" candy available at Honeydukes.

Transfiguration Today: A publication for the wizarding community.

Transmogrifian Torture: A curse cited by Gilderoy Lockhart to explain the petrification of Mrs. Norris, a cat belonging to Filch. (Lockhart, as usual, volunteers that if only he had been present, he could have provided the appropriate counter-curse to keep the cat from being afflicted.)

Travels with Trolls: A classroom textbook by Gilderoy Lockhart.

Travers: A supporter of the Dark Lord, he helped in the murder of the McKinnons. Travers was betrayed by Karkaroff.

Treacle Pudding: A favorite dessert of Harry Potter's.

Treacle Tart: A dessert served in the Great Hall at Hogwarts Castle.

Trelawney, Sibyll: A faculty member at Hogwarts who teaches Divination in a decidedly odd classroom that recalls a fortune-teller's chamber. She is, herself, a decidedly odd-looking person from Harry Potter's perspective. Rowling describes her through his eyes as "a large, glittering insect." She is a great-great-granddaughter of a well-regarded Seer, Cassandra Trelawney.

Trevor: The name of Neville Longbottom's pet toad.

Trimble, Quentin: Author of *The Dark Forces: A Guide to Self-Protection,* a required course book for Defense Against the Dark Arts classes.

Triwizard Cup: A Portkey that transports Harry Potter and Cedric Diggory to a graveyard where Tom Riddle, Lord Voldemort's father, is buried, near the Riddle family home; Voldemort and his Death Eaters have been lying in wait here for Harry Potter.

Triwizard Tournament: A wizarding competition among the three largest wizardry schools in Europe (Hogwarts, Beauxbatons, and Durmstrang) to enhance interschool ties. Each school offers up one champion to compete in the tournament, who must face three magical tasks. Besides bragging rights, the winning school gets the coveted Triwizard Cup; its champion wins 1,000 Galleons. Entry is limited to those 17 years old or older. It was organized by Ludo Bagman.

Turpin, Lisa: Ravenclaw student.

Two Predictions: According to Dumbledore, Professor Trelawney has made, by his estimation, only two real predictions.

U

Umbridge, Dolores Jane: A Senior Undersecretary to the Minister of Magic, this toadlike witch assumes the post of Defense Against the Dark Arts teacher at Hogwarts and, with the endorsement of the Ministry of Magic, becomes not only a High Inquisitor at the school, but also its Headmistress. She's the teacher everyone loves to hate.

Umgubular Slashkilter: This is a fearsome weapon that Luna Lovegood, who believes in all the conspiracy theories about the Ministry of Magic, cites as evidence to "prove" her meritless claim that Cornelius Fudge is a magical mastermind. She also asserts he assassinates goblins and feeds poison to his enemies.

Undetectable Poisons: An essay Harry Potter writes for Professor Snape's class.

Undiluted Bubotuber Pus: Hermione Granger gets a hate letter tainted with this liquid, which produces boils on her hands, sending her to the school infirmary.

Unfogging the Future: A basic textbook by Cassandra Vablatsky, required for Divination classes taught by Professor Trelawney. It provides instruction on fortune-telling methods.

Unicorn: A magical creature resembling a horse with a spiral horn on its forehead, it sheds silver-colored blood when wounded. The blood of a unicorn can keep anyone alive, but one will live a cursed life for killing such a

pure creature. As foals, unicorns are the color of pure gold; at age two they change to a silver color; at four, a horn emerges on the forehead; at seven, when full grown, they turn white.

Unplottable: A charm put on a house to render it impossible for Muggles to find, it was put on the Black family house in London.

V

Vanishing Spell: A difficult spell taught to fifth-year students, it causes one to disappear.

Vault 713: A vault heavily guarded by magic because of its invaluable treasure, the Philosopher's Stone, created by Nicholas Flamel. Hagrid retrieves the small package from this vault at Dumbledore's request. Soon thereafter, the vault is broken into by dark wizards, who attempt to steal it. Because the bank is considered inpregnable, the break-in makes headlines in the *Daily Prophet*.

Venomous Tentacula Seeds: These are "shriveled black pods" that Fred and George Weasley need for their Skiving Snackboxes. They are difficult to obtain because they're controlled items (Class C non-tradeable substances).

Veritaserum: A powerful truth potion, it is a controlled substance that can only be used under "very strict Ministry guidelines."

Victims of Lord Voldemort: According to Hagrid, the Potters, the McKinnons, the Bones, and the Prewetts.

Violet: This witch rushes from picture to picture hanging in Hogwarts, searching for the Fat Lady to tell her that Harry Potter was selected as a champion for the Triwizard Tournament.

Visitor's Entrance, Ministry of Magic: A red phone booth, designed to look innocuous.

Voldemort, Lord: A powerful dark wizard who is so feared that even his name is rarely uttered, he is responsible for killing scores of people, including Harry Potter's parents. He also attempted, but failed, to kill Harry, which is why Harry is known in the wizarding community as "the boy who lived," the only one to have ever survived the Killing Curse. The consensus is that Headmaster Dumbledore is the only one who might possibly defeat Voldemort in a wizards' duel, owing to Dumbledore's greater skill and knowledge—a notion he downplays. Be that as it may, Voldemort is growing in strength, gathering his Death Eaters around him, and making active plans to finish what he started: to kill Harry Potter. (Voldemort was a Slytherin student at Hogworts; see Tom Marvolo Riddle.)

Voyages with Vampires: A textbook required by Gilderoy Lockhart for his class, Defense Against the Dark Arts.

W

Waddiwasi: After Peeves put chewing gum in a keyhole, Professor Lupin uses this spell to expel it and insert it up Peeves's left nostril.

Waffling, Adalbert: Author of *Magical Theory,* a required course book for first-year students at Hogwarts.

Wandering with Werewolves: An autobiographical, fanciful book by Gilderoy Lockhart. The book recounts how he saved a village from werewolves, though proper credit should go to an unnamed Armenian warlock.

Warbeck, Celestina: A singing sorceress who can be heard on a radio program, *Witching Hour.*

Weasley, Arthur: He works at the Ministry of Magic in the Misuse of Muggles Artifacts Office. He and his wife, Molly, have seven children: daughter Ginny, and sons Ron, Percy, Fred and George (twins), Charlie, and Bill.

Weasley, Bill: A head boy when he was a Gryffindor student at Hogwarts, he is currently living in Egypt and works for Gringotts Bank as a curse breaker. Harry Potter considers him cool, and he is. He sports an earring, wears long hair, and dresses fashionably—a sharp contrast to the other Weasley boys.

Weasley, Charlie: Though we don't know for whom Charlie works, we know that he has spent time in Romania studying dragons. As a Gryffindor student at Hogwarts, he specialized in the Care of Magical Creatures; he was also a celebrated Seeker for his house.

Weasley, Fred and George: The Weasley twins are both in Gryffindor (as are all the other Weasley children), and both are Beaters flying outdated brooms, Cleansweep Fives, which are the best they can afford. Their real interest is not academic, to the consternation of their parents, who had hoped they would follow after their father, Arthur, who works at the Ministry of Magic. The boys' career ambition is to open a retail joke shop for the wizarding community.

Weasley, Ginny: Initially starstruck by Harry Potter, Ginny develops a crush on him. The youngest child in the Weasley family, she is their only daughter. Like her brothers, she has flaming red hair—the family trademark. In the second book, she is duped and then victimized by Lord Voldemort. In the fifth book, she replaces Harry Potter as the Gryffindor Seeker after Professor Umbridge bans him for life from playing Quidditch.

Weasley, Molly: Married to Arthur Weasley, she is a witch. She and her husband have seven children (see Arthur Weasley).

Weasley, Percy: One of the Weasleys, Percy is the most career-minded. A former Gryffindor prefect and head boy who took his duties at Hogwarts seriously, he is the quintessential career-seeking bureaucrat who rises up through the ranks of the Ministry of Magic. His career goal, of course, is to become the Minister of Magic. In the fifth book, he must make a decision to side with the Ministry or his family, and he, regrettably, chooses the former. He is a career climber who tests the winds of fortune and rides them accordingly.

Weasley, Ron: One of six Weasley sons, he is Harry Potter's best friend. They met on the train to Hogwarts and struck up a lasting friendship. The youngest son in the Weasley family, Ron gets the hand-me-downs. More than any of the others in the family, he's acutely aware that his family is not well off, and it's a source of constant embarrassment—especially so when reminded of it at every opportunity by a rich, supercilious snot named Draco Malfoy, who enjoys taunting him, Harry Potter, and Hermione Granger. In his fifth year, Ron becomes a prefect and a Keeper for the Gryffindor house Quidditch team.

"Weasley Is Our King": A song Slytherin students came up with to mock Ron Weasley after he began playing on the Gryffindor Quidditch team.

Weatherby, Mr.: Mr. Crouch, from the Ministry of Magic, misremembers Percy Weasley's name and calls him, to Percy's chagrin, Mr. Weatherby. Weasley is left in charge when Crouch, who helped arranged the Triwizard Tournament, meets with Ludo Bagman, Dumbledore, and others to make arrangements.

Weighing of the Wands: Before the first challenge for the Triwizard Tournament, the champions from each school must submit their wands to Mr. Ollivander for weighing.

Weird Sisters: The nickname for the Parvati sisters.

Weird Wizarding Dilemmas and Their Solutions: A library book Hermione Granger consults in hopes that it will help Harry Potter prepare for his second trial at the Triwizard Tournament.

Welsh Green: The dragon Fleur Delacour must face in her first trial at the Triwizard Tournament.

Wendelin the Weird: A witch who was addicted to the tickling sensation produced by the flame freezing charm; she enjoyed being burned at the stake so much that she deliberately and repeatedly changed her appearance to get caught again and "burned." This may account for her name.

Where There's a Wand, There's a Way: A library book Harry Potter consults in hopes that it will help him with his second trial at the Triwizard Tournament.

Which Broomstick?: A guide to the various models of broomsticks available. After his Nimbus Two Thousand is destroyed by the Whomping Willow, Harry Potter borrows this book from Oliver Wood. Ron consults it after he's assured of getting a new broom, a Comet Two Ninety.

Whitby, Kevin: A Hufflepuff student.

Whizzing Worms: An item sold at Zonko's Joke Shop, favored by Hogwarts students.

Whomping Willow: Located on the grounds of Hogwarts, this tree lives up to its name: It whomps the Ford Anglia with Ron Weasley and Harry Potter inside, after their car loses power and flies into this malevolent tree.

Widdershins, Willy: The perpetrator of the regurgitating toilets, he overhears Harry Potter and company talk in the Hog's Head about their secret class and rats on them to the High Inquisitor. He knows she has a direct tie to the Ministry of Magic and hopes his loyalty will be taken into consideration and leniency will be forthcoming for his transgressions involving the regurgitating toilets in the Muggles' world.

Wilkes: A Death Eater killed by an Auror.

Wimple, Gilbert: A member of the Committee on Experimental Charms at the Ministry of Magic.

Windgardium Leviosa: A levitation charm that must be properly pronounced to work, as Hermione Granger points out to a frustrated Ron Weasley, who can't get his feather to levitate.

Winky: A female house-elf belonging to Barty Crouch. She is of the firm opinion that Harry Potter made a mistake in freeing another house-elf, Dobby, who now wants to rise above his station. She becomes one of more than a hundred house-elves at Hogwarts Castle, which has the largest number of them in England.

Wisteria Walk: The street Mrs. Figg lives on.

Witch Weekly: A magazine with saucy tidbits of news; Rita Skeeter is a contributor, of course. One of its contests is the "Most-Charming-Smile Award," which Gilderoy Lockhart has won five consecutive times.

Wizards at the Department of Mysteries: Dumbledore, Sirius, Lupin, Moody, Tonks, and Kingsley show up to assist Harry Potter in a battle against Lord Voldemort and his Death Eaters.

Wizards' Duel: Accompanied by their seconds in case they are killed, wand-armed wizards face off in a fight to the finish.

Wizengamot: The Wizard High Court, the highest authority in the magical community in England.

Wolfsbane Potion: A fairly recent discovery, this potion prevented Professor Lupin ("lupus" = wolf) from assuming the shape of a werewolf.

Wonky-Faint: Hermione Granger, a star student, can't bother to remember the Wronski Feint, which Viktor Krum uses in Quidditch matches. She calls it by this name, which pains Harry Potter, who is a Quidditch expert.

Wood, Oliver: A former Quidditch team captain for Gryffindor. After graduation, Wood becomes a member of the Puddlemere United reserve team. In his first year, Harry Potter is brought to Wood's attention by Professor McGonagall, who declares that she has found their house a new Seeker, the youngest in a century.

Wormtail: (1) An obsequious toad, he's a servant to Lord Voldemort, who considers him beneath contempt. Wormtail brought Bertha Jorkins, whom he met at a wayside inn, to Lord Voldemort, who used magic to extract information from her. A cowardly wizard with a petulant nature, Wormtail more than lives up to his name. (2) Nickname for Peter Pettigrew when he was a student at Hogwarts. As an animagus, he assumed the shape of a rat after his supposed death and, for protection, hid in a wizarding family, the Weasleys.

Wronski Defensive Feint: A dangerous, diversionary tactic used by a Seeker in a Quidditch game.

WWN: Wizarding Wireless Network.

Y

Year with the Yeti: An autobiographical, likely fanciful, book by Gilderoy Lockhart.

Yule Ball: A tradition of the Triwizard Tournament, it's a formal dance restricted to fourth-year (and above) students, encouraging the students from all three magical schools to mix. Part of the tradition is that the selected champions open the ball with dance partners of their choice, which comes as an unpleasant surprise to Harry Potter, who wasn't expecting it.

Z

Zamojski, Ladislaw: A Polish International Chaser who went up against Barry Ryan, an Irish International Keeper.

A List of Harry Potter Book Publishers Worldwide

Note: These websites are accessible via links at www.jkrowling.com, from which this list was compiled.

Albania: Publishing House Dituria
Australia: Allen and Unwin
Bangladesh: Ankur Prakashani
Brazil: Editora Rocco
Bulgaria: Egmont Bulgaria
Canada: Raincoast Books
China: People's Literature
   Publishing House
Croatia: Algoritam
Czech Republic: Albatros
   Publishing House
Denmark: Glydendal
Egypt: Nahdet Misr
Estonia: Varrak Publishers
Faroe Islands: Bokadeildi Foroya
   Laerarafelags
Finland: Tammi Publishers
France: Gallimard Jeunesse

Georgia: Bakur Sulakauri
   Publishing
Germany: Carlsen Verlag GmbH
Germany (Low German): Verlag
   Michael Jung
Greece: Psichogios Publications S.A.
Greenland: Atuakkiorfik Greenland
   Publishers
Hungary: Animus Publishing
Iceland: Bjartur
Indonesia: Penerbit PT Gramedia
   Pustaka Utama
Israel: Books in the Attic/Miskal
Italy: Adriano Salani Editore
Japan: Say-zan-sha Publications
Korea: Moonhak Soochup
   Publishing
Latvia: Jumava
Lithuania: Alma Littera

Macedonia: Publishing House Kultura

Malaysia: Penerbitan Pelangi Sdn. Bhd

Netherlands: Uitgerij De Harmonie

Norway: N.W. Damm and Son A.S.

Pakistan: Oxford University Press

Poland: Harbor Point/Media Rodzina

Portugal: Editorial Presenca

Romania: Egmont Romania

Russia: Rosman Publishing

Siberia: Alfa-Narodna Knjiga

Slovak Republic: Ikar

Slovenia: Epta d.o.o.

South Africa: Human & Rousseau (pty) Ltd.

Spain (Castillian/Basque/Galician): Publicaciones y Editiones

Spain (World Catalan): Editorial Empuries

Sweden: Tiden Young Books

Taiwan: Crown Publishing

Thailand: Nanmeebooks

Turkey: Yapi Kredi Kultur Sanat Yayincilik

United Kingdom (England): Bloomsbury Publishing

Ukraine: A-BA-BA-HA-LA-MA-HA

USA: Scholastic

USA (large-print edition): Thorndike Press

Vietnam: Tre Publishing House

Yugoslavia: Alfa-Narodna Knjiga

HARRY POTTER ET PHILOSOPHI LAPIS

If you can't read it, Latin will be Greek to you; but if you *can* read Latin, you'll find out that far from being a dead language, it's quite alive, thanks in part to Harry Potter.

Unless a writer is a philologist like J. R. R. Tolkien, inventing languages is a real, sometimes insurmountable, challenge. Often, fantasy writers simply make it all up, with the result that the words don't ring true. They sound wrong because their linguistics are not consistent.

Rowling could have conjured up a language like the other writers, but she seized upon the idea of having the spells spoken in Latin.

And if you want to read a Harry Potter novel in Latin, the first one is available in hardback in the U.S. for $21.95. You might want to buy a copy of *Collins Gem Latin Dictionary: Second Edition,* published by HarperCollins, to help you out if you get stuck.

At the very least, you should know the Hogwarts school motto: *Draco dormiens numquam titillandus.*

It's actually pretty good advice!

The Final Exam: A Trivia Quiz for Muggles about J. K. Rowling and Harry Potter

Of course *you're* an expert on Rowling and Harry Potter, but how much do your friends *really* know about the writer and her work? Test their knowledge with this quiz, a final exam, which has questions ranging from easy to difficult, and bonus questions that are for real experts only.

Biographical

1. Pete Rowling and Anne Volant—Joanne Rowling's parents—were both in the military when they first met. Where did they meet?

2. Joanne Rowling has one sibling, a sister. What is her name?

3. What does the "K" in Joanne K. Rowling stand for?

4. When Joanne was growing up, she wanted a specific pet but could not have one. Years later, as an adult, she did get the childhood pet denied her. What kind of pet?

5. As a teenager, what school did Joanne Rowling attend?

6. The literary inspiration for one of the main characters in the Harry Potter novels is Rowling herself. Who is that character?

7. What position of responsibility did Joanne Rowling hold as a student at Wyedean Comprehensive?

8. Who is Joanne Rowling's favorite author?

9. On what public transportation did Joanne Rowling first get the idea to write a series of novels about Harry Potter?

10. What childhood friend of Rowling's is the model for Harry Potter's best friend, Ron Weasley?

11. Long before Rowling began writing the Harry Potter novels, she decided to limit the books to a specific number, one for each year of school he would attend. How many novels did she plan to write?

12. What college did Joanne Rowling graduate from?

13. What did Joanne Rowling major in when in college?

14. After graduation, Joanne Rowling took a teaching position overseas. Where did she go?

15. When Joanne Rowling returned to England, where did she move to?

16. Joanne Rowling went to a restaurant in Edinburgh, half-owned by her brother-in-law, to write in longhand the first Harry Potter novel. What was the restaurant's name?

17. What literary agency "discovered" Joanne Rowling?

18. Who at the literary agency initially championed Rowling's fledgling manuscript?

19. Which British publisher bought the first Harry Potter novel?

20. What sum was paid to Joanne Rowling for her first Harry Potter novel?

21. What U.S. publisher bought the rights to the Harry Potter novels?

22. What sum was paid to Joanne Rowling for the U.S. rights to the first Harry Potter novel?

23. Why did Joanne Rowling's literary agent recommend she use initials for her name instead of simply "Joanne Rowling"?

24. Joanne Rowling received a sizable grant from the Scottish Arts Council. What was her principal purchase with the grant money?

25. Joanne Rowling, who has sold a quarter-billion books to date, saw her first book published on June 26, 1997. What was its first print run?

26. *Harry Potter and the Philosopher's Stone* is the original title of the first novel in the series. When published in the U.S., what was its name changed to?

27. How many copies did Scholastic publish for the first printing of the first Harry Potter book?

28. What major literary prize did *Harry Potter and the Philosopher's Stone* win?

29. Who is the cover artist in the U.S. for the Harry Potter novels?

30. In terms of sales, which country accounts for the majority of all copies sold in the world?

31. What is Joanne Rowling's favorite house at Hogwarts?

32. Where does Joanne Rowling currently live?

HARRY POTTER AND THE SORCERER'S STONE

33. How young was Harry Potter when he was orphaned?

34. How old was Harry Potter when he discovered, after being told by Rubeus Hagrid, that he was a wizard?

35. What mark is on Harry Potter's forehead?

36. What is Harry Potter's late father's name?

37. What is Harry Potter's late mother's name?

38. Who killed Harry Potter's parents?

39. After Harry Potter was orphaned, a decision was made to leave him on the doorstep of his mother's sister, Petunia Dursley. Who made that decision?

40. What is the word used to describe a non-magic person? (Hint: Look in *Oxford English Dictionary*.)

41. Harry Potter is brought to the Dursley residence by Rubeus Hagrid, who is riding a vehicle owned by Sirius Black. What kind of vehicle?

42. What is the name of Vernon and Petunia Dursley's spoiled son?

43. When we first meet Harry Potter, he doesn't have his own room at the Dursley residence. Where in the house *does* he stay?

44. Acceptance letters arrive from Hogwarts, but Harry Potter never receives them because they are intercepted by Uncle Vernon. How are these letters delivered?

45. After the letters fail to reach Harry Potter, an emissary is sent from Hogwarts to hand-deliver an acceptance letter and, if necessary, personally fetch him. Who arrives to perform this necessary task?

46. Why is Rubeus Hagrid such an imposing physical figure?

47. What gift does Hagrid bring Harry Potter when he arrives at the shack by the sea?

48. What is the name of the school to which Harry Potter has been accepted?

49. Where does Harry Potter go to buy his school supplies?

50. Where does Harry Potter go to get money to pay for his school supplies?

51. What kind of creatures run Gringotts?

52. What fearsome creatures are reputed to reside deep in the bowels of Gringotts?

53. What is the name of the newspaper that serves the wizarding community?

54. What essential school supply must Harry Potter buy at Ollivanders?

55. What birthday gift does Rubeus Hagrid give to Harry Potter?

56. What item is forbidden for first-year students to purchase?

57. Harry Potter first meets Professor Quirrell at the Leaky Cauldron and learns that he's the latest addition to the Hogwarts faculty. What subject does he teach?

58. Wizard currency comes in three coins. What are their names?

59. Where does Harry Potter buy his school robes?

60. What is the favorite wizarding sport?

61. Harry Potter's wand, like all wands, has a key component. What is that component in his wand?

62. From where does Harry Potter leave in London to go to Hogwarts?

63. Who does Harry Potter befriend on the train to Hogwarts?

64. There are four houses at Hogwarts. What are they named?

65. A Sorting Ceremony is held to determine each student's house. Who—or what—is responsible for the sorting?

66. Into what house is Harry Potter sorted?

67. Into what house is his new friend, Ron Weasley, sorted?

68. Into what house does Hermione Granger get sorted?

BONUS QUESTION #1:

How many staircases are there at Hogwarts?

---

69. Who is the instructor for Harry Potter's flying lessons?

70. Who guards the entrance to the Gryffindor common room?

71. After seeing Harry Potter's skill at flying a broom, Professor McGonagall realizes that he's a natural for their Quidditch team. What position does Harry Potter play? (Hint: His father played the same position when he was a student at Hogwarts.)

72. First-year students are, of course, forbidden to own a broom, but the rule is broken for Harry Potter, who needs one as a Seeker. What model broom does he receive as a gift?

73. The goal of Quidditch is to score as many points as possible—best achieved by catching the elusive Golden Snitch, which is the principal responsibility of each team's Seeker. How many points does the Seeker earn when he catches the Snitch?

BONUS QUESTION #2:

How tall is a mountain troll?

---

74. What unusual animal does Hagrid buy from a "Greek chappie" whom he met at a pub?

75. What does Hagrid name this unusually dangerous pet?

76. Harry Potter gets a glimpse of his long-lost parents in an unusual magical item found at Hogwarts. What is that item called?

> **BONUS QUESTION #3:**
>
> Who is the librarian at Hogwarts?

77. A friendship develops between Harry Potter and Ron Weasley; soon a third friend enters the picture—a self-assured "swot," a brainy girl. Who is she?

78. For Christmas at his first year at Hogwarts, Harry Potter receives an anonymous gift. The gift belonged to Harry Potter's father, James. What is that gift?

79. What geographical area near Hogwarts is off-limits to students?

80. What unusual, and illegal, pet does Hagrid breed at his home on school grounds?

81. When Hagrid, Harry Potter, and Hermione Granger go into the Forbidden Forest, they encounter mythical, starstruck creatures. What kind of creatures are they?

82. What was Fluffy guarding?

83. Deep under Hogwarts, Harry Potter, Hermione Granger, and Ron Weasley are ensnared by a deadly plant. What is it called?

84. What popular strategy-based game is played out life-size by Harry Potter, Hermione Granger, and Ron Weasley?

85. Lord Voldemort is rarely referred to by name, though Hermione Granger correctly points out (in the second book) that "fear of the name only increases fear of the thing itself." Rather than call him by his real name, how is Lord Voldemort obliquely referred to?

> **BONUS QUESTION #4:**
>
> At the end of the first year, each house at Hogwarts is awarded points. Gryffindor and Slytherin are tied, but the tie is broken when Neville Longbottom earns ten points for Gryffindor. How many points did each house have *before* the tie-breaker?

HARRY POTTER AND THE CHAMBER OF SECRETS

86. Dobby, a house-elf, comes to visit Harry to warn him against returning to Hogwarts. To convince Harry not to return, he deliberately disrupts the dinner party to draw unwanted attention to Harry. What exactly does Dobby do?

87. The unauthorized use of magic at the Dursley residence results in an owl-delivered letter from the Ministry of Magic. Who sends the letter?

88. Harry has moved from the cupboard under the stairs to a spare bedroom that once belonged to Dudley Dursley. But he's a prisoner in his own room, since the windows have been barred and the door locked. How does he escape from his confinement?

89. At what office at the Ministry of Magic does Ron's father, Arthur Weasley, work?

90. What is the address of the Weasley residence?

BONUS QUESTION #5:

Who is Celestina Warbeck?

---

91. After breakfast, what task does Mrs. Weasley assign her sons George, Fred, and Ron?

BONUS QUESTION #6:

Which is Ron Weasley's favorite Quidditch team?

---

92. When it's time to head off to Diagon Alley to get school supplies for the upcoming term, the entire Weasley family travels by an unusual method— transportation via chimney flue. What is actually used to make the transport occur?

93. This is Harry Potter's first time transporting by this method, but he doesn't arrive where he should because he didn't speak clearly. Instead of arriving at Diagon Alley, where does Harry turn up?

> ## BONUS QUESTION #7:
>
> Who did Harry unexpectedly see in Mr. Borgin's store?

94. Harry encounters a rough-looking group of witches and wizards who obviously want to steer him in the wrong direction. Who just happens to be in the area and sees Harry and rescues him from his predicament?

95. Where does the Weasley family go to buy books for the upcoming school year?

96. Who is signing books at the bookstore when the Weasleys show up?

97. The author signing books at the store is the newest addition to the faculty at Hogwarts. What position does he hold?

98. Previously, Harry escapes the confines of his barred and locked room at the Dursleys by means of a flying car. What are the make and model of the car?

99. When Harry and Ron are unable to catch the Hogwarts Express, they use the flying car to get to school. Unfortunately, their arrival is anything but smooth. In fact, they have a crash landing. Where do they crash?

100. As a result of "hijacking" the car to get to school, Ron Weasley is humiliated in front of his classmates by his mother. What does she send that embarrasses him?

> ## BONUS QUESTION #8:
>
> Picture this: a new student, Colin Creevey, is awestruck by Harry Potter. What item does Colin have with him at all times?

101. At his first class with Professor Lockhart, Harry is surprised to have to take a pop quiz. Even more surprising is the nature of the questions. Why would those questions be surprising?

102. When Harry Potter goes to Quidditch practice, he's surprised, and then dismayed, to learn that the Slytherin team has a new Seeker. Who is the team's new Seeker?

103. Nearly Headless Nick, who is usually in a good mood, is unhappy because of a rejection letter he receives from Sir Patrick Delaney-Podmore, who says he doesn't fill the principal requirement for which group?

104. Mr. Argus Filch is a Squib—a non-magical person born in a wizard family. To make up for his lack of natural aptitude, he takes a beginner's course in magic. What is the course title?

BONUS QUESTION #9:

Nearly Headless Nick doesn't celebrate his birthday but his deathday. What is that date?

---

105. The Hogwarts school houses are named after their four founders, powerful witches and wizards. Who, by name, were the original founders?

106. After getting struck by a rogue Bludger in a Quidditch match, Harry Potter's arm is broken. Unfortunately, Professor Lockhart volunteers to fix his arm and, in doing so, makes things worse! What is used by Madam Pomfrey to cure Harry?

107. To arm the students with knowledge, two Hogwarts professors conduct a dueling class. Who are those two professors?

108. The professors suggest that, as a teaching lesson, two students square off. Who are those students?

109. Harry is surprised when he speaks in a language associated with Slytherin house—he can speak to snakes. What is that language?

110. When Ron Weasley and Harry Potter drove off to Hogwarts in a flying car seen by Muggles, Ron's father, Arthur, was fined by the Ministry of Magic. How much was the fine?

111. Gilderoy Lockhart, effusive in his thanks after getting Valentine cards, uses the opportunity to deliver cards to students. Whom does he retain as delivery persons?

112. When Tom Riddle was a student at Hogwarts, who was its headmaster?

113. Using the attacks on the students as a pretext, Lucius Malfoy delivers an order to Headmaster Dumbledore, removing him from his post. What is that order?

114. What creature do Ron Weasley and Harry Potter encounter in the Forbidden Forest?

115. What creature does Harry Potter encounter in the Chamber of Secrets?

116. Dobby receives an unexpected gift of clothing from his owner, freeing him from a lifetime of involuntary servitude. What gift does Dobby receive?

HARRY POTTER AND THE PRISONER OF AZKABAN

117. Who *is* the prisoner of Azkaban?

118. In a *Daily Prophet* drawing, an astonished Arthur Weasley wins the annual Grand Prize Galleon Draw. How much does he win and what does he do with most of the money?

119. One of the required texts for third-year students is a very unusual book required by Rubeus Hagrid for his class, Care of Magical Creatures. What is the title of that unusual book?

120. What is the only magical community in England?

121. Third-year students are allowed on weekends to visit the nearby magical community, but Harry Potter cannot. Why?

122. The excuse the Dursleys use to explain Harry Potter's absence during the school year is his attendance at which school?

BONUS QUESTION #10:

When Aunt Marge comes to visit the Dursleys, she leaves her beloved dogs in the care of whom?

---

123. Unable to control himself, and without planning to do so, Harry Potter performs a magical act on Aunt Marge. What exactly does he do?

124. Thrown out of the Dursley residence after this magical incident, how does Harry Potter, burdened with a heavy trunk and other possessions, get to Diagon Alley?

BONUS QUESTION #11:

How much does it cost for Harry Potter to go from Privet Drive to London on the aforementioned wizard transportation?

---

125. How many people did Sirius Black reportedly kill?

126. In Diagon Alley at one of his favorite stores, Quality Quidditch Supplies, what object does Harry Potter see in the showcase window that he covets?

127. What is the name of Ron Weasley's pet rat?

128. When the Weasley children head off to King's Cross station, they travel in grand style. What means of transportation is used?

129. When Dementors show up on the Hogwarts Express, looking for Sirius Black, Professor Lupin dismisses them. Afterward, he passes around an antidote to counter the pervasive feeling of perpetual gloom the Dementors instill in people. What antidote is offered?

130. A Boggart is a shapeshifter that can be countered, and bested, with a specific charm. What is that charm?

131. George and Fred Weasley give Harry Potter a very unusual gift, something they discovered in Filch's office in a file cabinet. What is that gift?

132. What is the name of the candy store in Hogsmeade favored by students?

133. The candy store in Hogsmeade has a wide assortment of irresistible candies, but some are for more specialized tastes. What special candy would appeal to vampires?

134. What is one of George and Fred Weasley's favorite shops in Hogsmeade?

135. In extreme cases, the Ministry of Magic has to dispatch special wizards to pursue criminals. What are those wizards called?

136. What does Harry Potter get for Christmas from an unknown person?

137. What is the physical form of Harry Potter's Patronus?

138. During a Quidditch match, the student commentator often offers extraneous personal observations to the dismay of the faculty advisor, Professor McGonagall. Who is the overenthusiastic student?

139. What unwelcome surprise does the hapless Neville Longbottom get during breakfast after he foolishly compromises security by writing down a week's worth of passwords to Gryffindor house?

140. When Professor Snape discovers that Harry Potter has what is obviously something he shouldn't own—the Marauder's Map—what surprise does Snape receive from the map?

141. To Hagrid's great dismay, as well as that of Harry Potter, Ron Weasley,

and Hermione Granger, one of Hagrid's beloved pets, a hippogriff, is sentenced to death. What is its name?

142. What is an O.W.L.?

143. What is a N.E.W.T.?

144. What was Professor Lupin's nickname when he was a student at Hogwarts?

145. Some witches and wizards can turn themselves into animal form. What are they called?

BONUS QUESTION #12:

Who is the appointed executioner for Hagrid's hippogriff?

---

146. When he was a Hogwarts student, what was James Potter's nickname?

147. When he was a student, what was Sirius Black's nickname?

148. What is the legal relationship between Harry Potter and Sirius Black?

HARRY POTTER AND THE GOBLET OF FIRE

149. What famous (or, more accurately, infamous) house can be found in the village of Little Hangleton?

150. Not all residents of the Riddle House are human. What slithering creature resides there?

151. Who at the Ministry of Magic was waylaid and subsequently killed by Lord Voldemort?

152. When Harry, along with the others in the Dursley household, is forced to eat small portions of diet food to provide moral support to a dieting Dudley, he requests his friends to send him food. What inedible food does Hagrid send him?

153. When Arthur, Fred, and George Weasley travel to the Dursley residence to pick up Harry Potter, how do they get there?

154. In one of the funniest scenes in any of the Harry Potter novels, pranksters George and Fred Weasley test out an engorgement charm cleverly disguised as candy on Dudley Dursley, with comical effect. What is the name of the candy?

155. What part of Dudley's anatomy grew to four feet in length after he ate enchanted candy?

156. Ron Weasley received a small gray owl as a gift. From whom did he receive it?

157. Percy Weasley, a company man, speaks incessantly about his boss at the Ministry of Magic. What is his boss's name?

158. When someone unsucessfully Apparates, there's the possibility that instead of transporting instantly to another location, the person is literally split in half. What is the term for that effect?

159. What is the expected attendance at the Quidditch World Cup tournament?

160. Transportation, obviously, is a problem when thousands of wizards and witches convene in one place at one time. Conventional (and unconventional) transportation modes are used, including a method new to Harry. What is that mode of transportation?

161. Who is the Bulgarian Seeker?

162. According to Percy Weasley, how many languages can his boss speak?

163. Who is the female house-elf who inspired Hermione Granger to take up the cause of house-elves?

164. Hogwarts is one of three major wizarding institutions in Europe. What are the other two?

165. What are the followers of Lord Voldemort called?

BONUS QUESTION #13:

Who at the Quidditch World Cup is the keeper of the Portkeys?

---

166. Wizards who hunt Dark wizards are among the elite in the wizarding world. What are they called?

167. In lieu of the usual Quidditch school tournament, this year an international competition is held. What is it called?

168. Besides covering oneself in glory for one's school and winning the Triwizard Cup, what else does the winner of the tournament get?

169. Which reporter at the *Daily Prophet*, who can best be described as a tabloid journalist, bedevils Harry Potter and company?

170. There are three Unforgivable Curses, including the dreaded *Avada Kedavra*, the killing curse, used against Harry Potter's parents and Harry himself, when he was an infant. Regarding the curse, what makes Harry unique in the wizarding world?

171. Outraged at the treatment of house-elves, especially those who work at Hogwarts in the kitchen, Hermione Granger takes up their cause and starts an organization to promote their rights. Her fledgling organization is called S.P.E.W. What does that stand for?

172. In what magnificent conveyance does the delegation from Beauxbatons arrive?

173. In what impressive conveyance does the delegation from Durmstrang arrive?

174. Potential competitors for the Triwizard Tournament are encouraged to put their names in the hat, so to speak, but only those of age can do so. What prevents the underage from submitting their names?

175. Three champions, representing their respective schools, are selected by the Goblet of Fire. Who are they and their respective schools?

176. Though only three are allowed to compete, the Goblet of Fire selects an unprecedented fourth competitor, to the surprise of all. Who is that fourth person?

177. For the Triwizard Tournament, each school champion must submit an item for inspection. What is that item?

178. In the first competition at the Triwizard Tournament, the contestants must individually face a dragon. What are the names of the four species of dragons on the premises?

179. Fred and George Weasley invent a special candy that turns the person who eats it into a large canary, which immediately begins molting, after which the person reappears as his or her normal self. What is this candy called?

180. The competitive Triwizard Tournament holds no fear for Harry Potter, but a social event associated with the Tournament—a long-standing tradition—is not an event he's looking forward to. What is that social event?

181. The contestants for the Triwizard Tournament compete not only physically but mentally. Each contestant must unravel the clue found in what object?

182. Mocking Hermione Granger, Ron Weasley asks her sarcastically if she's starting a new organization called S.P.U.G. What does that stand for?

183. What kind of people reside in the lake on the Hogwarts school grounds?

184. What plant allows Harry Potter to breathe underwater?

185. Cedric Diggory and Fleur Delacour don't use the plant Harry Potter used to breathe underwater. How do they manage to breathe underwater?

186. What is Veritaserum?

187. Still at large, Sirius Black suggests to Harry Potter that when he and his close friends (Ron Weasley and Hermione Granger) are discussing Sirius, they should refer to him by another name. What is that name?

188. A popular student beverage among the students acts like liquor to house-elves. What is that drink?

189. It's a "shallow stone basin" into which one can empty one's excess thoughts. Dumbledore shows it to Harry Potter. What's it called?

190. The Triwizard Cup is more than it seems. What is its sinister purpose?

191. Reporter Rita Skeeter, who is able to get stories that no one else can, has a secret that Hermione Granger discovers. What is that secret?

HARRY POTTER AND THE ORDER OF THE PHOENIX

192. What *is* the Order of the Phoenix?

193. To Harry Potter's great surprise, he encounters unexpected visitors in the Dursleys' neighborhood. Who are the visitors?

194. After several owls drop off messages to Harry Potter at the Dursley residence, the last owl delivers a message to Aunt Petunia. Who sent that message?

195. Where is the headquarters of the Order of the Phoenix located?

196. Fred and George Weasley invent an unusual magical listening device. What is it called?

197. Percy Weasley, formerly working for Barty Crouch at the Ministry of Defense, is rising rapidly at the Ministry of Magic. What's his new job?

198. The residential house that serves as the headquarters for the Order of the Phoenix belongs to whom?

199. When Arthur Weasley accompanies Harry Potter to his hearing at the Ministry of Magic, he takes him to a Muggle-disguised entrance. What is its disguise?

BONUS QUESTION #14:

How many floors does the Ministry of Magic building have?

---

200. At the hearing, who are witnesses for Harry Potter's defense?

201. Hogwarts student Luna Lovegood's father is the editor of which tabloid newspaper?

202. Who is the new Defense Against the Dark Arts teacher?

203. Who is the new Quidditch Keeper?

204. In an attempt to enforce new Magic of Ministry approved standards for Hogwarts, the Ministry has appointed Professor Umbridge to an additional position besides teaching Defense Against the Dark Arts. What is her other position?

BONUS QUESTION #15:

What is the highest grade possible on an O.W.L. exam?

---

205. Needing a confidential place to hold his unofficial Defense Against the Dark Arts classes, Harry Potter finds out from Dobby that there is a room that can be entered only when a person *needs* it, as Harry does. What is that room called?

206. In coming up with a name for Harry Potter's informal group of students who meet in secrecy to practice Defense Against the Dark Arts, the initials D.A. are finally agreed upon by all. What does that stand for?

207. Thestrals are unusual creatures in appearance—*if* one can see them. Who *can* see them?

208. What is the name of the wizarding community's hospital?

BONUS QUESTION #16:

To Muggles, the hospital looks like a different building. What do Muggles see when they look at the hospital?

---

209. Who can be found in the hospital ward for those who have suffered permanent spell damage?

210. At the request of Headmaster Dumbledore, Professor Snape teaches Harry Potter the art of Occlumency. What is it?

211. What is the opposite of Occlumency?

212. Since the *Daily Prophet* cannot be fair and balanced in its reportage—the Ministry of Magic exercises undue influence on its editorial content—the news of Lord Voldemort's return must be published elsewhere. What newspaper prints an interview with Harry Potter that causes everyone in the magical community to take notice?

213. When Professor Trelawney is fired by the High Inquisitor, whom does Dumbledore find to replace her?

214. In a shocking development that's the talk of Hogwarts, the High Inquisitor assumes what new position?

215. To assist her, to be the eyes and ears at Hogwarts, Umbridge handpicks student spies. What are those spies called?

216. In the grandest prank ever pulled by Fred and George Weasley, what do they conjure up to bedevil the hated new head of Hogwarts?

217. To the great surprise of Harry Potter and Hermione Granger, Hagrid harbors a big secret in the Forbidden Forest. What is that secret?

218. Veritaserum is the most powerful truth potion available, but what might be an effective second choice?

219. After suffering repeated insults from Draco Malfoy and his fellow Slytherins, Harry Potter's D.A. members exact revenge. After their handiwork, what form do Malfoy and his stooges Crabbe and Goyle take?

ANSWERS

Biographical
1. On a train that left from London's King's Cross station, headed north.
2. Dianne Rowling.
3. Kathleen, after her grandmother on her father's side.
4. A rabbit.
5. Wyedean Comprehensive.
6. Hermione Granger.
7. Head girl.
8. British novelist Jane Austen.
9. A train.
10. Séan Harris.
11. Seven.
12. The University of Excter.
13. French and Classics.
14. To Porto, Portugal.
15. Edinburgh, Scotland.
16. Nicolson's.
17. The Christopher Little Literary Agency.
18. Bryony Evens.
19. Bloomsbury.
20. £1,500
21. Scholastic.
22. $100,000.
23. Because he was concerned that if she used her real name, boys wouldn't buy her books, since they tended not to buy books written by women—or so he thought.
24. A word processor.
25. 500 copies: 300 in hardback, 200 in paperback.
26. *Harry Potter and the Sorcerer's Stone.*
27. 50,000 copies.
28. The Smarties Prize for children's literature, voted upon by children.
29. Mary GrandPré.
30. The U.S.
31. Gryffindor.
32. In Edinburgh, Scotland, where she has her principal residence. (She owns two other homes.)

Harry Potter and the Sorcerer's Stone
33. One year old.
34. 11 years old.

35. A lightning-shaped scar.
36. James Potter.
37. Lily Potter.
38. Lord Voldemort.
39. Albus Dumbledore.
40. Muggle.
41. A motorcycle.
42. Dudley Dursley.
43. In a cupboard under the stairs.
44. By owl mail.
45. Rubeus Hagrid.
46. His height—he's a giant.
47. A homemade cake.
48. Hogwarts School of Witchcraft and Wizardry.
49. Diagon Alley.
50. Gringotts, the wizards' bank.
51. Goblins.
52. Dragons.
53. *The Daily Prophet.*
54. A wand.
55. An owl.
56. A flying broom.
57. Defense Against the Dark Arts.
58. Galleons (gold), Sickles (silver), and Knuts (bronze).
59. From Madam Malkin's Robes for All Occasions.
60. Quidditch.
61. A phoenix feather.
62. King's Cross station, train Platform Nine and Three-Quarters.
63. Ronald Weasley.
64. Slytherin, Hufflepuff, Ravenclaw, and Gryffindor.
65. The Sorting Hat.
66. Gryffindor.
67. Gryffindor.
68. Gryffindor.
69. Madam Hooch.
70. The Fat Lady, who resides in her own picture frame.
71. Seeker.
72. A Nimbus 2000.
73. 150 points.
74. A three-headed dog.
75. Fluffy.
76. The Mirror of Erised.

77. Hermione Granger.
78. An invisibility cloak.
79. The Forbidden Forest.
80. A baby dragon.
81. Centaurs.
82. The Sorcerer's Stone.
83. The Devil's Snare, a sentient, malicious vine.
84. Wizards' Chess.
85. You-Know-Who, or He-Who-Must-Not-Be-Named.

Harry Potter and the Chamber of Secrets

86. He levitates a pudding, the dessert for the dinner guests, and drops it on the floor.
87. Mafalda Hopkirk, from the office of Improper Use of Magic Office.
88. Ron Weasley and his brothers George and Fred arrive in a flying car and rip the bars off his window.
89. The Misuse of Muggle Artifacts Office.
90. The Burrow.
91. De-Gnome the garden.
92. Floo powder.
93. At a retail store in Knockturn Alley.
94. Rubeus Hagrid.
95. Flourish and Blotts.
96. Gilderoy Lockhart.
97. Defense Against the Dark Arts teacher.
98. A Ford Anglia.
99. Into a malicious tree, a Whomping Willow, on school grounds.
100. A Howler.
101. Because all the questions had nothing to do with the class per se; they were all questions about Lockhart himself.
102. Draco Malfoy.
103. The Headless Hunt.
104. Kwikspell.
105. Godric Gryffindor, Helga Hufflepuff, Rowena Ravenclaw, and Salazar Slytherin.
106. Skele-Gro.
107. Gilderoy Lockhart and Severus Snape.
108. Harry Potter and Draco Malfoy.
109. Parseltongue.
110. 50 Galleons.
111. Dwarves.
112. Headmaster Dippet.

113. An Order of Suspension.
114. Aragog, a giant spider.
115. A basilisk.
116. A sock.

Harry Potter and the Prisoner of Azkaban

117. Sirius Black.
118. He wins 700 Galleons and takes the family on a summer vacation to Egypt.
119. *The Monster Book of Monsters*.
120. Hogsmeade.
121. Because he needs a signed letter from a parent or guardian, but Vernon Dursley won't give him one. (He's such a git!)
122. St. Brutus's Secure Center for Incurably Criminal Boys.
123. Inflates her—she's a living, floating balloon.
124. He accidentally summons the Knight Bus.
125. 13.
126. A Firebolt racing broom.
127. Scabbers.
128. Two chauffeured cars provided by the Ministry of Magic.
129. Chocolate.
130. *Riddikulus.*
131. The Marauder's Map.
132. Honeydukes.
133. Blood-flavored lollipops.
134. Zonkos, a novelty store.
135. Hit wizards.
136. A Firebolt racing broom.
137. A silver stag.
138. Lee Jordan.
139. A Howler.
140. An insulting round of replies.
141. Buckbeak.
142. Ordinary Wizarding Level, examinations given to students when they reach age 15.
143. Nastily Exhausting Wizarding Tests, the highest level of qualification offered at Hogwarts.
144. Moony.
145. Animagi (the singular is Animagus).
146. Prongs.
147. Padfoot.
148. Black is his godfather.

Harry Potter and the Goblet of Fire

149. The Riddle House.
150. A snake named Nagini.
151. Bertha Jorkins.
152. Homemade rock cakes.
153. By floo powder.
154. Ton-Tongue Toffee.
155. His tongue.
156. Sirius Black.
157. Mr. Barty Crouch.
158. Splinching.
159. 100,000.
160. A Portkey.
161. Viktor Krum
162. Over 200.
163. Winky.
164. Beauxbatons Academy of Magic and Durmstrang.
165. Death Eaters.
166. Aurors.
167. The Triwizard Tournament.
168. 1,000 Galleons.
169. Rita Skeeter.
170. He's the only one who ever survived an attack.
171. The Society for the Promotion of Elfish Welfare.
172. A gigantic airborne carriage drawn by flying horses.
173. A sailing ship.
174. An Age Line.
175. Viktor Krum for Durmstrang, Cedric Diggory for Hogwarts, Fleur Delacour for Beauxbatons.
176. Harry Potter.
177. The competitors' wands.
178. Hungarian Horntail, Common Welsh Green, Swedish Short Snout, and Chinese Fireball.
179. Canary Cream.
180. A Yule Ball, for which he'll need a dancing partner—his first formal dance.
181. A golden egg.
182. Society for the Protection of Ugly Goblins.
183. Merpeople.
184. Gillyweed.
185. By performing a Bubble-Head Charm.
186. A Truth Potion—very powerful; its use is strictly regulated by the Ministry of Magic.
187. Snuffles.

188. Butterbeer.
189. A Pensieve.
190. It's a Portkey.
191. Skeeter, an unregistered animagus, can turn into a beetle.

Harry Potter and the Order of the Phoenix

192. A secret order of witches and wizards loyal to Dumbledore, who resist the return of Lord Voldemort.
193. Dementors.
194. Albus Dumbledore.
195. Number 12, Grimmauld Place, London.
196. Extendable Ears.
197. Junior Assistant to the Minister of Magic, Cornelius Fudge.
198. Sirius Black.
199. A telephone booth.
200. Albus Dumbledore and Arabella Doreen Figg.
201. The *Quibbler.*
202. Professor Dolores Jane Umbridge.
203. Ron Weasley.
204. High Inquisitor.
205. It has two names: The Room of Requirement and The Come and Go Room.
206. Dumbledore's Army.
207. Only people who have witnessed death firsthand.
208. St. Mungo's Hospital for Magical Maladies and Injuries.
209. Neville Longbottom's parents.
210. A magical form of mind defense—sealing off one's mind to external penetration.
211. Legilimency.
212. The *Quibbler.*
213. A centaur named Firenze.
214. Head of Hogwarts, replacing Dumbledore.
215. The Inquisitorial Squad.
216. A Portable Swamp.
217. He's taking care of his half-brother Grawp, whom he's trying to civilize.
218. A Babbling Beverage.
219. Human-sized slugs.

Bonus Questions

1. 142.
2. 12 feet tall.

3. Madam Pince.
4. 472 points.
5. Heard on the radio, on the *Witching Hour,* she's a popular singer, a sorceress.
6. The Chudley Cannons.
7. Lucius Malfoy and his son, Draco.
8. A camera.
9. October 31, 1492.
10. Colonel Fubster.
11. 11 Sickles.
12. Walden Macnair, from the Ministry of Magic.
13. Basil.
14. Seven.
15. E (for "Exceeds Expectations").
16. A department store closed for "refurbishment."

Tim Kirk

Books about Rowling and Harry Potter

All About J. K. Rowling, by Shaun McCarthy. Steck-Vaughn, 2003. 32 pages. A brief biography.

Beacham's Sourcebook for Teaching Young Adult Fiction: Exploring Harry Potter, by Elizabeth D. Schafer and Elizabeth D. Sullivan. Beacham, 2000. 528 pages. A resource guide especially useful to students and teachers, this book's 20 chapters provide background information and a chapter-by-chapter and book-by-book look at the Potter novels with projects and activities appropriate for students. Most useful for its excellent bibliography.

Beatrix Potter to Harry Potter: Portraits of Children's Writers, by Julia Eccleshare. England: National Portrait Gallery Publications, 2002. 136 pages. According to the publisher, "Julia Eccleshare illuminates the lives of British authors from the last 100 years, exploring their inspirations, influences, and ideas. Illustrated throughout with photographs, paintings, and drawings, as well as manuscripts and covers."

A Charmed Life: The Spirituality of Potterworld, by Francis Bridger. Image Books, 2002. 176 pages. A theologian and principal of Trinity College (Bristol, England) examines the Potter novels in the context of J. R. R. Tolkien's and C. S. Lewis's novels, steeped in Christian faith.

Fantasy and Your Family: Exploring The Lord of the Rings, *Harry Potter, and Modern Magick,* by Richard Abanes. Horizon Books, 2002. 300 pages. A thought-provoking discussion organized in four sections: an overview of fantasy literature, Tolkien's *The Lord of the Rings,* Harry Potter, and pro/con arguments about Harry Potter.

From Alice to Harry Potter: Children's Fantasy in England, by Colin Manlove. Cybereditions, 2003. An e-book available online from Amazon.com in Adobe Reader format. An overview of children's literature spanning 150 years and 400 English classics, where the genre flourishes. An in-depth and informed discussion that puts this wide body of literature in broad context.

God, the Devil, and Harry Potter: A Christian Minister's Defense of the Beloved Novels, by John Killinger. New York: St. Martin's/Griffin, 2004. 208 pages. A defense of the Harry Potter novels written by an ordained clergyman who has doctorates in theology and literature. (For a similar discussion, see *A Charmed Life.*)

The Gospel According to Harry Potter: Spirituality in the Stories of the World's Most Famous Seeker, by Connie Neal. Westminister John Knox Press, 2002. 166 pages. An explication of the Potter texts in light of Christian beliefs. Read this instead of books by other Christian writers who see her texts as platforms espousing occultism.

Harry Potter and the Bible: The Menace Behind the Magick, by Richard Abanes. Horizon Books, 2001. 275 pages. A former minister, Abanes specializes in writing about the occult. This book is divided into two parts: the first part summarizes the first four Potter novels and discusses the elements of occultism to be found; the second part is an overview of occult in the U.S., putting it in the context of fantasy literature as a genre, with a discussion of the controversy of Potter books used as texts in public schools.

Harry Potter's World: Multidisciplinary Critical Perspectives (Pedagogy and Popular Culture), ed. Elizabeth E. Heilman. Routledge, 2003. 304 pages. A welcome addition to the growing body of books on Harry Potter from the academic community. Edited by a college professor, this collection of essays is organized in four sections: Cultural Studies Perspectives; Reader Response and Interpretive Perspectives; Literary Perspectives: The Hero, Myth and Genre; and Sociological Perspective. This is an illuminating book that sheds considerable light on the Harry Potter phenomenon in all its varied dimensions.

Harry Potter, You're the Best: A Tribute from Fans the World Over, ed. Sharon Moore. Griffin, 2001. 128 pages. A follow-up book to *We Love Harry Potter!,* this book is a tribute, with letters from young readers and fun stuff for them as well; she includes crossword puzzles, word jumbles, and a resource list of books recommended for Potter fans.

The Hidden Key to Harry Potter: Understanding the Meaning, Genius, and

Popularity of Joanne Rowling's Harry Potter Novels, by John Granger. Zossima Press, 2002. 384 pages. Its thesis is that, like C. S. Lewis and J. R. R. Tolkien, Rowling is at heart a Christian writer—the hidden key, as it were, to unlocking her fiction. Whether or not you agree, the fact remains that Christians are divided as to whether or not her books should be banned or bought. There are advocates within the Christian community for both positions. For everyone else without an axe to grind, this speculative book is fascinating reading, as it is neither a spirited defense nor a polemic against the perceived "evils" of Harry Potter novels.

An Interview with J. K. Rowling. Egmont Children's Books, 2002. 74 pages. The title is somewhat misleading, since the interviews herein are conducted with four authors, only one of whom is Rowling. (The others are Anne Fine, Michael Morpurgo, and Jacqueline Wilson.)

Irresistible Rise of Harry Potter, by Andrew Blake. Verso Books, 2002. 118 pages. The Head of Cultural Studies at King Alfred's College (England), Blake examines the Harry Potter phenomenon and its popularity in light of Rowling's depiction of the English boarding school and its relationship to the book and film industries. Both, Blake asserts, help explain the phenomenal success of the Potter books. A fascinating, thought-provoking look at Harry Potter.

The book was at the center of a legal battle when its original cover design smacked too obviously of the colors, typography, and elements found on Potter's book covers. The published book was pulled from bookstores nationwide and then reissued with a new cover, with a new disclaimer prominently displayed: "This book is not endorsed by Warner Bros., J. K. Rowling, or Bloomsbury Publishing PLC." That met the legal requirement to ensure that it didn't confuse Potter fans who might mistakenly think it was official, but Verso Books took it a step further and needlessly chided Warner Bros. "Verso is delighted to make it clear that this book is not part of the Harry Potter series. Neither the font nor the colour is intended to confuse readers—after all, Warner Bros., J. K. Rowling, and Bloomsbury Publishing PLC have spent very substantial sums of money marketing, advertising, and protecting the Harry Potter brand."

The Ivory Tower and Harry Potter: Perspectives on a Literary Phenomenon, ed. Lana A. Whited. University of Missouri Press, 2003. 408 pages. A Professor of English at Ferrum College (Virginia), Whited collected 16 essays, most of which vigorously defend the Potter novels on the grounds that they are literary classics that offer a lot to children and adults.

J. K. Rowling, by P.M. Boekhoff and Stuart A. Kallen. Gale Group, 2002. 48 pages. A short biography written for older children, ages 9–12.

J. K. Rowling, by William Compson. Rosen Publishing Group, 2003. 112 pages. Part of a series (Library of Author Biographies), this is a general biography that discusses her life and works.

J. K. Rowling, by Ann Gaines. Mitchell Lane Publishers, 2001. 32 pages. A short biography for children, which needs updating.

J. K. Rowling, by Mary Hill. Children's Press, 2003. 24 pages. A magazine-length article in book form written especially for young children, ages 4–8.

J. K. Rowling, by Carl Meister. Checkerboard Library, 2002. 24 pages. A very short biography written especially for young children.

J. K. Rowling, by Bradley Steffens. Lucent Books, 2002. 104 pages. This one provides an overview of the Harry Potter phenomenon, a short biography, discussions about the Potter books, the Potter movies, and speculations on what Rowling may do after she's finished with the series. Recommended.

J. K. Rowling: A Biography, by Connie Ann Kirk. Greenwood Publishing, 2003. 155 pages. The middle ground between the short and skimpy biographies and Sean Smith's (so far) definitive biography. Kirk has done her homework and conducted extensive research, which shows. Recommended, especially for students.

J. K. Rowling: A Biography, by Sean Smith. Michael O'Mara Books (distributed in the U.S. by Andrews McMeel Publishing), 2003. 240 pages. An eight-page color photo insert; the book is indexed. This is an expanded edition of this book, originally published in England in 2001. Sean Smith is the author of *Kylie Confidential,* a biography of pop star Kylie Minogue, published by Michael O'Mara Books (U.K.). His previous writing credits include writing a column for a national newspaper in England.

A straightforward accounting of her life, this biography draws principally on the author's firsthand trips and on selected interviews with people who knew her (notably Bryony Evens). Smith did not have the benefit of having the participation of Rowling, her family members, or her close friends.

Not surprisingly, Rowling has distanced herself from this unauthorized book, reportedly because of its emphasis on her personal life, which she now

aggressively shields from the media; but overall there's more to like about this book than not.

The book covers her life in sufficient detail to give the reader a sense of Rowling's love for her fictional creation, Harry Potter. Unfortunately, it also suffers from padding, as seen in a tedious recounting of her accepting an honorary degree from her alma mater.

For this U.S. edition, prices have been converted from pounds to dollars, but there are many instances in which words or phrases of British origin have not been Americanized, which will be confusing to readers.

Though unauthorized, this is a book worth adding to your collection. More useful for its scope than for its revelations, it's recommended, though with my reservations duly noted.

J. K. Rowling: Her Life and Works, staff-written for SparkNotes, 2003. 176 pages. A brief overview of her life and her Harry Potter novels. Intended as a study guide for students writing papers.

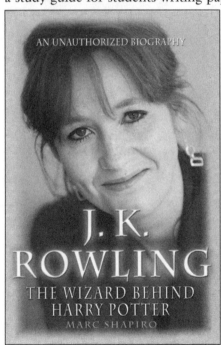

J. K. Rowling: The Wizard Behind Harry Potter, by Marc Shapiro. New York: St. Martin's/Griffin, 2001. 164 pages. Billed as "new and revised," this book badly needs updating. It lacks information about the most recent novel *(Harry Potter and the Order of the Phoenix)*. It also has no mention about Rowling's new husband or son—two serious omissions. A "freelance entertainment journalist," Shapiro has published a dozen celebrity biographies, most (if not all) unauthorized. Lacking an index, this biography, aimed mostly toward young readers, draws entirely from secondary sources, like magazines, newspapers, and electronic media profiles and interviews. A basic introduction to Rowling and her fictional universe, this book lacks the depth that makes Sean Smith's book the better choice. Recommended for those who want a general, not detailed, biography.

J. K. Rowling's Harry Potter Novels: A Reader's Guide, by Philip Nel. Continuum Publishing Group, 2001. 96 pages. A general overview, with a brief biography, an examination and review of the novels, and recommendations for further reading and discussion.

Kids' Letters to Harry Potter from Around the World, ed. Bill Adler. Carroll and Graf, 2002. 195 pages. Compiler Bill Adler has solicited assistance from booksellers who have forwarded letters to him written by children worldwide. It's a cute idea, but the letters tend to sameness. Compounding the problem, follow-up interviews merely echo what has gone before.

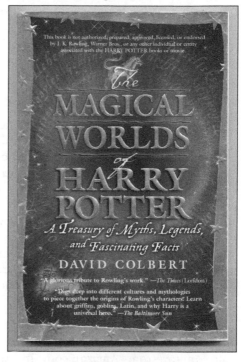

The Magical Worlds of Harry Potter: A Treasury of Myths, Legends, and Fascinating Facts, by David Colbert. Berkley Publishing Group, 2002. 209 pages. Fifty-three alphabetized essays ranging in length up to six pages, posing questions about the myths and legends alluded to in the Potter novels, as in "Did alchemists really search for a magic stone?" and "Have witches always flown on broomsticks?" Since Rowling does not answer these questions, it's up to others to explain the linkages between her fiction and myth and history texts. Recommended.

Meet J. K. Rowling, by S. Ward. Powerkids Press, 2003. 24 pages. A very short biography written for children.

My Year with Harry Potter: How I Discovered My Own Magical World, by Ben Buchanan. Lantern Books, 2001. 112 pages. The magic of Harry Potter's novels can be found in their transformational effect on readers. An inspiring memoir written by an 11-year-old boy who was inspired by the Potter universe to create a board game, which he entered in his school's Invention Convention.

Mythmaker: The Story of J. K. Rowling, by Charles J. Shields. Chelsea House Publishers, 2002. 112 pages. Another short biography on Rowling that is too similar to its competition and, therefore, doesn't stand out. Reviewers have pointed out that there are errors that mar the book.

New Clues to Harry Potter, Book 5, by Galadriel Waters, illustrated by Professor Astre Mithrandir. Wizarding World Press, 2003. 88 pages. A supplementary book to her previous book *(Ultimate Unofficial Guide to the Mysteries of Harry Potter),* this book discusses clues found in *Harry Potter and the Order of the Phoenix.*

Reading Harry Potter: Critical Essays, by Giselle Liza Anatol. Praeger Publishers, 2003. 248 pages. An assistant professor of English at Kansas State

University, Anatol has edited an excellent collection of essays that students, scholars, and teachers will find useful.

Readings on J. K. Rowling, by Peggy J. Parks. Greenhaven Press, 2003. 192 pages. Part of the "Literary Companion Series." From the publisher's website, "Authors in this anthology examine Rowling's life and work and tackle the controversies, both artistic and moral, surrounding the Harry Potter books."

Re-Reading Harry Potter, by Suman Gupta. Palgrave Macmillan, 2003. 224 pages. Suman Gupta teaches at the Open University (UK). From the publisher's website:

> This book is the first extended analysis of the social and political implications of the Harry Potter phenomenon. Arguments are primarily based on close readings of the first four Harry Potter books and the first two films, and a "text-to-world" method is followed. This study does not assume that the phenomenon concerns children alone, or should be lightly dismissed as a matter of pure entertainment as the amount of money, media coverage, and ideological unease involved indicates otherwise. The first part of the study provides a survey of responses (both of general readers and critics) to the Harry Potter books. The second part examines the presentation of certain themes, including gender, race, and desire, with a view to understanding how these may impinge on social and political concerns of our world.

Return of the Heroes: The Lord of the Rings, Star Wars, Harry Potter, and Social Conflict, by Hal G. P. Colebatch. Cybereditions, 2003. An e-book available online from Amazon.com in Adobe Reader format. We live, as Colebatch asserts, in a cynical age; why, then, are works of heroic fantasy like LotR, *Star Wars,* and the Harry Potter novels so phenomenally successful? Far from being reflective of our age, this book celebrates a different age, when traditional values held sway, and speaks of the health, not the demise, of our culture.

The Science of Harry Potter: How Magic Really Works, by Roger Highfield. Viking Press, 2002. 256 pages. Highfield, a British science writer, takes the position that it's possible "to show how many elements of [Rowling's] books can be found in and explained by modern science." Though there is some imaginative stretching to make the linkages, readers who approach this book with an open mind may find the speculations thought-provoking.

The Sorcerer's Companion: A Guide to the Magical World of Harry Potter, by Allan Zola Kronzek and Elizabeth Kronzek. Broadway Books, 2001. 304 pages. Allan Kronzek is a professional magician (see *A Book of Magic for Young Magicians: The Secrets of Alkazar*) and Elizabeth Kronzek (his daughter) is a writer. For readers who want to know more about magic as practiced in the real world, this book is indispensable. Drawing on diverse sources, the Kronzeks bring a wealth of knowledge about magic to bear. The Potter fan who isn't aware of all the historical references to the magical elements of Rowling's fiction will find this book compulsively readable and entertaining.

SparkNotes: Harry Potter and the Sorcerer's Stone. Sterling, 2003. 72 pages. The first (presumably) in a series of study guides, like CliffsNotes, this provides an overview of the book, a chapter-by-chapter breakdown, its literary motifs, and resources for students. Useful for students writing papers, this series is celebrated by students but condemned by teachers, who view them as what they are often used for: a substitute for reading the required text in question.

Storybook Travels: From Eloise's New York to Harry Potter's London, Visits to 30 of the Best-Loved Landmarks in Children's Literature, by Colleen Dunn Bates. Harmony Books, 2002. 288 pages. A fascinating and fun tour guide to literary landscapes worldwide that populate children's literature, including *Harry Potter and the Sorcerer's Stone* (London, Windsor, and Durham: all in England).

Triumph of the Imagination: The Story of Writer J. K. Rowling, by Lisa Chippendale. Chelsea House Publishers, 2001. 112 pages. This is a book in a series that celebrates "Overcoming Adversities." It's a biography for young adults, with a discussion of Harry Potter books one to four.

Ultimate Unofficial Guide to the Mysteries of Harry Potter, by Galadriel Waters and Astre Mithrandir. Wizarding World Press, 2003. 442 pages. The name of the publishing house, as well as the pen names drawn from Tolkien (Galadriel = Lady Galadriel, Mithrandir = Gandalf), suggest that it's a fun-filled look at the Potter books, taking its cue from Rowling's in-depth, celebrated plotting. Arranged by Potter book, with short summaries and a discussion of all the clues, this book is for the die-hard fan who recognizes that the game's afoot and, like Sherlock Holmes, enjoys tracking down clues.

We Love Harry Potter!, ed. Sharon Moore. New York: St. Martin's Press, 1999. 120 pages. A collection of letters from children praising the Potter novels. The term "Déjà vu" comes to mind.

What's a Christian to Do with Harry Potter?, by Connie Neal. Waterbrook Press, 2001. 224 pages. A balanced book that looks on both sides of the fence: those who feel the Potter books are the work of the devil, and those who don't.

The Wisdom of Harry Potter: What Our Favorite Hero Teaches Us About Moral Choices, by Edmund M. Kern. Prometheus Books, 2003. 296 pages. An associate professor of history at Lawrence University (in Appleton, Wisconsin), Kern explores the moral dimensions of the Potter novels in a nonsecular framework.

Part Five:
Harry Potter Merchandise
(a selection)

Tim Kirk

The following list gives an idea as to the scope and depth of the existing licensing program.

Obviously, not all licensed product lines are equally profitable. The Harry Potter Lego toys have seen flagging sales, but the electronic games are so profitable that Warner Bros. has recently set up a separate division to manufacture, sell, and distribute its own line.

Lego Toys
Mattel: Action Figures
 and Toys
Computer Games
Collectibles
Clothes
Posters
Household Items
Candy
Miscellaneous Print
 Products

School Supplies
Miscellaneous
 Educational Products
Spells and Potions Kits
Health Products
Plush Products from
 Gund
Trading Card Games
Games
Magical Minis Figures
Ornaments

Collector's Stones
Watches and Charm
 Links
Harry Potter Trading
 Cards: Movies
Harry Potter 3-D Viewer
 Windows
Coins
Wizard Cards

Lego Toys

1. Dumbledore's Office (LEGO Systems). Construct "a spire with parapets, potion books, letters, and golden keys," says Amazon.com. It has 446 pieces.

2. Aragog in the Forest. A 178-piece LEGO set, with the giant spider Aragog, Harry Potter, and Ron Weasley with a forest background. The Spider has an "action" web feature to capture Harry and Ron.

3. Escape from Privet Drive. The Dursley residence, with car, and figurines of Harry Potter, Ron Weasley, and Mr. Dursley.

4. Quality Quidditch Supplies. Construct this retail store, the place where witches and wizards go to get their Quidditch supplies. It has 120 pieces.

5. Knockturn Alley. Construct the dangerous alley off Diagon Alley where Harry gets lost. It has 209 pieces.

6. Chamber of Secrets. An elaborate set based on the book, it has 591 pieces.

7. Dueling Club. Gilderoy Lockhart's dueling club. It has 129 pieces.

8. Dobby's Release. House-elf Dobby is freed! It has 70 pieces.

9. Quidditch Practice. A Quidditch set. It has 128 pieces.

10. Slytherin. The Slytherin common room. It has 90 pieces.

11. Flying Lesson. Harry Potter and Draco Malfoy in a battle for Longbottom's Remembrall. It has 23 pieces.

12. Troll on the Loose. Harry combats a troll! It has 71 pieces.

13. Gringotts Bank. An elaborate set; the key is to find the treasure within. It has 250 pieces.

14. Sorting Hat. Spin the Sorting Hat to determine which house Harry will be put in. It has 48 pieces.

15. Hagrid's Hut. An elaborate set reconstructing Rubeus Hagrid's house on the Hogwarts grounds. It has 299 pieces.

16. Hogwarts Classrooms. Construct a classroom. It has 73 pieces.

17. Diagon Alley Shops. Construct two rooms for the shops. It has 90 pieces.

18. House of Gryffindor. The Fat Lady's portrait is the key to get through her frame. It has 73 pieces.

19. The Final Challenge. Based on *The Sorcerer's Stone*, Harry finally confronts Professor Quirrell. It has 60 pieces.

20. The Forbidden Corridor. Based on *The Sorcerer's Stone*, the goal is for Harry, Ron, and Hermione to get past the three-headed dog, Fluffy. It has 238 pieces.

21. Snape's Class. Set design for Professor Snape's Potions class. It has 163 pieces.

22. The Chamber of the Winged Keys. Construct the Key Room and the Chess Room from *The Sorcerer's Stone*. It has 175 pieces.

23. Hogwarts Castle. An elaborate set, design the Castle itself. It has 680 pieces.

24. Hogwarts Express. Construct the railroad train, the Hogwarts Express, and its loading platform—Platform Nine and Three-Quarters. It has 410 pieces.

Mattel: Action Figures and Toys

A. Action Figures

1. Chamber Series Action Figure: Harry. An articulated figurine of Harry Potter with wand in hand, with a black cauldron. Comes with colored slime to put in the cauldron.

2. Aragog. Eight poseable legs and moving pincers.

3. Dobby. Accessorized with lamp, iron, and other items.

4. Harry Potter Action Figure: Seeker Harry. An articulated figure, Harry on his Quidditch broom.

5. Seeker Malfoy. Comes with detachable flight cord and Nimbus 2001 broom.

6. Harry Potter Action Figure: Cast-a-Spell Harry. Harry Potter casts a spell.

7. Harry Potter Action Figure: Cast-a-Spell Ron. Ron Weasley with wand in hand casts a spell.

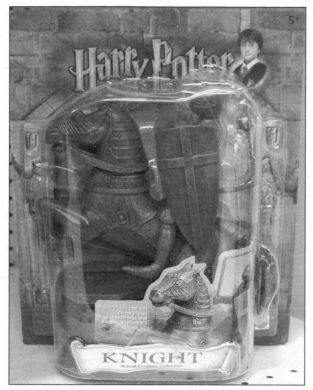

8. Tom Riddle. Articulated. Glows in the dark. Accessorized with a diary.

9. Professor Lockhart. Articulated. Accessorized with a cage of blue cornish pixies.

10. Professor Snape. Casting spell.

11. Professor Flitwick.

12. Snitch Chasing Harry.

13. Norbert Deluxe Movie Figure. This toy dragon figurine can flap its wings when its legs are pulled. The wingspan is 20 inches.

14. Centaur Movie Figure. Accessorized with a crossbow, this is a generic centaur. Moveable legs.

15. Hermione. Comes with potion bottle and magic wand.

16. Hermione: Magical Powers. Comes with magic wand, cauldron, and trunk.

B. Action Figures: Chamber of Secrets Toys
1. Harry Potter Chamber of Secrets: Harry with Gryffindor sword.

2. Harry Potter Slime Chamber Series: Harry with cauldron and slime compound.

3. Harry Potter Slime Chamber Series: Draco Malfoy with cauldron and slime.

4. Harry Potter Slime Chamber Series: Ron Weasley with wand in hand and cauldron with red slime.

5. Chamber of Secrets: Fred Weasley with wand in hand and cauldron.

6. Chamber of Secrets: George Weasley with wand in hand and cauldron.

7. Chamber of Secrets: Hermione Granger with wand in hand and cauldron.

C. Deluxe Creature Collections

1. Harry Potter Deluxe Creature Collection: Knight. Knight on horse; can be dismounted, wielding a star of David (mace with chain attachment). When its legs are squeezed, the Knight "explodes."

2. Harry Potter Deluxe Creature Collection: Fluffy.

D. Dolls

1. Wizard's Sweet Hermione. A Hermione Granger doll in winter fashion. Comes with a scented bracelet for wear.

2. Wizard's Sweet Harry. A Harry Potter doll. Comes with a scented bracelet for wear.

3. Magic Talking Hermione. A Hermione Granger doll with witch's hat and cloak. The doll's recorded messages encourage girls to be creative. Comes with charms for the owner to make a bracelet.

4. Harry Potter. A Harry Potter doll, with his owl, Hedwig, and her cage.

5. Ron Weasley. A Ron Weasley doll, with his pet rat, Scabbers.

6. Hermione Granger. A Hermione Granger doll, with her pet cat, Crookshanks.

E. Dueling Clubs

1. Harry Potter Dueling Club: Harry Potter with wand in hand.

2. Lockhart: Dueling Club. Articulated. Accessorized with robe, magic wand, and footpeg tile.

F. Games/Puzzles

1. Harry Potter Uno Game. An adaptation of the popular Uno card game. The goal: to discard all of your cards before the other player can.

2. Dicers. Three different games can be played with its six dice. Comes with an instruction sheet.

3. Harry Potter Puzzle 1–4. Each puzzle is 100 pieces. The images are drawn from the films.

4. Whomping Willow. Players win by removing luggage from the limbs of the tree, which is motorized and spins. He who collects the most luggage wins.

G. Hogwarts Heroes

1. Hogwarts Heroes: Harry Potter. Comes with wand and Sorcerer's Stone.

2. Hogwarts Heroes: Hermione Granger. In Hogwarts school uniform, she comes with wand and Sorcerer's Stone.

3. Hogwarts Heroes: Ron Weasley. In Hogwarts school uniform, with wand and Sorcerer's Stone.

H. Miscellaneous

Harry Potter Sword of Gryffindor. Facsimile of the sword used by Potter to vanquish the basilisk in *The Chamber of Secrets*.

I. Playsets

1. Harry Potter and Draco Malfoy face off in a wizards' duel. Accessorized with a backdrop of Hogwarts and play pieces.

2. Harry Potter: The Slime Chamber. A tower capped with the figurehead of a serpent.

3. Harry Basilisk Attack. A basilisk with eyes and mouth that light up, it makes menacing sounds. Move the basilisk's tail to control movement. Comes with a backdrop of the Chamber of Secrets and accessorized with a sword and other implements.

J. Quidditch Team Action Figures

1. Harry Potter Quidditch Team Action Figure: George. George Weasley on his broom and holding a club.

2. Harry Potter Quidditch Team Action Figure: Harry.

K. Sorcerer's Stone Toys

1. Harry Potter and the Sorcerer's Stone: Wizard Collection, Gryffindor Harry. Comes with Hedwig and wand.

2. Ron Weasley. Comes with magic wand and Scabbers.

3. Harry Potter: Invisibility Cloak Harry Potter.

4. Lord Voldemort.

5. Mountain Troll.

6. Professor Snape.

7. Draco Malfoy.

L. Wizard Collection

1. Harry Potter Wizard Collection Action Figure: Griphook the Gringotts Goblin. Articulated goblin with cart and accessories.

2. Harry Potter Wizard Collection Action Figure: Hermione Granger. Comes with schoolbooks, wand, and magic trick.

3. Lord Voldemort: Wizard Collection. Accessorized with a garlic necklace.

4. Harry Potter Pumpkin Drink Maker with Refill. Makes an iced pumpkin drink; comes with ice shaver machine, a serving/ mixing cup, measuring spoon, and two packets each of Wizard Sprinkles Powdered Mix and Pumpkin Spice Powdered Mix.

5. Harry Potter Edibles Activity Set Refill. A kit to make "Snake Bites," a candy, with candy coating mix, artificially flavored tangerine powdered candy mix, and artificially flavored sour apple powdered candy mix.

6. Harry Potter Teleidoscope Construction Toy. Build a teleidoscope. Comes with activity guide.

7. Harry Potter Chamber of Secrets Trivia. You are in either Gryffindor or Slytherin; by answering questions ranging from easy to difficult, you gain points. Answering a Golden Snitch question—equivalent to catching one in the game itself—gets you 150 points. But it doesn't mean you've automatically won for your house, because the house that has accumulated the most points wins in the end.

8. Polyjuice Potion Maker Edible Activity Set. A kit to make a potion, polyjuice. Mixing in different ingredients causes the potion to change color.

Computer Games

1. Harry Potter: Quidditch World Cup (Electronic Arts). Playable on most popular platforms. According to Electronic Arts: "Take to the air in the first game that allows players to fully experience the magical speed, power, and competition of Quidditch, the favorite sport of witches and wizards, in the Harry Potter: Quidditch World Cup game." Generally, reviews on the game have been mixed, despite its strong sales. Matt Woo of PC Gameworld: "For a first attempt, EA does an admirable job of bringing *Quidditch* to gamers." Richard Clifford for ferrago.com: "The developers have obviously been limited to the rules as laid out in the books. Unfortunately they appear to have been unable to combine the ideas in a way that lends the game much depth, or any depth to be exact."

2. Harry Potter and the Sorcerer's Stone (Electronic Arts). "Harry Potter and the Sorcerer's Stone is the perfect game for Potter fans who've read the books, seen the movie, and still want more of J. K. Rowling's amazing world. As would-be wizard Harry Potter, you can run amuck in a virtual Hogwarts, learn to cast spells, play Quidditch, eat chocolate frogs, talk with teachers and classmates, and, of course, try to defeat You-Know-Who. This is one of those rare games that both very young kids and their parents will be able to enjoy. You don't need the hair-trigger reflexes of a 13-year-old Nintendo ninja to explore the complex and mysterious world of Hogwarts School of Witchcraft and Wizardry. In fact, exploring the school is half the fun. There are secret passages, shifting staircases, and dangerous shrubbery wherever you look. The ultimate battle at the end is suitably challenging, but overall, the game is fairly forgiving. And you don't have

to discover every single nook and cranny in order to pass to the next level." (Review by Eric Fredrickson from www.buy-everything-online.com.)

3. Harry Potter and the Chamber of Secrets (Electronic Arts). "You ask me is this game fun? Oh, yeah! You meet Ron Weasley and Hermione Granger. Personally, I think this game is adventurous and dangerous. You play Harry, who has to sneak past students to complete his tasks at night. (Hint: Drink the Polyjuice potion, which transforms you into Crabbe, and let students see you at night, so you can win the house cup.) Save Ron from the Whomping Willow Tree, sneak past the owner of the Magical Menagerie, play a Quidditch match, complete a task in the classroom to retrieve the spell book. Make sure you explore Hogwarts grounds because there are secrets hidden everywhere and ways you can collect Gryffindor housepoints. Are you ready for this magical, adventurous, dangerous game? Are your wands ready? Do you have the Spell Book and the potion vial? They'll come in handy. I guess you'll be ready." (An edited review from an uncredited reviewer on Amazon.com.)

4. Harry Potter and the Prisoner of Azkaban (Electronic Arts, spring 2004). From a company press release: "For the first time gamers will play as friends Ron Weasley and Hermione Granger as well as Harry Potter, switching between characters and utilizing their key attributes and skills to resolve challenges and overcome enemies. The three friends will need to combine their strengths and master a variety of new spells as they face Harry's most terrifying opponents yet: the escaped convict Sirius Black and the Dementors, the sinister guards of Azkaban prison."

5. LEGO Creator: Harry Potter (LEGO Media International, Windows platform only). Based on the LEGO Harry Potter line, this computerized game allows you to build interactive LEGO-shaped characters of your own design, construct LEGO interiors, and build a train track for the Hogwarts Express, and offers challenges. Recommendation: If you want to play with LEGO, get the actual pieces, available in Harry Potter configurations; and if you want to play a computer game, there are several to choose from. This game, however, is neither fish nor fowl—not LEGO and not a full-fledged computer game, but an awkward hybrid of the two.

Collectibles

Harry Potter: Giclee Print by Fred Bode. A limited edition of 100 copies on canvas, signed and numbered by the artist. Measuring 23 x 32.5 inches, the print is under plexiglas and framed.

Sculptures

1. Harry Potter Victory. A limited edition of 5,000 pieces. Cold-cast resin sculpture of Potter on his Nimbus Two Thousand broomstick. He is pursuing the Golden Snitch. It is accompanied by a numbered certificate of authenticity.

2. Battling the Mountain Troll. A limited edition of 5,000. Cold-cast resin sculpture of Potter atop a mountain troll holding a club, with Hermione Granger and Ron Weasley looking up. It is accompanied by a numbered certificate of authenticity.

3. Hagrid's New Arrival. A limited edition of 5,000. Cold-cast resin sculpture of Hagrid in his hut. He's holding Norbert, a baby dragon. It is accompanied by a numbered certificate of authenticity.

Clothes

1. Harry Potter Dress-Up Boxed Set (Rubies Costume Company). Hogwarts cape with wand, glasses, and stickers.

2. Harry Potter: Hogwarts Student Hat (Elope). Constructed of black velvet, this is a wizard's cone-shaped hat.

3. Harry Potter Chamber of Secrets Student Hat. Constructed of black velvet, with a Hogwarts crest.

4. Harry Potter New Sorting Hat and Glasses Set (Elope). A brown Hogwarts-style sorting hat with a pair of Harry Potter glasses.

5. Harry Potter Robe: Children's Costume (Rubies Costume Company). The full-length cape. (You will need to accessorize with hat, wand, glasses, broomstick, and black shirt/pants.)

6. Ron Weasley Kids' Costume Set. From toddler to large, Ron's Hogwarts robe, accessorized with his pet, Scabbers.

7. Harry Potter Briefs for Boys (Hanes). A three-pack.

8. Harry Potter Socks. Two designs, one in color and one in black-and-white, from child's to youth size.

9. Harry Potter Embroidered Adult Polo Shirt. Blue shirt with a gold embroidered logo "HP."

10. Harry Potter Chamber of Secrets T-Shirt. Blue T-shirt showing a golden Snitch against a backdrop of clouds.

11. Harry Potter Hedwig Kids' Costume. For sizes from toddler to large, a white jumpsuit with headpiece.

12. Harry Potter Kids' Scarf and Hat Set (Elope). Matching hat and scarf with a Hogwarts crest on both.

13. Harry Potter Professor McGonagall's Hat (Elope). A replica of her hat.

Posters

A. *Sorcerer's/Philosopher's Stone*

1. Harry Potter and the Sorcerer's Stone (Barewalls). In color, measures 27 x 40 inches.

2. Harry Potter and the Philosopher's Stone (Art.com). In color, measures 27 x 41 inches. Shows an Owl bearing an envelope addressed to Harry Potter at Privet Drive. Also available as an advance poster, sheet A, with the same image.

3. Harry Potter and the Sorcerer's Stone (Art.com). In color, measures 27 x 41 inches.

4. Harry Potter and the Sorcerer's Stone (Barewalls). In color, an advance poster, sheet B. Measures 27 x 40 inches. Shows students in lantern-lit boats heading to Hogwarts under a moonlit sky.

5. Harry Potter: Flying Lessons (Barewalls). Harry highlighted, and beneath, two rows of students flanking teacher.

6. Harry Potter: Gringotts (Art.com). In color, measures 24.25 x 36.25 inches. Harry Potter and a Gringotts goblin size each other up.

7. Harry Potter (Art.com). In color, measures 23 x 35 inches. Shows Harry holding a broom, superimposed on the flying scene. The text: "The first flying lesson: Grip it tight. We don't want you sliding off the end."

8. Harry Potter and the Philosopher's Stone (Art.com). In color, measures 27 x 38 inches. A reprint of the movie poster, this shows Harry, Dumbledore, Hagrid, Hermione, Ron, Professor Snape, and Professor McGonagall.

B. *Chamber of Secrets*

1. Harry Potter and the Chamber of Secrets (Art.com). In color, double-sided, measures 27 x 41 inches.

2. Harry Potter and the Chamber of Secrets (Art.com). In color, measures 26.5 x 38.5 inches.

3. Harry Potter and the Chamber of Secrets (Art.com). In color, measures 30 x 40 inches. Shows Dobby the house-elf against a red/green background.

4. Harry Potter and the Chamber of Secrets (Barewalls). In color, measures 27 x 40 inches. Shows Dobby the house-elf against a spotlight.

5. Harry Potter and the Chamber of Secrets (Barewalls). In color, measures 27 x 40 inches. Shows Harry brandishing a sword, as Ron wields his wand and Hermione brandishes a book.

6. Harry Potter and the Chamber of Secrets (Art.com). In color, measures 27 x 41 inches. Shows Harry with his head stuck out of a Ford Anglia.

7. Harry Potter and the Chamber of Secrets (Art.com). In color, measures 26.5 x 38.5 inches. Shows Harry superimposed over a shot of Hogwarts at night.

8. Harry Potter and the Chamber of Secrets (Art.com). In color, measures 23 x 25 inches. Shows Harry superimposed over a shot of Hogwarts at night, with the Ford Anglia soaring over the school.

9. Harry Potter and the Chamber of Secrets (Art.com). In color, measures 27 x 41 inches. The original movie poster. Shows Dobby the House-elf in a spotlight.

10. Harry Potter and the Chamber of Secrets (Art.com). Close-up of Harry, flanked with smaller portraits of Ron and Hermione. The text reads: "Something tells me we're going to REGRET this."

C. *Goblet of Fire*

Harry Potter and the Goblet of Fire (Art.com). In color, measures 24 x 34 inches. A promotional poster. Reprints the child's art cover for the book, with text beneath the image.

D. General

1. Harry Potter (Barewalls). In color, measures 24 x 35 inches. Shows a head-and-shoulder shot of Harry wearing his house sweater.

2. Harry Potter (Art.com). In color, measures 23 x 35 inches. Shows a head-and-shoulder shot of Harry wearing his house sweater.

3. Harry Potter: Life at Hogwarts (Art.com). In color, measures 21 x 62 inches. A vertical composition showing three "panels" of art: Harry in his Potions Class under the watchful eye of Professor Snape; Hagrid playing with his dragon, Norbert, as Ron, Hermione, and Harry look on; and Ron, Hermione, and Harry looking out from behind a wall.

4. Harry Potter: Gryffindor (Art.com). In color, measures 23 x 35 inches. Shows the lion crest for the house of Gryffindor at Hogwarts.

5. Harry Potter: Flying over Hogwarts (Art.com). In color, measures 24.5 x 36.5 inches. Cartoon by Dick Dietrich. Art depicts Harry, Ron, and Hermione on brooms, flying in front of Hogwarts castle during the day; in the lower left corner, a white, snowy owl; in the lower right, an emblem of Hogwarts.

6. Harry Potter: First Quidditch Game (Art.com). In color, measures 24.5 x 36.5 inches. Shows Harry on a broom with other figures on brooms behind him; Harry is highlighted by a circle; in the corners are the house banners of Hogwarts.

7. Harry Potter's Journey to Hogwarts (CSA Worldwide Gifts). In color. A cartoon of Harry and other students in a small rowboat headed to Hogwarts at night.

Household Items

1. Pillow: Harry Potter and the Snitch (CSA Worldwide). Measuring 13 inches square, the cartoon on the top shows Harry reaching for the Golden Snitch.

2. Pillow: Harry Potter, Grand Wizard (CSA Worldwide). Shows Harry swishing his wand.

3. Pillow: Harry Potter, Magic Mirror (CSA Worldwide). Shows Harry looking in the Mirror of Erised.

4. Harry Potter Chamber of Secrets Sleeping Bag. Polyester hollow fiber fill, the bag measures 30 x 57 inches. Features a color image of Ron and Harry in the Ford Anglia flying over the Hogwarts Express, headed to Hogwarts.

5. Harry Potter Herbology Class Tapestry Throw. In color, a scene from Professor Sprout's Herbology class. Measures 50 x 60 inches.

6. Harry Potter and the Chamber of Secrets Spell and Charms Fleece.

7. Harry Potter and Ron Weasley Alarm Clock. Battery operated, twin bell alarm, measuring 4.5 x 6.5 inches. On the face, Ron and Harry with Hedwig in the back seat of the flying Ford Anglia. The words "Mind That Tree" appear on its face.

8. Harry Potter Holiday Stocking. Christmas stocking, red and white, measuring 20 inches. With a picture of Harry holding a wand, and a hanging Golden Snitch.

9. Harry Potter Polystone Miniature Clock. Harry with book in hand, seated with his back against a brick wall adorned with a Gryffindor school crest.

10. Harry Potter Waterball. Harry looking down at a waterball containing Norbert, the baby dragon. Stands 5 inches tall.

11. Hermione Granger Waterball. Hermione looking down at a waterball containing potion bottles.

12. Ron Weasley Waterball. Ron with potion book in hand as he conjures up a potion at his cauldron.

13. Harry Potter Polonaise Quidditch Ornament. Measuring 4 x 7 inches, made from Polonaise glass, this ornament shows Harry on his Nimbus 2000, with the Golden Snitch in hand.

14. Harry Potter Children's Character Handle Umbrella. A black umbrella with a Harry Potter figurine handle.

15. Harry Potter with Gifts Fabric Mache Tabletop Figure. A table centerpiece standing 7 inches tall, Harry has his arms filled with gifts.

16. Harry Potter Kids' Umbrella. Black with images of Fluffy the three-headed dog, Hedwig the owl, Norbert the baby dragon, and the caretaker's cat, Mrs. Norris.

17. Harry Potter Wall Hanger (Book 1). A canvas wall hanger, in color, measuring 20 x 30 inches.

18. Harry Potter Wall Hanger (Book 2). A canvas wall hanger, in color, measuring 20 x 30 inches.

19. Harry Potter Wall Hanger (Book 3). A canvas wall hanger, in color, measuring 20 x 30 inches.

20. Harry Potter Felt Banner: Hufflepuff. Felt banner, yellow and black, measuring 14 x 48 inches.

21. Harry Potter Felt Banner: Ravenclaw. Felt banner, measuring 14 x 48 inches.

22. Soup Bowls (four). Holding 16 ounces, black with color image imprinted on one side—Hogwarts, Gryffindor, Slytherin, or Quidditch.

23. Drinking Mugs (eight)
    Slytherin, black mug
    Quidditch, black mug
    Quidditch Match, white mug
    Dobby Drops In, white mug
    The Final Chapter, white mug
    Watch the Bludger, white mug
    Brewing Up Trouble, white mug
    Driving to Hogwarts, white mug

Candy

   Jellybean flavors include banana, blueberry, black forest cake, black pepper, booger, bubblegum, buttered popcorn, buttered toast, cantaloupe, cherry, chocolate pudding, cinnamon, coconut, cotton candy, fruit punch, grape jelly, grass, green apple, honey graham cracker, horseradish, kiwi, lemon drop, orange sherbet, peach, pear, peppermint stick, pink grapefruit, pineapple, pumpkin pie, raspberry, red apple, root beer, sardine, strawberry jam, toasted marshmallow, tutti-frutti, and watermelon.

1. Harry Potter Discover Gift Box (Jelly Belly Candy Co.; www.jellybelly.com). A boxed assortment of 20 mild-to-wild flavors of jellybeans.

2. Bertie Bott's Beans (Jelly Belly Candy Co.). An assortment of 20 mild-to-wild flavors of jellybeans. The bag weighs 3.5 ounces and contains banana, black pepper, blueberry, booger, bubblegum, buttered popcorn, cherry, cinnamon, dirt, earwax, grape jelly, grass, green apple, lemon drop, sardine, spinach, toasted marshmallow, tutti-frutti, vomit, and watermelon.

3. Bertie Bott's Beans (Jelly Belly Candy Co.). A small box, an assortment of 20 mild-to-wild flavors of jellybeans. The box weighs 1.75 ounces.

4. Harry Potter Extravaganza Birthday Cake Decorating Kit (TheParty Works.com). Contains everything needed to decorate and customize a cake. It consists of 92 pieces.

5. Harry Potter Bookmark Pics Cupcake or Cake Decorating Kit (ThePartyWorks.com). Everything needed to decorate and customize cupcakes or a traditional cake. It consists of 25 pieces.

6. Harry Potter Shield Pics Cupcake or Cake Decorating Kit (TheParty Works.com). Contains 25 pieces.

7. Chocolate Frog with Lenticular/Holographic Motion Wizard Card. Each pack contains one chocolate frog and one wizard card (the text written by Rowling):

Adalbert Waffling, Magical Theoretician

Beaumont Majoribanks, Herbology Specialist

Bertie Bott, Inventor

Bowman Wright, Metal Charmer

Cliodne, Bird Animagus

Cornelius Agrippa, Author

Daisy Dodderidge, Tavern Owner

Derwent Shimpling, Comedian

Devlin Whitehorn, Inventor

Donaghan Tremlett, Entertainer

Gifford Ollerton, Giant-Slayer

Gunhilda of Gorsemoor, Healer

Gwenog Jones, Quidditch Captain

Helga Hufflepuff, Cofounder of Hogwarts

Hengist of Woodcroft, Founder of Hogsmeade

Ignatia Wildsmith, Inventor

Lord Stoddard Withers, Magical Creatures Specialist

Merlin, Charms Specialist

Morgan Le Fay, Bird Animagus

Newt Scamander, Author

Quong Po, Magical Creatures Specialist

Rowena Ravenclaw, Cofounder of Hogwarts

Sacharissa Tugwood, Inventor

Uric the Oddball, Eccentric

Miscellaneous Print Products

1. *Harry Potter and the Sorcerer's Stone: Postcard Book*. Contains 32 mailable postcards with scenes from the movie.

2. 2004 Harry Potter Wall Calendar: Heroic Moments (Andrews and McMeel). Scenes from *Sorcerer's Stone* and *Chamber of Secrets*. (This is an annual publication.)

3. 2004 Day-to-Day Calendar (Andrews and McMeel). A 365-page calendar. (This is an annual publication.)

4. 2004 Student Planner (Cedco). Measures 7 x 9 inches, a student activity/study planner running from August 2003 to August 2004 (the school year). Note: Cedco (www.cedco.com) publishes a full line of related Harry Potter themed products, including journals, notecards, address books, and photo albums.

School Supplies

1. Harry Potter Double Buckle Leather Briefcase. Measures 11 x 14.5 inches, with a 3-inch depth. Sports a metal "Hogwarts" logo on the front.

2. Harry Potter Leather Backpack. Measures 9 x 11 inches. Sports a metal "Hogwarts" logo on the front.

3. Harry Potter Denim Backpack. Measures 13 x 16 inches, with a "Hogwarts" design on the back.

4. Harry Potter Remembrall Book. A spiral-bound notebook with places to put essential student information: addresses, homework assignments, special dates, and personal information.

5. Magnet: Harry in Potions Class.

6. Magnet: Harry Gets Rescued.

7. Magnet: Harry with Wand.

8. Die Cut Erasers.

9. Harry Potter Big Sticker Book. Measuring 3 x 9 inches, this book contains 24 stickers designed to be put on bumpers, notebooks, lockers, and so forth.

Miscellaneous Educational Products

Quantum Pad Interactive Book and Cartridge: Making Movies—The Inside Scoop. For very young children, an interactive primer on moviemaking.

Spells and Potions Kits

Note: As with all toys of this nature, designed for young children, adult supervision is *highly* recommended!

1. Harry Potter Activities Plus Kit. A boxed set containing a plastic case; includes an illustrated book and 10 activities from *Harry Potter and the Chamber of Secrets.* For instance, making a Howler, swelling Malfoy's nose, and making invisible diary entries.

2. Harry Potter Spells and Potions Kit. A chemistry work kit for children, with tools, chemicals, safety gear (gloves and eyewear), and an activity guide for step-by-step instructions on how to concoct basic spells and potions, packed in a 10 x 13-inch box.

3. Slithering Slime Potion: Apothecary Kit. Comes with an activity poster and the ingredients necessary to create slime.

4. Potion of Draught: Apothecary Kit. Activity poster and the ingredients necessary to make water appear and disappear.

5. Sorcerer's Stone GloGear Amulet Necklace. A kit to make a light-up stone necklace. (Note: adult supervision is especially recommended for this item, since it does contain real chemicals.)

Health Products

1. Harry Potter Band-Aids (Johnson and Johnson). Glow-in-the-dark band-aids, an assortment of 25.

2. Harry Potter Toothpaste (Johnson and Johnson). An anticavity fluoride toothpaste with a bubble gum flavor.

3. Harry Potter Toothbrush (Johnson and Johnson). Soft-head toothbrush, in a variety of colors, and various designs of Harry.

4. Hermione Granger Toothbrush (Johnson and Johnson). Soft-head toothbrush, in a variety of colors, and various designs of Hermione Granger.

Plush Products from Gund

1. Hedwig Keyring. A miniature white owl.

2. Sorting Hat Keyring. A black sorting hat.

3. Golden Snitch Keyring. A golden ball with wings.

4. Harry Potter Plush Doll. Standing 11.5 inches tall, Harry is wearing a black Hogwarts robe over a red-and-white shirt, blue jeans, and sneakers.

5. Hermione Granger Plush Doll. Standing 11 inches tall, Hermione is wearing a black Hogwarts robe over a pink shirt, blue jeans, and sneakers.

6. Ron Weasley Plush Doll. Standing 11.5 inches tall, Ron is wearing a black Hogwarts robe over a purple shirt and, presumably, blue jeans and sneakers.

7. Scabbers Plush Doll. Approximately 8 inches tall.

8. Mrs. Norris Plush Doll. Approximately 8 inches tall and 10 inches wide (excluding tail).

9. Hagrid Plush Doll. Approximately 16 inches tall, Hagrid is dressed from head to toe in brown, matching his beard, and sports a colorful scarf.

10. Dobby Plush Doll. Dressed in green rags and wearing purple socks.

11. Basilisk Plush Doll. A 4-foot-long green basilisk.

12. Fluffy Plush Doll. Three-headed watch dog, 13 inches tall.

13. Hedwig Plush Doll.

14. Golden Snitch Bean Bag. A gold-colored ball with wings, measuring 2 inches in diameter.

15. Scabbers Bean Bag. An upright, 5-inch-tall bean bag.

16. Mrs. Norris Bean Bag. Approximately 5 inches wide.

Trading Card Games

Wizards of the Coast, a subsidiary of Hasbro, has discontinued the trading card game. For collectors seeking a list of the cards and related links, go to http://www.harrypotter.warnerbros.co.uk/wotc/card_list1.html.

Games

1. Aragog Chapter Game. Includes fold-out map-book with figurines of Ron and Harry, two small spiders, dice, a blue car, and a large spider. The goal of the game is to avoid Aragog and get to the Flying Car.

2. Harry Potter: Dicers (Collectible Dice Game Starting Set). Includes 6 Dicers: Nimbus 2000, Quidditch Harry, Fred and George Weasley, Oliver Wood, the Snitch, and Professor McGonagall.

3. Harry Potter: Wizard Chess. The chess pieces are modeled after those in the movie. The set consists of the board and the modeled chess pieces.

4. Harry Potter: Uno Card Game. For 2–10 players. Includes 110 cards and Command Cards.

5. Harry Potter: Casting Stones Starter Game. For 2 players.

Magical Minis Figures

1. Albus Dumbledore. Comes with wand and the phoenix, Fawkes.

2. Hermione Granger. Comes with her cat, Crookshanks.

3. Harry Potter. Comes with a caged Hedgwig.

4. Harry Potter. Comes with broom and trunk.

5. Ron Weasley.

6. Ginny Weasley. Comes with inkwell and Tom Riddle's diary.

7. Rubeus Hagrid. Comes with pink umbrella and Norbert the dragon.

Ornaments

1. Harry Potter and Hedwig (Kurt Adler).

2. Harry Potter Polonaise Ornament Boxed Set. In a collector's box, four ornaments: the Golden Snitch (3 inches in diameter), and Harry, Ron, and Hermione (each 7 inches tall), made of Polonaise glass.

3. Harry and Ron in Flying Car Resin Ornament. A resin ornament with Harry and Ron in the Ford Anglia, flanked by Hedwig.

Collector's Stones

A. Series 1

1. The Golden Snitch. White/clear stone with Snitch embedded.

2. Harry. Purple stone with head portrait of him; the stone is in the shape of a lightning bolt.

3. Hermione. Red stone with head portrait of her; the stone is a teardrop shape.

4. Ron Weasley. Red stone with head portrait of him; the stone is diamond-shaped.

5. Mrs. Norris. Blue stone with head portrait of the cat; the stone is diamond-shaped.

6. Severus Snape. Amber stone with portrait of Snape; the stone is oval.

7. Fluffy. Red stone with head portrait of the three-headed guard dog. The stone is diamond-shaped.

8. Flying Keys. Purple stone with picture of a flying key. The stone is jagged.

9. Spells. Green stone with a picture of a spell book. The stone is diamond-shaped.

10. Sorcerer's Stone. Red stone with a picture of a stone. The stone is square.

11. Bertie Botts Beans. Amber stone with the words "Bertie Botts Beans." The stone is jagged.

12. The Sorting Hat. Red stone with a picture of the Sorting Hat. The stone is a teardrop shape.

13. Potions. Red stone with a picture of a stoppered potion. The stone is diamond-shaped.

14. Gryffindor. Purple stone with a picture of a lion's head. The stone is jagged.

15. Slytherin. Blue stone with a picture of a snake's head. The stone is roughly oval.

16. Ravenclaw. Yellow/amber stone with the picture of a raven's head. The stone is roughly a parallelogram.

17. Hufflepuff. Green stone with a picture of what appears to be a wolf. The stone is roughly square.

18. Hogwarts. Red stone with a picture of the school seal. The stone is roughly diamond-shaped.

19. You-Know-Who (Lord Voldemort). Purple stone with a pair of snakelike eyes, and the words "You Know Who." The stone is roughly diamond-shaped.

20. Hedgwig. Red stone with a picture of Harry's owl. The stone is jagged.

21. Scabbers. Green stone with a picture of Ron's pet rat. Roughly teardrop-shaped.

22. Fluffy. Red stone with a picture of the awakened three-headed dog. Roughly diamond-shaped.

23. Norbert. Blue stone with a picture of the dragon. Jagged shape.

24. Harry's Glasses. Green stone with a picture of his glasses. Roughly diamond-shaped.

B. Series 2

1. Sorcerer's Stone. Red stone with the words "The Sorcerer's Stone" on its face. Irregularly shaped.

2. Madam Malkin's. Clear stone with the words "Madam Malkin's Robes for all Occasions" on its face. Teardrop shape.

3. Invisibility Cloak. Clear stone with a picture of Harry putting it on. The stone is square.

4. Baby Norbert. Red stone with a picture of the baby dragon's head. Roughly a teardrop shape.

5. *Daily Prophet*. Red stone with a globe and the words "Daily Prophet" on its face. Square in shape.

6. Platform Nine and Three-Quarters. Red stone with the words "Platform 9³/₄." Square in shape.

7. Flourish and Blotts. Clear stone with the words "Flourish and Blotts" on the face. Diamond-shaped.

8. Apothecary. Purple stone with the word "Apothecary" on the face. Jagged shape.

9. Scabbers. Clear stone with a head portrait of Hermione's pet cat. Jagged shape.

10. Harry Potter. Purple stone with a head portrait of him. Diamond-shaped.

11. Ron Weasley. Purple stone with a head portrait of him. Square in shape.

12. Hedwig. Purple stone with a head portrait of Harry's pet owl. Teardrop in shape.

13. Goblin. Salmon-colored stone with a head portrait of a goblin. Diamond-shaped.

14. Ollivanders. Green stone with the legend "Ollivanders: Maker of Fine Wands." Roughly teardrop-shaped.

15. Gringotts. Green stone with the legend "Gringotts: Wizards' Bank." Roughly diamond-shaped.

16. Rubeus Hagrid. Salmon-colored stone with a head portrait of him. Roughly teardrop-shaped.

17. Hourglass. Green stone with a picture of an hourglass. Jagged in shape.

18. Hogwarts Express. Clear stone with a picture of a railroad train engine. Diamond-shaped.

19. Drooble's. Salmon-colored stone with a drawing of a pack of wizard bubble gum. Irregularly shaped.

20. Gold Galleons. Green stone with two pictures of Galleons. Diamond-shaped.

21. Bronze Knuts. Blue stone with three pictures of bronze Knuts. Diamond-shaped.

22. Books. Blue stone with a picture of a book. Irregularly shaped.

23. Silver Sickles. Blue stone with two pictures of silver sickles. Roughly teardrop-shaped.

24. Cauldron. Blue stone with a picture of a cauldron. Square shaped.

Watches and Charm Links

A. Watches

1. Harry Potter Quidditch Pocket Watch (Fossil). Comes in a black pouch in a Quidditch-themed trunk tin, limited to 2,000 copies, this stainless steel watch has a traditional clock face; at the 12-3-6-9 o'clock marks, Hogwarts houses are represented with icons.

2. The following watches are designed so that the links can be changed with various images relating to Harry Potter:
   - Hedwig. The watch has a purple face, with white lettering and Hedwig, the white owl, imprinted on its face. The watch has a silver-colored case. Round watch design.
   - Harry Potter. A plain face with a white background and the words "Harry Potter" imprinted; the face has a pink border on its outer edge. Round watch design.
   - Harry Potter Blue Potions Bottle. A small, rectangular face with a blue potion bottle in the center.
   - Harry Potter Potions Bottle. A circular face with a potions bottle imprinted.

B. Charm Links

1. Harry Potter Book 1 Cover.
2. Harry Potter Book 2 Cover.
3. Harry Potter Book 3 Cover.
4. Harry Potter Book 4 Cover.
5. Harry Potter Book 5 Cover.
6. Harry Potter Enamel Italian Charm.
7. Harry Potter Custom Blue Logo.
8. Harry Potter Custom Pink Logo.
9. Harry Potter Custom Purple Logo.
10. Harry Potter Custom Movie 1.
11. Harry Potter Custom Movie 2.
12. Harry Potter Custom Movie 3.
13. Harry Potter Custom Potion Class.
14. Harry Potter in Robe.
15. Harry Potter Custom Laser.

Harry Potter Trading Cards: Movies

On the front side, each card has a still image, with descriptive banner; and on the back side, explanatory text.

1. A Few More Words
2. A Few Words
3. Announcing . . . Lee Jordan!
4. Caught!
5. Christmas Gift
6. Classes at Hogwarts
7. Dangerous Detention
8. Detention Begins
9. Express to Hogwarts
10. Figuring Out Transfigurations
11. Filch Leads the Way
12. Flitwick, Charms Professor
13. Gringotts Goblin
14. Hagrid of Hogwarts
15. Hagrid's Errand
16. Hagrid's Hut
17. Harry and Hedwig
18. Harry Enters Gringotts
19. Harry in the Forest
20. Harry of Gryffindor House
21. Head Table
22. Hermione in the Forest
23. Hermione's Sorted
24. Heroic Ron
25. In the Library
26. Into the Dark Forest
27. Introducing . . . Hagrid!
28. Letters From No One
29. Oops!
30. Plots and Pain?
31. Portrait of the Fat Lady
32. Quiet Moment
33. Restricted Section
34. Ron's Sorted
35. Safest Place in the World
36. Through the Barrier!
37. Transfigurations
38. Up!
39. What Was That?
40. Wingardium Leviosa!
41. At the Zoo
42. Bags and Baggage
43. Bank Clerk
44. Beginning Flying
45. Cupboard Under the Stairs
46. Down for the Count
47. Draco Investigates
48. Dudley's New Clothes
49. Fang the Boarhound
50. Flee!
51. Flying Instructor
52. Gryffindor Quidditch Team

53. Hagrid and Fang
54. Hagrid and Friends
55. Hagrid as Host
56. Hagrid's Heart
57. Harry and a Quaffle
58. Harry Makes a Friend
59. Harry Takes Flight
60. Harry, Ron, and Hermione
61. Help Arrives
62. Hermione the Scholar
63. Hogwarts Challenges
64. Inside the Leaky Cauldron
65. Keeping the Accounts
66. Letter for Harry
67. Malfoy and Flying
68. Manners Lesson
69. Meeting "The Boy Who Lived"
70. Mother and Son
71. Mysterious Potions Master
72. On the Same Side
73. Professor Minerva McGonagall
74. Quirrell, Defense Against the Dark Arts Professor
75. Remembrall Trouble
76. Seamus's Flying Lesson
77. Serious Considerations
78. Showing Off
79. To the Skies!
80. Watching Harry's Flight

Harry Potter 3-D Viewer Windows

With the binocular viewer, the pictures on these slides become three-dimensional. The individual windows include:

1. Hagrid on the Cycle
2. Platform Nine and Three-Quarters—Decoder
3. Harry in the Cupboard
4. Dumbledore and Baby Harry
5. Letters from Hogwarts
6. Hagrid's Gift for Harry
7. Wild Ride under Gringotts
8. Mrs. Norris on Patrol
9. Inside Gringotts
10. Norbert—Decoder
11. Ron and the Potions
12. Albus Dumbledore
13. Devil's Snare—Decoder
14. Harry Casts a Magic Spell
15. Slytherin or Gryffindor
16. Ron and the Sorting Hat
17. Potions Class
18. Invisibility Cloak
19. Pig Snout
20. Mirror of Erised
22. The Key among All Keys
21. Ron on Broom
23. Hermione Levitation—Decoder
24. Hedwig with a Message

Coins

Harry Potter and the Chamber of Secrets Collectible Coins. Five nickel alloy medallions in a cardboard case, accessorize with stickers. Medallions include Harry Potter, Professor Lockhart, Tom Riddle, Ginny Weasley, and Dobby the house-elf.

Wizard Cards

The cards, with names and biographies provided by Rowling, can be found within the video games from Electronic Arts. Here's a list of the cards:

1. Paracelsus
2. Andros the Invincible
3. Circe
4. Herpo the Foul
5. Mopsus
6. Cliodne
7. Ethelred the Ever-Ready
8. Morgan le Fay
9. Gregory the Smarmy
10. Godric Gryffindor
11. Hengist of Woodcroft
12. Helga Hufflepuff
13. Queen Maeve
14. Merlin
15. Merwyn the Malicious
16. Rowena Ravenclaw
17. Salazar Slytherin
18. Uric the Oddball
19. Wendelin the Weird
20. Fulbert the Fearful
21. Wilfred Elphick
22. Bridget Wenlock
23. Ignatia Wildsmith
24. Cyprian Youdle
25. Chauncey Oldridge
26. Gifford Ollerton
27. Alberta Toothill
28. Burdock Muldoon
29. Quong Po
30. Yardley Platt
31. Felix Summerbee
32. Daisy Dodderidge
33. Cornelius Agrippa
34. Bowman Wright
35. Montague Knightley
36. Musidora Barkwith
37. Gunhilda of Gorsemoor
38. Mungo Bonham
39. Balfour Bane
40. Archibald Alderton
41. Elfrida Clagg
42. Dymphna Furmage
43. Thaddeus Thurkell
44. Havelock Sweeting

45. Elladora Ketteridge

46. Honoria Nutcombe

47. Lord Stoddard Withers

48. Glanmore Peakes

49. Edgar Stoulger

50. Flavius Belby

51. Gondoline Oliphant

52. Glover Hipworth

53. Beaumont Marjoribanks

54. Gulliver Pokeby

55. Xavier Rastrick

56. Artemisia Lufkin

57. Grogan Stump

58. Beatrix Bloxam

59. Crispin Cronk

60. Alberic Gunnion

61. Dorcas Wellbeloved

62. Laverne de Montmorency

63. Leopoldina Smethwyck

64. Mirabella Plunkett

65. Oswald Beamish

66. Justus Pilliwickle

67. Sacharissa Tugwood

68. Hesper Starkey

69. Norvel Twonk

70. Roderick Plumpton

71. Cassandra Vablatsky

72. Newt Scamander

73. Adalbert Waffling

74. Perpetua Fancourt

75. Roland Kegg

76. Tilly Toke

77. Joscelind Wadcock

78. Derwent Shimpling

79. Jocunda Sykes

80. Celestina Warbeck

81. Blenheim Stalk

82. Miranda Goshawk

83. Carlotta Pinkstone

84. Bertie Bott

85. Devlin Whitehorn

86. Gaspard Shingleton

87. Greta Catchlove

88. Glenda Chittock

89. Gwenog Jones

90. Dunbar Oglethorpe

91. Myron Wagtail

92. Kirley Duke

93. Donaghan Tremlett

94. Heathcote Barbary

95. Herman Wintringham

96. Gideon Crumb

97. Orsino Thruston

98. Merton Graves

99. Harry Potter

100. Albus Dumbledore

Part Six:
Harry Potter Websites

Tim Kirk

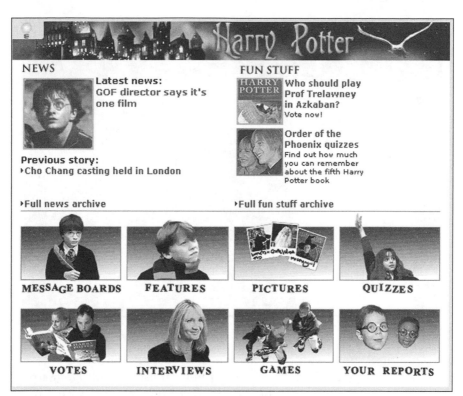

NEWS

Latest news:
GOF director says it's one film

Previous story:
▸Cho Chang casting held in London

▸Full news archive

FUN STUFF

Who should play Prof Trelawney in Azkaban?
Vote now!

Order of the Phoenix quizzes
Find out how much you can remember about the fifth Harry Potter book

▸Full fun stuff archive

MESSAGE BOARDS   FEATURES   PICTURES   QUIZZES

VOTES   INTERVIEWS   GAMES   YOUR REPORTS

British Broadcasting Corporation (BBC)

An official site at www.bbc.co.uk.

For Rowling fans hungering for real news, this is the source: the British Broadcasting System covers all the Potter news fit to print, with a special section devoted just to "The Harry Potter Phenomenon."

Though fan websites tend to report every tidbit, even tangential items of possible interest, the BBC is necessarily selective and does a good job covering not only what's going on with Rowling's books but her film adaptations as well.

Scholastic

An official site at www.scholastic.com/harrypotter/home.asp.

An owl carrying a letter flies across a hilly landscape with Hogwarts in the background, accompanied by the sounds of tinkling music. The string-wrapped letter is released and fills the screen. An envelope, sealed with red wax, has a white note on it bearing the major subject areas of this website: (1) about the books, (2) reference guide, (3) discussion chamber, (4) wizard challenge, and (5) screensaver.

1. About the Books

The pronunciation guide is alphabetical and, when a word is selected, it's spoken aloud. This is very useful, since you can see how to read it phonetically and then hear it. (You'll be speaking Potter-tongue in no time at all!)

The discussion guide, written by Kylene Beers (an assistant professor of reading at the University of Houston, Texas), discusses the first four Potter novels and offers summaries of the plot, theme, characters, settings, and characterizations of each, followed by questions.

"Meet J. K. Rowling" is the official biography, supplemented with three selected interviews: one from Comic Relief, a charity organization that she supports, and two from this website.

"Meet Mary GrandPré" is a brief biographical sketch of the artist well known in illustration circles for her "soft geometry" art (as she explains it) and best known for her art that graces the U.S. editions (and some foreign editions) of the Harry Potter novels.

2. Reference Guide

"Did You Know?" poses and answers questions drawn from the novels. The pronunciation guide (see "About the Books").

An alphabetized glossary to the people, places, and things in Harry Potter's fictional universe.

3. Discussion Chamber

A provocative question is posed: you send your answer to the website. Sample question: "You are applying for a job at the Ministry of Magic. What job are you applying for? Why do you think you are the right person for this job?"

4. Wizard Challenge

Think you know everything there is to know about Harry Potter? Well, guess again! You can play this trivia quiz game—until you get a total of three answers wrong. What makes this fun is that website visitors submitted the questions, but it's not child's play. (A listing of top-ranking "students" shows that "BJR" from Pennsylvania, got 53 questions right; the second place is also held by "BJR", with 37 right.)

5. Screensaver

What website is complete without a screensaver? It shows scenes from the first four years of Harry at Hogwarts. A bonus: the preview scenes are interactive.

The bottom line: A first-rate website for budding and aged wizards alike.

Warner Bros.

Harry Potter, the official movie site at http://www.harrypotter.com.

On the Internet, the trick is not only to get the attention of the Web surfer but, more importantly, to hold it.

Insofar as its official Harry Potter movie tie-in website is concerned, Warner Bros. need not worry: The official Harry Potter book website is good, but this is better.

The site opens with a Flash animation, showing a Quidditch game that you can play.

Some of the key features of this site:

1. Hogwarts: Enroll and Be Sorted

After signing in as a student, a form letter on parchment appears. "We are pleased to inform you that you have been accepted at Hogwarts School of Witchcraft and Wizardry," it begins. Signed by Draco Dormiens Nunquam Titillandos and Professor McGonagall, it prompts you to check on the "supplies list."

A list of supplies—clothes and books—appears, including items that Muggles would find decidedly odd, like "One pair of dragon-hide gloves" and a copy of Emeric Switch's classic book, *A Beginner's Guide to Transfiguration.*

Optionally, "an owl, a cat, or a toad" can be brought, as well. (Recommendation: Get an owl, so you can communicate by air mail.)

The list is signed by Lucinda Thomsonicle-Pocus, the Chief Attendant of Witchcraft Provisions.

Then the sorting begins. You have two choices: you can be automatically sorted—what's the fun in that?—or you can answer a few questions and let the sorting hat decide where you ought to be.

Most readers will want to be in Gryffindor, which is the house where Harry Potter, Ron Weasley, and Hermione reside; and it's the house that Rowling would like to be in, too.

Once sorted into your house, you're on your own, free to roam the halls of Hogwarts.

2. Fun and Games

All work and no play makes Harry a dull boy. Fortunately, on this page, there's a little of both, and all in good fun.

School activities including trying out as a Seeker, practicing Quidditch, and drawing swords in the Fencing Club.

Games include Weasley's Kitchen Game, Escape from the Dursleys' (in the flying car), and the Staircase Game.

Extras include sending mail by house-elf, exploring the library, and designing your own Hogwarts hallway.

3. Beyond Hogwarts: Venture off School Grounds

When you've had enough of cramming for your O.W.L.s (Ordinary Wizarding Levels) and need a change of scenery, three appealing destinations are available: a walk-through of Diagon Alley; a 360-degree room-by-room tour of the Burrow (the Weasley residence); and Touring the Set, a 360-degree exploration of various parts of the Potter universe, including the Dursley home, Dumbledore's Office, and Lockhart's Class.

4. *Daily Prophet:* News and Events

As expected, this section focuses only on the movie adaptations, with news about the third Potter movie, interviews with the principal cast, and a link to a message board for fellow Potterites.

As the FAQs section explains, "The *Daily Prophet* area is where you should go to get the latest news on *Harry Potter and Prisoner of Azkaban.* We try to complement news from the set with interviews with some of the actors, actresses, and key people related to the movie's filming."

5. Platform Nine and Three-Quarters: The Online Community

Sign up for the e-mailed newsletter, create and submit your Potter website,

send an Instant Message, or discuss topics of interest on the message board. (The most popular message board? At 6,717 postings, House Board: Gryffindor.) The obligatory FAQs appears in this section.

6. Wizard's Shop: Official Merchandise

Potter fans can be divided into two camps: purists or collectors. The former want only the books, audiobook adaptations, and film adaptations, but the latter want *everything*—the books, the DVDs, the toys, clothing, posters, stationary, and so forth.

If you're in the market for Potter merchandise, this online store offers a wide range of products if you've got Galleons to spare.

7. Live the Magic: Magical Fun and Activities

This category needs to be expanded and brought up to the level of play that can be found in "Beyond Hogwarts" and "Fun and Games." In other words, someone needs to conjure up a few more interactive features for this section. As is, it includes a link to an external site by Coca-Cola, to promote StoryTraveler (a reading program that tours the U.S.), and a 3-D game (catch the escaped magical pixies), which requires the Shockwave plug-in.

The bottom line: A vastly entertaining website that offers a wealth of information and extensive interactive features, including 360-degree visual tours of places in the Potter universe. This website is a "must" for new and old Potter fans alike. Though its principal purpose is, obviously, to showcase the movie adaptations, it stands on its own as a website especially useful to new fans who want to explore the world of Potter at their own pace before plunging into the books.

Bloomsbury Publishing

An official site at www.bloomsbury.com/harrypotter.

Bloomsbury Publishing, Harry Potter's U.K. publisher, provides information on the Potter novels as well as other titles.

Less elaborate than Scholastic, this website features two major Harry Potter areas: (1) Witches and Wizards, and (2) Muggles.

1. Witches and Wizards

This catch-all section is the interactive portion of the site, with information about the books (including foreign editions), interviews with Rowling, a message board for fans, a biography of Rowling, news, three screensavers, and FAQs. Of course, you can send e-mail as well, with a banner e-card (think electronic postcard), a book cover e-card, and most fun of all, a Howler (rant) or Owler (thanks/praise). My favorite Howler: "You Muggle!" My favorite Owler: "You're a star!"

2. Muggles

This information-only section cites Rowling's awards and offers capsule book reviews and a glossary, among other information.

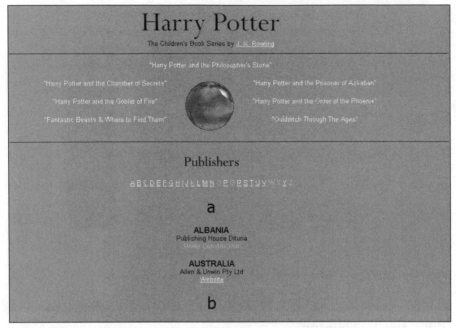

J. K. Rowling (Christopher Little Literary Agency)

An official website at www.jkrowling.com. Launch date: May 14, 2004. Plug-ins: Flash. (A plain text version is also available.)

Finally, something to write home about! Get your quill pen and parchment out, and jot a quick note to the folks at home and send it by owl mail as soon as possible!

Wizards and muggles alike will be glad to know that J. K. Rowling ("Jo" to you) has not only put up what has to be the most enchanting website devoted to a single author, but has taken a hands-on approach to its design and, more important, its content.

Recreating Rowling's desk, the website uses the Flash plug-in to allow visitors to navigate this delightful site packed with information. A nice touch: as in her novels, Portkeys are used for traveling on-site, accompanied by a whooshing visual and sound effect. Bloody brilliant!

Dispelling rumors, providing news, and offering an illustrated autobiography, Rowling serves up a palatable feast of words and pictures that delights, entertains, and most important, informs fans on the goings on in her muggles and wizarding worlds.

Generating over 17 million hits in its first week, Rowling's website is pure magic for fans worldwide who, finally, have an indisputably reliable source of information for all things Rowling.

The Harry Potter Lexicon

An unofficial fan site at www.hp-lexicon.org.

"Our goal is to make this website the most complete and thorough resource about the Harry Potter universe available anywhere, in any format."

Accurately subtitled as "The most complete and amazing reference to the wonderful world of Harry Potter!" this is required reading for anyone who wants to get up to speed on the Harry Potter universe.

For the five Potter novels, this website provides a large scan of the front cover (U.S. edition), a chapter-by-chapter synopsis, a daily calendar of events to help get a sense of place, a listing of the differences between the U.K. and U.S. editions, and, depending on the book, a reader's guide. This information is supplemented with facts and trivia, comments by Rowling gleaned from interviews, and a listing of awards (if applicable).

Rowling's charity book projects (*Fantastic Beasts and Where to Find Them,* by Newt Scamander, and *Quidditch Through the Ages,* by Kennilworthy Whisp) are also discussed, with bibliographic information, facts and trivia, comments by Rowling gleaned from interviews, and a chapter-by-chapter outline.

Beyond the books, there's an exhaustive look at everything in the Potter universe, including:

• "The Muggle World" provides detailed information about the people and places in Rowling's fiction.

- "Support the Lexicon" asks for donations using PayPal and provides links to Amazon.com, which gives this website a referral fee for the initial purchase.

- "What's New?" provides information about news and updates relative to this website.

- "The Harry Potter Universe: A to Z," is a thorough, alphabetized listing of the people, places, and things in the Harry Potter Universe—accurate, exhaustive, and definitive.

- "Explore the Wizarding World" provides detailed menus for the magic, people, places, and things in the Potter Universe, including a wizard's atlas, a Who's Who in the wizard world, an encyclopedia of spells and potions, a directory of magical items, a Quidditch handbook, and "The Bestiary," which describes the imaginary beasts populating Harry's magical universe.
  Subsections include:

  - "Encyclopedia of Spells," alphabetized for easy reference.

  - "The Wizarding World: An Atlas and Gazetteer" offers visual speculations based on the books, but in no way definitive.

  - "Magic and Magical Theory" is especially useful for Muggles to explain magic, which they can't do.

  - "Wizarding Through the Ages," with timelines, calendars, and essays.

  - "Lexicon Forum" is a message board.

Bottom line: This is by far the most detailed, authoritative, and updated Potter website of its kind. A "must" view for any Potter fan, but especially useful to the new fan who came to the Potter universe through the movies and not the books.

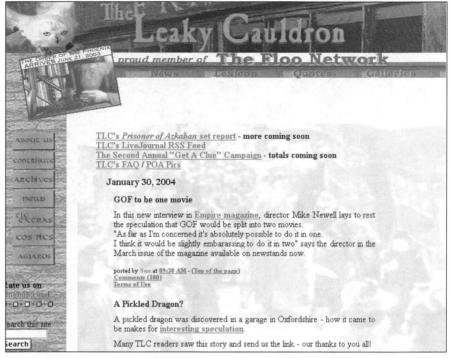

The Leaky Cauldron

An unofficial news site, at www.the-leaky-cauldron.org.

This website is named after a nondescript fictional inn located on Charing Cross Road in London, where Harry was taken by Hagrid, who escorted him through this bar and into the courtyard at its back, which is the entrance to Diagon Alley.

As stated in its FAQs, "The Leaky Cauldron, www.the-leaky-cauldron.org, is a nonprofit, volunteer-run website. It is a news source and archive for all news relating to the Harry Potter franchise. Here you will find up-to-the-minute reports on the books, films, interviews, merchandise, and events, as well as all pertinent peripheral Harry Potter news."

If you want to bookmark one site for news, filtered through fans' eyes, this is the site to watch. (For news reportage from traditional sources, your best bet is the BBC website.)

MuggleNet

An unofficial news site, at www.mugglenet.com/jk.shtml.

The best general interest site about Rowling and Harry Potter, divided into sections:

- MuggleNet (editorials and news archives).

- Books (information about the books, quotes, funny excerpts, name origins, mistakes noted by eagle-eyed readers, book covers, chapter pictures, anagrams, and information gleaned from various sources about the forthcoming books).

- Games (trivia, puzzles, downloads, MuggleNet interactive, and a caption contest).

- Movies (cast, crew, still photos, promotional photos, magazine covers, trailers, reviews, and release dates).

- Info (Hogwarts, Quidditch, Ministry of Magic, creatures, characters, Rowling, and other information).

- Media (TCG, Videogames, LEGO, merchandise, action figures, wallpaper, and Photoshop fun).

- Fans (fan art, chat, chat transcripts, forums, and a spotlight on the fan of the week).

- Miscellaneous (color-ins, parallels, Too Big a Fan, AIM Stuff, Rejected Titles, License Plates, Spoofs, Song Parodies, the Book Trolley, and Rosmerta's Recipes).

All in all, an excellent overview of the entire fictional universe by dedicated fans who know the books and the movies inside and out.

Other Recommended Sites

1. Rowling on the Web. Philip Nel, author of *J. K. Rowling's Harry Potter Novels: A Reader's Guide,* has compiled a handy list of links to other sites, especially useful to students seeking more information about Rowling and Harry Potter. Go to: www.ksu.edu/english/nelp/rowling.

2. Amazon.com (U.S.). The premier online bookseller that sells not only books but DVDs, music soundtracks, and toys through its affiliation with Toys'R'Us. If you want anything available by or about Harry Potter, this is the first place to go.

3. Amazon.co.uk (U.K.). The premier online bookseller branches out overseas. For those wanting British editions of the Potter books, this is the first place to go.

4. The Sugar Quill. Another site with many useful informative links. Go to: www.sugarquill.net.

5. Harry Potter Fan Fiction. There are plenty of sites, but you may want to start with www.fanfiction.net or www.fictionalley.org.

6. Scotsman.com. The official online web presence of the *Scotsman,* the newspaper that serves Edinburgh, Scotland, which is where Rowling lives. By registering, you can freely access its extensive inventory of stories about Rowling from a local perspective.

7. The Harry Potter Automatic News Aggregator. This site uses special

software to continually harvest the Internet on an ongoing basis for news by and about Rowling and Harry Potter. It provides a summary of each major news story with a corresponding link to its original source. Go to: www.hpana.com.

8. TheSnitch.co.uk. An excellent, all-round, U.K.-based website; this one is worth your time and attention.

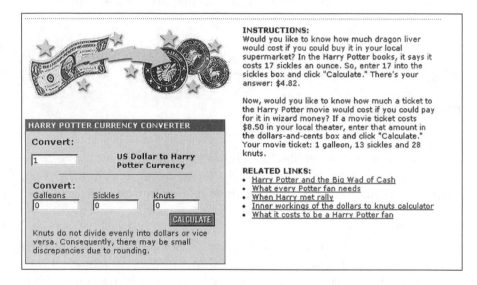

INSTRUCTIONS:
Would you like to know how much dragon liver would cost if you could buy it in your local supermarket? In the Harry Potter books, it says it costs 17 sickles an ounce. So, enter 17 into the sickles box and click "Calculate." There's your answer: $4.82.

Now, would you like to know how much a ticket to the Harry Potter movie would cost if you could pay for it in wizard money? If a movie ticket costs $8.50 in your local theater, enter that amount in the dollars-and-cents box and click "Calculate." Your movie ticket: 1 galleon, 13 sickles and 28 knuts.

RELATED LINKS:
• Harry Potter and the Big Wad of Cash
• What every Potter fan needs
• When Harry met rally
• Inner workings of the dollars to knuts calculator
• What it costs to be a Harry Potter fan

HARRY POTTER CURRENCY CONVERTER

Convert:

| 1 | US Dollar to Harry Potter Currency |

Convert:

| Galleons | Sickles | Knuts |
| 0 | 0 | 0 |

CALCULATE

Knuts do not divide evenly into dollars or vice versa. Consequently, there may be small discrepancies due to rounding.

9. Harry Potter Currency Converter, from CNN and *Money* magazine. You'd have to be a little "knuts," so to speak, to put too much currency in this website, but it's fun and addictive! Enter the U.S. dollar amount and the converter will instantly tell you your fortune in Galleons, Sickles, and Knuts.

Appendices

Tim Kirk

Appendix A
Books by J. K. Rowling: In Print and Audio

Note: In the U.S., Scholastic publishes the Harry Potter novels; in the U.K., Bloomsbury is the publisher. All other publishers are duly noted. The prices are the suggested retail prices.

U.S. Editions

Harry Potter and the Sorcerer's Stone
1. Hardback, $19.95

2. Paperback, $6.99

3. Audiocassette (unabridged) read by Jim Dale, $35

4. Compact disc (unabridged) read by Jim Dale, $49.95

5. Gift edition, out of print

Harry Potter and the Chamber of Secrets
1. Hardback, $19.95

2. Paperback, $6.99

3. Audiocassette (unabridged) read by Jim Dale, $35

4. Compact disc (unabridged) read by Jim Dale, $24.95

5. Gift edition, out of print

Harry Potter and the Prisoner of Azkaban

1. Hardback, $19.95

2. Paperback, $6.99

3. Audiocassette (unabridged) read by Jim Dale, $35

4. Compact disc (unabridged) read by Jim Dale, $49.95

5. Gift edition, out of print

Harry Potter and the Goblet of Fire

1. Hardback, $25.95

2. Paperback, $8.99

3. Audiocassette (unabridged) read by Jim Dale, $25.95

4. Compact disc (unabridged) read by Jim Dale, $69.95

5. Gift edition, out of print

6. Large print (Thorndike Press), $25.95

Harry Potter and the Order of the Phoenix

1. Hardback, $29.99

2. Paperback: not yet published

3. Audiocassette (unabridged) read by Jim Dale, $45

4. Compact disc (unabridged) read by Jim Dale, $75

5. Deluxe edition, slipcased: $60. (Note: The dust jacket features new art by Mary GrandPré; the art used for the dust jacket of the trade hardback is printed in color as its endpapers.)

Boxed Sets

1. In hardback, books 1–4 in a cardboard slipcase, $85

2. In trade paperback, books 1–4 in a cardboard slipcase, $30.96

3. In hardback, books 1–5 in a cardboard slipcase. $100. Comes with a leather bookmark. Packaged as "Books 1–5 Limited Edition Box Set."

4. Harry Potter Schoolbooks Boxed Set: Two Classic Books from the Library of Hogwarts School of Witchcraft and Wizardry; cardboard slipcase con-

taining two "BT bound" (hardback) books written under Rowling's pen names: *Quidditch Through the Ages,* by Kennilworthy Whisp, and *Fantastic Beasts and Where to Find Them,* by Newt Scamander. These books are available separately for $11 each.

U.K. Editions

Note: In the U.K., two editions of the books and audiotapes were published: one edition for children, and one edition for adults. There is no difference in the texts; however, the cover art is changed to reflect the age difference.

Harry Potter and the Philosopher's Stone

1. Hardback
   a. Children's edition, £11.99
   b. Adult edition, out of print

2. Paperback
   a. Children's edition, £5.99
   b. Adult edition, £6.99

3. Unabridged audiocassette read by Stephen Fry
   a. Children's edition, £21.99
   b. Adult edition, £21.99
   c. Cassettes and travel bag, £23.99

4. Unabridged compact disc read by Stephen Fry
   a. Children's edition, £25.99
   b. Adult edition, £49.99
   c. CD and travel bag, £39.99

5. Special edition in hardback, £10

Harry Potter and the Chamber of Secrets

1. Hardback
   a. Children's edition, £11.99
   b. Adult edition, out of print

2. Paperback
   a. Children's edition, £5.99
   b. Adult edition, £6.99

3. Unabridged audiocassette read by Stephen Fry
   a. Children's edition, £21.99
   b. Adult edition, £21.99

373

4. Unabridged compact disc read by Stephen Fry
   a. Children's edition, £25.99
   b. Adult edition, none

5. Special edition, £10

6. Large-print edition, £13.95

Harry Potter and the Prisoner of Azkaban

1. Hardback
   a. Children's edition, £11.99
   b. Adult edition, out of print

2. Paperback
   a. Children's edition, £5.99
   b. Adult edition, £6.99

3. Unabridged audiocassette read by Stephen Fry
   a. Children's edition, £26.99
   b. Adult edition, £26.99

4. Unabridged compact disc read by Stephen Fry
   a. Children's edition, £31.99
   b. Adult edition, no information available

5. Special edition, £10

6. Large-print trade paperback, £13.95

Harry Potter and the Goblet of Fire

1. Hardback
   a. Children's edition, £14.99
   b. Adult edition, not available

2. Paperback
   a. Children's edition, £6.99
   b. Adult edition, £6.99

3. Unabridged audiocassette read by Stephen Fry
   a. Children's edition, £49.99
   b. Adult edition, no information available

4. Unabridged compact disc read by Stephen Fry
   a. Children's edition, £59.99
   b. Adult edition, no information available

5. Special edition, £25

Harry Potter and the Order of the Phoenix

1. Hardback
    a. Children's edition, £16.99
    b. Adult edition, £16.99

2. Paperback
    a. Children's edition, not yet published
    b. Adult edition, not yet published

3. Unabridged audiocassette read by Stephen Fry
    a. Children's edition, £65
    b. Adult edition, £65

4. Unabridged compact disc read by Stephen Fry
    a. Children's edition, £75
    b. Adult edition, £75

5. Special edition, £30

Boxed Sets

1. *The Harry Potter Quartet Collection* (books 1–4) in lunch-box-style case, audiocassette, £99.99

Appendix B
Filmography and Videography

DVDs

Discovering the Real World of Harry Potter, $15, from Questar, May 2002. Running time, 74 minutes.

An authorized profile narrated by British actor Hugh Laurie, this is a professionally produced documentary that aired on PBS. It focuses on real-world places associated with Rowling, supplemented by interviews with David Colbert (producer of the Harry Potter films), and Lindsey Fraser (author of *Conversations with J. K. Rowling*). Recommended.

The Magical World of Harry Potter: The Unauthorized Story of J. K. Rowling, out-of-print, from Eaton Entertainment, August 2000. Running time, 30 minutes. An unauthorized profile.

The coverage of Rowling is limited to two public appearances; the bulk of the footage focuses on interviews with booksellers and children. The most interesting footage is an interview with members of the Potter family, whom Rowling knew in her early years.

Harry Potter Film Adaptations

Note: DVD has replaced VHS as the preferred home entertainment format. Offering a better picture, clearer sound, and more storage capacity, the DVD format is clearly superior in every way.

Two DVD formats are available: a widescreen, sometimes called letterboxing, in which you see the same proportions as seen at the theater; and fullscreen, in which the left and right sides of the frame are chopped off to fit a conventional television screen.

Harry Potter and the Sorcerer's Stone [#1], $26.99, from Warner Home Video, 2002. Available in VHS and in two DVD formats: widescreen and fullscreen. (The DVD set is comprised of two discs: #1 is the movie itself, with 34 scenes, end credits, and theatrical trailers; and #2 is comprised of supplementary material.

For Potter fans, the bonus disk is packed with material especially designed for younger fans:

Additional Scenes: There are deleted scenes from the theatrical release available on the disk, but they are hidden. You must find the clues in the areas below to access the hidden scenes.

Diagon Alley: In a courtyard behind the Leaky Cauldron, a brick wall bars the way to Diagon Alley. But if you choose the right bricks in the right order, the brick wall reshuffles itself, so you can enter Diagon Alley, where you'll need to shop for school supplies. You'll need a wand, so be sure to stop at Ollivanders; you won't have to choose a wand, for the wand will choose *you*. The Owl Emporium is your next stop and, as the narrator suggests, an owl is air mail, whereas only a Muggle would want to use the slower, and less reliable, Muggle Mail for delivery. The third stop is, of course, Gringotts Bank, where you'll need to go to get money to buy the wand and owl. (Hint: Go to the bank first.)

Common Room, Great Hall, Harry's Room: These are self-navigated tours using Apple's Quicktime to provide a 360-degree view of these rooms as seen in the films.

Library: This is like no other library you've ever seen. Pull a book off the shelf, open it, and be prepared for anything. See pictures talk on the walls and watch ghosts walk.

Classes: As a student you'll be expected to learn how to prepare potions and cast spells. Here's where you get a little hands-on experience.

Quidditch: Learn more about wizards' favorite sport and see if you, like Harry Potter, can catch the Golden Snitch. (It's harder than it looks!) You can also look for the Mirror of Erised, where you may be able to find your heart's desire.

Bonus: If you have a CD-ROM drive on your PC-compatible computer (there's no Mac version available), you can access special features. "Be Sorted. Receive owl messages. Collect Wizard cards. Enhance your Hogwarts tour. Transform your computer with downloadable features. Sample Harry Potter games, and more."

Harry Potter and the Chamber of Secrets [#2], $29.95, from Warner Home Video, 2003. Available in VHS and in two DVD formats: widescreen and fullscreen. (The DVD set is comprised of two discs: #1 is the movie itself, with 36 scenes and end credits, and some special features, such as cast and crew, year one at Hogwarts, and the theatrical trailer; and #2 is comprised of bonus material, with more elaborate [and imaginative] fare than on the first DVD.)

Behind Hogwarts: An in-depth interview with Rowling, conducted by Steve Kloves, opens this section, followed by interviews with the principal cast. Also in this section, an extensive gallery of production sketches and a look at Professor Dumbledore's office, where you can simply take a tour or, alternately, build a scene.

Activities: Tour the Chamber of Secrets and take the Chamber Challenge, if you're up to it. After screwing your courage to the sticking place, ask yourself if you're up to Forbidden Forest Challenge. For weaker hearts, stick to a tour of Colin's photographic Darkroom, or tour Diagon Alley with your fellow wizards.

Gilderoy Lockhart's Classroom: Check out his list of required reading, see Certificates, and view a photo gallery.

Spellcaster Knowledge: Think you know your spells? Test your knowledge in this section.

The second disc also has a demo of the EA Game based on the movie and, unlike the first DVD *(Harry Potter and the Sorcerer's Stone)*, readily available additional scenes, which can be played individually or collectively.

Appendix C
Key Collectibles: Books

The word *collectible* has acquired a pejorative meaning in today's market. The word has become cheapened with overusage, even in the Harry Potter community, and consumers are thinking (erroneously, as it turns out) that they are buying bona fide collectibles, even when they are not.

For instance, the U.S. edition of *Order of the Phoenix* had a record-breaking first printing of 8.6 million copies, which means that it will *never* be collectible—unless Rowling happens to sign your copy.

As for licensed products through Warner Bros., few are collectible because they are mass produced; when the stock runs low, more are manufactured.

If you are in the market for a genuine Harry Potter collectible, think in terms of books: a first edition, preferably signed, and purchased through an antiquarian book dealer who knows his stock, grades the books accurately, and buys only from other reputable dealers, to minimize the chance of selling you a book with a forged signature—a problem most often encountered at online auction sites.

The gold standard in collectibles can be simply summed up: demand versus supply.

Though Rowling's recent titles went to press with multimillion-copy print runs, the early editions—especially in the U.K.—went to press with significantly smaller print runs, which makes them scarce.

The demand for those early copies has steadily increased, because of the additional exposure Rowling has experienced due to book sales and film adaptations. The supply also dwindles with each passing year, since many collectors hold on to their copies. The result is that fewer copies of Rowling's earlier books appear in the secondary marketplace.

Original Manuscripts

With the exception of a brief outline for *Order of the Phoenix,* which was expected to fetch $9,400 but sold at auction for $45,314, no manuscripts have reached the marketplace. Should Rowling sell her original manuscripts, they would be auctioned off by Sotheby's and command record sums.

Signed Postcards/Letters

Rowling does answer some fan mail, but it's very much the exception, not the rule. I've not seen any postcards or letters on the open market, though some may eventually surface. Expect to see them offered on eBay or through rare book dealers. (Of course, you should be very concerned about provenance!)

Signed Books

Through book four, Rowling supported book signings and made the obligatory author's tour to promote them; but if book five is any indication, we will see controlled public appearances and no announced book signings. Though she may drop in unannounced at Waterstone's in Edinburgh on publication day for Harry Potter books six and seven, don't count on it.

The following list of Potter novels (proofs and first editions) show a representative sampling from a website that offers stock from antiquarian booksellers, who scrupulously list the flaws and attributes of each book offered. Go to www.abebooks.com and use the search engine to check its database of existing stock.

General Considerations Affecting Price

1. Condition. The better the condition, the more expensive the book. In the book world, the highest grade is "fine."

2. Intact book jacket. With few exceptions, all of the Potter novels in the U.K. and the U.S. have dust jackets. The exceptions: the first printing of the British edition of *Harry Potter and the Philosopher's Stone,* which had a laminated hardback cover, and the British Special editions, which have a color illustration inset on the front cover.

3. Markings. Books are often given as gifts and, on the inside front cover or flyleaf, a cheery birthday or holiday greeting may be found. Such markings devalue the book.

4. Clipped prices. The retail price of a book is usually printed on the top of the front dust jacket flap. Some people clip it off when giving a book as a gift because they don't want you to know how much they spent—an antiquated notion, since anyone can simply look it up on amazon.com. Clipping devalues a book because the book jacket has been mutilated.

5. Signature. Rowling always signs on the title page, and appends a European-style date (e.g., 29-6-98 for June 29, 1998). If she knows the person, she will warmly inscribe it. Obviously, if you are not associated with Rowling and get a general inscription, it is not as valuable as a flat-signed (signature only) copy to booksellers. But an "associational" copy, signed for someone she knows, will be valuable, depending on who the person is. Case in point: Several associational copies given by Rowling to her father commanded record sums at Sotheby's in December 2003, including a first edition of *Harry Potter and the Goblet of Fire*, which sold for $48,000 because of its inscription.

6. Bookplates. When these are pasted in a book, permanently defacing it, the book is devalued.

U.K. Editions from Bloomsbury

Note: This listing is intended to provide an overview of the current fair market values as reflected on the Internet through antiquarian book dealers. It provides a representative sampling only and should be used as a general guide. Check with antiquarian booksellers for current pricing.

First editions for all the Potter novels are marked by a row of descending numbers to indicate their printing: Thus, first editions are marked: 10 9 8 7 6 5 4 3 2 1. The *exception* to this rule is *Goblet of Fire*, which states "First Edition."

Harry Potter and the Philosopher's Stone (U.K.)

The first edition had a minuscule print run—500 copies, of which 300 were hardback and the remaining 200 were paperbacks. Because this is the first edition (marked "10 9 8 7 6 5 4 3 2 1" on the copyright page), it is the rarest and most desirable Rowling collectible in book form. As expected, copies in fine condition are very scarce, since many were sold to libraries; and those copies are usually in fair (or poor) condition due to excessive handling. The hardback had a laminated color cover and, as such, did not require a dust jacket.

Generally, a hardback copy in fine condition will command $30,000, owing to its tiny print run and the fact that few copies are in private hands.

1. In hardback, this first edition copy is in an aftermarket clamshell box with a dust wrapper from a later printing, the wrapper signed by Thomas Taylor, the artist. $46,200.

2. In hardback, a first edition copy of the Special Edition, this copy has a watercolor by Taylor drawn on the dedication page, bearing the artist's signature, as well. $9,700.

3. In paperback, with wrappers, in an aftermarket box, this first edition copy shows signs of wear. $9,240.

4. In hardback, a signed copy of the first edition of the Special Edition, with an event ticket dated December 9, 2000, stating "JK ROWLING BRINGS HARRY POTTER TO GLASGOW." $4,160.

5. Proof copy in paperback, with the misspelled name: J.A. Rowling. A copy sold at an auction house, Bonhams in Bath, for £1,250.

Harry Potter and the Chamber of Secrets

The first edition had a small print run in hardback, with dust jacket. On the copyright page the following numbers appear, identifying it as a first edition: 10 9 8 7 6 5 4 3 2 1.

1. A signed copy, with the dust jacket signed by the cover artist, Cliff Wright. $9,700.

2. Another signed copy. $8,300.

3. A signed uncorrected proof with provenance. $7,860.

4. An inscribed copy. $6,500.

Harry Potter and the Prisoner of Azkaban

The first edition was published in hardback, with dust jacket. On the copyright page the following numbers appear, identifying it as a first edition: 10 9 8 7 6 5 4 3 2 1.

There are two states: the first issue has, on page 7, a misaligned text block. It also states, on the copyright page, "Copyright Joanne Rowling"; the second, more common, state indicates the copyright is by "J. K. Rowling" and the text on page 7 is corrected.

1. A first issue copy signed by Rowling and artist Cliff Wright. $11,000.

2. A first issue copy signed by artist Cliff Wright. $5,080.

3. The Book People. A licensed hardback edition with dust jacket printed by Clays (the printer for Bloomsbury) for British millionaire Ted Smart. First edition. $930.

3. A second printing of the first edition. $460.

Harry Potter and the Goblet of Fire

The first edition was published in hardback with dust jacket. The first edition is thus marked: "First Edition." (It does *not* have the usual row of numbers found in books 1–4.)

1. A signed first edition copy, also signed by cover artist Giles Greenfield. $5,000.

2. A signed deluxe first edition copy, with a row of numbers to indicate the first edition. $3,230.

3. A first edition copy signed by Rowling. $1,200.

4. A limited, signed edition from Rowling's Canadian publisher, Bloomsbury Raincoast, one of 400 issued. As issued, with a four-page color brochure and a Certificate of Authenticity. The occasion: the International Festival of Authors. $1,200.

Harry Potter and the Order of the Phoenix

The first edition was published in hardback with dust jacket.

1. A copy signed at the Edinburgh bookstore on publication date. $4,070.

2. A copy with Rowling's signature on a Bloomsbury bookplate. $3,700.

3. A copy signed by the cover artist, Jason Cockroft. $330.

4. A copy of the adult edition. $50.

5. A copy of the children's edition. $50.

U.S. Editions from Scholastic

All the U.S. editions were issued with dust jackets. The text is different from the British edition, since it has been Americanized.

Rowling in Dough: Peter J. Rowling Sells His Harry Potter Novels

It's not unusual to see first editions of the Harry Potter novels up for auction at the prestigious Sotheby's, but four copies that sold in December 2003 stood out; in fact, they were unique: presentation copies from Joanne Rowling to her father, Peter. Of the seven offered for sale, four sold for a total of $87,600:

Book 1: *Harry Potter and the Philosopher's Stone* (U.K., paperback, first edition), for $9,600.

Book 2: *Harry Potter and the Chamber of Secrets* (U.K., hardback, first edition), for $10,800.

Book 3: *Harry Potter and the Prisoner of Azkaban* (U.K., hardback, first edition), for $19,200. (On the copyright page, Rowling circled the number "one" to indicate it is a first edition copy, with a pointing arrow highlighting a cautionary comment, "Guard it with your lives!!!")

Book 4: *Harry Potter and the Goblet of Fire* (U.K., hardback, first edition), for $48,000. What made this copy unusual was a lengthy handwritten note by Joanne in which she talked about the origins of a fictional character, Ron Weasley, with cartoons drawn on the bottom of the page.

Harry Potter and the Sorcerer's Stone

The first edition was published in hardback with dust jacket. The first edition bears the numbers: 1 3 5 7 9 10 8 6 4 2. The lowest number indicates the printing.

1. Signed first edition. $5,000.

2. Review copy signed at a publisher's dinner. $4,600.

3. Signed first edition, with minor defects. $4,500.

4. First collector's edition. $150.

Harry Potter and the Chamber of Secrets

Two states: the first state has a $17.95 cover price on the flap of the book jacket and does NOT have "Year 2" on the spine of the jacket or the book itself.

1. A signed first edition, first state: $1,500.

2. A signed first edition, second state: $720.

Harry Potter and the Prisoner of Azkaban

1. Signed on a bookplate, a first edition: $1,300.

2. Signed first edition copy. $600 to $1,000.

Harry Potter and the Goblet of Fire

1. Signed first edition copy. $450 to $600.

2. First edition copy. $29.

I really don't believe in magic. I believe in some kinds—the magic of imagination and the magic of love.

—*Joanne Rowling, during a Q&A*
at the Royal Albert Hall in London,
June 2003

About the Author

George Beahm has published numerous books, among them *The Essential J. R. R. Tolkien Sourcebook, The Stephen King Companion, The Unauthorized Anne Rice Companion, The Unofficial Patricia Cornwell Companion, Stephen King from A to Z: An Encyclopedia of His Life and Work*, and *War of Words: The Censorship Debate*.

Actively involved in the book industry since 1975, Beahm has also been a self-publisher, regional publisher, book marketing director, book publishing consultant, and book packager.

Beahm is a lifelong fan of fantasy and science fiction; his first two books focused on fantasy artists Vaughn Bode, Tim Kirk, and Richard Corben.

His websites are at www.GeorgeBeahm.com, www.beahmworks.com, and www.FlightsofImagination.com.

About the Contributors

Colleen Doran is the creator (writer and artist) of *A Distant Soil* from Image Comics. Doran is a cartoonist with hundreds of books from D.C., Marvel, and independent publishers. Her recent books include *Orbiter* (with Warren Ellis) and *Reign of the Zodiac* (with Keith Giffen). The illustrator of *The Essential J. R. R. Tolkien Sourcebook*, Doran is a member of the National Cartoonists Society, the Association of Science Fiction and Fantasy Artists, and the American Society of Portrait Artists. She is currently completing a fourth *A Distant Soil* graphic novel and *Stealth Tribes*, a graphic novel with Warren Ellis.

Her websites are at www.colleendoran.com and www.adistantsoil.com.

Stephen McGinty is a senior feature writer with the *Scotsman* newspaper and author of *This Turbulent Priest: A Life of Cardinal Thomas Winning*, a critically acclaimed biography published in 2003 by HarperCollins.

Allan Harvey is a lifelong fantasy, science fiction, and comic book fan who lives in London. He currently works as a technical manager at an independent laboratory on the outskirts of London. He is an aspiring comic book artist; his website is at www.thefifthbranch.com.

Photographer Nick Derene is a graduate student at the University of Wisconsin–Stevens Point. While working on his master's degree in wildlife, he volunteers as a rehabilitator and public educator at Raptor Education Group, Inc. (REGI) in Antigo, Wisconsin.

Tim Kirk is a celebrated fantasy artist whose work has graced countless fanzines, magazines, and books. Best known for his calendar illustrations for the 1975 J. R. R. Tolkein Calendar, Kirk has worked for Hallmark Cards and, more recently, for Disney as a senior designer in its famed Imagineering division. His most recent design project is the Science Fiction Experience, a musem in Seattle, Washington, devoted to the history of science fiction.

Hampton Roads Publishing Company

. . . . for the evolving human spirit

Hampton Roads Publishing Company
publishes books on a variety of subjects,
including metaphysics, health,
visionary fiction, and other related topics.

For a copy of our latest catalog, call toll-free
(800) 766-8009, or send your name and address to:

Hampton Roads Publishing Company, Inc.
1125 Stoney Ridge Road
Charlottesville, VA 22902

e-mail: hrpc@hrpub.com
www.hrpub.com